THE PRENTICE HALL

MIRACLE SALES GUIDE

FOURTH EDITION

THE BUREAU OF BUSINESS PRACTICE /
PRENTICE HALL EDITORIAL STAFF

PRENTICE HALL
Englewood Cliffs, New Jersey 07632

Prentice-Hall International, (UK) Limited, *London*
Prentice-Hall of Australia, Pty. Limited., *Sydney*
Prentice-Hall of Canada, Inc., *Toronto*
Prentice-Hall Hispanoamericana, S.A., *Mexico*
Prentice-Hall of India Private Limited., *New Delhi*
Prentice-Hall of Japan, Inc., *Tokyo*
Simon & Schuster Southeast Asia Pte., Ltd., *Singapore*
Editora Prentice-Hall do Brasil, Ltda., *Rio de Janeiro*

10 9 8 7 6 5 4 3 2 1

Library of Congress Cataloging-in-Publication Data

Thr Prentice Hall miracle salesguide. — 4th ed.
    p. cm.

    Includes index.
    ISBN 0-13-756263-2
    1. Selling—Handbooks, manuals, etc. I. Prentice Hall, Inc.
HF5438.25.P734   1993
658.85—dc20   92-46123
                                                         CIP

ISBN 0-13-756263-2

PRENTICE HALL
Career & Personal Development
Englewood Cliffs, NJ 07632

Simon & Schuster, A Paramount Communications Company

PRINTED IN THE UNITED STATES OF AMERICA

INTRODUCTION

The *Prentice Hall Miracle Sales Guide* has been used by over 500,000 salespeople to multiply their income, save themselves precious time, and build successful territories. It contains hundreds of creative ideas, proven techniques, and valuable action plans that allow you to reach the top of this tough and demanding profession.

For more than 30 years, salespeople have used *The Prentice Hall Miracle Sales Guide* to recharge their batteries, find new approaches to old problems, and fine-tune their selling skills. The techniques and ideas presented in the *Guide* work—because they've been tested and proven in real-world situations. Thousands of letters from salespeople are testimony to the fact that the *Guide* can help you turn an ordinary career into an extraordinary one.

This updated version of *The Prentice Hall Miracle Sales Guide* is an invaluable tool for today's salesperson. It covers every aspect of the selling process. Its unique index allows you to focus in on a particular problem and find a variety of methods for solving it. And the real-life examples throughout the *Guide* show you how ideas and techniques can be applied to your specific selling situation.

Here are some of the topics covered in the *Guide:*

- **Breaking into big selling** (Chapter One): Covers how to determine the value of your time, five ways to increase your production, techniques for selling more to your present customers, moving up to bigger buyers, breaking into big selling through better time planning, and keeping up with the latest selling techniques.

- **Prospecting for volume business** (Chapter Two): Includes finding full-potential prospects, using the help of others to find good leads, ideas for finding leads on your own, qualifying prospects for buying potential, finding and rating the key prospect in a group, and guidelines for better territory coverage.

- **Ideas for creative selling** (Chapter Three): Contains how to train your mind to create ideas, stepping up your creativity, a sampling of creative ideas that make bigger buyers, and ideas to keep you constantly creative.

- **Successful strategies for preapproach, making them listen, callbacks** (Chapter Four): Provides information on finding out about a prospect, getting the interview, making appointments by telephone and by letter, getting in without an appointment, making the prospect listen, putting your finger on the prospect's reason to buy, and making callbacks pay off.

- **Making a great presentation** (Chapter Five): Explains the reasons for a thorough preparation, preliminary steps in your preparation, creating an effective outline, guidelines for a surefire demonstration, masterful use of sales tools, how to handle price, putting your presentation into words, building interest and turning that interest into desire, and making your presentation convincing.

- **Power-closing techniques** (Chapter Six): Describes dozens of ways to make a close in a variety of situations, why your hook is an essential ingredient of every sale, and ways that you can develop personal closing techniques that will increase your selling power.

- **Making objections work for you** (Chapter Seven): Demonstrates the four basic rules for turning objections into sales, the answer attitude that wins, and the answer guide to specific objections: multiple comebacks for 25 common objections.

- **Selling at concert pitch** (Chapter Eight): Shares insight into how you can build and maintain your selling enthusiasm, self-management techniques that will gain selling time and make a positive impression, and how to make the most of your personality.

- **Salesperson's personal money kit** (Chapter Nine): Details how you should handle your everyday expenses (including entertainment, travel, and transportation), how the tough new rules on company-paid transportation and entertainment affect you, how to make your deductions stand up.

- **Helpful personal records to reach high-bracket goals** (Chapter Ten): Describes how to get the most out of your personal records—to keep track of prospects, sales calls, callbacks, possible reorders, route schedules, and your own productivity.

- **How to find information about people and companies** (Appendix): Lists valuable reference sources that are readily available and that you can use to gather information to help you in your day-to-day selling.

In short, *The Prentice Hall Miracle Sales Guide* provides you with all the tools you need to build your sales success. Follow the lead of the top salespeople who have used the *Guide* as a blueprint to send their careers soaring. Put these techniques to work right away—and find out what thousands of men and women already know: That *The Prentice Hall Miracle Sales Guide* can truly work miracles in any sales career.

CONTENTS

Chapter One

BREAKING INTO BIG SELLING 1

Chapter Two

Prospecting For Volume Business   70

Chapter Three

IDEAS FOR CREATIVE SELLING 121

Chapter Four

PLANNING YOUR PREAPPROACH, MAKING PROSPECTS LISTEN, AND GETTING CALLBACKS 172

Chapter Five

MAKING A GREAT PRESENTATION 232

Chapter Six

POWER CLOSING TECHNIQUES 323

Chapter Seven

MAKING OBJECTIONS WORK FOR YOU 350

Chapter Eight

SELLING AT CONCERT PITCH 427

Chapter Nine

SALESPERSON'S PERSONAL MONEY KIT 479

Chapter Ten

HELPFUL PERSONAL RECORDS TO REACH HIGH-BRACKET GOALS 530

Appendix

HOW TO FIND INFORMATION ABOUT PEOPLE AND COMPANIES 547

INDEX 558

CHAPTER ONE

BREAKING INTO BIG SELLING

It's just as easy to sell big buyers as smaller ones—and it's definitely more profitable.

Any salesperson who wants to make real money—who wants to earn $50,000, $75,000, or more a year—faces a real challenge in today's economy. A lot of customers are buying less. Some are just buying more wisely. All are putting a lot more thought into what they buy and whom they buy from. Everyone wants to get maximum value for the money he or she spends on goods and services.

This doesn't mean that there aren't still opportunities there for salespeople who know how to recognize and take advantage of them. If you're ambitious for high-bracket earnings, the *Guide* will give you the surefire selling techniques that will permit you to write your own ticket.

The seven keys to taking the first step on the ladder to success are right here in this chapter:

1

1. Know what your time is worth, and work with an awareness of that value.

2. Set your sights on higher earnings. Then make sure you've mastered the six essentials for success in reaching your goal.

3. Increase your total volume of sales by tapping the five sources for increased business.

4. Sell more to your present customers by dedicating yourself to them. Use tested ideas for turning dedication into more income.

5. Move up to bigger buyers. It takes no more ability to sell a big buyer than it does to sell a small one.

6. Break into big selling with a time-value approach to planning your work schedule.

7. Stay up to date on the latest selling techniques.

Refer to the *Guide* on a daily basis, and you will pick up ideas, hints, techniques, and inspiration that will help you reach your higher earnings goals.

A SIMPLE FORMULA FOR VALUING YOUR TIME

How to Make Every Customer a Profitable One

You can earn big money in selling only by putting the right value on your time and never forgetting how valuable it is. If you want to take home a bigger paycheck, you must be acutely aware of just how much each hour of your working day is worth in terms of dollars and cents. About the only time that you can safely forget that "time is money" is when you are getting the well-earned relaxation and rest that tune you up for the next day's successful selling.

Place your own value on your working time. Fix it in relation to what you want to earn. Then earn it by working with prospects and customers whose orders can yield earnings that are commensurate with your time value.

REMEMBER Time is capital. You must invest it for maximum return—the return that you yourself have determined it is worth.

How to Figure Your Time Value

All you need to know to calculate the value of your time is how much you'd like to earn each year. There are 244 working days in a year, or 1,952 working hours. Divide your earnings goal by 1,952, and you'll know how much your time is worth.

Here are the figures for some attainable goals:

Earnings Goal per Year	Value of an Hour
$ 35,000	$17.93
45,000	23.05
55,000	28.18
65,000	33.30
75,000	38.42
100,000	51.23
125,000	64.04

How Simple Arithmetic Can Bring You More Dollars

Now that you know how much each hour of your time is worth, you can see the importance of using your time as judiciously as possible. And you'll probably agree that the most profitable hours are those you spend in a selling interview, telling the story of your product.

Of the 1,952 hours in a working year, most salespeople spend only 976 hours face to face with their prospects trying to close the sale. Notice what this does to the value of those 976 hours:

Earnings Goal per Year	Value of an Hour Spent in Actual Selling
$ 35,000	$ 35.86
45,000	46.11
55,000	56.35
65,000	66.59
75,000	76.84
100,000	102.46
125,000	128.07

Obviously, those "presentation" hours with prospects are not going to yield their money's worth to you unless the calls you make produce a commensurate volume of business.

WHAT TO DO The conclusion is clear: You must eliminate as far as possible those calls that do not pay, as measured by the dollar value of the orders obtained. Whether you are selling a product that requires you to call back periodically on each customer, or one that involves no repeat sales, time must still be measured against sales results.

How Much Must A Prospect Be Worth For You To Make A Call?

Put yourself in the place of the salesperson who asked himself that question and then took action on what he discovered.

■ IDEA IN ACTION

Gordon Miller calls on hospitals to fill their needs for supplies and equipment. He averages 25 calls per week, and since he visits each account every 4 weeks, his selling list totals exactly 100 names.

Gordon's total net sales per year run about $550,000. His commissions average 8% or $44,000. Of this sum, $7,000 goes into traveling expenses; the balance of $37,000 is his net annual income.

Gordon knows that if he wants to increase his net earnings by $10,000, he has to get more value out of each of his working hours. So he analyzes his previous year's sales and discovers that one-third of his customers gave him only 10% of his total business, while the top two-thirds of his accounts produced 90% of his overall sales. These are the figures he comes up with:

- Thirty-three accounts yielded net sales of $55,000, or an average of $1,666 of net sales per account ($55,000 divided by 33).

- Sixty-seven accounts yielded net sales of $495,000, or an average of $7,388 of net sales per account ($495,000 divided by 67).

He realizes that it took just as much time, effort, attention, and expense to get the average of $1,666 net sales from each of the 33 accounts as it took to get the average $7,388 net sales from each of his 67 accounts. In fact, as he thinks about the 33 accounts, he realizes that some of them take a lot more time and effort than the better accounts.

"Well," he says to himself, "I guess if I want to get more of those big accounts, I've got to stop making calls on the small ones."

So Gordon Miller decides that on his next trip, he will eliminate calling on the 33 accounts that took up one-third of his time while contributing only 10% of his sales. He uses the time this saves to call on other hospitals in his territory and begins to develop still more higher quality prospects.

A few of these new prospects place an order on his first visit; others begin buying on the second or third.

Twelve months after making his analysis, Gordon finds that by dropping the one-third of his accounts that were yielding only $55,000 in volume and using the same time and effort to solicit new accounts, he has added $128,000 of business, for a net gain of $73,000.

Since Gordon's travel expenses remain unchanged, the $5,840 in additional commissions he is now earning mark an increase of 16%, boosting his income from $37,000 to $42,920— and this is only the beginning.

WHAT TO DO

1. Analyze your own selling record for the past year.

2. Identify the accounts that are lowering the value of your time.

3. Decide whether any of these accounts are worth keeping because they're growing rapidly and may soon be in the category you're aiming at.

4. Drop the remaining unprofitable accounts.

5. Go after prospects with a potential unit size order that will pay you what your time is worth.

When you make your analysis for the purpose of weeding out the small customers who aren't really worth your time in terms of potential earnings, you should guard against the following common fallacies:

1. "Since I pass right by their door, it doesn't cost me anything to stop in and get a small order." Wrong. It *does* cost you something: your valuable time. You are dissipating your capital.

2. "They've been buying from us for years, so I can't stop calling even if their volume is small." You can and you must. You cannot afford to give your time away at bargain rates.

3. "They haven't given me any business yet, but I know that sooner or later I'll get a break and make up for all the past calls." Persistency counts when it is applied properly—in getting interviews with high caliber prospects, for example. But you've also got to know when to cut your losses and move on.

Block thoughts like these out of your mind. It's easy—just head for the next prospect, someone whose size and importance in the industry are more in line with what your time is worth.

Don't Let the "Whopper Sale" Deceive You

By keeping the value of your time uppermost in your mind, you can make the occasional "whopper" sale without losing out on other business. Here is what frequently happens, but it won't happen to you if you are careful about how you utilize your time.

■ IDEA IN ACTION

Nancy Taylor sells a nationally advertised cosmetic line to retailers in the metropolitan Chicago area. Her orders normally run between $500 and $4,000, depending on the size of the individual store. She writes four orders a day, on the average.

One day, Nancy calls on a chain store that has about 20 retail outlets in the territory. The buyer says, "We're thinking about running a big promotion on cosmetics in a few weeks, right at the height of the season. If we do, we'll probably want to include your line. Stop back and see me in about a week and I may have a larger order for you."

Nancy is elated. She does some quick estimating and decides that if the plan goes through, the order would be at least $15,000—perhaps even more!

"Let's see," she says to herself, "I'm supposed to check back next Thursday. I'd planned to be working out around Evanston that day, but I'll put that off until Friday. That big order is worth going after, so I'll just work right here in Chicago next Thursday."

Then Nancy realizes that on Friday she had planned to work in Forest Park—had a couple of appointments there, as a matter of fact.

"Well, I can't put Evanston off too long—so I'll just phone my customers in Forest Park and explain why I can't see them until the following Monday."

When Nancy calls back to get her "big order" on Thursday, the buyer says to her, "We're going to have a final meeting on this first thing Monday morning. Can you call back at around 11 o'clock on Monday? Everything will be settled by then."

Nancy replies, "Well, I guess I'll be seeing you at 11 o'clock on Monday, then."

When she eventually lands the order, it totals $9,000. The buyer tells her that the final plans had to be "trimmed down a bit."

In reality, Nancy lost out on much more than the business she'd had to postpone. While she was pleased to write an order more than twice as large as her usual "top" orders, she was puzzled to discover that her final sales figures for the month were well below her normal monthly average.

WHAT TO DO

1. Get the "plum" order without disrupting your work schedule. Use the telephone. (What Nancy should have said when her appointment with the chain buyer was postponed is this: "I'm sorry, but I've simply got to be in Forest Park on Monday. I've postponed my appointments there once already, and I can't do it again. Why don't I telephone you from there?") The buyer will respect you for keeping your appointments with other customers. You'll be displaying the kind of attitude that all buyers appreciate, and you'll be showing confidence that you'll get the large order anyway.

2. Show the buyer that you're not walking away from this extraordinary opportunity by thinking of some way in which he or she can push your product during the promotion. If you can't come up with any creative ideas on your own, review the successful promotion efforts of some of your other customers: striking displays that have been used or how one of your customers linked its cosmetic promotion to a community event.

In this way you will guard against paying too high a price for the "plum" order in terms of lost time, disrupted plans, and any other departures from sound work habits.

REMEMBER Normal work habits frequently produce more total sales than what is gained from dropping them to try for a "plum" order.

Once you've raised the level of your customers' potential value, you won't be as dependent on the "whopper sale" to bring your earnings up to par. The "whopper sale" will still come your way, because both large buyers and small buyers have special promotions from time to time that call for larger than average orders.

You Put Yourself in Front When You Select Your Customers

You are in the vanguard of selling when you search for and discover the unprofitable segments of your customer list. You are doing what the most progressive companies are doing to convert losses into profits. They are analyzing their marketing costs to see how many and what kinds of customers to sell to, what territories to cover, and which products to sell and at what price. Not many companies have learned and applied all the available analysis techniques. But you're giving yourself an enormous head start when you apply the formula outlined shortly to improve your own profit picture by weeding out the small buyers and moving up to bigger ones.

SETTING YOUR SIGHTS FOR HIGHER EARNINGS

Six Essentials for Success in Reaching High Goals

Top-flight salespeople always set their sights for bigger earnings. Whenever a salesperson falls short of his or her goal, it is usually because there is a deficiency in one or more of six key areas. The degree to which you meet these qualifications rests entirely on your shoulders. Generally speaking, you must meet the following standards:

1. **Have the necessary qualifications to sell your product.** Your qualifications include such things as morale, ethical conduct, appearance, health, enthusiasm, and other personal attributes.

2. **Have an attractive product to sell.** You must have all the necessary product information and be able to visualize your

product's application. You must also understand its sales features, know the competition, and learn how to present your product properly.

3. **Know your territory.** You must know how and where to find prospects. You must understand how to handle the various types of people you encounter. You must keep proper follow-up records or your territory will fail to live up to its full potential.

4. **Go to the right places at the right times.** You must plan your work and work your plan.

5. **Do and say the right things during the interview.** You must be skilled in all phases of what is called "selling technique."

6. **Apply yourself wholeheartedly to your work.** You must be mentally and physically able and willing to do a full day's work. Salespeople who are recognized for being successful don't stop working when 5 o'clock rolls around. The vast majority of those who have achieved high earnings owe their success to their willingness to handle business during leisure hours as well.

This *Guide* is designed to give you the instructions, suggestions, ideas, and inspiration you will need to live up to your potential in each of these six areas. Everything you read in this *Guide* is drawn from the experience of salespeople with outstanding records. The ideas that worked for them will work for you if you apply them correctly.

Use the Law of Averages to Raise Your Sales Volume and Dollar Income

When applied to selling, the law of averages works this way: The more you do, the more you achieve. In other words, the more carefully selected calls you make, the more interviews you obtain. The more interviews you have, the greater the number of presentations you make. The larger the number of presentations, the more opportunities you have to close sales. And the higher the number of closings, the larger your volume of sales and income will be.

TIP You can perform more selling jobs in the same amount of time simply by planning your work more carefully.(Time planning is covered in greater detail lataer in this chapter.)

☐ EXAMPLE

You find that from an average of 40 calls per week, you obtain 30 interviews (75%). By preplanning your day's work and cutting down on travel time, you find you can average 38 interviews in 50 calls. You're still averaging around 75%, but you've gained 8 interviews.

Answer these questions and increase your sales volume and dollar income:

- How can I raise the number of calls I make each week?
- How can I raise the number of interviews I obtain per call made?
- How can I raise the number of presentations I give per interview obtained?
- How can I raise the number of closes I secure per presentation given?
- How can I raise the number of new prospects I see each week?
- How can I raise the number of repeat sales I succeed in making each quarter?
- How can I raise the dollar value of my selling time?
- How can I lower the travel time I spend between calls?
- How can I lower the number of minutes I spend waiting for my customers?

Achieve Your Goals Through Dynamic Planning

Long-range goals are achieved only if the many separate steps leading up to the goal are accomplished. Learn to plan and execute these smaller steps, and you will take giant strides toward your goal of success in selling.

WHAT TO DO Choose one or more long-range goals. Make a three-column chart with these headings: "Time Period," "Proposed Increase," and "Actual Increase." Divide your time period and proposed increase into equal, corresponding subdivisions.

□ EXAMPLE

Your present number of repeat sales is 120 per year. Your goal is to double your repeat sales in one year. Break down the coming year into quarters and assign a goal of 60 repeat sales to each three-month period.

Time Period	*Proposed Increase of Repeat Sales (cumulative)*	*Actual Increase of Repeat Sales*
1st quarter (March 31)	60	
2nd quarter (June 30)	120	
3rd quarter (September 30)	180	
4th quarter (December 31)	240	

Now determine the simplest and most direct methods of attaining your ultimate goal of increasing repeat sales. You might try some of these techniques:

- Use follow-up letters.
- Schedule periodic checkup calls.
- Leave your card with an invitation to call if your customer needs information or service.
- Send customers literature describing your new products.
- Look for opportunities to remind your customers that you have their interests in mind.

Watch your deadlines as though your job depended on your meeting them. At the end of each quarter, fill in the number of repeat sales you have made.

Check your progress from time to time by comparing your actual progress with the planned progress shown on your chart. If you find yourself falling behind, reexamine the methods you are using for possible improvement, or check with this *Guide* for other ideas and methods that will be effective.

Every salesperson who is aiming for top-flight results must increase the number of new customers. To do this you must increase the number of prospects, the number of calls, the number of presentations, and the number of interviews that result in closings.

Look at Selling as a Continuous Process

Each step in the selling process is related to all of the others. The final outcome of an interview is determined not by your ability to close successfully or by any other single factor, but by the use of the proper techniques at each and every point throughout the planning and execution of the sale.

▪ IDEA IN ACTION

Ted Hughes's appearance and manner of handling prospects are good. He makes a strong presentation and is an excellent closer. But he turns in only an average volume of business.

Why? Because his technique is under par in two areas: (1) meeting objections and (2) handling necessary selling details, such as arranging financing, explaining the trade-in allowance offer, and so forth.

By correcting these two weaknesses, Ted could immediately increase his sales volume by at least 25%. Until he does this, he will continue to be a mediocre salesperson. For no one can really succeed in sales until he or she understands that each step in the sale affects the final outcome.

Wind Up Each Day with a Review and Analysis

Your workday should not be considered finished until you have retraced every hour of the day, step by step, to measure your accomplishments. Without a purposeful analysis, you cannot hope to reach new ambitious goals.

When you review your day's selling experience, look for the answers to the following questions:

- Did I get my own dollar and cents time value out of the day's work?

- At which points did my enthusiasm falter? What could I have done to bolster it?

- What new strong point did I develop today that I must be sure to use again and again? (It was a strong point if you got the right response from the customer.)

Analyze the day's nonsuccesses by asking:

- Why didn't I get the interview?

- Why didn't I get the prospect's attention?

- What went wrong with my presentation that kept me from bringing my prospect to close?

- Why didn't I close?

- How can I correct the weaknesses I have discovered?

End your analysis for the day with an entry on a weekly performance record.

The record in Exhibit 1.1 was filled out by a salesperson who sells a tangible product in a territory covering several counties. It demonstrates how to spot weaknesses in each of the related steps of the selling process.

EXHIBIT 1.1

Weekly Performance Record

	Calls	Interviews	Got Attention	Gave Presentation	Got Chance to Close	Closed
Monday	5	3	3	3	2	1
Tuesday	12	8	6	6	3	2
Wednesday	7	6	6	5	2	2
Thursday	10	8	7	6	3	1
Friday	5	5	5	4	2	0
Saturday	2	2	2	2	2	0
Total	41	32	29	26	14	6

Now let's look for the areas of weakness revealed in the salesperson's tabulation of his work.

- Nine calls were a waste of time. Why wasn't his prospect in and free to see him? Poor planning is probably at the root of this problem.

- He lost out three times because he didn't get the prospect's attention. If he analyzed each day's work conscientiously, he would know why he failed.

- He lost out three more times by not being permitted to make the presentation. The daily analysis should show what stopped him from getting started on the presentation.

- He had numerous opportunities to close, having made 26 presentations, but he tried only 14 times. He might not see this weakness as clearly in his daily analysis as he would at the end of the week. The record makes it clear that he is not trying often enough to close the sale.

- Of the trial closings, six worked. It's time for him to review his presentation very carefully to see how it can be improved so that more of his prospects will close.

Rate yourself honestly on each step as shown in the analysis. If your rating shows that you are stronger in some of these areas than in others, you know that these are the areas you must focus on if you want to reach the earnings goal you've set for yourself. This *Guide* will show you how and where to begin.

SUGGESTION You might think that you have corrected each of your shortcomings after diligently applying the ideas and training suggested in this *Guide* and still not succeed in closing on sales that you feel you should have made. There are some situations in which you simply won't know why you were unable to close. If this is your problem, get someone whose selling ability you respect to accompany you on one of your calls. Let him or her observe you in action. There's a good chance that he or she will be able to spot the weakness for you.

How to Turn Failures into Success

Begin to analyze your failures so that you can find the causes and get rid of them. The benefits of this practice are twofold: (1) It makes for better selling and therefore larger volume, and (2) it forces you to confront your errors and thus saves you from deluding yourself and repeating the same mistakes.

> **HOW TO ANALYZE** Set aside a period of time each night—say, 15 minutes—to analyze your failures. Ask yourself: "Why did I fail to make that sale? What did I do wrong? How can I do better next time under similar circumstances?" Keep a written record of the reasons for failure so that you will be able to recognize those weaknesses that crop up most frequently. These are the ones you'll want to concentrate on rectifying first.

If you find that your sales volume is falling, examine your presentation. Perhaps it lacks the old "zing" you used to get into it. Perhaps it has become dull because it is not attuned to today's requirements. (For ideas on how to strengthen your presentation, see Chapter Five.)

FIVE WAYS TO INCREASE PRODUCTION

The Five Sources for Increased Sales

Regardless of the type of selling in which you may be engaged, there are only five ways in which you can achieve an increase in your total volume of sales. Unless you manage to tap at least one of these five sources, whatever effort you make or whatever plan of work you set up is doomed to failure.

■ **Source 1.** Call on a greater number of high-potential prospects or customers. For example, make nine calls per day instead of eight.

> **HOW TO DO IT** Plan your work better and devote more of your time to actual selling. (Detailed guidelines to better time planning are provided later in this chapter and in Chapter Eight.)

■ **Source 2.** Close a greater percentage of the prospects and customers you call on. For example, close three prospects out of eight instead of two out of eight.

HOW TO DO IT Develop your closing power. (Chapter Six covers closing techniques in detail.)

■ **Source 3.** Sell larger quantities per order. For example, sell 10 gross instead of 5 or a $100,000 life insurance policy instead of one for $50,000.

HOW TO DO IT Plan each interview and prepare for it in advance. (See Chapter Four for interview strategies.) Also, use a planned presentation instead of a hit-or-miss sales talk; perfect your sales presentation.(Chapter Five focuses on improving presentation skills.)

■ **Source 4.** Sell a wider range of products. For example, sell the full line rather than just the "easy-to-sell" items; sell related items rather than individual products.

HOW TO DO IT Acquire a thorough knowledge of your product and make the most effective use of it. (See Chapter Five for tips on increasing product knowledge.)

■ **Source 5.** Sell higher-priced units. For example, sell quality items instead of price items; sell the "economy size" or the large-screen television set instead of smaller, lower-priced units. (Selling higher-priced units is discussed later in this chapter.)

■ IDEA IN ACTION

Helen Burke's sales manager asks her why her selling record has been so poor in the year she's been with the company.

"If I had a larger territory," answers Burke, "I would do a lot better. There simply isn't enough business in the state of Maine. Give me Vermont and New Hampshire, and I'll double my business."

The sales manager agrees to this proposal, but on a three-month trial basis.

Rather than showing the promised increase, Burke's sales actually decline. The reason is that in covering the larger territory, Burke's travel time is increased, with the result that she makes fewer calls than before.

This experience causes Burke to review her selling habits. In analyzing her methods, she discovers a better way of closing.

Three months later, Burke reports to her sales manager. "I'm so busy closing sales that I find I can't cover three states after all. There are more prospects in Maine than I had realized, so I guess I'll have to drop the two other states."

COMMENT The first step Burke took (covering a larger territory) failed in this instance because it did not tap any of the five sources from which *all* sales increases must come. The second step Burke took (closing a greater percentage of prospects) did bring an increase in volume because it successfully tapped one of the sources just listed.

There are times, of course, when working a larger territory will result in making more calls, or in selling more "quantity users," or in some other way tapping one of the sources from which more business can be obtained. But unless you have a plan to accomplish this, it will not succeed as a means to greater sales.

WHAT TO DO NOW Examine your selling habits, your selling plan, and your selling activities in terms of the five sources of increased sales. Not every salesperson can use all these five sources, but you can at least try to focus your efforts along these lines.

Give Your Knowledge and Get Orders

You must give your customers the information about your product that will make them want to buy before you can expect to get their orders.

Find out if you have the right information by asking yourself the following questions:

- Do I know why my customer is buying my product?
- Do I know what my customer expects from my product?
- Do I know how my customer is planning to use my product?
- Do I know other ways the customer can use my product?
- Do I know when my customer expects delivery?

- Have I informed my customer of my product's limitations as well as its advantages?

- If a callback is necessary, have I left my customer with an impression of my product strong enough to overcome a competitor's sales talk?

> **N**ever accept an order for goods or services that the buyer cannot use, does not need, or for any other reason that you know of ought not to buy. To do so is never consistent with the principles of selling, and the results can eventually undermine your success.

REMEMBER Knowledge of your product and your job increases your customer's confidence and raises your own enthusiasm. If you know your product thoroughly, you'll never have to misrepresent it to make a sale.

SELLING MORE TO YOUR PRESENT CUSTOMERS

Dedicate Yourself to the Customer

An important factor in achieving the upbeat, hopeful frame of mind that is basic to success in selling more to your present customers is dedication—putting their interests first, doing your best for them, looking at things from their point of view, and selling from their point of view.

Dedicating yourself to your present customers can revolutionize your selling career and bring an explosion of success. Here's why:

- Like everyone else, salespeople must live with themselves. They keep track of the things they know they're doing right and continually weigh them against the things they know they're doing wrong.

- When you dedicate yourself to your clients' best interests, you know you're doing the right thing. This puts you in the expectant, hopeful frame of mind that is so necessary to selling success by making you feel that you have something good coming to you.

- It puts an end to the inner feelings of guilt that can inhibit your effectiveness. Salespeople who do something because it's to their own advantage often try to kid themselves that it's being done for the customer's sake. But at some level they know they're being dishonest with themselves and the customer.

- When you honestly dedicate yourself to your customers' best interests, it puts you on the side of what is right and immediately fills your mind with the expectation of good to come. This feeling can make an enormous difference in terms of self-confidence. It gives you an air of self-assurance that nothing else can.

One of the big changes you will notice at once when you dedicate yourself to your customers' welfare is the freeing of your own creative imagination, which often takes place under the emotional stimulus of dedication to the right side of a moral issue. Ideas for helping your customers will come thick and fast—your imagination will catch fire—you'll see hundreds of opportunities to serve them which were never apparent before.

Here are a few practical suggestions to further your work in this exciting direction:

- **Learn all about your customers' problems.** Talk with them, and listen while they talk. If you turn a sympathetic ear you'll get to know what their concerns are, and how you can give them the kind of help they need.

- **When you make a call, try to come up with a way of helping the customer.** Don't just go in there to sell something; go in with an idea that will be of some use to your customer.

  HOW TO DO IT By talking to your customer, you may have discovered that he or she is worried about a large supply of slow-moving stock. Instead of just making a call, offer a promotion suggestion that can be used to solve the problem. It might be a consumer contest, a sampling table (if it's a food item), a trade-in special (if it's a household product), or a premium offer.

- **Keep an idea book—with a page for each customer.** Jot down notes on each customer's problems—and his or her special concerns and interests. On the same page, put down ideas for helping him—as they come to you.

  HOW TO DO IT You may see a piece in the newspaper that your customer could capitalize on. Mail it to him or her.

- **As you move about your territory, keep an eye open for tips and information that you can pass along to your customers.** For example, you might know something that one customer is doing that would be helpful to another. Obviously you wouldn't want to pass information between competitors, but there are lots of other ideas that can be shared.

- **Consider putting in a little extra time at the office.** One salesperson we know spends Saturday in the office, checking on the new goods that have come in. First thing Monday morning, she makes long-distance phone calls to her people—with attractive offers—and does as much business in one day as most salespeople do in a week.

Getting into the Habit of Thinking of the Customers' Needs

Dedication to your customers may seem like an unusual approach at first. But it's not. You're merely applying the soundest of all selling principles: Constantly think of how you can best serve the interests of your customers.

Remember that this approach not only changes what takes place within you, but also changes other people's attitudes toward you. Consider the following case studies of three salespeople who made short-term sacrifices to serve their customers better.

Case 1: The "Dream House" That Wasn't

A real estate agent was approached by a woman who wanted to buy a $250,000 home he had listed. It was an old colonial place and she was completely taken with its charm.

But the agent knew she would be in for trouble if she bought it. It would cost thousands of dollars to get it in working order—and it was far too large for her purposes. The water supply was inadequate, and she would eventually have to drill a new well. The paint was falling off and the roof looked as though it would need replacing in the next few years. It might be the perfect house for someone who had plenty of money to reclaim its charm. But it wasn't the right house for his client. So he advised her not to buy it—and told her exactly why. The woman told all her friends about how helpful the agent had been. And the story got around. Eventually, the agent became known as a person who looks out for his clients. People placed their faith in him—and his business thrived.

Case 2: Know Your Customer's Business

A salesperson who wholesaled dresses to retail stores was working with a small retailer who normally sold "better" dresses costing $100 and up. This retailer told the salesperson that he wanted to take on a line of $35 dresses and wanted to give her a big order for a full line of less expensive styles.

The salesperson (who knew the dress business) advised against it. She told the customer that when it came to dresses in the $35 range, he could not hope to compete with the big-volume stores, that they could sell them for about what he would have to pay for them. The salesperson lost the order, of course, but the retailer was impressed with how much she knew about the business. He was particularly impressed by the fact that she wouldn't take an order for something she didn't feel was right for her customer.

Case 3: Understanding the Customer's Needs

A small business owner wanted to buy $100,000 of life insurance. He called up an agent and told her that his friend had recommended her and he wanted to place the order right there on the phone.

The insurance salesperson thanked him—but told him she would rather not take the order until she'd had a chance to review his situation and find out what he really wanted the policy for—and if it would answer his purposes.

The prospect was surprised and said, "I thought you would leap at the chance to sell a $100,000 policy."

The insurance salesperson called on the prospect at his office and asked him what he wanted the insurance for. She found out that he wanted it to protect his wife and three children.

The salesperson found that they would need at least $50,000 a year to keep going without the husband's income and that he would need $250,000 additional insurance to give him the protection he was after.

The executive took out $250,000 worth of insurance instead of $100,000.

REMEMBER The point of all three cases is that they show the value of looking at things from the prospect's point of view. It gets people eating out of your hand. It makes them go out of their way for you. They'll do you a good turn whenever they can. And it will end in your selling more to your present customers.

The Attitude That Sells More to Present Customers

Here is the successful salesperson's attitude about selling more to existing customers: A customer who already finds it profitable to give you a substantial amount of business is usually more than willing to listen to facts that show why it makes sense for him or her to use even more.

The only time a customer is likely to feel that your suggestion is out of order is if you simply ask for the additional business as a favor, without bothering to show how the customer will profit as well.

IMPORTANT You'll never sell more to your existing customers if you don't have the right attitude. Cultivate this attitude by avoiding the following mistakes:

- **Mistake No. 1.** Since you're already getting a substantial volume of business from this customer, you decide to "leave well enough alone."

- **Mistake No. 2.** You assume that if your existing customers were interested in having more of your product, they would say so.

- **Mistake No. 3.** You assume that the customer has a good reason for not buying more from you, without first having discussed why he or she should buy. The burden of stating the reasons why a customer should buy rests on you, not on the buyer.

- **Mistake No. 4.** When a customer decides to buy a particular item, you don't have the courage to suggest a full-sized order. The only risk you run in suggesting a larger order is that the customer will turn you down. But if the item is profitable, there's an equally good chance that he or she will agree to the higher limit.

IMPORTANT Be sure to find out how your customer uses your product, especially if you're selling raw materials. Only then will you stand the best chance of selling the quantity he or she really needs.

Selling more to your present customers doesn't mean that your objective is to become the customer's sole supplier, unless (1) the customer has a small business or (2) your product or service is not a raw material. Companies selling raw materials generally do not want all of a big company's business. Nor do they want to be the 100% supplier for too many small accounts.

Creative Selling Is the Key to Boosting Sales to Present Customers

Creative selling is the key if you want to sell more to your present customers. And if you want to sell creatively, you've got to be willing to use your imagination.

Chapter Three provides myriad ideas that great salespeople have used to boost sales to present buyers; here is a brief list of some of the techniques used:

1. Upgrade a customer.
2. Find a hidden application for a product.
3. Find a new use for raw materials.
4. Expand a small customer's buying.

5. Open up a whole new field of prospects, among which are some big buyers.

6. Get the product resold and reordered by a dealer-customer.

These ideas and others in Chapter Three demonstrate that creative thinking helps in each step of the selling process. They show that by using your imagination, you can yield creative ideas regardless of what you are selling.

Sell Across the Board

The more products in your line, the more opportunity there is for you to sell more to your present customers and prospects. It's all a matter of knowing how to build up a big order—in other words, how to sell across the board.

■ IDEA IN ACTION

In selling millwork products, John Mohr has several stock items to offer his customers. He asks for the order for one item at a time, starting, say, with window frames. He offers first the highest-priced frame that he has. When he closes on that item, he says, "Do you think 250 will be enough?" and starts writing up the order.

John then moves on to other items that the prospect might need, using the same technique of starting with the highest price, trying to increase the quantity, and then writing up the order as he continues to sell.

Failure to sell the complete line usually reduces the degree of success. Neglect of certain products might well result in an unbalanced and potentially dangerous sales picture in the territory. It is an invitation for the competition to step in and fill this need—and possibly to take over the other business as well.

WHAT TO DO Establish a breakdown ratio of selling time that allows for coverage of the complete line. For example, suppose your product line divides itself into three groups. You might decide to spend 30% of your time on group 1, 35% on group 2, and 35% on group 3. Establishing such a breakdown ratio does not necessarily mean that you *always* separate your time in exactly this way. It simply means that you never fail to look into every product possibility.

Concentrate on Selling Higher-Priced Units

The higher-priced units are usually the more profitable units, and they take no more of your selling time and energy than the lower-priced, less profitable ones. You should therefore concentrate on those items that yield the maximum profit. This means, of course, that you must also select prospects who are likely to buy the bigger items.

■ IDEA IN ACTION

Betty Strand has spent six years on the road representing a manufacturer of women's clothing. Her sales and income have increased only 15% in the past three years, whereas other salespeople who started out around the same time as Betty have more than doubled their sales in the same three years.

Betty has almost concluded that selling just isn't the right job for her. But when she examines her selling habits and activities in terms of the five sources of increased sales described earlier, she realizes that she's been concentrating on selling the low-priced items in her line. On her next trip around the territory, she concentrates on selling the higher-end items.

The result is that Betty's sales increase 40% almost immediately, and by the end of a year she has more than doubled her sales.

COMMENT Here is a concrete example of how much can be accomplished by a salesperson who makes a sincere and intelligent effort to apply the principle that there are only five ways to increase sales: (1) making more calls, (2) making better closings, (3) selling larger quantities, (4) selling wider variety, and (5) selling higher-priced units. In this instance cited, selling higher-priced items had an immediate and fundamental effect on Betty's career.

REMEMBER The caliber of the sale counts. A high-priced product usually offers better than average opportunities for earning big commissions. But selling such a product takes hard work, imagination, and skill. Those who excel at industrial selling, for example, which usually involves a high-priced product, get rejected just like every salesperson does. But they snap back quickly from their disappointments because they know that there's real profit in the next sale.

Strike at the Prospect's Biggest Need and the Sale Is Yours

Little sales can often be turned into big ones if you strike at the prospect's most important need. This technique works especially well in situations where the prospect starts by setting a limit on the size of his or her purchase.

■ IDEA IN ACTION

Charles Hampton, a real estate broker, sold a $400,000 building to a client who wanted income property at a top cost of $100,000. He did it by selling financial security, which was the client's primary need.

"Our client," says Mr. Hampton, "was 69 years old; his wife was 68 and in a wheelchair. He was looking for a two- or three-family house in good condition that he could rent to supplement his income, something located near his current home so that he wouldn't have to travel far to keep an eye on it." Here's how the sale was made:

- **Salesperson gets an idea.** The client was currently living in a two-story house. But because his wife used a wheelchair, they'd had to move their bedroom downstairs and the spacious upstairs, which had five bedrooms, was seldom used. Hampton suggested that his client sell his current home and buy a multiple-family dwelling with a first-floor apartment in which he and his wife could live comfortably. They could then use the profit from their original home to help finance the purchase of the new building and at the same time cut down on the cost of maintaining a large, two-story home that they didn't need any more.

- **Prospect likes idea but hesitates.** Hampton's idea made sense, but the client was worried that he wouldn't be able to sell his current home, which had five bedrooms and needed a costly paint job. There were very few families that required such a house—especially one that needed work. And without selling, the client wouldn't be able to afford the down payment and mortgage on the much larger building.

▪ **Salesperson resolves major stumbling block.** The real estate firm solved this difficulty. It approached a medical center in a nearby city that was looking for a place to house the parents of seriously ill children. The medical center agreed that the house's size and location were ideal and that, with the addition of another bath, it could easily house half a dozen couples in need of a place to stay while their children were hospitalized. Better yet, the medical center said it could make the necessary renovations using its own carpenters and maintenance staff.

▪ **Sale is made.** The client received what he wanted— additional income, as well as a more convenient living environment for himself and his wife. Mr. Hampton earned a nice commission. The deal was made possible because the salesperson understood and met the prospect's biggest need—financial security. Here was a creative idea thought up by associating the prospect's need with a knowledge of real estate needs in the surrounding area.

Get Customers to Think of You When They Need Advice

Frequently, a company seeks or needs the advice of suppliers when it is contemplating a change in a method or procedure that involves some product or service it is using. You may be one of several suppliers it can turn to. You stand a better chance than competitors to benefit from the change if you have shown your customer that you are eager to serve. You'll get the nod when a chance for bigger orders comes along.

▪ IDEA IN ACTION

Barney Bachman made a point of calling frequently on a publishing house that used his envelopes. His visits were brief but regular. Barney wanted to show the customer that he appreciated their business and that he had a genuine interest in being of service to them.

Just when he had begun to wonder if there was any hope of increasing his sales to this customer, the buyer called Barney in and asked if he could help them. The company wanted to increase the number of enclosures in the invoice envelopes that were glued to the outside of each package before shipment. The added thickness posed gluing and handling problems with the equipment they had in their shipping department.

Barney found that the problem could be overcome by using a new type of label-pocket envelope that was easier to stuff and easier to glue. Barney's company had the facilities to alter the customer's machines to handle the new envelopes. They offered to adjust the equipment without charge.

Pleased with the solution, the publisher agreed to adopt the new method. Barney got a large order and considerable repeat business, all because he had been the first salesperson the buyer thought of when advice was needed.

Upgrade Customers by Showing Them How to Use the Product

"Stepping up" a customer to a higher-priced item is often a by-product of seeing that the customer is getting full value from what he or she has already purchased. In discovering that a customer is not using the product properly, for example, you might also discover that his or her needs have changed and that a higher-priced product will serve these needs better.

Show the Loss Involved in Excessive Splitting of Business

Savings on transportation costs through quantity buying is often a convincing reason for getting customers to increase the size of their orders. This is especially true if a customer wants to divide his or her business among a larger number of suppliers than is really necessary. Here's one salesperson's response to the customer who says, "We prefer to divide our business":

"That's a very charitable approach. Still, you wouldn't open your purse and give your money away just to be fair, would you? Instead of buying in carload lots at carload bulk discounts, you are spending an additional 7% to split up the same business among, say, four suppliers and pay the case price. On your requirements for next month, that would mean a loss of $1,163."

Assume Responsibility, Based on Confidence and Knowledge

Big buyers are self-confident and invariably look for self-confidence in the salespeople who approach them. They want to do business with someone who knows everything there is to know about what he or she is selling, who considers the prospect's requirements as paramount, and who is not afraid to assume responsibility.

■ IDEA IN ACTION

Maureen Howitzer was determined to do business with a big contractor. She got the architect's specifications for a contemplated project and, upon examining them, found some items specified that were comparable to those handled by her firm.

After requesting a copy of the plans so that she could estimate the quantity required, she introduced herself to the contractor and explained that while her company's products were not specified, she had taken the privilege of estimating the quantities of materials that the contractor could use.

The contractor requested the figures and Howitzer told him the quantities that would be shipped if the order were accepted.

"No," said the contractor. "Your estimates are too high. You're just like the other salespeople who come around. They try to oversell on the job."

Howitzer gathered that the contractor was looking for someone to take responsibility for the quantities involved so that he wouldn't be caught with materials on hand that he couldn't return. She therefore said emphatically, "No! I'm certain my quantities are correct." Then she listed the dimensions of the building and computed the number of square feet in the area.

"If this order is based on my computation, I will accept full responsibility for the amount ordered," Howitzer promised.

The contractor signed the order, saying, "I'd have turned down the other salespeople because they had no confidence in their own figures and would not accept responsibility for quantities."

User Calls Help You Sell More to Present Customers

Many good salespeople make the mistake of not developing to the fullest the potential for increased business with their present customers. They fail to make the "user calls" that are essential to stepping up a customer's purchases. If yours is the kind of product that can be stepped up, you have much to gain by making user calls a regular part of your selling activities.

A follow-up call after a sale is the responsibility of the salesperson who got the order. During the call, you should make certain that the customer received what you sold him or her, and that price, shipping data, method of shipment, terms, and the like were carried out as promised. If you neglect to do this, you stand a good chance of losing your customer.

Consider the many advantages of following up on the customer who has purchased your product:

- You see your product in use and can check to make sure that it is performing satisfactorily. Many a customer has been lost because the product that was sold was not used properly. A simple bit of instruction, a slight adjustment, or a little extra technical assistance might have saved these customers.

- You gain the goodwill of the customer and the employees who are concerned with your product.

- You build the basis for repeat business without going through all the steps of selling.

- You get a chance to clear the air if the customer is harboring any resentment about unsatisfactory previous purchases, poor service, or other complaints that he or she may not have registered with your company. By nipping the hostility in the bud, you save the account. If you do more than the customer expects, for example, by offering a credit, refund, replacement, or other adjustment, you build goodwill and lay the groundwork for increased sales.

- You avert customer dissatisfaction before it arises.

- You pick up information that may reveal other customer needs.

SUGGESTION Plan your user calls so that they occur at regular intervals. Some of your customers might deserve weekly calls, others biweekly calls, or monthly or quarterly calls. When you can't meet your schedule, write a letter to your customer or telephone to let him or her know that you haven't forgotten the company's needs.

If you sell an industrial product, regular service calls must be made to protect your customer's investment in you and your product and to assure repeat business. Timing the calls properly depends upon the amount of service demanded and the number of customers to be covered.

CAUTION Do not confuse service calls with sales calls. The purpose of a service call is to render service. Although repeat sales will often result from service calls, you should let your customer bring up the subject of buying at these times.

Information Picked Up on User Calls Leads to More Sales

Every call on a customer should be thought of as the beginning of the next sale. With this thought in mind, you will always be alert to new selling opportunities.

■ IDEA IN ACTION

Ben Frost made a user call on a hospital and found that a new director had been appointed. He was the individual who would have to be "sold" in the future. Frost used the call to get acquainted and casually pointed out that he had observed a significant increase in the hospital's activities. The interview ended in the sale of additional hospital equipment.

■ IDEA IN ACTION

While making a user call, Marion Denberg learned from the purchasing agent that the company was building a new plant in New Jersey. She asked the purchasing agent who was in charge of the project. This lead eventually resulted in additional sales.

■ IDEA IN ACTION

Frank Atkins was on a user call when he picked up his first clue to the customer's need for more of his product. Operators said they were overloaded with work. However, this was not sufficient evidence of the need for additional equipment. On the next user call, Atkins learned that the increase in business was leading to excessive overtime. Later he was told that an independent contractor was being used to relieve the operators. Now he had enough information to justify making an "approach" call to the right person, and he was able to make the sale.

SUGGESTION If you have no reason for going back to see a customer at a particular time, create one. Send your customers some of your company's literature; then call to see if they have received it. Tie in your call with whatever is valuable in the printed material that helps you sell other products in your line.

A Little "Extra" Service Can Lead to Big Sales

Responding "beyond the call of duty" to a customer's request for help has opened many a door to bigger sales. It may even give you access to the individual you've been trying, without success, to see.

■ IDEA IN ACTION

A succession of changes in personnel involving operators of the product sold by John Lamb had led to a deterioration in the quality of the work produced by the product. The personnel problem had also caused the customer to miss important deadlines. The customer phoned John for help.

On his call, John ran off an eight-page price list for the customer to help him meet a deadline; he also started a new course of instruction. In a few days he had the department running smoothly.

The vice president, who was the "important person" to see for additional sales and with whom John had never been able to get an appointment, was naturally pleased with John's accomplishment. He now developed a friendly attitude. This was an excellent opportunity, John felt, to get the customer to buy more.

Here is what John did that led to an order for a larger unit of the product currently in use—and, later on, to sales of other products that had other applications.

- He started to discuss forms and promotional work for which new equipment could be used profitably.

- He gave the customer a new idea—sending a weekly price list to every customer.

- He showed samples of work that was being done by similar organizations.

- He overcame the customer's fear that employees would not be able to handle the operation. This was easy because the customer had renewed confidence in the seller's equipment, methods, and organization as a whole. All John had to do was to say that with his help, the installation would be successful. This experience shows how important it is to talk to the right individual. (Chapter Two offers tips on how to qualify prospects to ensure that your customer has the necessary buying authority.)

WARNING Don't confuse customer service that builds goodwill and leads to bigger sales with service that merely eats into your time and gets you nowhere. If you recognize that a customer is trying to "use you," it's better to say "No" politely to the request. And don't make promises unless you know you can and will fulfill them. A broken promise is not forgotten; it undermines your customer's confidence in you.

A Special Service Turns a Small Account into a Big One

Maybe you are getting a small share of a customer's total buying requirements because of your firm's location. A customer often favors nearby suppliers because he or she assumes that nearness is essential for service. The nearby suppliers, taking for granted that proximity gives them a hold on the account, may become lax in rendering service. By giving your customer better service than your competitors, you can become the favored supplier.

■ IDEA IN ACTION

Four competitive suppliers were selling cartons to a large manufacturer. Three of them were near to the manufacturer and the fourth, whom Charles Boland represented, was some distance away.

The manufacturer was angling for a $500,000 contract. If it could reduce the cost of the packaging, it was sure it could win that contract. So the manufacturer asked the nearby carton suppliers to help it solve the problem. After waiting a reasonable time without getting the service it wanted, the manufacturer presented the problem to Charles Boland.

Charles had been on the lookout for just such an opportunity to serve the manufacturer. If he could beat the competitors in finding a solution, he knew he'd get more of the manufacturer's carton business in the future.

Charles and his carton designer worked around the clock to redesign the manufacturer's carton. By cutting out part of the inner packing, they came up with a carton that served the purpose perfectly and cost less. Charles was in the manufacturer's plant bright and early the next morning with a sample of the redesigned carton.

The manufacturer got his $500,000 contract, and Charles got the carton order. This was only the beginning of a steady increase in the volume of business he brought in from this manufacturer.

Successful Repeat Sales May Depend on Your Knowing Top Executives

Business with your customer may be going along nicely enough until, one day, you drop in and the executive with whom you have been dealing is no longer there. A stranger is at his or her desk. This new manager may not feel as friendly toward your firm. He or she may have different ideas about whom to buy from. It may look like an uphill climb to get the account back on your side.

To prepare for such a situation, it may be wise to get to know your customer's top officials at the time you open the account.

■ IDEA IN ACTION

Dotty Stark, who sells advertising remembrance products, follows the practice of becoming acquainted with her customer's top personnel when she opens a new account. She says to the purchasing manager, the executive who usually makes the buying decision,

"Bill, you know my firm offers a unique line of greetings for the exclusive use of business firms and executives. I know your president and many of the officers of your company use a greeting of some kind at the holiday season and it is important to keep up these friendly contacts. We sell our distinctive line of greetings exclusively to businesspeople as a personal service, and it occurred to me that some of your officers would like to take advantage of making selections from our line. If you will introduce me, I will be only too glad to show them our line. In fact, it would be a pleasure for me to do so."

TIP Make as many friends as possible in every prospect's or customer's place of business. Your chances of selling the prospect or keeping the customer may be small if the only person you know is the buyer. Every organization has some very influential people who may not hold jobs of obvious importance. Get to know who they are and be friendly with them.

"Easy-to-Sell" Items Can Open the Way to Bigger Orders

If there are "easy-to-sell" items in your product list, you might apply this slogan: "Reach for the product instead of your hat." Even though you can't make big money by sticking to the easy-to-sell items, you *can* use them to make each interview count. You can also use them to keep the door open for a later sale of the more expensive item.

■ IDEA IN ACTION

Walter Keyser, who sold large wall calendars known as "quarterly planners," was calling on an insurance firm that was using a competitor's calendar. Walter wanted their business, but he was told that the company wouldn't change calendars under any circumstances. At this point he thought of the easy-to-sell pocket calendars that many companies handed out as holiday gifts and asked how many the firm sent out each year. He was told they sent about 1,000.

So Walter went into his pocket calendar story and made the interview pay off with a $3,000 order. When he left, Walter felt sure he would eventually be able to sell this firm the more expensive quarterly planners as well.

Sell by Telephone to Get Quick Customer Coverage

Sales to current customers can often be made quickly and inexpensively by using the phone. Local and even long-distance telephone calls pay off for the occasional selling opportunity when circumstances like the following, which have an element of urgency and importance, occur:

- **An increase in the product's price or service is scheduled.** A phone call gives current customers an opportunity to take advantage of buying during the period while the lower price is still in effect.

- **A limited-time "special" is being offered.** This may be a clean-out of merchandise at inventory time, or a special price for a particular line or item that is being dropped. Longtime customers are the logical prospects for such offerings.

- **A new line, a seasonal opening, or a new product is to be available at a certain time.** Longtime customers are given the first opportunity to get the new merchandise.

- **A pending event will increase the demand for the product.** For example, when a new law is about to be passed that affects the operation of a business or an individual's property, it often opens opportunities to get in under a deadline. The telephone can be used to reach as many customers or hot prospects as possible in a limited amount of time, so they can buy the product before the law goes into effect.

Telephone selling at such times calls for thorough preparation of the sales presentation that is best suited to the telephone. The techniques for selling over the phone are similar to those described for telephoning for an appointment. (Covered in Chapter Four).

Can You Increase Volume with Mail Orders?

Most salespeople are hired to do personal selling. If mail order were just as effective, salespeople wouldn't be needed. But when it comes to reordering, fill-ins, and orders on the basis of sample purchases, mail orders can serve a useful purpose. You can leave order blanks with customers and invite them to mail their orders or phone them in. But to depend upon mail orders for repeat business is foolhardy, even if you have developed the very best customer relations. Why? Because you leave an opening for your competitor to do on-the-spot selling. You miss the opportunity to make full-quantity sales and to upgrade. You encourage bad habits in the customer, such as asking for rush shipments. You just aren't selling, so you can't win.

HOW TO MOVE UP TO BIGGER BUYERS

You Can Move Up to Bigger Buyers

You must move up to bigger buyers if you want to reach your earnings goal. You must feel that no company is too big, and no single individual too important, for you to sell to. Experience has proved that it takes no more ability to sell a big buyer than it does to sell a small one. It may take more perseverance, more creative thinking, more planning of particular sales. But it does not take a greater knowledge of selling techniques than you need for everyday successful selling.

Follow these three simple rules and you will be able to face any big buyer, big executive, or person of prominence with as much ease as you would your best friend:

Rule 1.

Don't be afraid! Some salespeople are relegated to the status of small producers because they don't have the courage to talk to big people. There's no place where courage pays off as magnificently as it does in approaching a high-caliber prospect. Before you tackle this individual, however, you must have complete knowledge of your product, faith in it and in your company, and skill in applying the selling strategies explained in this *Guide*.

Rule 2.

Get started right away. Jump right in and begin to call on important prospects. After a few successful interviews, your fears will dissipate.

Rule 3.

Be fully prepared for each interview. Have a profitable idea to offer your "big prospect." Your idea should interest the prospect because it will benefit him or her particularly. The idea should come from your product knowledge and what you learn about your prospect before you go in for the interview. In other words, your sales plan should fit your prospect's needs so well that you know you have something great to offer him or her. Then, when you give your presentation, you'll be so engrossed in it that you'll completely forget that you're facing a very important person.

A Simple Plan for Selling to Bigger Buyers

Doing business with bigger buyers is largely a matter of intelligent prospecting and comparing the potential of prospects in different categories.

In almost all lines of business, the market comprises several groups of prospects. In each of these groups there may be small-, medium-, and big-potential prospects. Thus, in planning a work schedule, you must answer two questions: (1) Which groups in the market are most lucrative? and (2) Within these lucrative groups, who are the big potential prospects? You must think in terms of both issues if you want to invest your time in the most profitable manner possible.

■ IDEA IN ACTION

The territory assigned to Fran Elbert, who sells business systems and forms, contains more potential business than one person can cover. Fran must analyze the business in her territory and determine which markets offer the best opportunity for commissions.

In Fran's business, buyers fall into the following categories: wholesale, manufacturing, retail, financial, and professional. She studies the potential in each category and decides that a sensible time allotment plan is 50% industrial, 35% wholesale and retail, and 15% miscellaneous.

In each of these categories Fran analyzes the potential business which may be secured from an account and then invests her time commensurate with the volume of buying she can expect. She knows, for example, that any good retailer or wholesaler should use from $1,000 to $5,000 of her products per year. In deciding how much time she will spend with wholesalers and retailers, she concentrates on prospects with at least that potential. She doesn't waste time with prospects who can't buy more than $300 or $400 worth a year.

Fran is always alert to changes in business conditions in the various industries that she serves. She knows that some are hit harder than others at different seasons or are more sensitive than others to changes in the business cycle. When business falls off among certain customers and prospects, her sales to them will fall off. So she adjusts her efforts and spends less time among the temporarily depressed businesses and more time selling to businesses that are enjoying good times.

WARNING Being selective in reaching for big buyers does not mean concentrating all your efforts on only a few large accounts. It's exceedingly dangerous to make that mistake, because the loss of one account can mean the loss of a substantial share of business and earnings in the territory. A territory composed of a distribution of accounts, of varying sizes but all profitable, is a stable territory that won't be affected by the loss of a few accounts.

Know How Your Customers Are Faring

Business is a dynamic venture. Some small businesses become big businesses overnight because they are in a growing industry and have a vigorous, progressive management. Big customers can get bigger for the same reasons—or something happens and they begin to go downhill.

Eternal vigilance is the key to success in keeping your customer list properly balanced with a good proportion of big buyers. You must know at all times how your customers are faring.

WHAT TO DO

1. **Keep your eyes and ears open** when you call on customers and cover your territory.

2. **Watch your sales records.** If a big buyer's orders keep declining over a period of time, look for the reason. Has a top executive become incapacitated? Has there been a change of management? Is the business suffering from inroads made by the competition? If so, should you go after the business of the competitor who is causing your customer's business to taper off?

3. **Consider dropping unprofitable accounts.** When a worthwhile account begins to deteriorate, and you no longer get value commensurate with the time you devote to it, consider adjusting your priorities and concentrating upon better potential accounts.

4. **Take advantage of rapid growth.** When a medium-sized buyer's record reflects vigorous growth, make the most of the added potential.

A Carefully Planned Sale Gets a Big Buyer to Order

A carefully planned sale, centered on a big creative idea from which a customer will profit, is a surefire way of making sales to big buyers. Planning such a sale means thinking through the entire proposal and doing all the necessary legwork and research. But once this groundwork is laid, you shouldn't have any trouble getting the prospect's attention, arousing his or her interest, creating desire, convincing the prospect, and closing the sale.

Quite often a thoroughly worked-out plan yields extra dividends. Little ideas turn up in the planning that make the sale actually grow bigger than you had anticipated.

■ IDEA IN ACTION

One of the reasons Jonathan Simms has been so successful as a salesperson for a company that makes decals is that he carefully works out an advertising program that will help his customer reap the full benefits of the sale. For example, his big sale to a large, progressive bank was built around the idea of getting the bank's name into the home of every Boy Scout and Girl Scout in the area. Since the Scouts were involved in a community outreach project on fire prevention, Simms suggested that the bank distribute brightly colored decals that could be put in the window of a child's room so that firefighters would know where to find the child in the event of a house fire. The actual distribution of the decals would be handled by the Scouts, which eliminated one of the bank's problems.

To accomplish this sale, Simms planned and took several steps before he approached the bank officials. When he was fully prepared, he presented the program to the bank and made the sale.

The plan that made the sale is outlined as follows.

- Simms first made several calls to Boy Scout and Girl Scout leaders in the area served by the bank.

- He learned from them the districts into which the area was divided for the purpose of selling Girl Scout cookies and conducting other scouting fund-raisers. There were five districts where the decals could be distributed.

- He obtained a large map of the town and pasted stars on this map, each one representing a meeting place for Scouts.

- He found out how many Scouts were in each of these districts, which gave him an accurate number of how many decals would be needed.

- He called on the bank officials and presented the idea of putting the bank's name on the decals and distributing them to every home with children in the area. Not only would the bank's name be associated with a valuable community service, but it would also be connected with the scouting movement. Simms pointed out in his sales presentation that promoting the bank's name through the distribution of the decals would invite new business from the Scouts themselves, their parents, Scout officials and all others who are connected with scouting.

- When he sat down with the bank officials to decide where the area of greatest influence would be and how many decals would be required to get complete coverage, Simms laid out his specially prepared map and membership figures while his prospects listened with interest.

The planning and presentation Simms did resulted not only in the sale of 9,000 decals but also opened up ideas for expanding coverage to include the schools and churches where the Scout troops hold their meetings.

BREAKING INTO BIG SELLING THROUGH BETTER TIME PLANNING

How You Use Your Time Means Everything

No salesperson—no matter how skilled—can attain a high degree of success unless he or she has learned, and put into effect, the practices that make for the sound utilization of time.

These practices are discussed in the following paragraphs. They show how to time each call to mesh, as far as possible, with the individual prospect's or buyer's own preferences and work habits. They explain how to time callbacks so that a "hot" prospect is not called back too late and a repeat call is not made too soon on a "lukewarm" prospect.

Also in this section are guides for eliminating "peak and valley" selling, as well as ideas for accomplishing immediate and long-term goals through the optimal use of time.

In addition to the planning techniques covered here, there are others in this *Guide* for gaining selling time through proper self-management. (See Chapter Eight).

Two Ways to Plan Your Calls to Save Time

Calls can be planned in two ways, depending on whether you are in "fixed route" selling or in "no-route" selling. This will determine whether you plan your calls by using route sheets or follow-up records.

Fixed-route salespeople.

Salespeople who call on each of their customers once a week usually make their calls in a fixed sequence, calling on each buyer on the same day at approximately the same hour. The same pattern prevails for salespeople who call once a month or at any other stated interval.

Planning your work under such circumstances is a relatively simple task, consisting of making a *route sheet* that will permit you to see as many customers in the least amount of travel time as possible. Be sure to include the following provisions, however:

- Allow time for calling on new prospects who have just started in business or moved into your territory.
- Find new customers to replace those who have moved out or stopped buying for some other reason.
- Adjust for buyers' vacations or other factors that might interfere with the normal call pattern.
- Pay proper attention to special matters, such as a rush order or some other unusual request or situation that you must act on yourself. For instance, you should inform your customers of an important price change, new products, or any other developments. Use these news items to increase sales.

No-route salespeople.

If you do not work on a fixed route involving calls at brief intervals, use the follow-up record approach to keep you informed without spending unnecessary time and trouble. This system involves nothing more than filling out a 3" × 5" index card for each prospect. Here is a typical card.

June 12, 19—

Woods Mfg. Co.
Mr. Grumback, Office Mgr.

Not interested now, but may need a #264 copier in about 60 days. Best time to call is before noon. Could use a #601, but won't spend that much.

Follow up Aug. 20

Now for the key to this system. File your card under "August 20." The next step occurs on or about that date. You call on this customer, without making another card, and simply add the following:

> Aug. 20—Grumback on vacation
> F/U Aug. 28

On that date the following notations are added:

> Aug. 28—Saw Grumback. He will try to get a purchase order put through. Telephone him 2 P.M., Aug. 29

The final note in this case might be:

> Aug. 29—Ordered one #264.
> F/U about Jan. 1 to see if he needs other items—they are expanding.

Note the advantages of this follow-up record system:

- Eliminates the need to rely on your memory.
- Does away with the need to *rewrite* data once recorded.
- Provides a healthy stream of callbacks on customers that you think merit a follow-up call.
- Provides a constant, foolproof source of definite appointments.
- Makes you decide and record immediately after each call the data you will find useful on your callback and the specific time when each callback should be made.

File each card so that it will "come up" again on the date you select as the appropriate one. You will find more suggested forms for planning calls in Chapter Ten.

How to Find the Best Time to Call on Customers in a New Territory

If you're in a new territory, you have no way of foretelling whether your prospect will be "too busy" the first time you call. A method to help you overcome this situation immediately and prevent its recurrence in future calls follows.

∎ IDEA IN ACTION

Bob Gray represents a distributor of radio and television receivers. He calls on retail dealers. Bob is transferred from Ohio to Massachusetts. His customer records for the new territory give him names, addresses, and the past buying record of each account.

On the day he starts out on his new assignment, Bob makes his first call at 9:20 A.M. He has selected an important account—a dealer with five branch stores.

"Mr. Cantrell is busy right now," says the receptionist. "He'll be tied up for another hour or so."

Most salespeople would say, "Well, I'll make another stop and then call back." But not Bob—he has a better method.

"Can you tell me," he asks the receptionist, "what is usually the best time of day to call on Mr. Cantrell?"

"Right after lunch," comes the reply. "Mr. Cantrell is rarely free in the morning, but he tries to save afternoons for salespeople and other callers."

Bob thanks the receptionist and immediately makes a note on his customer record: "Call only after lunch."

At about 1:45 Bob returns. He gets not only an interview but a good-sized order.

"Mr. Cantrell," Bob says as he is about to leave, "I mentioned a promotion we're going to launch in about three weeks. As soon as I get the material to show you, I'd like to stop by again. Would you prefer to have me telephone you for an appointment, or shall I just drop in?"

"You needn't phone in advance," says the customer. "Just make it in the afternoon—any day except Friday."

Bob now has two more clues to help in his timing. He adds to his notation, "Needn't phone—but don't call on Fridays." By the time Bob has made his first swing around his territory, he has "timing" notes on practically every account.

Because he has taken the trouble to find out about his customers' habits and preferences, Bob has accomplished these two important things: (1) He knows how to avoid calling at the *wrong* time. (2) Because enough of his customers prefer to see salespeople either early in the morning or late in the day, Bob can always plan to "sell" from at least 9 A.M. to 5:30 P.M.

How You Can Double the Working Day and Get to Your Goal Faster

A good planner works up a call schedule for a long enough period in advance to assure high goal earnings over the period. Then he or she follows up with a day-to-day plan, making each day count for two, that enables him or her to keep pace with the long-term plan.

■ IDEA IN ACTION

Sarah Graham sells a printed business service on a subscription basis. She earns at least $55,000 a year because she's one of the best planners in the sales organization.

During Christmas week Sarah blocked out the next 60 working days. Into each block she inserted, according to her itinerary, her four best prospects for the day. She then added four renewal prospects who could use an additional service (she determined this by servicing the accounts). She therefore had eight prospects each and every day for 60 days. Her goal was to close two or three orders a day—and with planning like this, why shouldn't she?

Sarah subscribes to the order-a-day philosophy. But she makes each of the 60 working days count for 2 days. How? By dividing each block into two parts. Thus she creates 120 theoretical working days. She then attempts to make one sale for each theoretical working day and gets her minimum of two orders a day.

"This approach," Sarah explains, "isn't difficult to do with the prospects aligned according to plan. I use it over a three-month period (the current month and the two months planned ahead). If I blank one day, I know that the sales of big-priced units will make up the dollar volume I want."

How to Avoid "Peak and Valley" Selling

A period of low or perhaps no productivity can discourage all but the strongest salespeople. When the valleys are hit, morale tends to sag. You may begin to wonder whether you've lost your touch. You begin to question whether your line and your territory are to blame. Indeed, the combination of financial hardship during the "slumps" and low morale has caused many salespeople to quit their jobs and in some cases to drop selling as a career. Such slumps usually follow a period of high productivity.

The first idea in action shows how the slump happens; the second shows how it can be avoided.

■ IDEA IN ACTION

Mike Milford sells space in a well-known trade magazine. Since there are no important seasonal factors involved, his selling pace should be a reasonably steady one. But in reality, Mike's record is one of "feast or famine."

The explanation for this is really rather simple. When Mike finds, as he periodically does, that he has "warmed up" a number of prospects whom he expects to close shortly, he concentrates his full attention on them, thus neglecting to do the prospecting and spade work needed to locate prospects whom he might close at a later date.

In due course Mike gets a "Yes" or "No" from each of his fully warmed-up prospects. The orders he gets make a rather impressive total, and he writes off his failures with the remark, "You can't sell them all."

At this point Mike is in the position of having had a fine month's business, with correspondingly high income. He isn't at all concerned, therefore, when he fails to close a sale for the next couple of weeks.

When two weeks stretch into four, however, Mike begins to get jittery. True, he has warmed up a few new prospects during this four-week period, but they aren't ready to be closed yet. Since Mike begins to feel himself under some pressure at this point, he tries to "rush" them into buying. When he finds that won't work, his morale begins to drop.

"Five weeks with only two quarter-page sales," Mike says to himself, "and I've got to sell two pages a week to make a living!" Wryly he recalls the extra bill he ran up some six weeks ago, when all those big contracts broke, one right after another!

Much as he dislikes doing it, Mike asks his sales manager for an advance. "Got some nice things lined up that will break any day, Ms. Davis," says Mike. "I've just had some tough breaks the last five weeks, that's all. You know, for about a month I was going great guns. Then, wham! It ended just like that!"

Ms. Davis knows all about it, of course. She also knows that all this could have been avoided if Mike Milford had only paced his warming-up efforts more evenly.

■ IDEA IN ACTION

Neal Sloan also sells space in a trade magazine. Several years ago, during a slump, he decided that if he couldn't somehow avoid "feast and famine" selling he'd change his job. His solution was simple. "I need two pages a week as a minimum. That means I ought to have four 'hot' prospects lined up at any given time. To do that, I'm going to make it an ironclad rule to spend every Tuesday and every Friday doing nothing but making 'warm-up' calls on cold prospects. That will leave three days each week—plenty of time to nurse along those who are about ready to buy. And if this plan works out the way I think it will, I'll always have at least a little backlog of 'hot' prospects, instead of a record-breaking month sandwiched in between two heart-breaking months." Neal's plan worked well, except the one or two times he violated his self-established rule about reserving two days each week for locating and warming up prospects.

WHAT TO DO If you don't have a fixed route, you should consider with care how you can best apply the rule in your own work. Some people find that it pays to devote every morning to prospecting and "warming up," thus limiting closing efforts to the afternoon hours. Others reverse the order. Still others find a different application most suitable. The point is that you can eliminate "peak and valley" selling in almost every instance if you arrange your work in such a way that there is a relatively constant stream, rather than an intermittent one, of prospects moving up the ladder from "cold" to "hot."

How to Lengthen the Seasonal Selling Period

If yours is a seasonal business in which the major portion of your sales is made in a concentrated period, you gain volume by lengthening the season. The method used by one creative salesperson, described next, is adaptable to most lines.

■ IDEA IN ACTION

Following a seasonal pattern in her trade, Alice Denton sold hard from April 10 to June 15, booking orders for merchandise to be delivered to retailers late in August. In those ten weeks she had to book practically all her year's business.

Alice began to look at her limited selling period as a problem. She thought, "How can I stretch the normal 10-week season into 12 weeks? If I call on the average retailer as early as April 1, he'll tell me it's too early. If I call as late as June 25, he'll tell me he's all bought up."

Having stated the problem, Alice then moved on to find a solution. Her creative thinking led to a successful plan:

■ She selected the names of five retailers who gave her the biggest orders and called on them a week ahead of the usual date. She had no trouble in getting them to place orders because the line meant a lot to them.

■ She called on other accounts ahead of the season and convinced them, by showing them the five big orders she already had, that there was nothing to be gained by waiting.

■ If the strategy didn't work, she would say, "Mr. Lane, I guess that since you prefer to buy considerably later in the season, I won't be too late if I call back on you, say, about June 15 or June 20?"

This salesperson recognized that her customers have buying habits. Some were "early" buyers, or could be encouraged to buy early; others by inclination were "late" buyers. With these facts at her command, it was easy to plan her way around obstacles.

Plan the Next Day's Work

At the end of each day review and analyze your selling performance for the day. Then, prepare for your next day's work. You should not consider your workday finished until you have outlined a detailed work schedule for the next day. With a planned order of work, your selling will become more efficient and effective, and you will have made it possible to earn the full dollar value of your selling time.

To arrange your calls in an orderly, economical, and effective plan is not enough. You must also provide an alternative plan in the event that someone you expected to spend time with goes out of town, is at a meeting, becomes ill, or cannot see you for some other reason.

☐ EXAMPLE

On a certain Monday you plan to make ten calls, but find that one appointment scheduled from 10 to 11 o'clock cannot be kept by your prospect. However, you have provided yourself with half a dozen carefully selected call cards for the vicinity. Had you not taken the precaution of these substitute calls, you would have had to "kill" the hour or spend it making random calls. Instead, you are able to use your time fruitfully.

How to plan for uncontrollable circumstances.

■ Determine which customers you will call on. Remember to double-check for appointments and to refer to your "follow-up" file described earlier in this chapter. (The number of customers you plan to see will depend largely on your estimate of how much time each interview takes as well as estimated travel time.)

■ Prepare several substitute calls for each customer to be called on. Be sure to choose alternatives located close to the customer you originally planned to see.

■ Estimate how much time to allot to each. Know just where you will be each quarter hour of the day, and stick to this schedule.

■ Decide upon an order of call which will take the least travel time. This means either arranging your calls into a continuous line which eliminates backtracking or arranging them in groups determined by their proximity to each other.

How to plan a successful day's work.

■ Review the past records of the customers you are going to call on. This will help you in deciding what items you should suggest they buy and in what quantities, colors, and so forth.

■ Refer to notes on your customer record card to see if there are any special matters you should take up with these accounts.

■ Mentally "make each call" by rehearsing what you will do and say when you get there.

You should also plan to

■ Spend more of your time with profitable customers.

■ Terminate your interviews when it becomes obvious that they are not going to be profitable. Customers will rob you of selling time by merely "chewing the fat." Learn to get away from these time-wasters as quickly and politely as you can.

■ Set a daily goal for yourself. Goals provide you with an important stimulus for your day's work.

TIP A well-planned day always lines up the minimum number of cold calls necessary to maintain a steady pace of earnings. It lines up more than the minimum if you are striving to reach a higher goal.

KEEPING UP WITH THE LATEST SELLING TECHNIQUES

New Developments Affect Your Selling

We are living in a dynamic world in which monumental changes affecting selling are occurring every day. You can't be blamed for missing these new developments; you just don't have the time—and maybe not the interest—to keep up with the discoveries made almost daily. But if you miss the import of the developments as they touch your own behavior as a seller of goods or services, you can and will pay the price—in lost orders.

Here are two suggestions:

1. Check your present selling methods and beliefs against the yardsticks presented in this section. This self-analysis will bring you up to date.

2. Have a healthy respect for your sales manager's constructive suggestions for better selling of your particular product or service. It's part of the sales managers job to alert the sales force to improved selling techniques as they are developed. He or she watches for changes that influence buyers' attitudes and finds out what is happening by reading current publications in the sales field, attending conferences of sales executives in all industries and exchanging ideas with them, studying the total market picture, and analyzing the reports of all the salespeople in the firm.

The "Natural-Born Salesperson" Is a Myth

The popular belief that some people are instinctively good at selling is a myth. The "natural salesperson" designation implies that the ability to sell is something you're born with. Actually, any normal person who is *interested in selling* can learn and, having learned, can practice selling successfully.

The spellbinder who cannot answer technical questions is likely to lose the order to a competing salesperson who may have a less glib tongue but can demonstrate the worth and application of his or her product.

▪ IDEA IN ACTION

Alfred Whiting is a salesperson from the "old school." He relies heavily on personality, hospitality, and the like to get the prospect to sign on the dotted line.

Alfred complains that business isn't as good as it used to be. The truth is that the people he calls on buy 50% more of his type of product today than they did 20 years ago, but they buy most of it from other salespeople. Why? Because Alfred continues to sell by being congenial, while his competitors devote the interview to showing charts, tables, analyses, reports, and other data that buyers require for decision making today.

Although he may not realize it, the world of buying and selling has left Alfred—and his like—behind.

Don't Oversell Yourself

Popularity and friendship are genuine assets when it comes to sales. But the days when salespeople reached the top by selling themselves is long gone.

▪ IDEA IN ACTION

Bill Albee covers New England, calling on hardware whole-salers with a specialty line. Although Bill has become friendly with many important buyers in the three years that he has called on them, he has not succeeded in opening as many new accounts as he had expected.

Several of Bill's competitors who have concentrated on *selling* rather than on building purely personal relationships are getting the very orders that Bill feels he has earned by three years of "cementing friendships."

If Bill understood that the real question is, "How much does my behavior contribute to the successful completion of this particular sale?" he would gear his thinking and activities toward getting orders rather than having friendly chats.

A "Prima Donna" Doesn't Fit into Today's Selling

Today's salesperson believes in and practices complete cooperation with his or her employer. He or she not only accepts supervision, but requests instruction and guidance. He or she participates in the company's sales meetings and does everything possible to make such an event succeed. He or she also joins wholeheartedly in planned "drives" and is an enthusiastic competitor in any contests that may be proposed.

Today, each person must be a member of "the team"—or make room for someone else who will join willingly and sincerely in the common effort.

Buying and Selling Have Become More Businesslike

The days when salespeople went around handing out expensive cigars, slapping people on the back, entertaining lavishly, and telling a new crop of stories on each visit are long gone. But some salespeople still believe that buyers will gravitate to the person who acts like everyone's best friend.

Buyers today favor the salesperson from whom they can buy most profitably.

Of course, buyers are still human, and still susceptible to attention and flattery, to friendly gestures, and to personal charm.

But today's competitive conditions and increased emphasis on ethical standards have shifted the emphasis from the social to the business aspects of sales transactions. The sales interview is no longer a time of persuasion by spellbinding. It has become, instead, a time of persuasion by education. Facts have replaced jokes and irrelevant stories; information is now preferred to cigars.

Everyone Values Time Today

The pace of business and of living is faster today than it was in former years. Everyone knows this, but not every salesperson remembers it while making presentations, for example. If you have not trimmed your sales presentation to take the minimum time necessary to interest and persuade your prospect, you haven't kept up with the changing pace of business.

Old-Time Persistence Is Not for You

While there may have been a time when persistence was regarded as a selling virtue, today's salesperson recognizes that each call and each working hour must pay for itself.

Exhibits 1.2 and 1.3 show the difference in the value of persistence. The first one was written by a sales manager 20 years ago, and the second was written just recently:

EXHIBIT 1.2

Memo Illustrating an Outdated Viewpoint Toward Sales Calls

To: Sam Hall, Sales Representative

From: William Green, Sales Manager

My hearty congratulations on the fine job you have done in opening the Lamson account! We have been trying to sell these people for 20 years, and as you may know, I visited them personally several years ago to try to get them started.

I know that you have called on them every three months for almost ten years. Now your persistence has been rewarded. Even though your opening order is for only 10 gross, you have finally cracked the ice, and I know that you will get a lot of business from them.

Hats off to you! I only wish we had more salespeople who had the guts to keep on calling after being turned down cold for ten years. If we had, we'd also have a lot more fine accounts like Lamson's on the books.

Congratulations and best wishes.

EXHIBIT 1.3

Memo Illustrating Today's Viewpoint Toward Sales Calls

To: Kevin Brown, Sales Representative

From: Karen Simpson, Sales Manager

In reviewing your reports I notice that there are about 20 accounts that you have been calling on for two years or more without getting any business.

As you know, Kevin, each call you make represents an investment on your part and on the company's. Four calls a year on each of 20 prospects means a total of 80 calls. Since our people average about 4 calls a day, these 80 calls are costing you approximately 20 working days per year.

There are about 20 working days in the average month, which means that this group of prospects is getting one-twelfth of your time and attention with absolutely no return. As a matter of fact, when you figure time out for vacations, holidays, sales meetings, and so forth, the percentage of your time really exceeds one-twelfth.

What correctives do you suggest for this situation? Unless you feel that you should try some other approach with these accounts, do you have any specific reason to believe that you can sell them within the near future? If not, I suggest that you drop them from your call list so that you can spend this valuable field time where you will get an adequate return.

Please let me hear from you on this within the next week or so.

"Low Pressure" Is Today's Byword

It's costly to be identified as a "high-pressure" salesperson. Buyers abhor tactics that they feel are high pressure. But don't think that pressure isn't an essential part of selling. It takes pressure to change a prospect's mind, for example, but this kind of pressure is seldom perceived as such. Every good salesperson uses a certain amount of pressure during the interview, but it is usually applied with such skill that the prospect is unaware of its use.

■ IDEA IN ACTION

Tony Merkle sells automobile tires to owners of fleets of trucks. He does a poor job of making his presentation, and as a result the prospect doesn't have a clear idea of the reasons to buy. Hence, when Tony goes into a close, the prospect thinks, "He's got his nerve! Offers me a proposition that has no appeal, and then acts as though I had said 'Yes'—I'm fed up with these high-pressure tactics!"

A few weeks later Tony's district manager, Lenore Todd, accompanies him on some calls, among which is a callback on the same prospect. Lenore makes such a skillful presentation that the prospect decides he is definitely interested.

Before the deal can be closed, however, the prospect must gather some data from his company records.

"Guess I'll have to ask for a day to get the data together, Ms. Todd," says the prospect.

"Mr. Main," Lenore says, "since I'm in town only for the day, do you think you could manage to have the data ready shortly before 5, so that we can get everything all set up while I'm here?"

Mr. Main agrees.

While in fact Lenore's pressure has been much greater than Tony's, it was not detected by the prospect, since it was applied with such skill that complying seemed the logical thing to do. In other words, an attempt to close an order that has been earned by a skillful presentation seems free from pressure to the prospect, while a much milder attempt to close an order that has not been earned seems to the prospect like high pressure.

Here's another example of this observation.

▪ IDEA IN ACTION

John Williams sells an employee pension program for a bank. He fails to open his presentation with a remark that gets instant and relevant attention, with the result that Mr. Fisher, the president of a large company, wants to terminate the interview after John has been with him for only a few minutes.

"No, I don't think we'd be interested, Mr. Williams," says the prospect.

"But, Mr. Fisher, there's so much more I want to tell you . . ."

"Not today, Mr. Williams. Perhaps some other time, when I'm not so busy."

What went wrong? Simply this: The salesperson did not arouse and maintain sufficient interest to keep the prospect from wanting to terminate the interview. Then he used a weak plea to try to get the prospect to give him a bit more time.

REMEMBER Any salesperson who fails to arouse and hold the prospect's interest will appear, to the prospect, to be unreasonable in asking for his or her time.

Now let's see how Leslie Burritt, another salesperson for the same company, approaches the same prospect:

▪ IDEA IN ACTION

Leslie makes such a skillful presentation that Mr. Fisher doesn't try to terminate this interview. She then proceeds to close the order.

"Well, Ms. Burritt," says the prospect, "you certainly have convinced me that your program has merit for a company like ours. I'll discuss it with my associates and let you know our decision before long."

"That's fine, Mr. Fisher," Leslie replies, "but do you mind if I make one suggestion? Your associates will have questions, just as you did, and some of them may be questions that we have not covered this morning. Wouldn't you like me to meet with your group, so that I can answer their questions right then and there?"

Mr. Fisher agrees.

This request represents much more pressure than did Williams' request for a few minutes of his prospect's time. But because Leslie Burritt used skill throughout the entire interview, and because her request was couched in terms that underscored the benefits for her prospect, it was granted.

Buyers and Prospects Are Usually Ready to Listen

Most business firms are at least willing to give every visitor a hearing. They may even have a policy that requires the purchasing agent to interview every salesperson who calls—except, of course, at times when this becomes a physical impossibility.

Such a policy makes good sense, because the company

- Wants to establish a reputation for being courteous.

- Knows that only by seeing a constant stream of salespeople can they be certain of buying to their advantage.

- Has learned that salespeople bring valuable "news of the trade." Even though the company may not be interested in what a particular salesperson has to offer, they often profit from his or her visit in terms of information about trends and developments that they might not get by other means.

- Knows that from time to time they are unable to get what they need from established resources. If they rebuff all salespeople except those from whom they buy regularly, they aggravate the problem of finding a source when they really need the material.

- Understands that if they want their own salespeople to get a hearing, they must return the courtesy by seeing the salespeople who call on them.

WHAT TO DO Keep the five reasons for an open-door policy in mind. You can use them in getting interviews and in making your presentation.

Competition Is a Stimulant

Competition is the motivating force behind the private enterprise system; it is a stimulant both for business and for individuals. But competition among salespeople is not as ruthless or as uncivilized as it was a few decades ago. In fact, competitors in most industries today cooperate through their trade associations to promote their mutual interests.

> **SUGGESTION** When you meet a competitor's salesperson in a hotel, be aloof without being unfriendly. You might talk to him or her about developments that affect the entire industry, but when it comes to direct competition, you're better off remaining silent. This attitude will reflect your conviction that your product is as good as, or better than, the product of the competitor.

Salespeople with absolute confidence in the superiority of their product have been known to make sales by boosting a competitive product. This procedure is not generally recommended, but the following story bears out the fact that under the right circumstances, confidence in the product can support highly unconventional selling techniques.

■ IDEA IN ACTION

When a prospect dropped into a car showroom, he told the salesperson that he had made up his mind to buy another make of car but just wanted to compare the two.

"I understand," the salesperson said, "but let me tell you about our car anyway." After he had cited all the car's features, the prospect was only half convinced and expressed a desire to examine the other car once more before he made up his mind.

"If you'll step into my car," said the salesperson, "I'll take you over to the other dealer. His car is a good one and deserves your consideration. If, after comparing it point for point with our car, you decide that ours is better, we will be very happy to serve you."

He drove the prospect to the rival showroom and left him there. Later the prospect came back and bought the car. He explained his decision: "Your willingness to let me see the other car, your admission that it was a good car, and your offer to take me to a competitor's place of business astonished me. I know that you wouldn't do that unless you had absolute confidence in your car. Obviously, you had no fear of competition. Your own belief made me believe."

When you succeed in winning the customer who has favored your competitor, your enthusiasm will naturally be high. But you shouldn't be devastated if you lose out. Instead, focus your attention on why it happened, and do whatever is necessary to prevent its happening again. Analyzing the results of your work each day is particularly helpful in rebuilding your enthusiasm.

Your problem is not so much how to act toward a competitive salesperson, but how to answer the customer who does not care to make a change, or the prospect who says that the other company puts out a better line. Guidance for dealing with these situations can be found in Chapter Seven, Making Objections Work *for* You.

Salespeople Must Be Experts

Buyers today are subject to greater management control than ever before. Their companies expect them to "buy right," and they look to the salesperson to aid them in this task. This means that salespeople must be equipped with facts, statistics, data, and knowledge of their product that would have surprised their predecessors only a few decades ago.

The demands on salespeople have been accelerated as the products themselves have become more technical. In many industries, the salesperson's responsibility as an educator has increased severalfold.

In our technologically oriented society, salespeople must have sufficient technical knowledge to give prospects the information they want and need about construction, use, economy, and features of the product offered. The way the information is given, how it is worked into the presentation, and how it is used to answer objections must be as up to date as the product itself.

■ IDEA IN ACTION

Theresa Smiley sells electronic typewriters. On her first call one morning, the office manager says, "I understand the ABC typewriter is faster than yours."

Theresa replies, "Oh, I don't think so. We sell a lot of our machines and nobody has ever raised that objection."

Of course, Theresa's competitor selling the ABC machine gets the sale. Her general statement, which merely expressed an opinion, failed to impress her prospect.

Theresa's second call works out differently. Her second prospect says, "We are interested in cutting down noise in our office. Will your machine help us do that?"

This time Theresa is equipped to meet this situation. She happens to have in her briefcase a study of the noise levels produced by her own product as compared to several leading competitive products. She makes the sale easily because she has earned it.

Salespeople Must Keep Pace

The day of the salesperson who "knows it all," who is a "natural" and who needs no instruction, is definitely gone. Sales has become a profession. It has become more of a science than an art. It is, furthermore, a science that is still being refined.

Today's salesperson, whether a novice or a veteran, must have a capacity for learning and must *want* to learn. Selling today relies as much on educating the prospect as it does on techniques of persuasion. But before you can educate your prospect, you must educate yourself.

As a salesperson, your education must take place largely through reading, study, and observation. You must get the facts about your company's history, development, growth, management, reputation, and place in the industry. You must know all about the products you have to sell and something about other products that might be sold through other divisions of the company. You must become acquainted with your customers' business as well, for the more you know about their selling problems—or manufacturing problems—the better chance you have of selling and serving them. You must know the specific types of competition you will meet in the field.

A "Psychological Moment" for Closing Is an Outdated Theory

Today's salespeople are the beneficiaries of some very revealing professional studies on the proper time to close the sale. There was a time when salespeople proceeded on the assumption that there was a specific moment in the interview called "the psychological moment" and that this was the "right" time for closing a sale. A good salesperson was supposed to be an expert at detecting this moment—the theory being that at this point in the interview the prospect's interest was at its peak and his or her resistance at its lowest. If the salesperson could "spot" that moment, the sale would be successful. But if he or she missed it, or so the myth would have us believe, all was lost.

Closing the sale is conducted today on an entirely different basis. Today's salespeople use what is called the "trial close" (or the "multiple close"). The trial close is in fact a series of attempts to close, spread throughout the entire interview. (Chapter Six offers extensive guidelines on how to use the multiple close.

Dickering or "Horse Trading" Is Frowned Upon

Special price concessions to selected buyers tend to be frowned upon these days as a matter of general policy. While dickering may have been the rule rather than the exception at one time, today it is engaged in only rarely. Most sellers pride themselves on practicing a one-price policy. Furthermore, there are legal restrictions covering many types of selling transactions that forbid or restrict more favorable treatment of one customer as opposed to others.

Nevertheless, there are close-outs and various other concession situations that can be taken advantage of to bring about an immediate decision to buy.

NOTE There is a difference between offering a concession that amounts to "horse trading" and offering an inducement to close. The inducement is available to anyone who takes advantage of it while the offer is in effect; the concession is not. (See Chapter Six for more information on using the inducement to close sales.)

How Changes in Management Have Improved Salespeople's Opportunities

Progressive companies today are focusing on the profitability of every product sold. There are systems available now through which the costs of distribution, which includes all the expenses associated with selling, are analyzed and allocated to various products, customers, and the like. For example, a dry goods wholesaler may keep statistical records on the number of orders invoiced, the number of items billed, the products sold, the size of the orders, the number of delivery stops made for each department, and so on.

These statistical controls enable the company to see exactly how productive each salesperson is from a profit standpoint. The studies may result in certain lines or products being dropped as unprofitable, certain items being taken out of the line and given to a specialty salesperson, and other changes.

Companies that pay attention to controlling distribution costs usually have their salespeople very much in mind. If, as a result of managerial control, a salesperson's territory is changed, or he or she is required to eliminate certain types of customers or products, his or her compensation will usually be adjusted so that he or she can continue to earn at the same level and make steady progress toward higher goals.

However, don't expect the company or its controller to give you a detailed explanation of the accounting by which it arrives at its decisions to make such changes. Most companies that once tried to explain their accounting practices to their salespeople have since abandoned the practice. They found that the salespeople were confused by figures that they did not understand and wasted time in useless discussions among themselves about the system.

"Selling" Includes Many Nonselling Duties

The increase in the number of non-selling duties has taken a big bite out of the salesperson's time. A salesperson's duties today include some or all of the following tasks in addition to the work of getting interviews and making sales:

- Giving your company your opinion about its existing products and competition's product lines, with criticisms and suggestions for changes.

- Helping your company to develop new products by offering ideas and giving advice on proposed new products.

- Supplying information about the territory, the local market, the competition, prospects' needs, and customers' credit position.

Salespeople are sometimes asked to conduct "survey interviews" to gather important facts about their present customers. They must come up with answers to such questions as: "Are customers buying as much as they should?" "Could they be sold additional lines?" "What is the competition?" "How can the competition be displaced?" "What is the customer's attitude toward the company?"

- Getting dealers to promote the company's merchandise, to display the product, to use the window display material, and to advertise and feature the product.

- Training distributors' salespeople to improve their selling ability.

- Instructing the jobbers' and dealers' salespeople in how to demonstrate the product.

- Handling complaints and adjustments, and collecting delinquent accounts.

- Handling correspondence with customers.

- Attending sales meetings, conferences, and training sessions.

- Keeping records and filing reports.

- Keeping samples, kits, literature, and related items neat, fresh, and up to date.

Few if any organizations require their salespeople to do all the jobs just mentioned. Employers know that their salespeople can increase their activity, and therefore the company's sales volume, only if they utilize their time effectively. To make up for the demands on their salespeople's time, the progressive company will often step up its training program to speed up the development of top-notch producers. It may also improve the equipment it furnishes to aid its salespeople in making the best presentation. If you happen to be selling for such a company, recognize the value of their sales training efforts. Use your equipment as you are instructed to use it.

The Right Attitude Toward Paperwork

Practically all sales work requires the keeping of certain records and filing daily or other reports with the home office. Those individuals who are not detail-minded will seek almost any escape from chores not directly connected with "signing up the customer." Others make the mistake of spending valuable hours in the office that might otherwise be spent in the field.

We have already pointed out how important it is to be constantly aware of the value you place upon your time and how detrimental it is to your earnings to waste precious hours that should be devoted to selling. Set a reasonable limit to the proportion of the selling day which you devote to paperwork. The forms and records you are required to fill out serve an important purpose, and the information they yield can often be turned to your advantage.

> **SUGGESTION** Do your paperwork during nonselling hours. (See Chapter Eight for suggestions for planning your work.)

Stay Aware of the Need for Change

Now that you have a better idea of the changes that have taken place over the years in business, in its attitude toward salespeople, and in salespeople's attitude toward their work, you should be ready to change your own outlook accordingly. No salesperson today can afford to use antiquated methods. Sooner or later you'll be brought up short if you continue to tell the same sales story and rely on the same strategies when you make your presentation.

Stay abreast of the changes going on in your field. Read the publications put out by sales experts. Talk to other salespeople you meet and find out what they've learned from their experiences. Life itself is a continuing process in which imperceptible changes are always taking place. They become discernible only when we stop to examine the present and make comparisons with the past. Since selling is, in a sense, a catering to human needs, selling strategies and techniques should change as often as human needs and behavior do. Get in the habit of stopping now and then to evaluate whether or not your selling methods have kept pace with the times.

CHAPTER TWO

PROSPECTING FOR VOLUME BUSINESS

"Big-league" salespeople concentrate on prospects with real potential

One of the fastest ways to reach the top income bracket is to call on top-level prospects. The quality of your prospects automatically sets the top limit of your income. It can relegate you to mediocrity or make you an explosive financial success.

This chapter shows you how to find a continuous supply of better prospects and, by focusing your calls on them, how to rapidly increase your income. It puts an end to indiscriminate calls—calls that are made in a random fashion. It shows you how to cut prospecting time by finding out *on the first try* which prospects are most likely to develop into customers.

Here's an overview:

- **Finding full-potential prospects:** Covers all you need to know about finding the blue-chip places to call.

- **Qualifying specific prospects for buying potential:** Includes tests and rating systems that eliminate "shotgun" prospecting and enable you to train your sights on the prospects who will buy.

- **Additional aids to profitable prospecting:** Contains additional ideas to help you get the best results from the time you spend on prospecting.

- **Guides to better territory coverage:** Includes ways to improve coverage of your territory through proper routing.

This chapter illustrates how salespeople who are serious about making money approach prospecting—salespeople who want sales, not just interviews.

Most salespeople must carefully select qualified prospects from a number of different sources. Only a few vendors—such as those who sell to garages, pharmacies, and other easily recognized buyers—can drive through a territory and spot prospects with little difficulty.

Finding full-potential prospects involves two main steps:

1. Discovering all the sources through which prospects might be located

2. Qualifying specific prospects for buying potential

Let's begin by looking at the two major sources of leads: the leads you get from others, and the leads you uncover yourself.

HOW TO FIND GOOD LEADS WITH THE HELP OF OTHERS

Who Might Supply You with Leads

Your prospecting work will be easier if you can get assistance from one or more of the following:

- **Your company.** It can supply you with specific leads, prospect lists, and the names of inactive accounts.

- **Your present customers.** They can help you keep your prospect list current and active by giving you the names of possible buyers and referrals.

- **Salespeople selling noncompeting products and services.**

- **Junior salespeople.**

- **Nonprospects.**

- **Social contacts.**

Each of these sources is described in detail in the following sections.

Always "Go Beyond" your Prospect List

Prospect lists provided by the sales manager are great aids, but they have their limitations. Often they are not up to date, and sometimes they don't pan out. You must go beyond your lists in prospecting for potential buyers.

■ IDEA IN ACTION

Ernest Dameron sells an improved type of sterilizing unit to hospitals. His company has furnished him with a list of hospitals in his territory. Ernest finds, however, that he can make numerous extra sales by "going beyond" this list of prospects.

In the first place, the list, which was compiled and published by the State Association of Hospitals, contains data that are two years old. It omits the names of institutions built or opened more recently. At each call, Ernest inquires for names of newly opened hospitals.

Second, Ernest happens to learn that a large company located in his territory operates a private industrial clinic.

After further investigation, Ernest finds that not only do many large industrial plants maintain such clinics, but also that some large nonmanufacturing concerns provide clinic service for their employees. All told, these extra prospects enable Ernest to earn about 25% more in commissions than he would earn if he confined his calls to those prospects whose names appear on the list provided by his company.

Inactive Accounts Can Be Prime Leads

Few types of leads are as rewarding as former buyers or "inactive accounts." This method of finding prime leads applies to most types of selling.

Why are former buyers or inactive accounts such prime prospects? It's very simple: A person (or company) who at one time found it advantageous to buy from a given salesperson or company is often more open to persuasion than is a new, cold prospect. In other words, an ex-customer usually has more reasons to buy again from a given seller than to place his or her business elsewhere.

∎ IDEA IN ACTION

Ruth McMahon is asked by her sales manager to call back every name on a list of 100 former customers who have stopped buying from the company.

Ruth reports to her manager at the end of this assignment as follows: Four customers have gone out of business, moved, or stopped selling such items. That leaves 96 former customers who buy the product Ruth's company sells but who have drifted away to the competition.

On her first call, Ruth is able to sell to 61 of these companies. The "reasons" they drifted away are typical of most inactive accounts:

- No one called on us for quite a while, so we began to buy elsewhere.

- We tried a cheaper product, but it hasn't worked out, so I guess we're ready to buy from you again.

- Your credit department wrote a strong letter that we didn't like. But we've found your competitors to be equally strict. Anyway, we have more working capital now, so I guess there's no reason why we shouldn't buy from you again.

- Once we had a shortage, and you couldn't supply our needs on time. So we shopped around and bought wherever we could. Now that things are normal again, and you are out seeking orders, we might as well buy from you as anyone else.

The common thread running through all the explanations given by these 61 customers who were willing to renew their former connection is simply this: None of these reasons was strong enough to cause the customer to say "No."

The remainder did not buy. The reasons for their refusal ranged as follows:

- We've tried out competitive sources and found one that we prefer to yours.

- We had a misunderstanding with your company that wasn't handled to our satisfaction.

Ruth found that 39% of these ex-customers were either no longer in a position to buy or simply would not return to their former buying habits. But 61% were ready to resume buying, merely because she asked them for their business again.

In calling upon inactive accounts you will sometimes run into a customer who stopped buying because of a grievance that was never settled properly. At the time, your firm might have been too busy to care. Now you want to bring the customer back into the fold. It might make sense to just listen while the disgruntled customer blows his or her top and then try to make a sale at a later date, after the person has had a chance to calm down.

Calls by Service Departments Turn Up Prospects

Service calls and good follow-up on service has brought many full-potential prospects to salespeople whose companies sell a product as well as service contracts.

▪ IDEA IN ACTION

Dick Meyers sells oil burners and oil burner service contracts. He spends part of his selling day calling up customers his company's service rep has called the day before, to see that everything is satisfactory. He is particularly sure to call new customers. This practice often leads to sales of new oil burners to replace worn-out ones.

TIP A customer who is given follow-up consideration will often mention other good prospects. He or she is especially likely to recommend your service to someone who complains about poor service from another company.

How to Get Prime Prospects from Customers

How you ask your satisfied customers for names of prospects often determines the results. What you want to avoid is the answer, "I can't think of anyone right now." Make your request for prospects in terms of the qualifications that fit your product, and you'll get your customer thinking harder for you.

▪ IDEA IN ACTION

Terry Lewis, an insurance salesperson, always asks her customers for names of prospects. If she should happen to get the reply, "I can't think of anyone right now," she comes to the aid of her customer's memory by saying, "You may not know anyone who has expressed an interest in buying life insurance. But the kind of people I'm interested in meeting are between 30 and 45 years of age, have children, and seem to be doing well financially. They've just had an addition to the family, or received a promotion, or gotten a raise. Do you know anyone who fits that picture?"

How to Use Customer Referrals as a Source of High-Potential Prospects

For certain types of selling, referral leads can be your best source of prospects. For example, if your product or service is of such a "personalized" nature that the recommendation of a friend carries great weight, you should work this source of prospects for all it's worth.

■ IDEA IN ACTION

Roy Terhune sells memberships in a local athletic club. He finds that cold-calling and other methods "pay off" to a certain extent but that his most important source of leads is referrals from present members.

"Yes," says one woman whom Roy has just signed up, "I'd be glad to give you the names of a few of my friends who might be interested. There's Ellen Larkin, the new credit manager in our office. Then there's Fred Day—we used to work out together at the Y. I think they'd both be good prospects for you."

Whenever Roy runs short of referral leads from new members, he calls on older members and asks whether they have anyone to suggest. He has found that referrals are better, in his particular type of selling, than any other leads he can develop.

Your new prospect will be more interested in what you have to say if you are able to state the name of the person who recommended him or her. There is a way to get this permission, even if it is denied at first.

■ IDEA IN ACTION

Kim Allen gets permission to use the name of the person who's just recommended prospects to her by saying, "I'm not going to call on your friends and simply try to sell them policies. I have a service to offer, the same kind of work I did for you, and I think that it will be interesting and valuable to them. Don't you? But I don't want to call on anyone unless I have an introduction, and I like to have cards so that my prospects will know I've done the same kind of work for their friends. They may even want to ask you about it. However, when I present your card, I will tell them that I requested it simply to make their acquaintance."

This approach is difficult to argue with, and since it points up the customer's importance, he or she is usually willing to grant permission without hesitation.

Introductions to valuable prospects can also be gained by using your own business cards. A customer who does not want to be bothered writing introductions to friends will be more likely to cooperate if you make it easier. Just hand him or her several business cards when you make your request.

■ IDEA IN ACTION

John Shiffman asks his customers for introductions to friends by handing him a number of his business cards. "Will you please write an introduction to a few of your friends on the back of these cards?" he says. "Don't try to sell me or my service. Simply write the person's name and then under it, write, 'Introducing John Shiffman' and sign your name. I'm sure your friends will appreciate your putting me in touch with them."

If the customer objects to writing on the cards, John tells him or her that without such an introduction, the customer's friends might miss out on a worthwhile opportunity.

Use Your Presentation to Get Fully Qualified Prospects

Ask a prospect for others who might be interested in the same information you have just provided in your presentation. This technique often will lead you to additional other full-potential prospects.

■ IDEA IN ACTION

Once Robert Parker has made his sale he says, "Ms. Jones, you say you like the job I've done for you and the methods I've used to work out your accounting problems. Do you know anyone else who might appreciate the same kind of help and information?" By integrating this step into his presentation, Parker is able to capitalize on the sale he's just made by taking advantage of his customer's knowledge.

How to Get Names of Prime Prospects from Prospects You Don't Sell

The extra time you've already spent on a "no-sale" prospect need not be lost. You can tactfully ask him or her to recognize your efforts by recommending other prospects. Most people who don't buy are still eager to show their appreciation, *if you have done a good selling job,* and will make every effort to give you names of prospects they feel sure will buy.

A Technique to Get Valuable Prospects from New Clients

Prime prospects will be recommended to you by new clients if you are careful to relate your request to the *same reason* that caused your new customer to buy.

■ IDEA IN ACTION

Diane Mason realizes that a new client she has just sold is primarily impressed with her service features. After the sale, Diane briefly reviews the customer's benefits and is quick to stress again that she always keeps in touch with her customers and is available any time they need her services.

At this point Diane says, "And if you have friends or colleagues who aren't getting that kind of service from their present supplier, I'd certainly like to talk with them." The customer usually admits that one of the reasons he or she switched to Diane was because of poor service elsewhere and recommends others who are experiencing the same dissatisfaction.

Noncompetitive Salespeople Can Furnish Excellent Leads

People selling noncompetitive products who cover the same territory as yours are prime sources for good prospects. Their specific knowledge of a prospect's business and background will qualify their leads as almost a sure sale.

■ IDEA IN ACTION

Janet Blake, who sells duplicating machines, had lunch with another woman who sold paper products in Janet's territory. In the course of their "shop talk," the paper vendor bemoaned the cut in a paper order by one of her biggest customers to one-tenth its former size. The reason for the decrease, she explained, was that the company was now having its shipping labels done by an outside printer.

Janet immediately contacted the paper company and aroused their interest by showing them how to cut their printing bill through the purchase of one of her machines. She made a sale.

TIP No one is better able to give you valuable information about a prospect than a salesperson of noncompetitive products who sells to the same prospects. He or she is usually able to tell you about the company's buying policy, the "key" people to contact, the best approach to use, and even the reason the prospect might buy your product. Though you should be wary about fraternizing with your competitors' salespeople, the opposite is true when it come to those selling noncompetitive products, especially if such products are indirectly related to your own. It pays to be friendly with these salespeople and to reciprocate when you can.

Junior Salespeople Can Find Highly Qualified Prospects for You

Here's an idea for the experienced salesperson who spends too much time seeking out qualified leads. If you feel that this is cutting into your selling time, the answer may be to employ a "junior" salesperson to locate prospects for you. Of course, in some fields this approach is simply not feasible—if, for example, it takes a veteran salesperson who knows all the answers to arouse a customer's interest. But there are other types of selling in which finding someone to do some of the "legwork" for you can really pay off.

Here's how the plan works. You delegate the job of finding worthwhile prospects to the junior salesperson. He or she then turns over to you only the names of prospects who are interested in buying your product. You do the actual selling.

The junior salesperson is your employee. You pay him or her a percentage of the commissions you receive on each completed sale. The payment must be large enough to assure your scout that he or she is being paid fairly and to stimulate him or her to put forth a real effort.

You train your assistant in how to uncover high-potential leads and how to make appointments. You teach him or her the facts about your product that will arouse the prospect's interest. You suggest the types of prospects that are most interested in your product. And you tell your assistant where such prospects can be found.

> **CAUTION** A junior salesperson should not give prospects your presentation. This will tempt the prospect to judge your product by what your assistant has said. The scout should tell only those facts that will arouse the prospect's interest and encourage setting up an interview. You might even want to write out a script for your junior salesperson to use and emphasize the importance of adhering to it.

■ IDEA IN ACTION

Tom Mullins sells a home study course. He finds that he must spend 75% of his time prospecting, leaving only 25% for actual selling.

Tom hires a junior salesperson who spends all his time seeking out prospects. When he locates a prospect, his job is to make a specific appointment for Tom, who then keeps the appointment and undertakes the more difficult task of making the presentation, overcoming objections, and closing the sale.

Tom pays his scout 25% of the commissions earned on completed sales. Since he now has four times as much selling time as he had before, Tom's sales—and hence his commissions—have increased fourfold.

A Nonprospect Can Help You Get Started

One way to get started successfully in a new area is to select a contact whom you know is a nonprospect, but who is familiar enough with your product to supply you with the names of other prospects. If you remember this rule—*your prospects are as good as their source*—then finding high-potential prospects will not be difficult.

■ IDEA IN ACTION

Hope Channing opened a branch office in a new territory to sell an advertising service that supplied advertising mats for retailers.

Hope's first call was on a leading retailer whom she knew would not be a good prospect. But she used this first contact as a starting point from which she developed one of her company's most successful branches.

She explained her business to the retailer and stated that she was fully aware that this particular store could not use her services. Then she asked for the names of up-and-coming retailers in the area who might benefit from her service.

Hope got the names of a number of retailers who were doing well, but who were too small to have advertising departments of their own. Each of these recommended retailers, in turn, supplied Hope with additional prospects.

Social Contacts Can Often Supply You with Prime Prospects

Certain types of selling lend themselves to gaining prospects through social contacts. For example, people who sell life insurance, automobiles, and luxury items, often make their social contacts an important source of prospects.

By "social contacts" we mean not only personal friends and acquaintances, but also neighbors; members of social, community, civic, and religious organizations; former classmates; and any other group whose members buy the type of product or service that you offer.

Be tactful when following up on these contacts. You don't want to come across as the kind of salesperson who's always looking for a lead—who looks at every social contact as a potential sale. However, this doesn't mean that you can't occasionally "talk business" as an indirect reminder that you're available to meet the needs of these acquaintances.

HOW TO FIND GOOD LEADS ON YOUR OWN

Depending on Yourself for Leads

Unless you supplement the leads supplied to you by others, you will probably find yourself floundering for calls to make. Most salespeople rely primarily on their own efforts to turn up worthwhile prospects. This section describes four basic approaches to keeping your prospect lists filled with potential buyers:

1. Cold-calling
2. Creative ideas
3. Direct mail
4. Trade exhibitions

Know the Markets for Your Product

By "markets" we mean all the classifications of buyers to whom your product can be sold. You'll find the greatest percentage of your prospects in these markets because (1) they have a need for your product and (2) they are available for contact.

☐ EXAMPLE

Bill Burley represents an electric tool company that offers a new power screwdriver. Bill's company furnishes him with the following list of markets for the product:

Automotive

- Car dealers
- Body shops
- Industrial repair shops

- Service stations
- Fleets
- Implement dealers

Industrial, Contractors, and Others

- Plant maintenance (all industries)
- Woodworking manufacturers
- Kitchen and other equipment fabricators
- Lumberyards
- Boat builders and repairers
- Electrical contractors
- Plumbing-heating contractors
- Air conditioning contractors
- Building contractors
- Heavy construction contractors
- Utilities contractors
- Vocational schools
- Technical schools

With this list, Bill can approach prospects on a systematic coverage schedule; he does not have to wait for leads to come to him from his company or from others. He has no difficulty in knowing where to call because the markets have been clearly defined for him.

> **SUGGESTION** If your company does not supply you with a list of markets for the product you sell, you can prepare your own list in much the same fashion as was just described.

How to Make Cold-Calling Yield High-Potential Prospects

Cold-calling is the backbone of good prospecting for most salespeople. But unless cold-calling is done properly, it will not yield high-potential prospects and could result in a disastrous waste of time.

Cold-canvassing is an organized program of calling on each member of a large group of prospects, *none of whom has been individually qualified as a high-potential prospect, but who, as a group, have been classified as such.* The points to remember are (1) find the qualified groups, and (2) call on each member of the group.

■ IDEA IN ACTION

Fran Tura sells a business information service to executives of large and medium-sized companies. She has been in her territory for 12 years but has opened only a few new accounts in the past 3 or 4 years because she is content to spend most of her time securing renewals to subscriptions she has previously sold.

Fran is alarmed to discover that the loss of established accounts that move out of her territory or that for some other reason fail to renew has caused a large drop in her business.

She goes to her manager, who suggests that she cold-call to increase her accounts and earnings. Fran doesn't like this suggestion. Like many salespeople who have been calling almost exclusively on people they already know, Fran has lost the "knack" of seeking new accounts. She decides, however, to take her manager's advice.

Fran begins by calling on companies whose names suggest that they might be likely prospects for her service. After trying this method for a week, Fran is very discouraged. Her total of new prospects is low, primarily because in seeking out *specific* individuals, she finds that she can see only three or four prospects a day.

Fran's manager suggests that she try calling on companies located in one building. "That will give you perhaps 40 opportunities a day to try to make a sale, as compared to the three or four you are now calling on."

Fran acts on this advice and finds that it pays off. The greatly increased number of calls bring her more prospects and sales than her more selective initial approach was bringing.

In about two weeks, however, Fran encounters another problem. Although she had decided to select larger office buildings so that she could call on more prospects at one time, this method actually resulted in fewer prospects than she was getting before.

Again, Fran's manager points out that she must be sure to select a building tenanted by companies that, *as a class,* justify a call. Many of the larger buildings she's been calling on have a large proportion of tenants who simply don't need her service. But since there are many other buildings in her territory with tenants who *do,* Fran should have no difficulty in carrying out her program.

Fran has learned two very important rules:

1. Cold-calling (seeing all or many members or a group) is frequently more rewarding than is seeking out specific prospects.

2. While cold-calling eliminates any previous evaluation of individual members of a group, it does require that the *group as a whole* be qualified.

In short, while cold calls can pay off, there is little reward for simply "opening lots of doors" indiscriminately. The status of the group must be promising to ensure a high rate of return on the time you invest.

How to Select the Right Groups For Cold-calling

To qualify as a good field for cold-calling, the group you select must, as a whole, have the qualities that you look for in individual prospects. For example, if you are selling investments, the group must include people who have money to invest. If you are selling a product, the group must have a need for the product. Once you have fixed the basic qualifications in your mind, finding the groups or individuals becomes easier.

■ IDEA IN ACTION

Carl Terry, who has recently been employed by a brokerage firm to sell shares in an open-end trust, makes over 20 calls during his first week in the field, but fails to locate a single good prospect. He has been assigned to a thriving city of about 100,000 population.

"Where have you been calling?" his sales manager asks when Carl explains his problem.

"I've called on the independent retailers who have stores on the main street in town," replies Carl. "I thought they would be good prospects, but they tell me they need their capital to carry on their business."

"Well," replies the sales manager, "I think you can do better than that. To begin with, there's an exclusive—and expensive—golf club in that town. Get a copy of the membership list—I bet you'll find quite a few preferred prospects on it.

"Then, find out who the most prosperous doctors, lawyers, accountants, and other professionals are. Get acquainted with some bank officials. Read the news about who just inherited some money. Next . . ."

But Carl interrupted at that point. "I get it," he said, "and I can see now where I've been making a mistake."

Four weeks later, Carl reported with pride, "That was great advice you gave me. I've closed nine sales in the last month and have a dozen good prospects warmed up as well. I guess the secret lies in knowing who really *is* a prospect."

Using Your Creative Abilities to Find Prospects

Beyond the usual sources for finding full-potential prospects, there is always the unexpected source that comes to you out of the blue—if, that is, you're creative. A number of examples are given in the following paragraphs.

Chapter Three offers detailed guidance for stimulating your creative abilities. The important point to remember is that you are more creative than you think.

Creative idea for improvement of customer's product turns up a high-potential prospect

An idea that shows a prospect how he or she can improve the company's product will almost automatically make him or her a full-potential prospect. There's only one catch: The idea must present a valid reason for buying.

■ IDEA IN ACTION

Lucy Stewart sells industrial chemicals. Lucy asks a friend of hers about the effectiveness of a new, easy-to-use cleaning compound. The reply is that it works very well but leaves a thin film that requires an extra rinse to remove.

Lucy asks her company's chemist to analyze the compound. As a result of the analysis, she writes a letter to the manufacturer explaining that the powdery film left by the compound can be eliminated by adding a solvent that her company manufactures. She also requests an interview.

Lucy receives an immediate reply with an appointment date that eventually leads to a large order.

A creative idea from a news item leads to a prospect

An apparently unrelated news item about an individual or a company will often lead you to a full-potential prospect. By interpreting what you read in light of how it might affect the need for your product, you can get the jump on your competitors by being the first to contact the individual or company involved.

■ IDEA IN ACTION

Al Holmes, who sells insulating materials, learned from an article in a trade publication that a manufacturer in his territory was planning a 100% increase in his advertising expenditure.

Al thought to himself, "That manufacturer has been operating at capacity for three years. This increase in advertising must mean that they're counting on a lot of new business. That means they need new facilities and buildings. What a prospect for insulating materials!"

Al contacted the manufacturer and found out that a major expansion was being planned. Because he was so quick to see the connection between the news item and the need for his product, he was able to contact his prospect well in advance of other salespeople and turn him into a customer who placed an order worth several thousand dollars.

TIP The creative salesperson reads the financial section of the newspaper or subscribes to a periodical that covers financial developments. This practice often leads to the type of opportunity just described. (Chapter Three provides additional tips on getting sales ideas through news clues.)

Creative idea, stimulated by chance remark, leads to prospect

The salesperson who is always thinking about what he or she has to sell can often profit from remarks overheard in ordinary conversation. The ability to associate chance remarks with a selling opportunity is one mark of the top-notch creative salesperson.

■ IDEA IN ACTION

Bill Mooney was returning from a convention of truck manufacturers when he struck up a conversation with a display salesperson who happened to mention to Bill that a large machine manufacturer she knew was making plans to put displays "on the road." The idea was to tour various sections of the country displaying equipment from specially designed trucks.

Bill contacted the manufacturer and set up an appointment. He convinced the purchasing agent and the company's engineers that with a few modifications, his trucks would suit their purposes perfectly. It would also save them the expense of buying specially designed trucks.

Bill sold this manufacturer three trucks.

Disaster situations point up prospects

One company's catastrophe can be another's opportunity. Alert salespeople know that while a fire or other disaster may be a tragedy for the individuals involved, it also creates a buying motive for products that must be replaced or for items or services that protect against future losses.

Use Direct Mail to Find Leads

Standard form letters sent to potential users of your product might be a source of good leads—if you know how to use direct mail intelligently. Sometimes your company will supply form letters for this purpose. In most cases, however, you must compose the letter and put together a list of names for the mailing. The classified section of the telephone directory is a good source for getting a mailing list started.

Companies that sell by direct mail use the services of "list brokers" to obtain lists for prospects. These lists might be of new firms in the area, passenger car registrations, buyers of certain types of products, and so on. A quick way to find the names of the list brokers in your territory is to ask someone who does a substantial mail order business—a publisher, for example. Once you have the list broker's name, ask for his or her catalog. Then decide which of the lists might yield the most promising leads.

The best way to use direct mail is to send out a small number of letters—10 or 15 at a time—and then follow them up with phone calls a few days later. You must plan your work methodically if you use direct mail to find prospects. Set aside part of a certain day each week, for example, to send out letters and make follow-up calls. You might decide to mail on Monday and devote a couple of hours every Thursday morning to telephone follow-ups, making appointments for Friday and the following Monday.

> **CAUTION** Don't assume that if you send out hundreds of letters you can sit back and wait for the orders to flow in. It doesn't work that way.

■ IDEA IN ACTION

Exhibit 2.1 is a letter composed by an office equipment salesperson, using a principal selling point to get the interview.

EXHIBIT 2.1

Sample Prospecting Letter

Dear Ms. Brown:

IF YOU WERE AN ELEPHANT . . .

Yes! If you were an elephant I know you would be interested in what I have to say, for I am talking about PEANUTS—peanuts in terms of dollars and cents, that is.

You have probably shied away from buying that new word processor you need because of the investment required to purchase it—but let's take a close look at the costs involved. The cost of a new ABC word processor is PEANUTS compared with what you pay the operator:

For example, suppose you pay a secretary $350.00 per week:

For 52 weeks	$18,200
For 5 years	$91,000

Now, by increasing this secretary's efficiency *only 15%* (and research has proved this is a conservative estimate), in five years you will have saved $13,650.

A new machine at this time costs $1,400. Your actual savings are $12,250.

If you buy one of our word processors now, you will be saving over $12,000—*and* you'll be using state-of-the-art equipment for the next five years.

Perhaps you are satisfied with your present word processor. The four leading manufacturers of word processors, of which ABC is one, have always led the world, both in sales and in technical excellence. Certainly no one of the four would be where it is today if it were a poor machine—they're all good.

But there *are* differences. Our claim is that when you add up what ABC offers, it comes to a more impressive total than any of the others. Even if our only point of difference was the on-site training we provide, we'd still be ahead.

We would be happy to come in and discuss this in more detail with you. Return the enclosed card or phone 555-1010.

Sincerely,

James R. Sovine
Exclusive ABC Agent

Trade Exhibitions Can Yield
Full-Potential Prospects

Trade shows have become an outstanding means of attracting buyers to a company's product. Salespeople who are assigned to "cover" these trade fairs are in a prime position to contact highly interested prospects.

These are the advantages you gain by using trade exhibitions as a source.

- You meet prospects from areas you might otherwise have overlooked.
- You meet more prospects than you could hope to contact in a normal workday.
- You encounter prospects in types of businesses you may not have considered as users of your product.
- You are in a position to talk with prospects on their "own level."
- You can consolidate your relationships with old customers you meet at such exhibitions.
- You can collect names of many valuable prospects at the exhibitions.

    TIP Exhibiting companies usually supply their salespeople with materials and information to help warm up new prospects. Cards are normally available for interested parties to fill out for further information.

QUALIFYING SPECIFIC PROSPECTS
FOR BUYING POTENTIAL

Qualifying Is Determined
by Your Product

Every prospect you contact, whether you get an order or not, represents an expense in terms of your time and transportation. A dead-end interview is good money lost. This is why you must qualify your prospects ahead of time. The extent of qualification will vary, depending upon the type of market to whom you're selling. Consider these examples:

The mass market (example: office equipment)

Little qualifying is necessary. The office equipment salesperson need identify only an office, business, or factory; all are prospects for his or her product. The main responsibility here is to determine the prospect's specific needs after he or she is contacted.

The selective market (example: junior encyclopedia)

Somewhat more qualifying is required to choose prospects who can be profitably contacted. This salesperson cannot identify prospects immediately or call indiscriminately. He or she must take at least these two steps to make sure that every call has selling possibilities:

1. Get the names of families with school-age children, using school registration lists or other sources.

2. Choose a residential area with families that can afford the product.

This salesperson can then further qualify the prospect's family: Do the parents belong to the PTA? What grade is their child in? What courses is he or she taking?

If your product calls for a careful selection of prospects, you must spend time qualifying them before your first call, to make the investment of your time profitable.

The highly selective market (example: pension or profit-sharing plan)

The salesperson who is selling a pension or profit-sharing plan for a life insurance company must fully qualify each prospect. Each company he or she approaches must have

■ A stable continuing management, a good record of earnings (past or prospective), and a reasonable outlook for a continuation of such earnings through its ability to market its products or services.

- A potential employee retirement problem that management is interested in solving.

- A sufficient number of permanent employees to make the establishment of the plan feasible, and yet not too many to make some other type of plan, such as a group annuity, a more practical funding vehicle.

The salesperson can check directories or contact the prospect's suppliers, an informed banker, or even one of the prospect's competitors to find this qualifying information. In addition, the salesperson has to "qualify" himself or herself: Is his or her influence at the prospect-company sufficient to guarantee purchase of this particular insurance if the firm decides to adopt an insured pension plan?

> **REMEMBER** Qualifying a prospect is an important initial step in the sales process. Do it well, and you'll have taken a big stride toward making the sale.

"Potential" Is the Key to Prospecting

For the salesperson who is aiming to make every selling hour yield full time value, it is important to test each prospect's potential as a customer. This doesn't mean, of course, that every initial sale to a new prospect must reach a fixed number of dollars or you've wasted your time. In many cases, repeat orders or additional orders will promise enough business in the long run to compensate you for your time.

The tests that follow are useful in determining a prospect's potential. You may be able to come up with other tests, based on your selling experience, that are better suited to your particular product or service.

Three-Point Test to Determine the Potential of Every Prospect

The key words to remember in this test are *need, authority,* and *capital.*

- Does this prospect have a need for my product? No matter how convincing your sales talk, your time is wasted if you give it to a prospect who has no need for your product.

- Does this prospect have the authority to buy? You may successfully "sell" a prospect who needs your product, but if he or she lacks the authority to buy, then your talk is wasted. (If your job requires group selling, however, one "sold" member will often influence the rest. This approach is described in greater detail later in this chapter, in the section on "Finding and Rating the 'Key' Prospect in a Group."

- Does this prospect have the necessary capital? Although a prospect may have a definite need for your product and may be authorized to purchase it, he or she cannot actually buy unless your company's credit requirements are met. Sometimes special credit arrangements will make a purchase possible.

Each of these points is discussed in detail.

Exploring the "need" test

If you're going to turn a prospect into a customer, your product must be able to help him or her in at least one of these three ways:

1. Your product must save the prospect money.
2. Your product must make money for the prospect.
3. Your product must help the prospect to do a better job.

You have a full-potential prospect if you can satisfy your prospect's need for *one* of the foregoing benefits.

A test of buying authority

Human vanity can be an obstacle when you're trying to find the individual who actually has buying authority. Sometimes the first person you contact will try to give you the impression that he or she is the person in charge. If you suspect that this individual doesn't have the authority to buy, your job is to get past him or her as quickly and tactfully as possible. Remember: You waste valuable time talking to the wrong person. Here are some questions to help you determine who has buying authority:

- **"Can you buy?"** After the introductions have been made and preliminary information has been exchanged, *but before you'll begin your presentation,* ask the person you're talking to if he or she is able to make the decision to buy. Be as polite as possible: "If you are interested, Mr. Johnson, will you be able to buy? Or do you suggest I see the purchasing agent first, as is the policy in most companies?" The "as is the policy" phrase will protect the individual's pride and invite his or her cooperation.

- **"When can I come back?"** If the individual to whom you're speaking puts you off with a remark to the effect that "I'll take care of it myself," it might indicate a reluctance to admit his or her lack of authority, or a wish to present your message personally to "the boss." It may also mean that the person you should see is busy. Whatever the reason, avoid leaving the ball in his or her court. Try to pin down a time for a second interview. Ask, "How about Thursday?" Then arrange a definite hour. Make it clear that you want to see whoever is going to participate in the purchasing decision. Say, "I'll look forward to seeing you, and anyone else you feel should hear my presentation."

  NOTE It's important to write down the time and date for the meeting in this individual's presence. It makes the commitment stronger and more definite. Don't use a scrap of paper, either. Use a formal callback card or the effect will be weakened.

- **"Can I see him/her now?"** If you get the feeling that another person's authority is needed, suggest that your contact call that person right now. If after listening to your opening he or she agrees to call in the boss, you're in an excellent position to strengthen your presentation. Don't try to undermine the first person's position, either. Make frequent references to the role he or she has played by saying, "As Ms. Johnson pointed out . . ."

- **"Do you have a buying policy guide?"** Some large companies offer booklets describing their buying policies. A booklet might give the company's purchasing aims, name the responsible buyers, and list the products or services they are interested in buying. Be sure to profit from this information when it is available.

■ "Who is the purchasing agent?" In many companies, salespeople are automatically directed to the purchasing agent, who then sends them to the department head or buyer concerned. The purchasing agent will usually sign an order based on their recommendations. But, remember, whenever the purchasing agent is involved, you usually run into competition. If the product involves a major expense or company policy, the decision may rest with a management team. (How to handle group selling is covered later in this chapter.)

CAUTION To assume that you are always being directed to the right individual can be costly. Check to see if there are others you can more profitably contact. One salesperson was directed to a buyer, whom she called on unsuccessfully for two years. Only by accident did she discover that it was the head of the maintenance department who had the authority to buy. Her second contact resulted in an immediate sale.

No rule can guide you unerringly to the "right" person. The authority to buy can range from a short verbal exchange in one company to a lengthy cosigned approval in another. Some companies have a formal procedure for salespeople to follow; in contacting others, you may have to rely on your wits alone.

A test of a prospect's ability to purchase

The key words to remember in this test are *observe, inquire, decide*.

■ **Observe.** Where is the business located? What kind of impression does the company make? How are local business conditions? Does the individual you've contacted appear to be "the one in charge"?

■ **Inquire.** What is the company's reputation? What is the experience and ability of its management team? Examine the financial data in its annual report or in other sources of information (see the Appendix for a list and description of various information sources).

- **Decide.** The facts about the prospect that you gather through observation and inquiry will enable you to decide whether he or she is a prime prospect.

A Test to Help You Select "Hot" Prospects

The "hot" prospect is one who will buy now. How do you know? Ask yourself these simple questions:

1. *"Is there a reason for the prospect to buy right now?"* If you can supply a strong reason to buy immediately, a prime prospect will automatically become a "hot" prospect. For example, someone who has just had a new baby will be a "hot" prospect for insurance.

2. *"Is this the time to follow up a postponed purchase?"* A prospect may have put you off temporarily because he or she is waiting for a new model to come out, or for a new budget period to begin, or for the buying season to start. Whatever the reason, when the time arrives, this prospect will be a "hot" prospect. The reason for postponement will become the reason to buy *now*.

   TIP Timing your follow-up to coincide with the prospect's readiness to buy makes a strong impression on the prospect and helps the sale along. Your reminder system must, therefore, be systematic and dependable. (See Chapter One for a suggested follow-up system.)

Qualifying a Prospect Who Comes to You

In some fields of selling, the prospect comes to you. You may know nothing about this individual and must begin to qualify the prospect on the spot to avoid wasting valuable time. You may be able to determine the three qualifying "musts" (i.e., need for product, ability to pay, authority to buy) fairly quickly. But a successful sale to a "cold" prospect usually depends on further qualifying information.

□ EXAMPLE

If you're selling real estate, you'll want to find out

- What the prospect is interested in buying
- The prospect's reasons for buying
- The extent of the prospect's inclination to buy
- The attitudes and influence of the prospect's family members
- How much looking the prospect's family has already done—what they've seen and why they didn't buy
- What real estate the prospect already owns
- If the prospect is looking for residential real estate, his or her requirements in terms of schools, transportation, recreation, and shopping districts
- If it is a business opportunity prospect, the extent of his or her experience

Try to find out all you need to know the first time you meet the prospect, drive him or her to the listed property, and show him or her around the premises. If your field of selling demands extensive qualifying of prospects, remember the value of your time and qualify as quickly—but accurately—as possible.

Sizing Up Prospects by Category in Cold Canvassing

The "mental picture" technique is a quick method of sizing up prospects at a glance to estimate their probable worth. In sizing up a prospect, you place him or her in a category that fits your particular needs. For example, it might suit your product to classify prospects as (1) a repeat business prospect, (2) a prospect to be won away from a competitor, or (3) a small-order prospect. Other categories may have to be created to identify a prospect's potential value.

This technique is particularly useful in cold canvassing.

WHAT TO DO

1. Decide on the categories into which your prospects should be classified.

2. When you are in the prospect's office or place of business, be as observant as possible and make mental notes of what you see that might place your prospect in a particular category.

3. When you leave, immediately jot down notes of what you have observed and enter them on your prospect record card.

▪ IDEA IN ACTION

Phil Grant, an office furniture salesperson, begins to cold canvass all the offices located in a large metropolitan office building. He has little idea of the kind of office that will meet his eyes when he opens a door, but he is prepared to make a quick mental picture of what he sees.

He has already appraised the appearance of the building itself. As he enters the first office, he quickly notices its general condition, size, the number of people, and the condition of the furnishings. He looks particularly at desks, chairs, and file cabinets and tries to determine their age and make.

Phil puts his ears to use as well. He notices that the office isn't carpeted and that the old metal desks and file cabinets currently in use make quite a bit of noise. Many of the chairs which are on casters, squeal as they're pushed across the floor. He also notices that space is at a premium.

If Phil is granted an interview during this first call, he already has a fair picture of the prospect's needs. He might talk in terms of the advantages of the new model chairs or the file cabinets whose drawers open horizontally rather than vertically.

As Phil calls on each prospect in the building he makes similar observations. In each case he immediately establishes a general approach that fits in with the prospect's needs. He can suggest to one prospect the advantages of his furniture over a competitor's; to another, he can suggest the advantages of adjustable chairs to relieve the strain on computer users.

After each call, Phil jots down the prospect's full name and what he has observed, as well as the results of his call. He does this promptly to avoid forgetting any details and to have a record for follow-up purposes.

After he finishes canvassing the entire building, he finds that most of his prospects fall into one of the following categories:

1. **Repeat business prospects.** Most of these prospects have definite replacement schedules and are prime prospects. Service organizations, legal firms, government offices, publishers, and insurance companies are examples.

2. **Prospects who buy from necessity.** This class of high-potential prospects includes new businesses, companies that are reorganizing their office space or moving to new offices, companies that are expanding, and others who for some reason are compelled to buy.

3. **Prospects who should replace old furnishings.** These prospects are using old, beat-up desks and file cabinets that look as though they've been there since World War II. They must be sold hard.

   TIP Notes made about these prospects will show whether, once sold, they will be big buyers or small.

4. **Prospects who are casual buyers.** Sales to these users can be made at any time, but usually depend solely upon the salesperson's capabilities, for example, prospects whose office furnishings are fairly new but don't quite fit their requirements.

This method of classification will help you to determine the amount of time you should spend on prospects after your first call (the value of your time compared with their potential business).

Sizing Up a Prospect's Needs on a Cold Call

When you call on someone with no advance information to help you determine his or her need for your product, you must find out as much as you can *while making the call*. Much of this information can be gained through observation.

■ IDEA IN ACTION

Jane Keely sells an internal communications system. As she approaches a cold-call prospect, she stops to look at the premises from the outside. Her observations help her determine the extent of the prospect's need for her product. Here are the questions she asks herself:

- Does the company occupy more than one floor?
- Is there a loading platform at the rear?
- Is there a separate building used as an annex or warehouse?
- Is there a showroom on the ground floor with offices at the rear or upstairs?

Once inside, Jane looks for more clues that tell her if her product is needed:

- Are there a number of separate offices?
- Is there an office in front and work rooms or processing rooms in the rear?
- Is some sort of public address or beeper system being used to summon persons to the telephone?
- Are employees walking around with papers in their hands?—a sure sign of the need for a communications system.

The answers to these questions tell Jane her prospect's specific needs, and also give her clues to what benefits she should emphasize during her demonstration.

How to Qualify Prospects You Contact by Telephone

Full-potential prospects can often be identified over the telephone by using the "probing" technique. Probing is a method of posing statements and questions to find the answers to your unasked questions: Does this prospect need my product? Does the company have the ability to pay for it?

If the answer to these questions is "yes," you can often proceed to close the sale over the phone. If your product does not lend itself to a telephone close, you should arrange for an appointment.

These guidelines will help you:

1. Increase your chances of finding full-potential prospects by calling from selective lists. If yours is a tangible product, constantly replaced by newer models, you can further refine your prospecting by calling only those possessing last year's model.

2. Maintain a flexible approach. Adjust your talk to the prospect's responses, using a written telephone approach as a guide. (See Chapter Four for tips on using the phone to get appointments.)

3. Use the "suspect's" responses as a lead-in to qualifying questions or to other parts of your talk.

4. If your prospect balks at an attempted close, shift the focus to the appointment. It's usually easier to make a sale when you're face-to-face with the prospect.

5. If your prospect mentions something that clearly disqualifies him or her as a potential buyer, further talk is probably useless.

▪ IDEA IN ACTION

Frank Flannery sells aluminum door and window frames to home owners. Frank makes 20 telephone calls a day to prospects located in an area heavily populated with private homes. (Frank has observed the first rule of prospecting by making sure the *group* he contacts is qualified. His job now is to qualify *individuals* in the group.)

"Hello, Mr. Mansfield?" Frank begins. "This is Frank Flannery of Aluminum Products Company. Mr. Mansfield, beginning this week we are offering home owners a special low-payment price on aluminum door and window frames."

If the prospect does not own the home he or she usually tells Frank immediately, and the conversation is over. No immediate response is the signal for Frank to begin his talk to gain an interview.

If an objection is raised, Frank overcomes it and proceeds to create a desire for his product. He mentions the money saved on heat bills and negligible replacement costs. As he talks, Frank continues to qualify the prospect.

"Just to give you an idea of how much money you can save on heating bills, how many windows are there in your home?"

From this and other qualifying questions, Frank determines the number of doors and windows in the prospect's home and the construction or condition of the home. When he mentions the special low-payment plan, the prospect's response gives Frank a clue to his or her ability to pay.

So Frank continues to guide the conversation, from statements that arouse interest to careful mention of a few important reasons to buy. He soon has a fairly accurate picture of the prospect's needs and his buying attitude and ability. To clinch an appointment, Frank capitalizes on the selling point he feels carried the most weight with the prospect.

Build your telephone approach around statements and questions that will qualify prospects for your product. Pay particular attention to the opening sentence. It should immediately identify nonprospects and arouse interest in prospects who might qualify further.

TIP It's usually wise to avoid giving details of installation, choice of product, and so on, over the phone. Don't make the picture complete; you don't want the prospect to make an immediate decision about buying. It's too easy to say "No" over the telephone. Remember, your goal in contacting prospects by telephone is to gain appointments, not to make sales.

FINDING AND RATING THE "KEY" PROSPECT IN A GROUP

Three Common Situations Requiring Group Decision

In three common situations—the family, partners, and industrial buyers—the approval of more than one person may be necessary before you can make a sale. In each of these situations, knowing the right combination of prospects to see can save you from making callbacks. It might even increase your valuable selling time if you give your sales talk only when the right prospects are present.

Finding the key prospect in the family situation

The purchase of big items, such as a home or a car, is almost always a joint decision between husband and wife. The opinions of other members may count as well. When the product does not concern the family as a unit, the "combination" approval is usually not needed. However, sales to "junior" members of the family must generally be approved by a senior member, even though the actual buyer is the younger prospect.

> **NOTE** An attempt is often made to get the wife or the husband to make an independent decision and sign the offer, even though the prospect has said that his or her spouse must be consulted. See Chapter Seven for ways to handle this situation.

Here is a workable system that will show you immediately which member of a husband-wife combination is the "key" prospect. It automatically identifies the prime prospect as the one who scores on two out of the three qualifying "tests":

1. Who will use my product more?
   - ❏ Husband
   - ❏ Wife
   - ❏ Both

2. Who knows more about this product or has been involved in its purchase in the past?
   - ❏ Husband
   - ❏ Wife
   - ❏ Both

3. Who appears to wield more decision-making power in this area?
   - ❏ Husband
   - ❏ Wife
   - ❏ Both

Finding the key partner in a partnership

It is often necessary and almost always advisable to gain the assent of all partners when a partnership is purchasing your product. However, there are times when only one partner can be successfully sold.

The best way to find the key partner in a firm is to tell the receptionist you'd like to see the individual who has the authority to buy. If he or she hesitates, simply explain that you want to see the right person first so that you don't waste the other partners' time. This will usually get you immediately to the person you want to see.

> **TIP** If you are fortunate enough to know another salesperson who has sold to your prospect before, or if you can check back to see who signed past orders with your company, your job will be easier. But better check your information with the secretary; there may have been a change. "Is Mr. Alvarez still in charge of buying?" or a similar verifying question will do the trick.

Here are some guidelines and cautions that will make your partnership prospecting easier:

- The senior partner—who is usually the key person in a smaller partnership—is often designated by the firm's name. The "Brown, Carter & Laughlin Company" would seem to indicate that Brown is the senior partner. Be sure to check, however; this may be merely an alphabetical arrangement.

- A firm's name may include the names of past or even deceased members, retained for prestige or identification reasons. "Brown, Carter & Laughlin" might turn out to be a partnership of only Carter and Laughlin.

> **TIP** Use the *Martindale-Hubbell Law Directory* to find information about law firms in the United States and Canada. Here you will find a list of lawyers and their addresses, firm names, the types of law practice in which the firm specializes, key personnel, and other background information that may be helpful in selling to lawyers. Every law library and almost every law office has this reference volume.

- Sometimes a salesperson "sells" one partner, only to have the sale canceled when the other partners do not okay the sale.

- A partner may wish to pass the buying decision on to someone else in the partnership. How to handle this situation is explained in Chapter Seven.

> **NOTE** In the absence of any contrary arrangement, each partner has an equal right to participate in the management of the partnership's affairs. Each partner has the authority to act as agent for the partnership and to bind it with respect to matters relating to the partnership's business. This power, however, may be limited by the terms of the partnership agreement or by any other agreement between the partners, but the limitation is not binding on outsiders who have no knowledge of it.

Finding the key prospect in an industrial situation

A large management team is usually responsible for major purchases in industrial sales. Because the industrial sales "prospect" is often a group of three or more, you may have difficulty in finding the one person whose decision to buy will carry the most weight.

This "key" prospect is usually determined by your product. If it is a major piece of machinery costing thousands of dollars, the prime prospect will most likely be a vice president in charge of operations. If it is a new kind of hand tool, the opinion of a supervisor or even a line worker may be the important one. Other prime prospects might be the plant manager, engineers, the head of the maintenance department, or the purchasing agent. Your job is to determine which one will influence the purchase most.

Here are some questions to help you locate this key individual:

- "Who is the head of the department that will use my product?"

- "Is this position just a 'title,' or does it carry real authority?"

- "Will my product be used by more than one department?"

- "Is this company concerned more with purchase price or with quality of performance?"

If possible, try to get the prospect's organizational chart outlining the positions and functions of the individuals in the company you are trying to sell. You may find such a chart in the company's annual report.

> **REMEMBER** Even if you identify the key person, it is always important to see the purchasing agent first.

Always contact the purchasing agent first. Most large companies clear buying decisions through the purchasing agent, even though the actual decision to buy might be made by another member of the management team, so it always pays to see him or her first.

If you attempt to pass over the purchasing agent and go directly to someone else, you're likely to incur his or her anger. You want the purchasing agent to be your ally—not your opponent—and it's his or her job to know the sources for as many products as possible.

In many cases it makes sense to contact the purchasing agent by letter or telephone. Often he or she will refer you directly to the key person.

In addition to enrolling the purchasing agent "on your side," you may be able to gain information about the company's policy toward purchasing your type of product. He or she can also tell you about the company's needs and whether they're already using your product or a similar one from another source.

ADDITIONAL GUIDELINES TO PROFITABLE PROSPECTING

Prepare Your Own Complete Prospect Source List

A complete source list is a constant reminder of all the places to find prospects. Without such a list, you might concentrate your prospecting efforts on a few "easy" sources and neglect or overlook others that could be equally profitable.

Identify the Sources of Your Leads

Knowing the source of your leads can mean the difference between wasting time on weak prospects and spending your time profitably in contacting high-potential prospects.

Use a symbol system to identify and evaluate your leads. It helps to keep your prospect lists in good shape. For example,

- "R"—prospects referred to you by steady customers
- "C"—prospects from your company prospect list
- "N"—prospects from a newspaper
- "J"—prospects provided by your junior salespeople

Each source is as valuable to you as your judgment and experience indicate.

First Sale in a New Field Opens the Way to New Prospects

As you gain knowledge of a prospect in an unfamiliar field, your approach to others in the same field will become stronger. The natural follow-up is to uncover more prospects in the same line of business.

■ IDEA IN ACTION

Henrietta Wallace sold a service to increase office efficiency. She was called in by a prospect in a field that was new to her—a local hospital—to analyze the admitting procedure.

During her visit, Henrietta also surveyed the hospital's general systems for discharging, billing, and so on. She found that she could propose a procedure that would eliminate duplication and cut expenditures by $15,000 annually.

Within a reasonably short time after her recommendations were put into practice, she was able to approach and sell three more hospitals on the basis of what she'd learned during her first hospital contact.

Word of Mouth Creates Prospects

The prospect-conscious salesperson never misses an opportunity to mention his or her profession and product. Here's the story of one salesperson who lost out by simply forgetting to say that he was in the real estate business.

∎ IDEA IN ACTION

Herb Walrath was furious with himself. One day on his way home from work, he walked into the grocery store to pick up a few items for dinner. For the first time in the four or five years he'd shopped there, the owner was nowhere to be seen.

"Where's Mr. Ortiz?" he asked one of the checkers.

"Oh, he's over at the new store," was the reply.

It was the first that Herb had ever heard about "the new store." He realized then that in all his casual conversations with Mr. Ortiz, he'd neglected to mention that he was in the real estate business.

Herb promised himself that he'd never forget again.

Increase Your Sales Through Well-kept Prospect and Customer Records

Your chances to make a sale will increase each time you add new information to a prospect or customer record card. When checked against the data you've already recorded, the new facts will often give you the clue to a sale.

Make certain that your records give you the exact name, title, and location of your prospect. Correct names are important. "Smith-Anderson Company" is incorrect if the proper name of the firm is "Smith and Anderson, Incorporated."

The first name or initials of individuals should also be carefully noted. A notation to see "Mr. Smith" is useless if there are several Smiths in the company. "Mr. John J. Smith" will enable you to contact the right person when you write, telephone, or make a personal call.

Titles, too, are important. When you approach a prospect with your proposition, it is essential to know if you're dealing with the assistant to the general manager, the assistant general manager, or the general manager himself or herself.

Be just as careful to record accurate department designations, room numbers, and street addresses.

Cooperation with the Credit Department Helps You in Prospecting

What may appear as a favor to your credit department may in fact be a favor to yourself. Your credit department may ask for your cooperation in any of the following ways; notice how you profit by doing the favor:

- A credit manager urges you to call on a new company that has just placed its first order. You're asked to take a look at the firm and report your observations. When you make the call, you are greeted warmly. You establish a strong personal contact with the new account and gain a profitable prospect for future sales—assuming that the firm is worthy of credit.

- An account has fallen behind on its payments, and the credit manager asks you to call on the customer to see what has happened. During the course of your visit, you advise the customer on ways to improve his or her business, thereby establishing a basis for future sales even if the credit department does not extend credit on present orders.

- You are asked to review a written form regarding the line of credit to be extended to a particular customer. Because you have also been asked for your advice, you use this opportunity to gather as much information as you can to help the credit department make the right decision. Whether your recommendations result in a suspension of credit or an extension of credit, you are doing yourself a favor by reassessing the customer's buying potential.

SUGGESTION When you get such a form from your credit department, don't just write "O.K." or "N.G." Jot down a few lines, or even paragraphs, on the back of the form. You might even attach a lengthier comment if the situation merits it. By cooperating fully with your credit department, you'll be the first to be offered a good lead when it comes along.

A good credit manager will help the company's salespeople whenever the opportunity arises. Here are some of the ways that credit departments can help:

- They will usually supply you with periodic information about the kind of purchases customers are making. A sharp salesperson knows how to use this information to make bigger sales.

- Credit checks on new prospects whose potential business looks good but whose credit acceptability may be doubtful can save you the trouble and disappointment of getting an order only to have it rejected.

TIP Some credit managers consider inactive accounts to be the "cream" of prospect sources. Their reasoning is as follows: If a company is still in business and you aren't selling them, then someone else is. The history of a former customer's business with your company can give you clues as to why the customer stopped buying (as described at the beginning of this chapter.)

GUIDES TO BETTER TERRITORY COVERAGE

Covering Your Territory Effectively

Unless your efforts follow a carefully thought-out plan, you are likely to find that time spent covering your territory is not yielding rewards that are proportionate in terms of earnings. Your goal should be to reach your contacts quickly and effectively, and to produce enough repeat and new business to compensate you fully for every minute spent "out in the field."

With planning and forethought you can almost always save time through careful routing of calls. You avoid backtracking, criss-crossing your route, making long trips to see just one customer, bypassing customers, and needless travel. This section describes basic routing plans that save time.

A Sampler of Basic Routing Plans

A routing plan that reduces total travel distance to a minimum

This plan works for the salesperson who calls on a definite number of dispersed customers, all of whom are equally important.

> **WHAT TO DO** Pinpoint your stops on a map. Try several alternative routes based on different groupings. Use a ruler to help you determine the shortest route.

Figure 2.1 illustrates how a salesperson has grouped his calls to cut travel distance to a minimum.

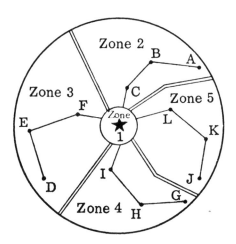

Figure 2.1

Customer Call Grouping Designed to Minimize
Travel Distance

The star in the center of the routing plan represents the salesperson's base of operation. He has divided his territory into zones and covers one zone each day.

If the salesperson is unable to cover all the towns in one zone on a particular day, he still works the next zone, as usual, on the following day. By not working one route two days in succession, the salesperson is able to take care of individual inquiries at the smallest possible transportation cost.

For example, on the first, second, third, and fourth days of the month, the salesperson may work towns in Zones 2, 3, 4, and 5, respectively. On the morning of the fifth day, he might receive a call from Town B in Zone 2 that he had been unable to cover thoroughly.

He can now gather all the prospect and customer cards in Town B, Zone 2 that he has been unable to call on or follow up. After he takes care of the inquiry, he can finish the rest of the calls in Town B and work Town C in any remaining time.

If he had interrupted his normal work schedule to spend two or three days in Zone 2 and complete his work there, he would have had to make a special trip back to Town B to take care of this single call.

NOTE By driving to the farthest point in each zone first and then working backward, the stops not covered are those *nearest* to your base of operations.

A plan to route calls around key customers

"Key" is defined here as those customers who demand immediate attention. A customer who must be seen right away to prevent him or her from giving a large order to a competitor is a key customer. So is a customer who needs an immediate service call or a prospect who is ready for closing and needs only a final interview.

Calls to key customers can be used as a routing guide by salespeople who sell in one city or in many. In either situation, the key customer becomes the one around whom all other calls are planned.

□ EXAMPLE

A salesperson who operates in three states may have to make a sudden call to a key customer in a distant city. Before he leaves, he checks his records for other prospects or customers he might profitably contact while he is there.

☐ EXAMPLE

A salesperson whose territory is one section of a large city is called for emergency service to the other end of her territory. She checks her files for others she might see who are located near the key customer.

Key customer routing is most advantageous to those salespeople who have

■ A limited number of accounts

■ A large proportion of service calls

■ Calls to make on prospects in various stages of closing

■ Less interest in territory coverage than in paying careful attention to accounts as they need it

CAUTION Because of its concentration on only a few customers, this routing plan does not assure you of thorough territory coverage. If you use this plan, be sure to avoid losing potential business through lack of contact and neglect.

A routing plan to stagger calls in order of customers' importance

This type of routing allows a salesperson to call on accounts with greater or less frequency according to their value. It is particularly valuable to the salesperson who has figured the dollar value of her customers and who wishes to make more calls to more valuable customers.

WHAT TO DO Divide your customers into categories labeled "excellent," "good," and "marginal." Plan to call on your best accounts every trip, the middle group every other trip, and the least important group every third or fourth trip.

■ IDEA IN ACTION

Joanna Filardi sells her product to customers located in 20 cities in two states. She has divided her accounts into the classifications just discussed. She calls on the accounts in the first group every time she is in their city and calls on the customers in the second group during alternate trips. The third group she sees whenever possible, or when it is necessary to call on them.

This "staggered" approach enables Joanna to spend more time with the customers who are most profitable to her.

CAUTION If the towns in your territory are very far apart, it may be advisable for you to use the "clean-up" plan described next.

A routing plan for salespeople who sell one town at a time

Here is a plan that is advantageous for salespeople who call on all prospects and customers in one town before they go on to the next. Because this plan allows the salesperson to finish his or her business in a particular town, its chief advantage is the economy of travel time and expense. This plan is especially valuable for salespeople who must travel long distances.

Although it should be followed as closely as possible, this plan does not preclude spending extra time in any town if the salesperson finds it necessary.

CAUTION Saving travel time is not an end in itself. It may pay for you to spend more time traveling if the end result is more selling time with worthwhile accounts.

A routing plan for salespeople who call on customers regularly and frequently

You will save travel time by using regular stop routing if your product (1) requires little selling, (2) appeals to an unlimited market, and (3) requires regular and frequent calls on customers. This type of routing is especially useful to those who sell food, tobacco products, a service that offers periodic checkup calls and repairs, and so on.

WHAT TO DO Purchase a map that includes your territory. Pinpoint the locations of your customers. Now trace a connecting route that *most nearly* represents a straight line. Use this map to guide you on your calls until your route becomes familiar.

NOTE Your customers need not be located close together. Regardless of the proximity of your stops, the route must follow a path that is as near a straight line as possible.

The broadside routing plan for door-to-door salespeople

Broadside routing can be used in selling to homes, stores, and offices. It guarantees complete territory coverage and is primarily valuable for one-call or first-call coverage. Figure 2.2 illustrates the route for thorough door-to-door coverage.

CAUTION Call at *every* door. You will undermine the purpose of broadside routing—*intensive territory coverage*—if you skip homes or offices to call on only those that appear promising to you.

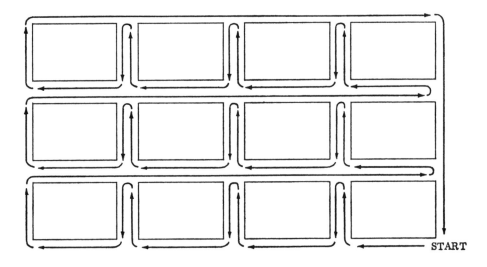

Figure 2.2

Door-to-Door Coverage of Contiguous Blocks

NOTE A sales manager whose product requires this type of territory coverage calls it the "hit 'em all" system. He warns his people against using the "horse race system"—wandering around in a random fashion, looking for a prospect who is a "natural." "It's a funny thing," he says, "but almost all new salespeople start out using the horse race system. They travel all over looking for 'naturals' and end up believing that there just aren't any good prospects. By relying on the horse race system, they're missing some of the best prospects. If they use the hit 'em all system, they *can't* miss them."

Maps Can Be Valuable

Territory management can be made more effective through the proper use of maps. Maps give you a precise picture of your territory, help you see your customer locations, and aid you in planning routes that will save travel time and assure complete coverage.

Maps of towns, cities, counties, states, and sections of the country may be obtained from these sources:

- State highway department (state and county maps)
- City or town clerk (maps of the city or town)
- Service stations (state maps, sometimes maps of larger cities)
- Travel bureaus
- Chambers of commerce
- Bookstores

TIP Maps obtained from the state highway department often contain information that will be valuable in planning your territory coverage. These maps usually pinpoint the locations of radio stations, town halls, hospitals, schools, factories, commercial buildings, and garages.

Use the Telephone to Increase Territory Coverage

Telephone calls to supplement your personal calls on bread-and-butter customers can keep your relationships with smaller customers active, improve your territory coverage, and result in extra sales.

▪ IDEA IN ACTION

Harry Brown thinks it's important to spend most of his time in face-to-face contact with his best customers. Although Harry's list of customers includes many other smaller buyers, he normally sacrifices contacting them in deference to his more profitable accounts.

Eventually, Harry finds that a large percentage of these seldom-contacted customers become inactive accounts or switch to competitors. His loss in earnings, although not large, is enough to spur Harry to try supplemental telephone coverage.

On the next trip around his territory, Harry stops long enough in each town to telephone nearby smaller accounts after he has seen his bigger customers. The result is threefold:

1. Contact is maintained with these accounts, assuring them that they haven't been forgotten.

2. Orders are sometimes taken over the telephone.

3. Arrangements are made for a personal call if Harry has a new line or if the customer has enjoyed an upswing in business.

Watch for Changes in the Demographics of Your Territory

You can bet that your company's executives—the president, sales manager, and others—are paying close attention to demographics these days. They know that the "baby boomers" are getting older. They're keeping an eye on widespread regional shifts in the population, and on the growth of certain metropolitan areas and their attached suburban, exurban, and interurban offshoots. All these changes affect marketing.

It is not enough for top executives to know how to capitalize on these changes. As a salesperson, you should be watching the developments and changes that are taking place in your own territory and be quick to cover the newcomers in the area.

> **NOTE** The shifts in industry that weaken a territory for some products strengthen it for others. For example, when farmlands are sold out for housing developments, the farm equipment salesperson loses out, but those who sell to builders, landscapers, and shopping centers move right in. Similarly, when rezoning permits the establishment of light industry in a formerly restricted area, the astute salesperson gets a line on what businesses are being "invited" in.

The more attention you pay to such developments, and the more responsive you are to them, the more likely it is that you'll get a jump on your competitors.

WHAT TO DO

- **Re-examine your routine for covering your territory.** If you haven't changed it for the past few years, there is only one possible conclusion: Your geographic area has remained stagnant while most of the country has been doing somersaults. Make it a point on your very next trip to compare the territory with what it was when you first took it on. That will clue you in to some of the sales opportunities you might have missed and will tell you whether you've been losing ground by following the old routine year in and year out.

- **Make it a point to know "what's cooking" in the community.** Local newspapers, chamber of commerce activities, business organization luncheons—these are just a few of the places to pick up news. And don't overlook your existing customers in the area. They can be a valuable source of information.

A Territory Cut Can Result in Bigger Volume

Don't worry about losing business volume when your territory is cut. Look upon it as a challenge to make bigger buyers of your present customers. This is the time to look for new profitable accounts among the prospects you never had time to develop. (Chapter Three shows how one salesperson got more volume out of a reduced territory by upgrading his customers.)

> **NOTE** Sales managers usually have a good reason for reducing a salesperson's territory. In most cases they know that there is more business in the old territory than any one individual can possibly handle. For example, if the company has put on a big sales promotion and advertising campaign, each salesperson must work his or her territory more intensively to get the maximum benefit from the promotion expenditure. This is easier to accomplish if everyone has less territory to cover.

IDEAS FOR CREATIVE SELLING

A creative salesperson always gets the lion's share of the business.

What is a creative salesperson? Someone who creates business where none existed before.

No one has a monopoly on creativity. In fact, most salespeople are far more creative than they think they are. They underestimate their creative talents because they don't really understand what creative selling is all about.

Picking up orders is not creative selling. You get that business without any special effort. Creative selling takes imagination. You alone can supply this vital spark. It's the key to selling greatness. This chapter will help you to:

- Utilize the full extent of your creative powers, by training your imagination.

- Step up your creative thinking by adopting the attitudes shared by the most creative people in your field.
- Start applying creative thinking to each step of your work—from finding prospects to closing sales.

To keep your creativity alive, borrow ideas from others—this *Guide* is full of them. Once you've trained yourself to look for ideas that you can adapt, you will find them everywhere—in what you read, observe, and hear in conversation.

Originate new ideas by thinking about your selling problems and trying to come up with innovative solutions. Then act on the solutions you think up.

The hard-to-crack prospect will eventually soften if you can leave just one idea with him or her every time you call. Others have won big accounts this way.

The biggest dividend from developing your creativity is the confidence you gain. Plan your interview around an idea that you have created, and you'll feel a new power to perform.

REMEMBER You can't be a star salesperson just by wanting to be. Willpower alone won't do it. But willpower combined with creative selling will get you there.

YOU MUST BE CREATIVE TO MAKE BIG MONEY

Creative People Are in Demand

Today, more than ever, business executives are looking for creativity in the people they hire. Why? Because our times demand originality. The salesperson who gets the account is not necessarily the most experienced, the most persistent, or the shrewdest. Companies that are going through rough economic times are not always going to respond to the same old approach that's worked for years, nor do they want to deal with someone who's going to grab on to them like a bulldog and never let go. But there's a good chance they'll respond to someone who understands the problems they're facing and comes up with an approach that addresses those problems and points the way toward a solution.

Today's salespeople must not only know their company's products but must also be able to see the relationship between those products and changing consumer needs and demands. For example, concern for the environment is a high priority for many customers today. While yesterday's salesperson might have been content to sell the product for what it does, today's salesperson must be prepared to promote the fact that it comes in a recyclable container or that the fluorocarbons have been removed. Tapping into both present and future market trends is the mark of a creative salesperson.

You Can Qualify as a Creative Salesperson

Any salesperson can pick up orders, check stocks, answer phone or mail inquiries, and cover a lot of miles in the car. These are necessary activities in selling, but they are *not* creative.

Creative salespeople earn big money because they bring their imagination into play at every step of the selling process. If you are going to make money, you have to know how to create a demand for what you sell. This is the heart of selling. It takes imagination—it takes ideas—but it pays off.

Have you got what it takes? Begin by answering the following questions:

- Have you ever found a prospect during cold calls?

- Have you ever gotten an appointment with a prospect who was hard to see?

- Have you ever created a desire for your product or service in a prospect who did not seem to be very interested when you first started your interview?

If you can answer "Yes" to any of these questions, you've already proved that you can be creative. Now the question is: Have you been creative enough?

We are going to show you how to develop your imagination and how to bring creativity into play in all your selling efforts.

HOW TO TRAIN YOUR MIND
TO CREATE IDEAS

Imagination Has Power

Everyone has imagination. It's what we use when we dream, visualize, invent, or create.

Imagination can lend a magical touch to your product or service. The power of imagination makes it possible for you to help your customers visualize the profit in your company's line, the value in your merchandise, and the desirability of your organization.

To be helpful, imagination must be constructive. Constructive imagination has a dramatic force that sweeps away resistance and draws the prospect into your fold. With this quality, you are miles ahead of your competitor; without it, he or she may be ahead of you.

Curiosity Is an Element
of Imagination

Salespeople who are imaginative are also curious. They are eager to obtain knowledge, to find out the "why," "how," "when," "where," and "what" of everything that pertains to their job. Curiosity becomes a habit. They are always asking questions, reading, looking for answers.

Without curiosity you cannot hope to open up new avenues for the sale of your products. All you can do is feed on the results already obtained by an inquisitive predecessor.

Imagination resides in the salesperson who sits down quietly every evening, reviews everything that happened during the day, and tries to think up better ways to handle those situations that didn't work out well. It resides to a greater extent in the salesperson who spends an hour at home each night thinking about his or her customers and their problems, trying to come up with ways to solve these problems and build up their business so that he or she can sell more to them. It resides to an even greater degree in the salesperson who tries to discover new ideas that will make his or her job bigger and better than it ever was before.

Wherever you fit in this picture, there is always room for further development of your imagination. In fact, it *must* be developed in every salesperson who has a bigger goal ahead than he or she has yet achieved.

Train your Imagination

Most people think that imagination is something you have to be born with. Fortunately, this isn't true. Imagination can be acquired and developed. Regardless of what you're selling, you can develop imagination with this simple exercise:

Imagine yourself handling your job like a star salesperson. Dissect your job piece by piece and imagine all the things you would do in difficult situations. Let your imagination have boundless horizons, but try to keep your ideas practical and realistic. Write down your ideas so you don't forget them—you never can tell when they will be needed.

Don't be afraid of wild ideas—they can frequently be adapted to more realistic situations when you think them through. Naturally, you can't expect to use every idea that comes to you. But as a rule, ideas go where they are welcome, which means that they develop and display themselves when and where you encourage them. Whatever it is you are doing, try to think of ways to do it better, more efficiently, more effectively, and more profitably for all concerned.

▪ IDEA IN ACTION

Regular practice in using imagination made a star salesperson out of James Renaldi. He spent half an hour a day, every evening, in thought. He asked himself where he could find new markets for his products, where and how he could discover new uses for them. Within a few years' time, the results of this routine became apparent, and his success has been outstanding for years. His specialty is "creative selling"—creating business where none existed before, finding customers where other salespeople didn't see them.

Whenever you are forced to sit still for a while—when you're waiting, traveling, or resting—think of something constructive, something connected with your job. If you read while waiting, do it with a conscious effort to find ideas that you can apply in your work. Follow your thoughts through to a definite conclusion so that your thinking results in an idea. You will be astounded at the number of helpful ideas you will come up with when you do this on a regular basis.

The more you use your imagination, the more imagination you will have available to use. "Use it or lose it!" is an apt warning. Imagination is not some magical quality that only a few gifted individuals possess. It is more like a muscle that everyone is born with. Some people develop it by exercising it constantly; others let it atrophy by never exercising it at all.

Creativity depends upon stimulation. If you let your imagination lapse, even for a short time, it may take a week or even a month to regain your creative momentum.

Getting Ideas for Creative Selling

Getting ideas to help you create sales means driving yourself to apply your imagination to your selling job. Drive is a vital part of creative thinking. Only with drive will you get ideas from the numerous sources that are available to every salesperson.

There is no secret to finding good ideas. All creative salespeople get their ideas from the same basic sources:

Borrow ideas from others

You can apply to your own uses an idea that someone else has used to create a sale. In the section that follows, you will find ideas that creative salespeople have used in the past. Many of them can be used exactly as they are given.

> **NOTE** When sales managers ask their salespeople to submit their best selling ideas for purposes of exchange, they are encouraging members of the sales team to borrow from each other.

Adapt ideas that others have used

With a little applied imagination, you can often use other people's ideas to help you create sales. Approach each creative idea in this *Guide* as having some elements that you can use. You can almost always find a way to adapt it to your needs.

Originate ideas

The ideas you originate to create sales may come from

- Reading
- Contacts with customers, prospects, and friends
- Observations
- The extra thinking you do to break special contest quotas
- Concentrating on a particular problem

These original ideas are nothing more than a new combination of old elements. It's the fresh twist you give to an old idea that makes it original.

Become Idea-Minded and You'll Find Ideas

To prove to yourself that you are more creative than you think, begin to focus on coming up with ideas. They may be ideas that will help you make a sale or ideas that you can pass along to a customer the next time you call, just to show your interest.

> **SUGGESTION** Since the idea-minded salesperson can find ideas anywhere and everywhere, use this list to stimulate your thinking. Use each of the sources mentioned in a concentrated effort to become idea-minded. Remember to look for *adaptable* ideas. When you spot one, make a written note of it. Spend a few minutes deciding how you are going to use it, and with whom.

- **Trade magazines.** Read the trade magazine in your field, if there is one. Then look at the trade magazines of the industries to which you sell.
- **Newspapers.** Scan local, regional, and national newspapers with the thought of finding ideas in them. You may spot an item that will be of special interest to a customer. Clip it, write your name on it, and send it to him or her.
- **Customers.** When you call on a customer, be on the lookout for ideas. These may come from conversation, from seeing

the customer's displays, or from hearing about new promotions.

■ **Conversations with coworkers.** The exchange of ideas can begin with your throwing one into your conversation. Your coworkers will probably have ideas to match it.

■ **Customers' in-house publications.** Do your customers publish a newsletter or in-house magazine? Get copies of these publications whenever you can. There's information about your customers in it that will get you thinking of ways to fit your product to their needs. You might read about a change in organization, a replacement of personnel, an upcoming expansion—any such information can spark a new idea.

Get Ideas from Satisfied Customers

Users of your product can be an excellent source of ideas. To take full advantage of this source, make a regular practice of calling upon your old customers, say, a few every week, to discuss how they are actually using the product. Here's what you gain from such a practice:

■ You might discover that the customer has found an application for your product that even your firm has not yet discovered.

■ Satisfied customers can provide valuable testimonials to be used in future selling. Some of these customers will even be willing to talk directly to your prospects about their experience with the product.

■ You win the goodwill of your old customers by making them feel that you have their interests at heart. And, of course, you can prove this by passing on to them any ideas you've picked up in visits to other longtime customers.

Build Up an "Idea Bank"

The more ideas you can dig up, the more chances you have of making sales. Once you become idea-minded, you'll discover that ideas come your way on a regular basis.

To preserve the ideas that come to you at odd moments, keep a notebook handy. Jot down in it the ideas you read, hear, see, or think about—or the ones that come to you out of the blue. This handy notebook is your idea bank.

Some of the ideas you come across will be in magazine articles, newspapers, or other sources that you can clip. It's a good idea to supplement your "idea notebook" with an "idea file" into which you place the clippings.

Your idea bank and file become valuable to you only if you use them. Get into the habit of "visiting" your idea bank regularly. Go to it not only when you have a problem to solve, but whenever you have a few spare minutes. Review the ideas you've clipped and jotted down, and you'll be surprised at how frequently one will come to life for you just at the moment you need it. And remember: If a creative idea works once for you, it will probably work again.

Give Your Ideas Freely

The salesperson who supplies customers and prospects with useful ideas as well as with good service builds goodwill and confidence, which in turn open the door to larger orders. Nothing will pique a prospect's interest more quickly than a new idea or even an old idea dressed up in new clothing.

Dig into your idea bank and idea file to find something that will help your customers get more for their money, or increase sales, or save a few hundred dollars through more efficient operations.

> **CAUTION** When you pick up an idea *from a customer* to put into your idea bank, be sure to note where you got it. No customer wants his or her ideas passed on to a competitor. Also, be careful *how* you offer your suggestions. You don't want to give the impression that you're telling a customer how to run his or her business.

STEPPING UP YOUR CREATIVITY

Adopt the Attitude of a Creative Salesperson

To begin to step up your creativity, you must adopt the attitude of a successful creative salesperson. Here's how creative salespeople approach their work:

- They know that there's a solution to the problem and that by thinking creatively, they can find it.

- They know that by discovering the bottleneck in a selling situation, they can accelerate their creative thinking.

- They know that by thinking creatively they can convert a "No" to a "Yes."

- They look at each step of the sale as a challenge to creative thinking.

The following sections offer guidelines to how you can adapt these approaches to your sales work.

Finding a Solution to Problems

Creative salespeople have learned that when it comes to selling, there is a solution to every problem—*if* they can only find it. Of course, they don't always find it. But their attitude is that a solution exists.

Every sales executive knows individuals who seem to have a knack for getting around obstacles that others have found insurmountable. These people achieve outstanding results largely because they "stay with" a given sales problem rather than throwing up their hands in defeat. It's a form of persistence, and they do it because they've learned from prior experience that tough problems, if they are to be solved at all, require a little extra "sweat."

■ IDEA IN ACTION

Ralph Saunders sells automotive supplies. He is the top salesperson in his organization, but even so he is unable to sell several large chain organizations which do a large volume of business. Other salespeople representing Ralph's company have also tried without success to "crack" these special accounts, so there is reason to believe that their minds are made up.

But Ralph won't accept this. Instead, he "stays with" this particular problem, hoping to come up with a solution. He realizes that persistence in calling will not provide the answer.

Finally, Ralph has a new idea. He carefully surveys several of the chain's outlets and determines exactly which competing brands they stock. He notes the resale prices of various items and compares them with his own. After considerable work, Ralph makes a discovery. He finds that his company offers an unusually attractive value on one particular specialty unit as compared with the lines that are established in these outlets.

Ralph telephones the buyer for one of the chains. "Mrs. Elton," he says, "I'm not calling you to ask you to consider our line. I'd like to have about 5 minutes of your time to tell you about an opportunity you're missing in some of your stores."

This "curiosity" approach wins him the interview. True to his word, he does not try to present his line as such, but instead focuses the buyer's attention on the one item which she is buying at a much higher cost from her present suppliers.

"Now here's my suggestion," concludes Ralph. "If you will select, say, six of your typical outlets and let me test out our #763 in them, I'm willing to let the results speak for themselves."

Mrs. Elton accepts this offer.

Ralph personally instructs the salespeople in the six test stores and persuades them to feature his #763 in their windows and to "talk it up" as a good item.

The added sales induce Mrs. Elton to place this item in their entire group of stores. Shortly thereafter she says to Ralph, "You're one of the few salespeople who have ever taken the time to *prove* to us how we could increase our sales and profits.

"We saw no reason to change suppliers before, but we now think you've earned a break. Next time you stop in, we'll be glad to listen to your suggestions as to how we can go about introducing some of your products."

Discovering the Bottleneck will Accelerate Creative Thinking

The creative salesperson looks for the "bottleneck" or obstacle in every selling assignment. It may be in finding prospects, in getting the interview, or in beating the competition.

No matter where the bottleneck lies, the creative salesperson concentrates on finding a means of overcoming this impediment. Once he or she has hit upon a successful formula, the same solution can be applied to similar situations in the future.

■ IDEA IN ACTION

How to beat competition was Jill Cordero's bottleneck. Here's how she beat it in one case, using methods that she had already applied in others.

The prospect, a large industrial concern, had already performed a time-and-motion study that broke down each of its processes into make-ready, set-up, and running time. Jill took these figures and translated them in terms of her company's new high-speed equipment. She determined that with her company's equipment, the prospect could achieve a 35% improvement in efficiency.

In the meantime, three competitive equipment producers were contacted by the prospect. Here's what Jill did that beat this competition:

- She prepared an attractive proposal, which was more convincing than that of at least one of the competitors because it recommended a specific piece of equipment.

- She arranged for a demonstration with the "key person."

- She cultivated a friendly relationship with the department head, who kept her informed about when the competitors were to make their demonstrations.

- She arranged a luncheon with the key buyer so that she would see him immediately after the most threatening competitor had finished his demonstration—and she brought her sales manager with her to the luncheon.

- She compared her own product with the competitor's (the one still in the running), whose equipment she knew thoroughly.

- She presented an impressive list of users and new customers who had recently purchased the same equipment.

- She brought the controller and the department head to see her company's exhibition at the Business Show.

Small wonder that Jill made the sale to this new customer, whose potential for future purchases ranked high. She knew exactly what her biggest obstacle would be and she set out deliberately to overcome it.

How "No" Can Be Overcome by Thinking Creatively

Creative salespeople adopt the attitude that a "No" is merely a challenge to their creative abilities. They apply their creative thinking to finding ways to stimulate desire. Notice how, in the following example, the salesperson gets the order in spite of the initial opposition of the prospect company's president. This kind of creative selling is characteristic of the salesperson who is determined to better his or her income every year.

▪ IDEA IN ACTION

A real estate multiple listing service advertised in a local newspaper. Salesperson George Bostwick saw a potential lead in this and decided to explore the "up-to-date methods" mentioned in the ad.

He called on the president of the listing service and was informed that the current system was working very smoothly. They weren't interested in changing anything.

That didn't stop George from finding out for himself how smooth the system for preparing listing reports really was. He found he could offer a much better system. This is how he won the president's cooperation and made the sale:

- He went to the office where the listing reports were prepared and spoke to the staff there. They had a number of complaints about the system and the equipment.

- He prepared a sample listing report using his own equipment.

- He sent copies of the sample to each member of the service and outlined the many advantages his method had over the existing method.

- He called back on the president and got permission to gain additional cost information.

- He presented his proposal at a meeting of the listing service's Operating Committee.

- He overcame an important objection of the Operating Committee concerning how photographs would be printed. In anticipation of this objection, he had already discussed the problem with a local photographic lab, and they came up with an even better way of getting the work done than he had originally proposed.

- He resubmitted his revised proposal to the listing service authorities, and it was unanimously accepted.

The natural sales curiosity of this creative salesperson, his determination even though the president endorsed the existing method, and the intrinsic qualities of the product he sold made this sale possible.

Each Step of the Sale Is a Challenge to Creative Thinking

The attitude that each step of the sale is a challenge to creative thinking makes it possible to create business where none existed before. In cold-calling, this attitude is the key to success.

Let's take each of the steps in a sale and see how a creative idea helped to win over a cold-call prospect. Creative ideas work the same way, of course, in selling to "hot" prospects and longtime customers. Obviously, creative selling is not limited to these methods.

Here are the steps, all of which will be familiar to you from your selling experience. Each creative idea is then discussed in detail in the following sections.

- You create the prospect—by making him or her recognize a need.

- You make the right preapproach—by creative thinking.

- You get the interview with the prospect—by getting around a secretary who won't let you in.

- You arouse the prospect's interest—by discovering the benefit that means most to the prospect.

- You stimulate the prospect's desire—by creatively building his or her desire for the benefits.

- You convince the prospect that the benefit can be achieved—by the creative quality of your demonstration.

- You overcome an unusual objection—by offering the prospect a new idea.

- You get the prospect to take action—by using a creative closing strategy.

In each of the factual situations described in the following sections, the salesperson found a new way of solving a problem; ordinary selling techniques did not work. That's what a creative idea is—it's a "new way" the first time the salesperson uses it. Another good thing about a creative idea is that it can be used again and again—by any smart salesperson who wants to adopt it.

Step 1: Creating prospects by using creative techniques

A creative salesperson doesn't just look for prospects; he or she creates them. Every time you make a cold call in cold-canvassing, you are creating a prospect.

☐ EXAMPLE

Most users of office computers don't "shop" for new machines. In fact, most of them do not even want, or realize they need, new computers until an enterprising salesperson convinces them of what a new machine can do. So in a sense it is the salesperson who *creates* the prospects rather than just looking for them.

The same is true of many other fields where each day's plan must include several cold calls. (Chapter Two offers more examples of creative ideas that lead to prospects.)

Step 2: Preparing your preapproach by creative thinking

Part of the preapproach to a sale is to aim your presentation at the right person. It takes creative thinking to find this individual, especially if you've been having trouble with the person you first encountered and are looking for an opportunity to make your presentation to someone else who has the authority to make the buying decision.

■ IDEA IN ACTION

The person Lynette Oakes had been trying to persuade to buy her product wouldn't budge from his established source. Lynette learned one day that this man had resigned from his position, and she saw the possibility of a more amenable prospect in his successor.

But Lynette didn't know who this successor was. So even though she knew that Mr. X had left, *Lynette still called for him by name.* The switchboard operator volunteered the name of the person who had assumed Mr. X's duties, and there Lynette was, ready to greet the newcomer by name and to congratulate her on her promotion.

Chapter Four provides additional tips on successful preapproach strategies.

Step 3: Getting by the secretary in cold-calling by using creative thinking

The very first step toward the interview in cold-calling—getting by the secretary—may call for imagination. This happens when the secretary guards his or her employer's time so carefully that you can't get in to see the prospect.

■ IDEA IN ACTION

Ordinary sales methods were of no avail to Tom Miller in trying to get an overly conscientious secretary to tell her boss that Tom wanted to see her. Tom had already tried his usual technique—"selling" the secretary on announcing him and fixing a time when he could see the boss. But this guardian of the boss's time could not be won over.

Tom would not let his effort end there. He knew, from what he had observed of the prospect's place of business, and from what he knew about the prospect through preapproach study, that he could make a sale easily if he could just get his foot in the door. So he pondered the situation and decided to do something bold: he would call his prospect at home after working hours.

"Ms. Smith," asked Tom, "do you have any influence with your secretary?"

"Why?" asked Ms. Smith, laughing good-naturedly.

"Because," said Tom, "I have some equipment that could save you a lot of money, and I can't convince her that she ought to let me in to see you."

The prospect fixed a convenient time for an appointment the next morning, and a week later Tom had a signed contract.

Step 4: Arousing your prospect's interest by showing more than savings

Suppose your best selling point for the product you offer is the savings it will achieve for your prospect. The weight of this argument may seem sufficient to you to convince any prospect to buy. But you can never be sure that it will be. You must be prepared to use your imagination and think creatively, should additional persuasion be necessary to help you make the sale.

▪ IDEA IN ACTION

Rita Fleming found that savings alone would not always "bring home the bacon." She was able to point out savings of more than $25,000 a year to her prospect, which to her way of thinking more than justified purchasing her product. But what finally made the sale was Rita's switching her selling point to the space-saving benefit of her equipment. She had observed that the prospect's office was overcrowded. The space-saving advantage solved the problem uppermost in the prospect's mind, and Rita made the sale.

Step 5: Stimulating your prospect's motive to buy by making a creative presentation

The motive to buy something often lies dormant and is not consciously felt. But when certain suggestions are made, or circumstances change, this hidden motive suddenly becomes clear.

Many selling jobs depend on channeling these motives to create a need that the prospect has not felt before—the need for your product or service.

☐ EXAMPLE

What businessperson would say, right off the bat, that he or she needs more than the ordinary steel cabinets to protect important documents against loss by fire? Probably none. To sell equipment that will protect papers against fire, the salesperson must first get the prospect to start thinking about the hazards. He or she must demonstrate to the prospect that records housed in steel containers will last only about 4 minutes in a fire. The skilled salesperson will make the prospect actually *smell* fire before convincing him or her that such equipment is needed.

In this type of selling, the salesperson channels two basic wants—security and protection—to create a need that the prospect has not felt before. He or she builds desire for the product that meets this need. (You can see this creative salesperson at work in the sample presentation described in Chapter Five.)

Step 6: Convincing your prospect by using creative ideas

You may want to use a demonstration to convince your prospect that the benefits you've pointed out are real. The entire demonstration takes creative thinking (as explained in Chapter Five). But an extra twist, in the form of a creative thought, can increase your demonstration's persuasive power.

Imagine having a prospect for whom you discover savings of $85,000 a year through the use of something you sell! If the savings are this big, chances are the investment required by the customer is a considerable one as well. When you add in your own commission, the whole proposition takes on mammoth proportions.

When you're headed for a big deal, you may have to convince your sales manager that the situation merits a deviation from your usual demonstration procedure. In the following example, the company went to the expense of shipping the product to the customer's office and making advance preparations so that a good demonstration, adapted to the prospect's specific needs, could be made. The trouble and expense all proved worthwhile: The big sale was made.

■ IDEA IN ACTION

Harold Thomson had a customer who used only one of his company's products. Thomson knew there was a potential need for much more equipment, if he could only get in and make a survey.

He "sold" the survey first. One of the recommendations he made on the basis of the facts disclosed was to decentralize the operation. This meant that a unit of the product he hoped to sell would be installed in five different places.

The most important phase of the sale was the demonstration. Twenty-one people from five different divisions had to see it. This fact, plus the size of the potential sale, justified a request that his company do everything necessary to permit an on-the-spot demonstration.

The demonstration was made in the customer's office. The on-the-spot display overcame all the objections raised by the 21 interested viewers.

NOTE This kind of deal won't happen to the salesperson who's merely there to take orders. It's for those who have confidence, courage, imagination, and a desire to tackle big buyers.

Step 7: Overcoming your prospect's objections with a creative response

It takes creative thinking to overcome an ordinary objection—one that you've encountered before—in that you must have a number of reasons on which to build your answer. But when an unusual objection arises, it takes an even higher level of creativity to make the sale.

■ IDEA IN ACTION

A Brooklyn real estate broker, Anna Bognossian, had an attractive investment property for her client, a corporate executive. It was just what the prospect wanted, and he made an acceptable offer to the owner. A few days later the prospect called at the broker's office to say that he could not buy the property.

"Ms. Bognossian," he said, "I can't go through with this deal. I know it's a good buy, but if anything should happen to me, my estate will need cash and too much would be tied up in that property."

The $8,500 commission looked too good to Bognossian to let it slip away. She thought quickly, using an idea that was new to the prospect.

"Mr. Investor," she said, "I understand what you're saying, but I'm sure I can show you how you can buy this property and still keep yourself in a cash-on-hand position."

The investor-prospect was eager to hear the solution.

"After all your expenses are deducted," said Ms. Bognossian, "the property will still earn profits of about $18,000 a year. Instead of $18,000, figure the return at $16,000 and use the other $2,000 a year to buy life insurance to give you the cash your estate will need. This way your estate will be completely protected in the event that something happens to you."

Bognossian closed the deal.

Step 8: Closing the deal by using creative closing techniques

Creative salespeople think of ways to make their presentations dramatic and carry the dramatic element right to the close. Asking for the order comes naturally as they bring their drama to a climax.

The following idea in action illustrates this point.

■ IDEA IN ACTION

Bill Carroll sells an intangible service: long-distance moving. He developed his presentation by devising a visual aid that made his service appear more tangible. Using a large briefcase with a cutaway side, he made it possible for the prospect to look into a large moving van packed with miniature furniture. Each packed piece was protected with cloth wrapping.

Bill unpacked the van in front of the prospect, showing as he did so why it was impossible for any furniture to be scratched, marred, or broken if packed the way his firm packed it.

As Bill unpacked the miniature van, he reiterated the advantages of his company's careful method of preparing goods for long-distance shipping. Then he began repacking the van. This was the dramatic action that led to the close.

Having repacked the van, he asked, "You would want your household goods handled in this safe, sure, and easy manner, wouldn't you?" Of course, there could be only one answer from the prospect, "Yes." He followed this up immediately by asking when the family expected to move, "so I can make all the arrangements and guarantee that your household goods will be in your new home when you get there."

CREATIVE IDEAS THAT MAKE BIGGER BUYERS

Creative Ideas Can Be Applied to Methods of Increasing Sales

Creative ideas can open doors to bigger buyers in many ways. For example, creative ideas have been used to

- Upgrade customers
- Increase the size of a sale
- Find hidden applications for a product
- Find new uses for raw materials
- Broaden a customer's buying
- Open up a whole new field of prospects among which there are some big buyers
- Win important new accounts
- Get the product resold and reordered

These ideas are described in the following sections: They worked for the salespeople who originated them, and they can work for you, too.

Upgrade Customers with Creative Thinking About How Their Business Will Benefit

You can raise the dollar volume of a customer's business by thinking creatively about how the business will benefit if he or she buys a better grade of the product or service you're selling. The creative ideas come to you through recalling past experiences and relating them to the problem at hand.

Go over your list of customers who already use the better grade product. Then ask: "How has each customer used the high-priced product?" "Can the person whom you are going to upgrade make a similar use of it?" "What is there about this individual's business that is similar to that of the customers who use the better grades?"

■ IDEA IN ACTION

The sales manager for a large envelope company noticed that Elizabeth Fleming had not only survived a territory cut but was actually producing more dollar volume than her old territory had yielded. It was especially noticeable because sales figures from the other territories showed no similar successes among the other salespeople. The sales manager called Fleming in and asked her how she did it.

"Well, I did add some new customers, but most of the increased sales came from old customers," Fleming said.

"What did you do, convince them to buy more envelopes than they could use?" asked the sales manager.

"No, although by concentrating on them I did get more volume. In most cases, however, I got them to buy better envelopes than they had been using—better paper, better design, better printing. Each time I'd call on an old customer, I'd talk about the benefits of using higher-quality, better-looking envelopes. Slowly but surely it worked, and now almost half my old customers are ordering higher-priced envelopes and are happy with them."

Make a Big Sale Out of a Little One with a Service Idea

By showing a prospect how to increase efficiency or otherwise improve operations, you may be able to increase the size of an original order. The suggestions you are able to offer come from the knowledge you gain about the company as you prepare to make the sale.

■ IDEA IN ACTION

The cashier of a bank was interested in buying a desk and called in Herb Brown, salesperson for an office supply house. As the prospect talked, Herb made mental notes of the condition and arrangement of the bank furniture and operating equipment. He made no effort to close the sale at the end of the interview, but told the prospect that he would see him the following morning.

That evening Herb prepared a scale drawing of the bank, incorporating his own ideas on how it should be modernized. He showed how rearranging the furniture and equipment would increase efficiency. The drawing interested the prospect, and that morning Herb received a $20,000 order for furniture and equipment.

Creative Salespeople Look for Hidden Applications of the Product

When a product has many applications, you may be inclined to select the most obvious one and make a proposal that meets that particular need. But the creative salesperson looks for hidden applications. A not-so-obvious application may be the one that opens the way to big orders.

■ IDEA IN ACTION

Sabina Ulrich had been calling for a long time on the circulation manager of a well-known firm that did a tremendous amount of direct mail advertising. The obvious application of one of her products was to save costs by using her company's machine to put out promotional literature.

Sabina called on the circulation manager, a top executive in this type of organization, and was brushed off. When she subsequently called on other departments, she was referred back to the circulation department or the purchasing agent, and neither would see her.

One day when the circulation manager was out sick, Sabina spoke with the assistant, who seemed quite interested. She made a survey, and a short time later she presented a proposal covering promotional literature. A savings of up to 70% was shown on one application, and a specific machine was recommended.

The assistant circulation manager presented the proposal to the circulation manager. The sale died.

Ulrich tried again the following year. This time, with the help of a colleague who sold another product to the same prospect, she hit upon a hidden application for a different machine and was able to get an order. Also, through this sale she got an "in" with the general manager, to whom she planned to reissue her original proposal.

This sale was the most important of the year for Ulrich for at least three reasons:

- It was the initial sale to a large nonuser of long standing.

- The sale opened the door to many new applications and additional equipment for this customer.

- The application was simple, though obscured by many larger and more obvious applications

NOTE In addition to showing how a hidden application can be used to make a sale, this story illustrates the value of "staying with" a big-buyer prospect. It also demonstrates the necessity for finding a way in when the "key person" for the obvious application won't buy. Of course, it is usually easier to find another "key person" in large organizations than in smaller companies.

New Uses for a Product Challenge the Creative Salesperson

A new use for a product is best illustrated by the strides that have been made in adapting new raw materials to products conventionally made of other materials. Plastic is an outstanding example.

Producers of raw materials are not the only ones thinking up new uses for their products. Salespeople can also catch the "creation fever" and make important creative contributions.

Your creative abilities are especially brought into play when you set out to sell a prospect on the new use of your materials. You work hand in hand with the firm's engineers on such an assignment. In fact, your role is even more important than the engineer's, because without your ability to create a desire for the product in the customer's mind, the engineer's idea would be worthless. An idea that has no value is not a creative idea.

The stimulant to selling a new use for your product is the extra sales you will make to new prospects and old customers. The very first sale of a new use opens the way to big buyers.

■ IDEA IN ACTION

Bryan Moore's firm, a manufacturer of paper cartons, had hit on the idea of making a carton that would replace wooden containers for a hardware item. Engineers perfected a sample self-locking carton. Before the firm could undertake production, the first sale had to be made.

Bryan made the sale by being creative in every step of the selling process. He qualified the prospect by selecting an important manufacturer of the hardware item. The name of this manufacturer, as a user, would carry weight when he approached other prospects. He "went for broke" to get in to see the firm's "key person." ("Going for broke" is one of the preapproach strategies described in Chapter Four.) He created a desire for the product by giving a presentation that emphasized the benefits of a carton as compared with wooden boxes. He demonstrated dramatically with his sample carton the security, lightness, and other advantages of his materials. And he closed the sale on the strength of the well-planned presentation he had created.

Creative Salespeople Look for Clues to Broader Selling

A customer may be purchasing all he or she needs of a certain item from you. But you may see a need for other items in your line, or for certain services your firm offers. Your normal efforts to sell across the board, however, have not brought results. Your customer has remained a one-item buyer.

As a creative salesperson, you know there must be a way to get the customer to buy other items in your line. You keep your eyes and ears open and your mind alert for the slightest hint of a need for other items on your product or service list. You get permission to watch the employees who use your product in performing their jobs. This kind of observation can provide valuable clues as to what that "something else" might be.

■ IDEA IN ACTION

A salesperson for an envelope company was pleased with the envelope orders from a large mail order company, but stayed alert for ways to make the publisher a bigger customer. Watching the operators prepare some envelopes for a special mailing, he discovered that many of the envelopes were "slugged" "Attention: Sales Manager" and that the company did this job itself.

Knowing that his company could do the same imprinting in one-sixth the time, the salesperson showed the customer how to save time, trouble, and expense by letting the envelope supplier perform this service. The mail order company was quick to see the convenience and the savings in time and money that preprinted envelopes would mean. And the salesperson was happy with the larger orders that resulted.

Open Up a New Prospect Group
with Creative Selling

Are you in a field where certain prospects will not buy because they say they get what they need through trade associations? There may be a sales appeal that will overcome this objection. In the situation described next, a creative salesperson was able to open up an entire group of prospects by coming up with a new approach.

■ IDEA IN ACTION

"Don't waste your time on the textile people in your territory," was the counsel given to Doris Bell by the salesperson whose territory she was taking over. "They don't want our business service because they have several trade associations that take care of these things for them."

Doris checked with her sales manager and found that the company had never done well with the textile people. The sales manager knew of no approach that would work, but he encouraged Doris to try to come up with something.

Doris looked upon the problem as a challenge. She investigated the services that the trade associations provided for their members and listed all that were similar to those offered by her company.

Then she began to make calls. Sure enough, she was brushed off with the objection that she had been warned about.

Her reply: "On this sheet of paper, I have listed all the help you get from those other sources. But over here on the right I have listed the things we provide that you can't get elsewhere.

"Now, do you honestly think that you don't need our service?"

That, in essence, was her presentation. Because the facts were on her side, and because she had presented them in such a clear and undisputable manner, she made sale after sale.

A Creative Idea Wins a New Important Account

Persistence in calling on a prospect who will be a big buyer once you land him or her is no waste of time. But it does take ingenuity and creative thinking, especially if you've already used every technique in the book for breaking through the barrier of competition. The day when you can plan your interview around a creative idea, you will probably make the sale.

■ IDEA IN ACTION

Thomas Docherty had his mind set on selling his company's calculators to a firm in his territory that had the potential for becoming his biggest account. Docherty knew that this firm was the largest user of office machines in the territory. For years he had called regularly on the purchasing agent but had never been able to break through the competition. At the same time, he couldn't afford to give up: The potential volume of sales, if he overcame the bottleneck, was too promising.

Docherty had the drive and persistence that are essential to creative thinking. He knew that some day he would come up with a creative idea that would lick his problem, but he didn't know when or how.

In the meantime, he made a practice of keeping himself informed about his prospect's business. He always read the prospect's in-house newsletter and its annual report. In following this routine, he got the idea that finally clinched the sale.

The prospect had a wonderful profit-sharing plan for its employees. Looking through the annual report of securities owned by the profit-sharing trust, Docherty noticed that a profitable investment had been made in shares of a company affiliated with his own.

Immediately the idea came to him that he could use this information to advantage. Surely the purchasing agent would be interested in knowing that she and her fellow employees were, in a sense, indirect "owners" of his company and would see the wisdom of buying their calculators from him. The idea worked. It proved to be the wedge that opened the way to an order.

Again we see the ramifications of creative thinking. Here it was not a product use that was involved, or a way to broaden a customer's buying. All that was needed was a fresh approach.

The Creative Salesperson Follows Through to Get His or Her Product Resold and Reordered

A salesperson who sells to companies who must resell the product—either wholesalers or retailers—must be deeply concerned with the effort his or her customer makes to complete the sale to the ultimate consumer. Reorders are almost completely dependent on the customer's ability to sell the product to the end user.

> **NOTE** It's human nature to shy away from things with which you're not familiar. If the customer or its employees are not fully informed about your product—how to use it, what it will do, its advantages, and so on—they may hesitate to promote it, fearing the embarrassment of not knowing the answers to the customer's questions. Given two competing products, the dealers' hands will naturally reach for the one with whose use and selling points he or she is most familiar.

Creative salespeople are keenly aware that all the devices their companies use to educate the dealer and the dealer's selling staff—advertising matter, sales manuals, company newsletters, dealers' conventions, dealers' contests, training programs for salespeople—are not enough. They must make an active contribution to the process.

■ IDEA IN ACTION

Charlene Kozlowski called on her dealer-customer and found that she couldn't get an order because the dealer was overstocked. Being a creative salesperson, she was very observant. She looked around and didn't see any evidence of the material that had been furnished by her company to publicize the product. She knew that this dealer would be selling the product if he himself, as well as people who come into the store, were reminded of the product and its benefits.

She approached the dealer this way: "The reason you're stocked up, Mr. Dealer, is that you aren't selling our Shino Polish fast enough. I think I know why, too. As I look around, I don't see a single one of our new lithographed displays that every one of our dealers is entitled to. As a matter of fact, I've gotten six reorders, today alone, from stores that are using this display. It's the best sales aid we've ever put out. Suppose I drop in tomorrow and put one up for you? Then I'll check with you again in a week or ten days—unless you need a restock sooner."

TIP Tons of promotional and display materials are allowed to gather dust in storerooms and basements simply because the wholesaler or retailer, to whom they've been furnished at great expense, forgets about them and the salesperson doesn't take the opportunity to remind the customer how useful they can be. Here's an enormous opportunity for the creative salesperson.

IDEAS TO KEEP YOU CONSTANTLY CREATIVE

A Creative Idea That Gets Repeat Orders

Repeat orders mean hefty commissions. You don't want to lose them. In some fields of selling, taking a survey to convince the customer that he or she cannot afford *not* to repeat the order will often bring in the renewal.

■ IDEA IN ACTION

Stanley Grant sells a line of remembrance advertising products. When Stanley's customer told him that he didn't plan to renew his desk pad program, Stanley suggested a post card survey.

"When the post cards started flooding the customer's office," says Stanley, "the customer was astonished. He had no idea anyone would be so enthusiastic about the desk pads. The return totaled more than 33%, and all but ten asked to be kept on the list."

As a result, Stanley got his renewal order.

A Special Service Idea Helps You Become the Main Supplier

You can increase your share of a customer's business by thinking up a better service for his or her needs. Offer something extra—perhaps a convenience that he or she will appreciate or some personal attention that will prove your interest in his or her business. This is one way that you, as a creative salesperson, can gain a customer's increasing dependence on you as a main supplier.

∎ IDEA IN ACTION

Knowing that she had plenty of competition for the stationery business of a large mail order firm, an ambitious salesperson decided that she had to be tops in service to win the bigger orders she wanted. She spent some time mulling over the customer's requirements and came up with a big "extra" that she discussed with her sales manager. The sales manager agreed that the potential in extra orders warranted giving the plan a try.

The great idea around which she planned her next interview was this: Her company would hold the customer's orders in stock and make shipments to the proper letter shops on the customer's release. This plan would save the customer the space and expense needed to stock stationery and the trouble and cost of frequent shipments to the letter shops that handled its mailings.

With this valuable extra on her side, the salesperson soon saw sizable increases in orders from the appreciative customer. The reward for better service was a better share of the customer's business.

Walking Through a Customer's Plant Gets You Thinking Creatively

Manufacturers of products that have many uses and applications are always on the lookout for creative salespeople because they make the best sales. They do it by never missing an opportunity to look around and pick up clues to different uses.

Even though creative salespeople may know that a prospect has a definite need in one area, they stay alert for signs of additional applications, because they know that the more uses they can find for the product, the easier it will be to make the sale.

The message here is clear: Look around, ask questions, and get away from the "over-the-desk" survey of requirements based entirely on the known needs of the customer.

■ IDEA IN ACTION

The most important factor leading to a large sale of equipment by Ralph Kemp was the walk he took through the plant on the way to the prospect's desk. He stopped to question what the employees in this clipping bureau plant were doing with certain 2" × 4" slips of paper. They were attached to each article, showing from which publication the article had been clipped. He learned that the clip slips were quite a headache to the prospect and also a bottleneck in the overall operation. The more questions he asked, the more interested his prospect became.

The proposal Ralph made focused on those slips. By showing how the equipment he recommended would eliminate the need for those slips and reduce costs and storage space, he sold two machines.

Ralph comments, "Without going through their plant I would never have realized the existence of the publication slips and the real need for our equipment."

An Idea That Got Dealers to Handle a Line

Uncover a few new accounts for a dealer whom you have been trying to get to handle your line, and you will probably succeed in breaking through the competition that has stood in the way.

■ IDEA IN ACTION

A salesperson for a company that made gas ranges was sent into a city where competition was strong and dealers were satisfied with competitive lines. Her problem was to open new outlets.

The salesperson concentrated on restaurant prospects. During her lunch hour she would have her soup in one restaurant, her main course in a second, and dessert and coffee in a third. In each instance she would praise the food and get into a friendly conversation with the proprietor. Capitalizing on the proprietor's natural courtesy to a patron, she would arrange for an appointment later on in the day. At the interview she offered to make an analysis of the restaurant's kitchen problems and in short order made a few sales which she turned over to dealers.

Within little more than a year, seven dealers were handling her line and 127 units had been sold.

Offer the Retailer Ideas for Selling Related Products

By helping retailers to sell related products, you win their goodwill and increase the sales of items on your product list.

■ IDEA IN ACTION

Ben Burke goes into a pharmacy and offers to set up a sales display. If, for instance, the display advertises a hair-grooming product that Ben sells, he asks the druggist for hairbrushes, combs, and other items related to a hair-grooming product.

He also asks the druggist for a few bottles of his company's hair-grooming product to use in the display. This gives the salesperson a chance to check the druggist's stock. Also, by using some of the stock in the display, he can more readily find the opportunity to ask the druggist for a reorder.

Offer an Idea for Using Existing Equipment Along with Your Product

Many a sale has been made by the creative salesperson who can find a way to fit his or her product to a company's use without forcing the prospect to discard equipment that is still good. The savings and other benefits to be gained by purchasing the new product look even better if the prospect knows that the equipment he or she has already purchased won't go to waste.

■ IDEA IN ACTION

Stanley Toff, who sells office duplicating equipment, thinks it's important to find out what auxiliary office equipment a prospect has. He then comes up with an idea for how the prospect can combine the existing equipment with the equipment he recommends, to perfect a process that reduces costs and speeds up production.

Toff found, for example, that the combination of his particular method and a small copying machine proved very successful for one of his prospects. He worked up a process by which both the old copying machine and the new machine could function together.

Knowledge of Product and Customer Needs Make You Creative

Knowledge of your business and a strong desire to win an order are a combination that often leads to creative thinking. This is especially true in businesses that manufacture largely to customers' specifications. You know what your firm can do, you know what your customer wants, and you think hard for a way to overcome every difficulty that might interfere with your getting the order. You sometimes come up with a solution that even the engineers have not hit upon. You discover that you are much more creative than you thought you were—in fact, you're quite an inventor.

■ IDEA IN ACTION

In Bev Turner's line, every order is a special order. Bev's customer wants a package for its canned juices that has an easy-opening feature. But to make the package just as the customer wants it, the sample maker at Bev's plant points out, will lead to gluing trouble.

The order is important to Bev and she starts thinking about the specifications. She gets an idea for how to retain the easy-opening feature and avoid the gluing difficulty. Her idea is to perforate the outer flaps. Even the sample maker considers the solution ingenious.

Plan the Sale Around Your Creative Idea

Small or large, the creative idea begins with thinking and ends with selling. Thinking in itself is not sufficient. Coming up with an idea is not enough. You must do something with it. Sometimes it takes planning to convert a big idea into a commission.

If it's a little idea—and some of the smallest have led to big sales—you merely apply it. If it's a big idea, you must develop it, plan your sale around it, and sell all the way down the line to make it count.

■ IDEA IN ACTION

A real estate manager makes his commission on the amount of income obtained from the properties he manages. The more income he can make a property yield, the higher his commission.

Kevin Watters creates a big idea for increasing the income from a three-story commercial building. It will cost money to make the changes he has in mind. The landlord is willing. But will the tenants pay the extra rent? There's the rub. The idea won't work unless he can think up a way to induce the tenants to accept the increase in rent.

Watters creates a plan. He puts it in writing to help him clarify his problem. Here are the steps he writes down:

- Survey the neighborhood and find out what rents are being paid for similar property in somewhat better condition.

- Find out if tenants would pay additional rent if the exterior were brightened up and interior redecorated.

- Convince the tenants that they would profit more if the property were improved.

- Sell the tenants on the idea that the increase in rent would be used *exclusively* to redecorate their particular unit.

His plan works. The income from the building is upped from $1,200 a month to $1,800 a month *without using a nickel of the original $1,200 a month.*

What a Camera Can Do, If You Use Your Imagination

Everyone knows how to use a camera. Creative salespeople find a use for photography that wins customer admiration for their ingenuity. But even more important, they save time in making the sale. Good selling techniques, when combined with the use of photography, can hasten the customer's buying decision. When customers are given a photograph to hold and look at, they are using their eyes—often considered the most powerful of the five senses.

Read the following examples of how salespeople have made the camera work for them, and then start thinking about how it might work for you.

☐ EXAMPLE

A San Francisco real estate broker has "before" and "after" pictures of renovated buildings that were sold before they were modernized. When a prospect doubts that anything can be done with an old building, he quickly convinces him with the display of photographs.

☐ EXAMPLE

A company that sells kitchens uses miniature cabinets and appliances to show the customer how the kitchen they recommend will look. But the miniatures alone don't seem to be doing the job. Customers usually want to talk over the plans at home, and all the designer can give them is a drawing.

The solution is a Polaroid camera. The designer photographs the miniature model that has been set up for the customer, and the customer takes the picture home if he or she can't make a decision on the spot. The photograph technique has made it easier for the company's designers to sell their individually planned kitchens.

□ EXAMPLE

A salesperson who deals in home appliances finds that the usual presentation is too impersonal. So he tries taking a picture of the prospect's house and using it in his approach. During the interview, he places the picture on the prospect's table and says, "I called to talk about that home of yours." This approach always arouses the prospect's interest and helps to make the sale.

Photography is widely used in industrial selling where installations of machinery and equipment entail considerable planning, blueprinting, and study by sales engineers to make the product fit the customer's needs and facilities. The photographs serve a variety of selling purposes. For example, plant interior photographs are taken to supplement old blueprints of factories that have been changed since their construction. The pictures help the salesperson work out accurate recommendations and cost estimates. Photographs of a piece of equipment being assembled before it has been dismantled for shipment helps to expedite the reassembling of the product at the customer's plant.

Reselling Demands Creative Selling and a Strong Attitude Against the "No"

Some salespeople have to fortify themselves against a prospect's "No" only long enough to make him or her say "Yes" once. The order that follows the "Yes" is final; the sale is made and the commission earned.

But in some fields, a prospect's "Yes" is only the beginning of a sale. A follow-through is necessary to turn the sale into a completed transaction. In the follow-through the prospect may say "No" again. The second "No" is an even greater challenge to the salesperson's stamina and creative ingenuity.

□ EXAMPLE

In the book publishing field, a salesperson who "sells" a professor the idea of writing a college text often has to resell this individual *after* the professor has consented to write the book. The reason is that before a contract can be signed, the professor must submit an outline of the book. Sometimes the professor gets bogged down in day-to-day activities and nothing happens. The salesperson must see the professor again and resell him or her. At this stage, a "No" from the professor-prospect can be devastating to an ordinary salesperson. The successful salesperson, however, looks upon it not as a refusal but as an attitude that can be changed. Let's see how this negative attitude can be changed.

■ IDEA IN ACTION

When John Bates first approached Professor Tirrell, he walked into the professor's office certain that he would have a series of "No's" to face before a contract could be signed. For him, the first "No" was the start—not the end—of the interview. Determined not to give up, John eventually "made the sale," and the professor agreed to submit an outline.

Weeks passed and nothing happened. The outline was not sent to the publisher.

John approached Professor Tirrell again. She had many "good" reasons for not having worked up the outline. Family obligations, illnesses, administrative details, and so on stood in her way. No, she just didn't have time to work up an outline.

John knew that if he quit now, the interview would be over. To him, Professor Tirrell's attitude was something he intended to change. John expressed his keen disappointment. He let Professor Tirrell know that he felt let down. He asked her to sketch out how she would be spending her time for the next three months to see if there was any time that could be set aside for writing.

In reselling his prospect, John made the professor see herself enjoying the benefits of royalties. In four to six years her children would be ready for college themselves. She could use the royalties to reduce her mortgage. If she needed a new car, the royalties would help her pay for it. And there was even a possibility that the European vacation the professor had been dreaming about could become a reality. John *created* the professor's desire to write the book.

Then John did something more. He helped the professor overcome her inertia. Right then and there he got the professor started on her outline. And this time the publisher began to receive the promised material. It was good and the contract was signed.

NOTE Nobody who is overwhelmed by the demands on his or her time is going to make a decision quickly. Something or someone must bring about the transition from *inertia* to *action*. The creative salesperson performs this function by moving an idea from the back of a prospect's mind to the front.

How to Use Showmanship in Creative Selling

How do you turn showmanship into a selling aid? It depends upon what you sell and to whom you sell it. What impression do you want to make, and what special techniques can you use to make it? Get your mind thinking along these lines, and you may hit upon an original idea for showmanship that suits your product and your customers.

■ IDEA IN ACTION

Hudson J. Force became known in the building industry of his town as a human dynamo with a flair for showmanship. In every aspect of his operation, from building homes to selling them, he displayed originality and inventiveness.

When calling on prospects, Mr. Force always carried a newspaper in his pocket. The reason? "I wear leather half-boots, so when I knock on the door and am invited in, I take the boots off and set them on the paper." By showing respect for the prospect's home, he indicates that he is just as careful in the construction of his homes.

To make sure that he was easily recognized and remembered, Mr. Force wore a large white hat at all times.

Look for Causes of Trouble and You'll Create a Solution

Before you can get started thinking creatively and effectively about a selling problem, you must first find the reason why you are having trouble. Let's say your sales to a certain wholesaler have fallen off. You don't know why, but you are certain that the dealer's salespeople are not pushing your product. Your next move should be to discover why. When you get the facts, the right solution will often suggest itself.

■ IDEA IN ACTION

Sales to one of Harriet Rodney's wholesaler-customers had fallen off drastically. Harriet called on the wholesaler, saying, "It's almost a year since I last talked with your salespeople. When are you having them in for a meeting? I'd like a few minutes of their time."

"Okay," came the reply. "Next Friday at 4:30."

Harriet was amazed to find that out of a group of 11, 5 of the salespeople were new. Here she had gone along for a whole year, confident that every salesperson employed by this wholesaler knew her line and how to push it. But in reality, not only had 5 of them never heard her presentation, but most of the other 6 had forgotten what they had been told.

At her meeting with the salespeople, Harriet told her story to the newcomers, refreshed the memories of the veteran salespeople, and cleared up a number of misunderstandings. In short, she "sold" her line to the salespeople themselves.

Sales to the wholesaler picked up dramatically.

Creative Salespeople Play Up Minor Sales Points When Big Ones Don't Do the Job

Special product features, quality, price, service, savings, and other big sales points in your presentation will usually make the sale. But when your prospect is not responding favorably to these big selling points, your creative thinking is challenged. What can you say about your product that will make your prospect buy?

Here is where you begin to think of the secondary sales points. What were the minor points you listed when you prepared your sales presentation? One of these will come to mind and you may be able to create a sale with it.

■ IDEA IN ACTION

When Pete Stringer listed the sales features of the valves he was selling, he included the packaging of the valves as a minor sales point. Individual boxing of each valve didn't add one iota of value to the valves themselves. Competitors weren't boxing their valves; they merely protected the outer ends.

Pete's prospect wasn't as impressed with the virtues of Pete's valves as other prospects were. So he thought quickly of the "extra" selling points that he ordinarily omitted from his presentation. The individual packaging might make his valve seem sufficiently different from his competitors' to strike a responding note in the prospect. It did, and Pete made the sale.

Creative Salespeople Help Customers Get Full Value from What They Buy

Making certain that your customers are getting the full value of your product is your best protection you have against losing them to a competitor. Customers who are not making the best use of what they bought from you are a poor prospect for repeat sales or sales of other products in your line. You can't afford to sell them and forget them. You must create the opportunities to test whether they're making the best use of your product. The simplest way is to

- Make a service call and ask about how your product is working out.
- Pass an idea along to your customer that helps him or her get more value out of the product—perhaps an idea you picked up from another customer who is enjoying the product fully.

Creative Salespeople Assume That Every Qualified Prospect Needs Their Product

Creative salespeople operate on the assumption that there is a need for their product in every company that fits into a category in which they already have customers. Acting on this assumption, they're able to turn up business where "it just couldn't exist." They may even sell their product to a competitor! Or they may sell it to a company that has apparently eliminated all need for such a product.

□ EXAMPLE

A salesperson sold her competitor a machine for preparing duplicate copies of proposals for the sale of competitive products. Reporting on this sale, she said, "Very often, in planning calls on nonusers, we stumble across the name of a large concern that is closely allied with our products. The usual response is to find reasons for not calling on them. Here is a concern that surely has complete knowledge of modern business methods, so why bother? I found, to my astonishment and pleasure, that this is not true." This salesperson takes nothing for granted.

□ EXAMPLE

A company that has recently introduced high-speed electronic equipment would seem to have no need for slower equipment. But the creative salesperson considers the possibility that the new equipment may not meet all the company's requirements. Perhaps there are some operations that can be served more economically by some of the equipment he sells, in conjunction with high-speed electronic methods. So he is always on the lookout for that kind of business—and he makes sales.

Creative Salespeople Win
Reciprocal Favors from Customers

Because creative salespeople are always on the lookout for ways to help their customers, they win reciprocal treatment. Customers reciprocate by writing a testimonial or expressing their willingness to tell another prospect how much they like the company's product. They may also willingly furnish leads to good prospects. But most gratifying of all are the unexpected ways in which a satisfied customer comes to the aid of the creative salesperson.

■ IDEA IN ACTION

One of Dave Blake's Brooklyn bank customers was grateful to him for having taken the time during a "user call" to watch the operators use the machines he'd sold to the bank. After observing the machines in use, Dave was able to point out some shortcuts that had apparently been overlooked when new operators were trained.

One day a Long Island bank prospect whom Dave had been trying to sell visited the Brooklyn bank to review some advanced accounting operations for which the Brooklyn bank was well known. During this visit, Dave's customer suggested to his Long Island guest that he take a look at the highly efficient operations that were being performed with the machines that George had sold the bank. This was the clincher for Dave's sale to the Long Island prospect. He got a signed order totaling more than $25,000 the very next day.

Reorganization of Customer Set-up
Demands Creative Thinking to Save
Accounts

What should you do when you find yourself in danger of losing an account because of a change in a customer's buying set-up? Such changes take place when one company sells out to another or merges to form a new corporation. It also happens when a big company "splits off" a subsidiary or creates new subsidiaries to take over certain divisions. It happens even more frequently when a company centralizes the purchasing function and takes purchasing out of the hands of branch offices, individual plants, branch stores, and so on.

Any change in a customer's corporate structure that introduces a new group of buyers or executives responsible for setting policies and making buying decisions, or that deprives those who have been doing the buying of their authority, or that waters down their authority may be a threat to good accounts.

Centralization that takes buying out of your territory

You can often succeed in salvaging accounts that might otherwise be lost during a reorganization by taking these steps:

- Find out who will do the buying of your product under the new set-up.

- Find out what purchasing will still be done in your territory.

   TIP A company that centralizes its purchasing authority usually prepares instructions for those who had purchasing authority under the old set-up. The memo explains the new procedures and may include a list of items that can still be bought locally, such as repair and maintenance services. A limit is usually placed on the dollar expenditures for such items.

   What can you do under these circumstances?

- Find out the motives for centralizing. Does the company want to speed up deliveries of raw materials? If so, perhaps you can keep the account by arranging for fast deliveries by air. Does it expect to get better prices through bulk buying? Perhaps you can prove that there are advantages in continuing to purchase from you that will offset the difference in price. You will probably have to contact and sell more than one executive to get your item on their list of exceptions.

■ Continue calling on the customer, but at longer intervals. You can never predict what changes might be made later that will affect local buying.

Decentralization that takes buying out of your territory

Your account may be with a central office that is to be decentralized. Instead of selling to one central office, you will now be required to deal with a number of purchasing departments. Again, you must find out the purpose of the decentralization, the personnel to deal with, and how your product will be affected. You must have the facts before you can think about ways to salvage the account.

There will be times when you'll lose an account because of a change in the customer's buying set-up. But this doesn't necessarily mean that your company will lose the business. It's your responsibility to try to salvage it for your company. Provide your sales manager with the facts, and he or she will take care of the rest.

Merger of customers

If your customer takes over another company, there are two possibilities: (1) you have an opportunity to sell more of your product, or (2) you have to watch out not to lose the account to a competitor who has been selling to the other firm. Being alert is essential:

■ Find out the purpose of the merger.

■ Find out what changes are to be made in the purchasing structure.

■ Get to know the new personnel who will have the buying authority.

If your customer loses its identity in the merger, there's always the possibility that some of its personnel will be retained. Again, if you discover the facts, you will know how to act to save your account.

REMEMBER You have the advantage over your competitor if you have been selling to the company that will continue to do the buying after the merger, and if your competitor was selling to the company that lost its identity. But that advantage can be lost in no time if you don't put forth a strong reselling effort to keep the account. This is a good time to share a valuable idea with your customer or to do anything that will mark you as the salesperson from whom to keep buying.

USING CREATIVE IDEAS ON YOURSELF

How to Apply Creativity to Your Own Work Habits

No salesperson is perfect. Each has his or her limitations, "blind spots," and other weaknesses.

One individual—a strong closer—would be a star if he could only make a more effective presentation. Another, whose presentation is all but perfect, falls down on the close. A third loses sales because her faulty diction distracts from her message; a fourth, because he fails to make enough calls.

These salespeople are "tough to buy from." If they would only add one more good work habit or skill to those they already possess, they would see their sales soar.

The proper starting place for those individuals who wish to use their creative talent to make themselves better salespeople is to face up to a fundamental truth: Every salesperson is, in some respect, "tough to buy from." The difference between the "dud" and the star is simply a matter of *how tough*.

Creative Salespeople Manage Themselves Well

The better the salesperson, the more he or she excels at "self-management." It is obvious that creativity in sales involves dedication and straight thinking, and an ability to spark and control one's own efforts. Salespeople who reach the top do so by performing well in the highly personal areas that are part of self-management.

The creative salesperson, like everyone else in the selling field, must maintain a high level of enthusiasm. This requires self-management of a high order, for enthusiasm is generated from *within*. Even if you don't feel enthusiastic, you can make yourself act enthusiastic. How-to-do-it guidance to selling with enthusiasm is covered fully in Chapter Eight.

∎ IDEA IN ACTION

Delia Marchand is a top-flight salesperson. She rates high in terms of "self-management"; that is, she performs well in those areas that are entirely under her control.

For instance, Delia never makes a call without proper planning. Her first call is always made promptly at 9:15—and she plans her work so effectively that she has less lost time than anyone else on the staff.

Delia has spent long and profitable hours—hours which no one else even knows about—studying her product, the competition, and her territory. She has worked harder at perfecting her presentation than she would care to admit. She has long since listed every objection she has encountered and has come up with just the right answer for each. None of these things could be done by anyone else. Delia is a star. She outsells the other salespeople because she has freely accepted and fully discharged the duties of self-management.

Creative Salespeople Use Selling Tools to the Greatest Advantage

Here we are talking about three kinds of selling tools:

1. What the company furnishes to its salespeople to help them do a better selling job

2. What the company furnishes to its wholesalers, dealers, and retailers to promote the sale of the product

3. The company's advertising to get its name and products known

What use does the creative salesperson make of these tools that the average salesperson does not? A few simple examples will illustrate.

☐ EXAMPLE

A heater company furnishes its sales force with a manual filled with information to help the sales reps sell automatic water heaters. Each salesperson uses the manual—more or less. But the creative salesperson uses it more, thinking up ways to dramatize the information provided in the manual.

For instance, the manual cites a survey stating that in the average home, the potential savings to be achieved by installing a gas hot water heater amounts to $800 a year. The creative salesperson dramatizes this fact by pulling eight one hundred dollar bills from his or her pocket and displaying them before the prospect's eyes.

"Do you have all of these you want?" he or she asks the prospect.

"No," replies the prospect.

"Well, you can have eight more of them every year with our automatic hot water heater."

☐ EXAMPLE

Counter space is extremely valuable to most dealers, who have a tendency to toss counter displays into the store room before they're even used. Creative salesperson Dan Brown has a customer who isn't using his company's display. Dan knows that the display will increase his customer's sales and consequently his reorders. He knows that the dealer's mark-up on the item is large enough to warrant pushing it. Also, the display is not too large for the customer's counter and will not interfere with his present set-up.

To get this uncooperative dealer to use the counter display, Dan must convince him that the display will be a source of extra sales. How does he do this? Dan makes a list of his big customers in whose stores the display is given the space it deserves. He enters on this list the amount of repeat orders he has gotten from these cooperative dealers in the last three months. Why are they selling more of the product than the uncooperative dealer? Their use of the counter display must be helping to move the product. The list is visible proof that it pays to use the counter display.

☐ EXAMPLE

Creative salespeople look for every opportunity to tie in their own selling efforts with their company's advertising and promotional campaigns. They make sure that they are informed of these plans *well in advance* and that they are supplied with the necessary layouts, tearsheets, proofs, or samples. This gives them time to study the material and to be prepared to explain what these resale aids can mean to each of their customers.

Keeping Up With Business and Economic Trends Is a Stimulant to Creative Salespeople

Creative salespeople get in the habit of reading the financial news to stay abreast of changes in the country's economy. Whatever the news, they are constantly thinking of how it affects their market and how they can use the news to make more sales.

Some large companies supply their salespeople with bulletins that point up important financial developments. For example, when the news shows that manufacturers are expanding their facilities, companies that sell industrial products alert their salespeople to the new sales opportunities. When industry is contracting, they provide guidance on how to overcome buyer resistance by stressing their products' cost-saving benefits.

Whether or not you are supplied with economic bulletins by your home office, you should always know what's happening in the business world. It pays to subscribe to one of the weekly financial publications, or to a newspaper like *The Wall Street Journal*. News magazines like *Business Week* and *U.S. News & World Report* also provide a good overview of what's going on.

The national economic situation is only part of the business picture. What is happening in the particular industries to which you sell is just as important, because there are always some businesses that are doing better or worse than others regardless of the general trend. (See the Appendix for a source of information on the state of trade in selected lines.)

▪ IDEA IN ACTION

Heather Bellows reads in the financial section of a New York newspaper that a large building materials corporation has inaugurated a companywide economy drive in the wake of the recent recession. This particular economy program is aimed at eliminating overstaffing and curtailing needless capital expenditures—in other words, the new emphasis will be on getting along *without*, wherever possible.

The gloomy news doesn't phase Bellows. Instead she thinks, *How can I find a use for our product that will contribute to this customer's economy program?* Result: She receives a $16,000 order for new equipment by showing a savings of $9,000 a year and a reduction of peak-period overtime.

A "Great" Creative Idea Gives You Confidence

The great idea around which you plan your interview must have merit; the benefits to your customer must be crystal clear. If your idea is "great" in this respect, you can be fully confident that the prospect will see it and act accordingly.

Sometimes, perhaps for a reason that defies logic, you will be turned down. But even then you should feel confident that someone will recognize your idea's merit some day and act. That is the beauty of a great creative idea. It remains good for as long as you "stay with" the prospect, assuming that the potential sales justify continuous calling. Eventually, you will make the sale.

▪ IDEA IN ACTION

Bill Stutts had a prospect whose needs he had already surveyed. He had a creative idea that could save the company approximately 50% of its mailing costs by installing certain equipment. The prospect could reduce the cost of its operation enough to write off the investment in a few months and show a large dollar savings on the books annually. But because all the company's branch offices couldn't utilize the same system, and because the bookkeeping profits didn't accrue to the particular prospect but to subsidiaries, the sale was not made.

Two years went by, during which time Bill continued to call on this prospect, trying to see various officers of the firm. Eventually, a change in management took place, and Bill was able to make the big sale. "This shows," he said, "that even after being turned down on a good application, sticking with it and calling back eventually paid off. Changes are always taking place, and if a proposal has merit, sooner or later someone will see it and act."

PLANNING YOUR PREAPPROACH MAKING PROSPECTS LISTEN, AND GETTING CALLBACKS

Your selling power soars as you keep on using successful strategies.

The selling strategies explained in this chapter bring you face to face with your prospect for a successful interview. Here are the actual selling techniques that high-bracket salespeople use to get to the right individual without wasting any time.

This chapter develops the strategies, techniques, and basic principles for winning through a successful preapproach. It tells you what to find out about a prospect before the interview, how to get the interview by making an appointment in advance, and how to get in without an appointment when you have to.

Your presentation is, of course, the most critical selling activity. But before we tackle that subject (which will be discussed in Chapter Five), we want to be sure you know how to handle individual prospects when they display certain types of behavior. Similarly, making a great presentation is easier if you understand buying motives and the techniques for putting your finger on the prospect's reason to buy.

Another prerequisite to successful selling is a knowledge of the techniques and strategies that make callbacks pay off. In addition to providing guidance for the preapproach, therefore, this chapter includes tips and information in the following areas:

- Making the prospect listen
- Putting your finger on the prospect's reason to buy
- Making callbacks pay off

You will sell your way into big money by mastering the selling strategies presented here.

WINNING SALES THROUGH A SUCCESSFUL PREAPPROACH

What the Preapproach Entails

To get your money's worth from the time you spend with your prospect, you must prepare in advance for the interview. This preapproach phase of selling involves two steps: (1) finding out all you can about the prospect and (2) getting the interview.

FINDING OUT ABOUT A PROSPECT IN ADVANCE OF THE INTERVIEW

What to Find Out About a Prospect

The better informed you are about your prospects and their needs, the better your presentation will be and the more confident you will be that you have something they will buy. Here are some of the things you'll want to learn about your prospect before making that initial contact:

- Exactly what the company makes or does.

- Its size—approximate number of employees, net worth, extent of operations (local or national).

- What its requirements are in your line—products and volume.

- Whether the company is growing.

- Whether its credit is good.

- Who is the right person to see (his or her *correct* and *full* name).

- Specific information you will need for a convincing presentation. For example, a chemical salesperson will want to know not only what the prospect manufactures but also which process the company uses.

WARNING You *could* get most of this information directly from the prospect by simply waiting until the interview. But don't make that mistake! The interview is for selling, not research.

NOTE There are some fields in which you simply cannot gather the necessary information about a prospect before seeing him or her. If, for example, you are selling life insurance, only the prospect can provide the information you need. Similarly, in businesses that require a great deal of specialized data before a sale can be made, not all the preapproach information can be obtained in advance of the first interview.

There are selling situations in which you may be warned by your sales manager not to spend valuable time on preliminary investigation. You must find out about the prospect's needs for your product *while making the call.*

You're more likely to win the prospect's respect and to gain his or her undivided attention if you show that you're interested enough to learn about the company in advance. The following illustration presents two approaches made by competing salespeople selling a stapling machine to a prospect who packages his product in cardboard cartons.

- **Poor approach:** "Mr. Allan, I'm Jack Smith from the ABC Staple Machine Company. We manufacture and distribute a full line of stapling machines. There is probably an application in your plant where we could save you considerable time in your packaging operations."

- **Good approach:** "Mr. Allan, my name is Fran Brown and I represent the Atlas Staple Machine Company. Let me explain briefly how you can triple your carton closing speed on overlap cartons, where I notice you're currently using tape."

The second salesperson, Fran Brown, has something definite to offer. She has taken the trouble to find out that there is a specific application for her company's stapling machine.

Where to Get Information About a Prospect

In general, there are two ways to get information about a prospect: You can ask someone, or you can get the information yourself from one of a number of sources, depending upon what you are looking for.

Who to ask

Any of the following people may know something about the prospect that will be useful to you.

- Another salesperson in your company, who may have called on this prospect in the past and can give you information based on his or her experience.
- Your present customers, especially those in the same business.
- Other salespeople in related but noncompetitive fields, who are usually willing to cooperate.
- People in the neighborhood of the company in which you are interested. The people you talk to at a local gas station or diner, for example, often know whether the company is hiring or laying off, is contemplating new construction, and so on.
- On a referral call, the person who referred you to the prospect can usually give you pertinent information about him or her.

Where to look up information

It may take a little time to look up information about companies and their executives in a printed publication or to get information from a chamber of commerce, but by using such sources to prepare yourself in advance of the interview, you fortify yourself with facts that make it easy to approach, please, and interest your prospect.

(See the Appendix for a list of some standard published sources and how chambers of commerce can help salespeople.)

How to Get Acquainted with Your Market

The more you know about the type of business in which your prospect is engaged, the easier it is to make the sale. You can visualize your product in use by the prospect, you can find new applications for it, and you can identify your product with the prospect's needs.

In addition, if you learn something of the language used in the trade, you can talk to your prospect at his or her own level and convince him or her that your product is ideally suited to his or her needs.

Get background information from trade publications

After you have classified your markets, (as described in Chapter Two), find out for each market the names of the leading trade publications in the field. You can get a world of useful information simply by looking at a few copies of the publication. Language of the trade can be picked up in almost any issue.

The trade association can tell you the name of the leading trade publication and the publisher's address. Or you can call up any large company in the industry and ask for the name and address of the best trade publication. If you are in a large city, you can usually find these publications in the public library. Otherwise, send for sample copies. (See the Appendix.)

Ask directly for information

People like to talk about what they are doing. When you express an interest in your prospect's business, you will usually find that he or she is more than willing to explain how the business works.

Use your company's guides

If your sales manager supplies you with special data about the markets that have a need for your product, use this information to the utmost.

GETTING THE INTERVIEW

Second Step of the Preapproach

The second step of the preapproach is to get the interview. Whenever possible, you should arrange to get the interview in advance. Sometimes, of course, you will be unable to do so, and your problem will then be how to walk into the prospect's office and get him or her to see you. (This is discussed later in this chapter.)

Rules for Getting the Interview

Regardless of the method used to get the interview, you should keep in mind the following three rules:

1. **It is up to you to get the interview.** You are never *entitled* to a person's time, regardless of the benefits he or she would receive from your product or service.

   NOTE Many companies have a policy of seeing as many of the salespeople who call on them each day as possible. (This policy was described in Chapter One.)

2. **Concentrate on seeing the right person.** There is no sense in interviewing someone who can't make the decision to buy from you.

3. **Sell the interview before you sell your product.** A prospect who is not convinced that the interview will be worth his or her time will either refuse to grant one or will listen only halfheartedly. Here is an example of a salesperson who learns this lesson.

■ IDEA IN ACTION

Herb Ward sells a collection service. He discovers that many prospects cut him short as soon as he reveals his company and service, even though most of them have had problems with past-due accounts. Herb decides to try a new approach.

"My name is Ward," he begins. "I stopped in to ask whether you'd be interested in something that amounts to insurance against losses from past-due accounts."

The usual answer is: "Yes, we might be interested. How does it work?"

Herb, having thus sold the idea of an interview, gets a chance to sell his service.

Why You Should Make Appointments

Every salesperson has had the experience of being told that the individual he or she made a special trip to see is simply not available: "Sorry, but Mr. Burton is at our other plant today. If you want to see him, it's best to make an appointment." The advantages of being expected by the prospect are obvious:

- You save yourself hours of wasted travel and waiting time.

- A prospect with whom you have made an appointment is at least familiar with your name and company—and, if your arrangements were made skillfully, he or she is already sold on the interview.

- Having an appointment adds prestige to your call.

MAKING APPOINTMENTS

The techniques described here are aimed chiefly at getting the initial interview. Your customers, and prospects on whom you call more than once, will usually let you know what to do about future interviews.

WHAT TO DO Use one of the following five means of arranging for an interview:

1. Make an appointment over the telephone.

2. Make an appointment by letter.

3. Have a mutual friend or acquaintance set up the interview for you, either by phone or in a letter.

4. Send advance sales material and follow it up with a request for an interview.

5. Send an advance card, announcing your intended call.

Each of these approaches is discussed in the following sections.

Making an Appointment over the Telephone

The telephone can be one of your most important sales aids, *if* it is used properly. Here's what it can do for you:

- It quickly and inexpensively establishes a definite time for an interview, without wasted travel or waiting.

- It enables you to get an idea of the prospect's potential for buying.

- It gives you a preliminary personalized contact that will ease the selling job later.

- In some cases, it will get you in to see someone whom you would not ordinarily be able to see merely by stopping in at his or her office.

The telephone has two serious drawbacks, however, that can kill sales before you even get started:

1. For many people, the phone makes it easier to say "No." For this reason your telephone approach must be well planned and well executed to get positive results.

2. The impersonal nature of the telephone can make it more difficult to cope with objections and unexpected problems. Salespeople who tell themselves they operate more effectively in a face-to-face situation are depriving themselves of

a useful tool, simply because they don't know how to make the telephone work for them.

When should you use the telephone?

These three points should help you decide:

1. If you already know the prospect, or if you feel that it will be just a matter of setting a time for an appointment, use the phone.

2. If you think that you will have to sell the interview, you'll have to be guided by your confidence over the phone. Just remember that you can *build* that confidence through experience and by learning good telephone techniques.

3. Experience will probably also teach you that certain kinds of prospects in your market are more receptive to telephone approaches than others. The following example is a case in point.

■ IDEA IN ACTION

Rita Whelan sells a home study course in sales techniques. Her first step is to convince the sales manager of a company to agree that, if she can sell the plan to the company's salespeople, the company will pay part of the cost. The second step is to sell the salespeople themselves on the idea.

Rita has learned from experience that when it comes to approaching the sales manager—or any busy executive, for that matter—she usually has better luck on the telephone. She, therefore, begins by calling the sales manager for an appointment.

She does not, however, try to make appointments by telephone with the salespeople. She knows from experience that she'll have more success if she visits the salespeople in the evening.

How to use the telephone to get an interview appointment

You will succeed in getting the interview you are after if you emulate top-flight salespeople who handle the telephone with great success. This is what they do:

- Plan the telephone conversation.
- Capture interest immediately.
- Say *only enough* to arouse interest.
- Never misrepresent just to get the interview.
- Persist without noticeable pressure.
- Use good telephone manners.
- Relax and enjoy the conversation.

These tips are discussed in detail in the following sections.

Plan what you have to say and say it

Carefully plan what you are going to say, write it out, and then read it that way over the phone. This process eliminates awkward hesitation, or forgetting or repeating anything, and it adds assurance to your words. Reading your words doesn't necessarily mean that your conversation lacks spontaneity, either. The more familiar you are with what you intend to say, the more natural it will sound.

Regardless of what you are selling, you'll want your initial telephone contact to convey the following information:

- Identify yourself and your company by name.
- Tell the prospect why he or she would benefit from seeing you.
- Ask him or her for an interview to explain these benefits.

Aim to capture interest immediately

You will probably speak to your prospect for less than a minute. This means that you have no time to waste, and since your whole purpose is to make the prospect curious enough to give you an interview, you should get to the point at once. Unless the prospect is a friend, avoid pleasantries or small talk; get right down to brass tacks and say what's on your mind.

Say only enough to arouse interest

Exactly how much you should say will depend to some extent on what you're selling. With some products, it's best to explain exactly what you want to talk about. Here's the direct approach:

□ EXAMPLE

"Mrs. Anderson, this is Mel Peters of the Paramount Automatic Machine Company calling. We know how important fast, accurate machining is in your business, and we think you might be interested in spending just 10 minutes to find out how you can reduce drilling costs by one-third with our multiple drill presses. May I arrange an appointment for Wednesday afternoon to tell you about it?"

Note that although the salesperson is specific about the purpose of the visit, he says only enough to get the interview. He saves the facts until later.

If you have a large territory, and your problem is confining your visits to those people who are definitely interested, then the direct approach is probably the most feasible one. It tells the prospect just enough to know whether he or she wants to hear more. If you have sent out advance material and are following it up for interviews, you will also use the direct approach, since the prospects already know what it is you sell from the literature you've sent them.

In many businesses, however, an indirect approach is best, especially if you anticipate a negative reaction to the nature of your offering. In such cases you should state the benefits that you're offering the prospect, and then ask for the time to explain just how those benefits work.

□ EXAMPLE

"Mr. Smith, this is Mary Ellen Temple. My firm specializes in ways to save home owners up to $1,000 a year on heating bills while making their homes more comfortable. Could I take 15 minutes some evening to explain what it is we offer? Naturally, there is no obligation on your part. Would Thursday evening be all right, say, about 7:30?"

Here the salesperson feels that referring directly to home insulation might create a barrier in the minds of some people, so she concentrates on the benefits of insulation without revealing exactly what it is that she sells.

With either approach, avoid answering questions if you can do so diplomatically. Here are some phrases to use:

- "That's one of several points I would like to explain in the interview."
- "I will be glad to explain that when I see you."
- "You would get a much better idea from seeing it than from hearing about it."

If the question cannot be avoided, or if the prospect insists on an answer, then by all means give a straightforward reply.

Do not misrepresent your purpose just to get the interview

If you sense resistance to your service or product, don't try to give your prospect the impression that you're selling something entirely different and then hope to dazzle him or her in the interview. A prospect who has been tricked into giving you his or her time is usually an angry one, and rightly so. The victim of this kind of deceitful approach usually catches on quickly and then refuses to see you under any conditions.

Be low pressure but persistent

In keeping with the best selling techniques, be strictly low pressure when you call for an appointment. It is wise to include in your few words the assurance that you will only take a minimum amount of time and that the interview will not obligate the prospect in any way.

You can and should, however, be persistent. If real success is your goal, you can't afford to let negative reactions side-track you.

Suppose you call a prospect and make a low-pressure approach on the subject of life insurance. His answer is: "I've already got several insurance policies." That should be your cue to try another tack.

□ EXAMPLE

"That's exactly why you would benefit from seeing me, Mr. Brown. My customers know that my job isn't to sell them as much insurance as I can, but to see that they carry the insurance they need. Why not let me estimate your coverage, free of charge, when I call? You might need *different* insurance, not more of it."

Use good telephone manners

Just as appearance and other personal details are important in the actual interview, the personal impression you make over the phone is important, too. Follow these instructions to assure success in using the telephone:

- Speak distinctly and loudly enough to be heard.
- Use a conversational tone, as you would in person.
- Try to sound cheerful and optimistic, no matter what the reaction on the other end has been.
- Keep your mouth close to the mouthpiece.

Avoid these disconcerting habits that spell failure in using the phone:

- Smoking or drinking water between phrases or sentences—in fact, smoking while you are on the phone should be strictly avoided.
- Putting your hand over the mouthpiece so that you can converse with someone else while the prospect is talking.
- Trying to keep the phone to your ear by hunching your shoulder; you affect both your hearing and your speaking.
- Talking against excessive background noise.
- Slamming the receiver down when you're through; the prospect may have an afterthought and still be on the line.
- Chewing gum.

These guidelines may be common sense, but they are included here because they are so often overlooked.

Relax and enjoy the conversation

If you are relaxed when you make your phone calls, your tone will be more conversational, your voice more natural and lively, and your attitude more friendly and optimistic. Follow these tips to help you relax on the telephone:

- Realize that you will not get an appointment from every call you make, no matter how good you are.
- Prepare thoroughly. This will help you feel more confident, and with confidence comes ease.
- Try taking a few deep breaths before you say anything to help you speak properly.
- Remind yourself to relax.

Making an Appointment by Letter

Aside from arranging a time for an appointment, a good letter can perform a very valuable service: it can *sell* the interview. If you word the letter skillfully, the prospect will not only expect you but will also welcome your visit. (Chapter Two offers sample prospect letters.)

On the other hand, sending a letter does have certain drawbacks. For example, your letter might arrive on a day when the prospect is preoccupied and will hardly do more than glance at it. Unlike a telephone call, a letter is out of your control once you mail it. When the conditions surrounding its arrival aren't favorable, even the best letter might be overlooked.

Therefore, to write letters that win interviews, remember these points:

- This is a selling job, and the same selling principles apply to the letter as to the interview.
- The more accurately your letter fits in with your prospect's wants, the more likely he or she is to give you the interview. The letter is an uninvited guest, and its only chance of making itself (and you) welcome is to hit on the benefits the prospect would like to have.
- Keep the letter short and uncomplicated. You can write yourself out of an interview just as you can talk yourself out of a sale.

Even in the shortest letter, you must lead the prospect through four stages:

1. Capture attention with the opening.

2. Turn interest into desire by describing the benefits you can offer and how they would fit the prospect's needs.

3. Show the prospect that he or she can secure these benefits.

4. Get him or her to agree to see you for further explanation.

Each stage is discussed in the following paragraphs.

Capture attention with the opening

Your opening must get the prospect's attention immediately. Most of the people you will contact are busy, and all of them are accustomed to getting sales material through the mail. They are therefore apt to glance hastily and with disinterest at mail that looks like another attempt to loosen their pocketbooks. Only a good opening will induce people to read a salesperson's letter carefully enough to be convinced by it.

> **NOTE** Many purchasing agents, buyers, and others encourage salespeople to make appointments with them. Your letter is only doing half its job if someone simply marks it "OK" and hands it to a secretary, or perhaps puts your name on his or her desk calendar. A good opening will make your prospect read the letter and will thus sell the interview as well as arrange it. Here are some tips to writing good openers.

First, be original. The letter that's *different* stands the best chance of getting a careful reading. You should, therefore, strive for originality, especially in the opening sentence. Originality does not mean that you must resort to spectacular, outlandish, or tricky forms of expression; it simply means a new or unexpected slant on the subject.

There is probably no service or product that will not benefit from a fresh viewpoint in its presentation. Even a straightforward approach is made more effective if the words in it have the spark of originality. For example, how often must a toy buyer in a department store read or hear that "Our toys can raise the sales volume in your department and increase your profits"? Certainly, the buyer wants to do both of these things, but his or her interest would be aroused more if it were put this way: "Watch your sales climb, your customers smile, *and* your pocketbook get fatter when you offer these popular toys."

The second sentence says basically the same thing as the first, except that it uses more vivid "picture" words.

Second, emphasize the "you." If an uninvited letter starts off with "The Brown Service Company is the world's largest . . ." or "The new Dandy Can Opener is the best . . .," the reader's attention will immediately lag. What does he or she care what you are or think? Your reader wants to know what's in it for him or her, and the fact that something is good doesn't necessarily mean that he or she wants to buy it.

The Dandy people, for example, would get a better response with an opening like this: "It's a fact: You will sell more automatic can openers, and make more friends, by carrying the new Dandy Can Opener . . . ."

Immediately, the prospect is personally involved, because the first thing mentioned is the advantage to him or her. Keep this "you" emphasis in mind no matter which method you are using to get your prospect's attention.

Third, get your prospect's attention. There are five proven techniques that will get your reader's attention at the start of a letter:

1. Promise a major benefit. People are attracted to a plan or product that promises increased profit or income, savings of time or effort, or some similar benefit. The prospect of making or saving a sizable sum of money is especially appealing. Consider these openers:

"Would a $10,000 boost in net profit next year interest you?"

"Stronger, neater package sealing in half the time—that's what you will get from . . ."

"Three machining operations instead of seven, and a better product as a result, if you use . . ."

Any prospect having a need for one of these benefits would probably read on to see if he or she could use the idea.

> **WARNING** If you can't deliver the benefits in full, by all means avoid this approach. It will be of use to you only if the claim means exactly what it says.

2. Tell a story to get your prospect's attention. A pertinent story that will lead the prospect into the rest of the letter is an effective opener.

□ EXAMPLE

"Remember the Greek myth about Icarus, the fellow whose homemade wings fell apart when the sun melted their wax fastenings? Well, your company, which is starting to take wing, will probably also meet some unexpected, serious problems. May I show you how the Benson Consultation Service has been of real help to . . . ."

3. Show the prospect how you can solve one of his or her problems. If the first thing a prospect sees in a letter is a possible solution to a persistent problem, or a better way to get the job done, he or she will naturally be interested. The more specific you can be in describing the problem, the more interested your prospect will be, but sometimes the use of common problems will work. For instance, construction firms are always interested in faster, easier methods. Speed means more jobs per year, less labor cost per job, and consequently a better bidding position. Here's an opening that capitalizes on this fact:

□ EXAMPLE

"Like other companies in the construction industry, you can save time and money on every job by using high-tension nut-and-bolt techniques where you now use rivets. Like to know how? . . . ."

4. Use a news item to get your prospect's attention. An interesting news item, especially if it touches the prospect personally, can be an excellent attention-getter. Perhaps you know of something in which your prospect would be interested, or maybe you will find something in a newspaper or trade magazine about the company or a local event. Your opening could then be something like this:

□ EXAMPLE

"Everyone in Millerville was understandably shocked when Dr. Frank's house burned to the ground the other night. There were only two things that saved the incident from being an even worse disaster: there was no loss of life or serious injury, and the Doctor sensibly carried enough insurance to cover even so terrible a fire. I would appreciate the opportunity to discuss the amount of fire insurance which you . . ."

Clippings from magazines and newspapers can be used as an opener for your letter also. Here is an opening for this kind of letter:

□ EXAMPLE

"From the enclosed clipping it looks like your buying responsibilities have been expanded to include the purchase of inks and dyes. So that your job can be made easier, I would like to show you the complete line of first quality inks and dyes made by . . ."

Note that the clipping is enclosed for added effect.

5. Get the prospect's attention through praise. Almost everyone is vulnerable to praise, and the prospect's vanity can be used as the target for your opening. Here is one example of opening a letter with praise:

□ EXAMPLE

"Someone who has reached your level of responsibility has one thing in common with successful individuals in any business or profession: Your time is extremely valuable and simply has to be conserved. Don't you agree that five of your valuable minutes on one day would be a good investment if you could be shown how you can save hours of time each week?"

WARNING False compliments must always be avoided. Also, if you feel that the prospect will not appreciate someone who flatters him or her, by all means choose another opening.

Guard against these openings

A good letter has a strong opening. You won't win your prospect's attention with an opening that is:

Timid. A timid opening will never get the prospect to do what you ask.

- **Timid opening:** "May I suggest a way in which you could increase your plant's production capacity?"
- **More forceful:** "You can increase your machine shop capacity 20% or more without adding a single machine or operator."

Negative. Anything that might create an unfavorable or unpleasant impression should be avoided. Strive for a pleasant and positive reaction.

- **Negative opening:** "You are probably not selling your share of sportswear this season, unless . . . ."
- **Positive:** "You are enjoying a busy and profitable season, we hope."

Indirect or vague. An opening should not leave the reader in doubt. Be direct and specific.

- **Vague opening:** "Does the idea of increased profit next year appeal to you?"
- **More specific:** "Would a $5,000 boost in net profit next year interest you?"

Irrelevant. A snappy opening followed by a sudden change in thought is confusing. The opening must lead logically to the message of the letter.

Turn your prospect's interest into desire by showing how your benefits will meet his or her needs

Your main job in a letter asking for an appointment is to make the prospect want to see you. The only reason he or she will agree to an interview is because the benefits you have described are appealing. It is with these benefits, then, that you whet your prospect's appetite once you have gained his or her attention. Tell your prospects that you can save them money, make them more comfortable, protect their children, solve their production problems, eliminate paperwork headaches, add to their prestige, and so on, according to what your commodity offers. Concentrate on *what your product or service can do for them* rather than on what the product is.

The most effective benefit is one that will satisfy a recognized need. Your letter will have the greatest success, therefore, if you have discovered exactly how your product can do something for the prospect.

> **IMPORTANT** Remember that wanting something represents an emotional state. The benefits that you describe should be aimed at *wants* more than just needs. A vacuum cleaner salesperson, for example, would do better appealing to the pride a homemaker takes in having a tidy home rather than to the underlying necessity for cleanliness.

Point out that the prospect can have these benefits

Once you've won the prospect's attention and kindled his or her desire, the person will now want to know what is involved in obtaining the advantages you have described. If this were a sales letter, you would explain your offer in some detail; but since this letter is designed only to get an interview, you should avoid giving too many facts. Some commodities have to be described at least partially, but generally speaking, the less you say about *how* they work, the better.

Instead, convey the impression that the benefits you describe can be had with a minimum of trouble and expense and will require only a few minutes to explain. For example,

> "This comfort and convenience can be yours at a cost of only pennies per day and without delay . . . ."

> "This easy-to-sell line could be boosting your sales level just as it has done for others, and with just as little effort on your part . . . ."

> "You will be amazed at how simple it is to put this plan to work for you . . . ."

The object is to make the transition from *wanting* to *having* seem like an easy one.

Get the prospect to agree to see you

Having led up to the interview as the next logical step, go ahead and ask for it. You can boost your average of "Yes" answers this way:

Suggest a time. Unless you do, you are forcing the prospect to come up with a time, which is bothersome to some people. You should not only suggest an appropriate time, but should also ask the prospect to advise you of a more suitable time if your suggestion is inconvenient.

> **SUGGESTION** If for some reason the date you suggest is the only one that would be convenient for you (for example, if you will only be in Cleveland on a certain day), state this in your letter. Most people will have the courtesy to make themselves available at that time if they want to see you, or will let you know if they *don't* want to see you then.

Point out that there is no obligation. With some people, this assurance can make the difference between giving you the interview and refusing to see you.

Make it easy to respond. You can include a stamped, self-addressed return card, printed so that the only action necessary on the part of the prospect is to mark the desired response with an "X" before putting it in the mail. Some salespeople have had success by simply stating in their letter that they will telephone soon to arrange for an appointment. This, of course, involves no action on the prospect's part.

SOME ADDITIONAL TECHNIQUES FOR GETTING AN INTERVIEW

Use the Influence of a Third Party to Get Interviews

One of the best ways to get an interview is to have a friend or business associate of the prospect arrange it for you, or give you a recommendation. Salespeople with the highest earnings use the third-party method for getting interviews. They aren't afraid to get others to do favors for them—and you shouldn't be, either.

Usually the mutual friend will telephone and make an appointment for you. In some cases, he or she may even introduce you personally. Someone who recommends you to a friend or business acquaintance is usually willing to answer questions about that person. Obviously, these questions should be business related and designed to obtain information pertinent to the interview.

> **CAUTION** Whatever personal information the third party might reveal about the prospect should be kept confidential—unless you are certain that the prospect will not resent the familiarity such personal knowledge implies.

Use a letter or card of introduction

A letter of introduction from someone you and your prospect both know conveys the same feeling of personal relationship and confidence as a phone call or face-to-face introduction. Such a letter can be written by the person recommending you, or you can ask him or her to use a standard letter that you've prepared and simply type it on his or her own stationery, adding a personal salutation and signature.

The letter must state the name of the person being introduced, the reason for the introduction, and enough personal or business details to make the introduction seem appropriate. If you're going to deliver the letter yourself, it should be left unsealed, the assumption being that it has been read before being presented.

You can pave the way for more of these letters of introduction by staying alert for opportunities to use them, and by making it a point to ask for one when the situation tells you it would be useful. Here are some ways to do this:

Have a sample letter available to serve as a guide for those who don't write easily. Exhibit 4.1 offers an example of such a letter.

EXHIBIT 4.1

Sample Letter of Introduction by a Third Party

Dear _____ :

This letter will be handed to you by Helen Bowes, a capable and dependable representative of _____ , whose services I have used to advantage many times.

Helen has untangled some of my worst administrative problems, and in doing so has learned a great deal about our business and how it works. Quite naturally she would like to extend her services to others in our industry who might gain from her experience.

For this reason she has asked me to introduce her to you. I recommend her both personally and professionally, and would appreciate any courtesy you may show her.

Sincerely yours,

Ask those who write well to give you a letter of introduction that isn't based on a model. Exhibit 4.2 is an example of this more informal style, using a first-name basis and written without a model.

EXHIBIT 4.2

Sample Informal Letter of Introduction by a Third Party

Dear Harry:

When we had lunch together, I mentioned Jack Hunt, who was doing some big things for one of our lines. Since that time he has decided that he's ready to tackle an even bigger challenge and has accepted a position with Blank & Company.

I don't know whether you're interested in the line he's introducing right now, but I do think he can show you some interesting ways to expand—unless, that is, you're too far behind in production as it is!

Seriously, talk to this fellow, won't you? Jack Hunt is a great guy and a real professional.

Sincerely,

Ask for a business card as a means of introduction. A simpler means of getting a written introduction is to use a personal or business card with a few words written in, such as "Introducing John Belden," and then have it signed by the introducer.

Use a verbal direct reference

Some of your customers and friends, for one reason or another, will decline to arrange an appointment for you or even write a letter or card of recommendation, but they will not object to your using their name as a reference, provided you ask for that privilege. The mention of someone's name as a direct reference, assuming the person is someone whom the prospect knows and respects, can be an effective interview-getter.

The impact of the reference will be increased if you get the prospect to acknowledge that he or she knows the individual who gave the reference. For example,

---

Salesperson: Mr. Prospect, you know Ms. Allison at All-Color Printing, don't you?

Prospect: Yes, I know Maryann.

Salesperson: Ms. Allison feels that you could benefit in the same way that she has from my product. Let me show you how it can help you, too.

CAUTION In direct references, you must obtain the person's permission before you say that he or she is recommending you. In indirect references, for example, merely stating that someone uses your product, permission is not necessary.

REMINDER Make a point of thanking those people who assist you in this way, and let them know what the results are. You will find that people who know that their favors are appreciated are usually willing to be helpful again.

Use Preapproach Sales Material to Soften the Prospect for the Interview

Top-bracket salespeople utilize every available means for making a prospect aware of them and their product before they attempt to get an interview. They reap the benefits of their company's advertising by using it. They also make use of preinterview mailing material, whether it is supplied by the company or it's something they've written themselves.

Make full use of company-supplied preapproach material

Your company probably advertises its product and has some kind of printed material that is designed to do part of the selling job. It's up to you to put this material to profitable use. Here are some suggestions:

- Know exactly what your company provides in the way of mailings, advertising, sales literature, sales letters, and so on.
- Select the material that is best suited for your purposes. Don't send more than is necessary to arouse the prospect's interest.
- Draw upon the material you're already using in your presentation. Some of it may be suitable for enclosure in a mailing. A small circular, for example, is easily mailed.
- Always follow up your mailings.
- When you interview prospects who have received your preinterview material, be sure to reinforce the original effect by mentioning it, or by using it in your opening remarks.

■ IDEA IN ACTION

Bill Hadley's company, a large insurance firm, sends out to a list of prospects (which Bill has okayed) a letter signed by the company president, on company stationery, and mailed from the central office. The letter mentions a new kind of policy that is available and states that a representative will call to explain its advantages. When Bill makes his call he begins this way: "Mr./Ms. Prospect, my name is Bill Hadley. A few days ago you received a letter from our president, Mr. _____ , mentioning a new kind of insurance plan now being offered by my company, XYZ Insurance. I am here to explain this new plan to you. May I tell you about it?"

Bill gets good results with this approach because he takes full advantage of the letter. He benefits both from the awareness that it creates and from the prestige of his president's signature.

SUGGESTION A good way to put company advertising to work is to use blowups or cutouts of ads that have appeared

In newspapers or magazines. Hand the ad to the prospect and ask whether he or she noticed it in such-and-such magazine.

Create your own preapproach material

Suppose your company doesn't offer you much advertising or mailing assistance. You can find your own ways to soften up prospects for an interview. For example, you might write your own series of interest-getting letters, send them to the prospect at regular intervals, and then follow up with a request for an appointment.

■ IDEA IN ACTION

Jean Blake's letters, mailed each week for three weeks, were short and simple. They stated that a certain company in the area had bought her product that week and had begun to save considerable time, effort, and money. The third letter included a request for an interview. By that time the prospect had gotten the message that Jean's product was doing a good job for other companies and might be able to help him or her as well. The interview was granted.

Letters of this kind, sent directly from the salesperson or from the local office, are usually more personal than are central office mailings. With imagination you can think of other types of mailings—post cards, samples, anything that will smooth the way for your approach. Just keep these two points in mind when you prepare your own preapproach materials:

Whatever you mail to a prospect should look good and be in good taste. Letters and envelopes should be neatly typed and the material carefully chosen.

CAUTION Humor and cleverness are effective only when used skillfully. Unless you're absolutely sure of your skill, don't try to be funny in your mailings.

You should send out only as much material as you can properly follow up. You can't afford to let a prospect wait too long before you contact him or her personally, or the effect of the mailing will be lost. Unless you normally canvass heavily by mail, warm up only a few prospects at a time.

Send an Advance Card
Announcing Your Intended Call

A quick, easy, and inexpensive way to arrange interviews is to mail out advance cards, informing customers or prospects that you plan to call on them at a certain time on a certain day. In many cases the company provides these cards, but if it does not, it is a simple matter to secure your own.

☐ EXAMPLE

Advance cards are frequently no more than standard post-cards, printed up as follows:

Our Ms./Mr./Mrs. _____
will call on you on _____
at about _____ -o'clock.

     Sincerely yours,
     Brink Mfg. Co.

Sometimes a phrase asking the reader to advise a more suitable time is added.

☐ EXAMPLE

Some salespeople prefer a more personalized or unusual card. It might begin: "Hold that order! I'll be there on . . . ."

☐ EXAMPLE

One card used successfully has a real quarter taped on it, under the heading "Yep! Its real!" followed by, "And so are the dollars you'll save when you start using _____ . I'll be in your neighborhood on _____ and would like to show you how it works."

The most common use of advance cards is to notify customers of a salesperson's intended visit. The customer will then expect him or her and can make plans (check stock, for example) if it is necessary. Advance cards can also be used to make appointments with prospects. But cards sent to prospects for this purpose should not be too informal or chummy.

> **IMPORTANT** Remember that an advance card, like a letter, does not obligate the prospect in any way to see you; it cannot take the place of a definite appointment.

GETTING IN WITHOUT AN APPOINTMENT

Sell the Interview First

No reasonable salesperson is disturbed when he or she is denied an interview for a valid reason, for instance, if the prospect is at a meeting. But in many cases the denial is not based on a valid reason. The buyer is always "too busy" to see salespeople in whose lines he or she does not have an active interest, or the buyer assumes that he or she knows all about the proposition and that its presentation would be a waste of time. Sometimes the buyer prejudges a proposition as not being of interest.

Such buyers and prospects usually give salespeople the brush-off through a secretary or other gatekeeper. Or they might agree to see the salesperson for a brief moment, only to explain why it would be a mutual waste of time for the salesperson to make his or her presentation.

Where the interview is not freely granted, the salesperson's task is to "sell the interview." It is rarely possible to succeed in selling the product when the prospect is still "unsold" on the idea that he or she should listen to the sales story.

The sale of the interview, like the sale of the product, must be thoroughly planned and rehearsed. All the steps, in short, that apply to the sale of the product (described in Chapter Five) apply to the sale of the interview as well. Special techniques must often be used to "get by" the receptionist, the secretary, or the assistant who seeks to bar the interview.

Let's look at this example of two salespeople trying to get interviews and see why one does poorly while the other succeeds.

■ IDEA IN ACTION

Scott King and Edwina Bryant sell life insurance. They work out of the same office.

One morning they are told that a new medical expense policy has just been made available. Their sales manager carefully explains the features and cost of the new policy and then tells them, "This is a real opportunity to go out and sign up a lot of people whom you couldn't sell before. Make the most of it!"

Scott and Edwina proceed to their desks to work up a list of people they will call on. At the end of the day they compare notes. "How many did you sign up, Scott?" asks Edwina.

"Two," is Scott's glum reply. "How about you?"

"Nine," says Edwina.

"That's great! I wonder what you're doing that I'm not? Would you mind sitting in on one of my calls in the morning so that you can tell me where I'm missing out?"

"It's a date," Edwina replies.

The next morning, with Edwina at his elbow, Scott sees his first client.

"Mr. Frisbie," he begins, "this is Ms. Bryant, who works in my office. I stopped in to tell you about a brand-new medical policy that has just become available. Here is what it offers you that makes it different from all other medical policies. First . . .

"But, Mr. King, I'm not interested in any medical policy, no matter how attractive it is," Frisbie interrupts. "I carry hospitalization, accident, and life, as you know. That's all I need, and I've got an appointment in 5 minutes, so if you'll excuse me . . . ."

"Well, Scott," says Edwina when they get outside, "suppose you tag along with me on my first call, and see if you like the way I present the new policy. Then we can compare notes."

Edwina leads the way to the office of a Mr. Klinger, who greets her with this remark: "I don't want to be rude, Ms. Bryant, but I don't need any more insurance—and I've got a conference coming up in a few minutes."

"Mr. Klinger," replied Edwina, "I want only 1 minute of your time. This is Mr. King, who is with our office. I just stopped by to ask you one question, Mr. Klinger. When you bought that new car a couple of months ago, didn't you tell me you wanted protection immediately against fire, theft, and collision?"

"Sure I did! Why run risks on an investment of twenty thousand dollars? I didn't drive it at all until you said I was covered."

"That's exactly what I thought, Mr. Klinger," Edwina smiled. "Now I want to talk to you about another risk that can run into hundreds of thousands of dollars, and against which you have absolutely no protection."

Klinger looks up quickly, "What's that?"

"Liability for medical expenses for yourself and family," Edwina replies.

"Well," her prospect says, "I'm not sure I'm interested, and i've got to go to a meeting in a few minutes. Can you stop back later?"

"I can, indeed. Say about 2 o'clock?"

"That's fine," answers Klinger.

As soon as they get outside, Scott says to Edwina, "Boy, am I grateful to you! Guess I'd forgotten the rule—'Never try to sell your product if the customer hasn't been sold on the interview.' Watch me go to town now!"

How to Handle a "Brush-Off" by a Gatekeeper

Receptionists and other gatekeepers are sometimes permitted, or even instructed, to "brush off" salespeople when, *in their judgment,* the executive who is being solicited would not be interested in seeing them. Some gatekeepers have highly developed skills for getting rid of unwanted salespeople. On the other hand, some salespeople become equally adept at "getting by" the gatekeeper.

Three techniques that work are described here: (1) the "outbluffing technique," (2) answering when the gatekeeper says, "Mr. Jones is busy," and (3) answering when he or she says, "I know Mr. Jones wouldn't be interested."

Outbluffing the gatekeeper

With this technique, your words and actions give the impression that you and your prospect know each other.

▪ IDEA IN ACTION

Jack Winchell sells folding boxes. He calls on a firm that uses large quantities of such boxes for shipping.

"May I help you?" inquires the receptionist.

"Yes, indeed," smiles Jack, hoping that this phase of his call will run smoothly, but laying the groundwork for any eventuality. "Will you please tell Mrs. Jones that Jack Winchell is calling?"

"Do you have a card?" asks the receptionist.

"No, I'm afraid I don't," says Jack, and then quickly adds, "Just tell Mrs. Jones that I'd like to ask her a question, but if she's tied up right now, ask her whether I can see her at 2 o'clock this afternoon." Jack promptly turns his back and examines some pictures on the wall in the reception room.

The receptionist hesitates for a moment, but then decides to announce the caller. Jack has created just the impression he feels is right for the situation. His words and his manner have implied several things that he has not actually said. The receptionist is thrown off guard by his apparent assumption that he will be announced and received—either then or at 2 P.M.—without question.

Jack's request that his name be sent in, without mention of his firm's name, makes the receptionist think that he already knows Mrs. Jones. His gesture in turning away makes it difficult for her to quiz him any further. All in all, Jack has outwitted her.

This game of "bluff" can be played in various ways—instructions for playing it are difficult to spell out. The alert salesperson learns by trial and error how this technique can best be used to advantage.

Some receptionists won't be outwitted. They'll persist in their attempts to "brush off" the salesperson without announcing him or her. Regardless of the exact words such a receptionist uses, the underlying message is the same: "So-and-so is busy right now, and I can't disturb him or her" or "I know he or she wouldn't be interested."

Answering the gatekeeper who says your prospect is busy

To a gatekeeper who uses the "busy" excuse for keeping you from seeing your prospect, say, "I see. When would be a good time for me to call back—how about 11:30?"

It's usually easy to tell from the person's reply whether your prospect is really busy at the moment or whether this is merely an attempt to "stall." If the gatekeeper says that 11:30—or any other time—would be better, then the chances are that his or her first statement was sincere.

But if the reply indicates that the gatekeeper doesn't want you to call back, then you can apply the same technique described next for answering the person who decides that your prospect wouldn't be interested.

Answering the gatekeeper who says your prospect wouldn't be interested

A gatekeeper who "knows" that your prospect won't be interested must be prepared to take the "strong medicine" such a remark invites. To break through this barrier, you must say, "You're making a very important decision that can be quite costly to your company. Are you certain you want to take the responsibility for this? Why don't you just tell Ms. Smith I'm here and let her decide whether she will see me?"

If this line of reasoning fails, there is one further step you can take. Ask, "May I have your name, please?" This question, politely voiced, usually wins the fray.

WARNING Few salespeople like to force such "strong medicine" on the receptionist, and some refuse to do so.

What to Do When You Are Received by a "Proxy" for the Prospect

What should you do when you are received by someone other than the executive you called to see? Sometimes a secretary or an assistant will stand in for a busy executive and try to determine whether or not your "message" is worth delivering.

The rule is: Do not try to "sell" a substitute listener on your proposition; instead, *sell him or her on the advisability of arranging for you to see the prospect personally.*

Determine whether the "proxy" listener has come forth at the specific request of the prospect or not, and make your approach fit the situation.

What to do if the prospect has sent a substitute to see you

In this case, concentrate on a few facts that will suffice to justify an interview with the prospect.

■ IDEA IN ACTION

Beth Krusewski asks to see Mr. Granger, head of a large company. The receptionist, after announcing her, tells her that Miss Davis, Mr. Granger's secretary, will be with her shortly.

"Ms. Krusewski," says Miss Davis, "Mr. Granger has a group meeting to attend in about five minutes. He's sorry that he can't see you at this time, and asked me to talk with you instead. May I ask what you wanted to discuss with him?"

Beth realizes from Miss Davis's remarks that she has actually been delegated to talk with her and that she has been further authorized to inquire about her mission.

"Let me give you the essence of the matter, Miss Davis," Beth begins.

This "opener" is designed to make it plain to Miss Davis that Beth—the salesperson—intends to tell her only enough of her story to persuade her that it would be advisable for Mr. Granger to hear the *whole presentation.*

"We offer a truck maintenance service, Miss Davis, that saves our customers from 8 to 20% of their delivery costs. Our service has been used for three years or more by the outstanding companies whose names appear on this list. That's what I want to discuss with Mr. Granger, and I wonder if you can suggest a time when we can go into the matter."

Beth has handled this situation with skill. She has told Miss Davis only a few facts to convince her that Mr. Granger would be interested in hearing the whole sales story. She has quoted no prices, offered no details, submitted no proof that her firm can actually save Mr. Granger's company from 8 to 20%. In other words, she has not given the information that would be absolutely necessary to make a decision on the offer itself.

By handling the matter in this way, she has completely bypassed the hazard that the prospect will attempt to make a decision on the basis of a secondhand presentation of her offer.

What to do if the "proxy" was not sent out by the prospect to see you

When you are sure that the person who receives you has not been sent by your prospect, and that he or she doesn't know of your presence, "sell" the proxy on announcing you to the prospect and fixing a time when you can speak to him or her directly.

■ IDEA IN ACTION

Dick Holden asks to see Ms. Rutherford, vice president of a large corporation.

The receptionist announces Dick by telephone, and then says, "Mr. Holden, will you wait just a moment, please? Ms. Rutherford's secretary, Miss White, will be with you shortly."

Dick thanks the receptionist and waits. He wonders whether Miss White is coming out because Ms. Rutherford suggested it or whether she is receiving him on her own volition as a matter of established routine.

"I'm Miss White, Mr. Holden—Ms. Rutherford's secretary. Can I help you?"

Dick decides to probe for the answer to his question. "Why, yes, Miss White," he replies, "I'm sure you can. I'd like about 10 minutes with Ms. Rutherford, and if this isn't a convenient time, I wonder if you can set an appointment for sometime tomorrow morning."

"Would you mind telling me what you have in mind, Mr. Holden? This is a very busy week for Ms. Rutherford, and I hesitate to make any more appointments for her. But I'll be glad to give her your message."

These remarks make it quite clear that Dick has not been announced to Ms. Rutherford herself.

Dick knows that "the other person" can't make his presentation for him. He also knows that in this instance, the secretary will somehow have to be "sold" on announcing him to his prospect.

So he says, "Well, Miss White, I don't think the matter I have in mind can be handled just that way. Can we set a time for some day next week?"

In short, Dick is trying hard to avoid having the decision as to whether he will be received made by anyone other than the prospect herself. Because he has followed the rules of sound sales strategy, Dick receives the answer he has earned.

"Can you come back about 10:30 tomorrow morning, Mr. Holden?" asks Miss White.

REMINDER *Never expect another person to tell your sales story as effectively as you would yourself.*

Getting In Without Naming Your Product

In selling certain specialty products, it is important to get in to see the prospect without mentioning the name of the product or your specific company. There is a reason for this tactic. In specialty selling, it is usually necessary, first, to prove to the prospect that a need exists (a need that the prospect is often not aware of) and, second, to show the prospect that your product or service is designed to fit that need.

If you mention the name of your product before you have proved a need for it, you are very likely to get a quick "We don't need it" or "We're not interested." You want to get in and explain the need first. How you can do this, making an ally of whoever greets you first, is demonstrated next.

■ IDEA IN ACTION

Kathy Foote sells a well-known communications device. Upon entering the outer office of one of her cold prospects, she walks up to the switchboard operator, intent upon making a friendly impression on the person who knows more than anyone else about the communication needs of the firm. The operator knows how often her lines get tied up by interoffice calls, how frequently long-distance calls are made, and so on. Kathy is determined to get this kind of information because it will help her establish the need for her product. Also, she's going to try to see the right person without letting the receptionist know what firm she represents.

"Good morning," Kathy says to the receptionist, adding in an easy, informal way, "I wonder if you can help me?"

Few people can flatly reject a friendly request for help. "What can I do for you?" the receptionist asks.

Then Kathy does a quick switch. Instead of answering the question, she asks one.

"You must have a pretty busy switchboard at times—do you have to handle all inside calls too?"

The receptionist is willing to give Kathy a few facts about their communications set-up—facts that Kathy can use later when she sees the boss. But eventually she comes back to the obvious question: "What do you want?"

This time Kathy's answer is: "I'd like to discuss a way to streamline your telecommunication system with Mr.—uh—what's his name?"

If the receptionist gives Kathy the name, she says, "That's the person I want to see—do you suppose you could get me in to see him?"

If at any stage of the conversation the receptionist mentions that the switchboard is overworked, or that communications are inadequate, Kathy says, "I have a new system that will solve many of your problems. Whom do I have to see about it?"

So far, Kathy has not revealed the product she is selling. If the receptionist insists on knowing, Kathy says, "Oh, I'm sorry—I didn't mean to be rude. I'm asking these questions because I have a service that will help your top executives—who is the head of this company?"

Kathy has made *three attempts* to see the boss without naming her product. Sometimes she succeeds on the first try, sometimes on the second, often on the third. If, however, the receptionist insists on learning exactly what company she is with and what she is selling, Kathy tells her.

She says, "I have a new product especially designed to help you in this kind of office." (The phrase "to help you" is an effective one and Kathy uses it often.)

If the boss asks what Kathy wants, she tells the receptionist, "I want 5 minutes of his time to show him a multiline telephone I know will help him." Or "Tell him I've made a survey of his office and that I have something here that is designed to help him."

If the executive asks, "What firm is she with?" Kathy answers the question. Putting some sell into it, she says, "I'd like to show him a new multiline telephone developed especially for offices like this one."

"Going for Broke" to Get In

There will be times when you feel dead certain you could get the order if you could only get your prospect to look at your product. But you can't get in to see him or her. You begin to feel that "you'll go for broke" if necessary, just to get in. You know this is a dangerous attitude, so you try again and again to get an appointment. Finally, you have exhausted all the usual strategies and are again thinking of "going for broke."

You want to try something different. If it works, you are in and you can proceed with the sale; if it doesn't work, you spoil your chances for approaching the prospect again. If the stakes are high enough, it might be worth trying out your "different" idea.

∎ IDEA IN ACTION

A whole new field of nonuser prospects would open up for Bryan Moore if he could get one important prospect to convert to paper cartons for packaging a hardware item that is normally packaged in wooden containers.

The product development engineers at Bryan's firm have designed a perfect self-locking carton for the purpose. But Bryan can't get in to see the right person. Receptionists, secretaries, and assistants keep telling him, "Ms. Ansell is too busy."

Bryan feels he should "go for broke." He calls before 9 o'clock, without an appointment, and brings with him the designer of the sample carton.

Again Bryan is given the brush-off.

"Ms. Ansell has an appointment at 9 o'clock," the receptionist says.

"Can I see someone else—even someone in the shipping department?" Bryan asks.

The receptionist senses an air of urgency about this unexpected call. She calls Ms. Ansell's secretary, who appears within minutes. Evidently, Bryan's wanting to go "under" Ms. Ansell's head has done the trick.

"Ms. Ansell will see you, but she has only 3 minutes," the secretary says.

Bryan and his designer are in. They leave with the order 25 minutes later.

How to Avoid the Reception Area Interview

It's advisable to give your presentation to a business prospect in his or her office. Ordinarily, you won't be able to do your most effective selling in a reception area. If your prospect leaves his or her office to come out to hear your presentation, you must try to maneuver your way back into the office. Sometimes this requires several attempts.

■ IDEA IN ACTION

Miranda Sears sells a specialty item. The major part of Miranda's presentation is the demonstration. It is essential that she give the demonstration in the prospect's office.

When an executive comes out to ask Miranda what her business is, she replies, "I want to show you something—can we step back into your office for a minute?" Although this simple request has worked for Miranda many times, this time the prospect persists and again asks what she wants. "I've made a survey of your office layout (an honest statement in Miranda's line), and I believe I have something that will help you," is her second response. As she says this, Miranda picks up her demonstration kit as if she assumes that her prospect will lead the way to his office.

But again Miranda's prospect balks. She then looks at him directly and says, "It'll take only a few minutes, and I'm sure you'll find it worthwhile." Miranda's prospect gives in to this third request and invites her into his office.

Miranda employs this same strategy effectively when she calls on retail stores. She says to the proprietor, "I have something here I'd like to show you. Do you have an office in the back?" If the prospect hesitates, Miranda uses her best interest-getting opener: "I believe I have something here that will enable your clerks to serve your customers better." If the prospect still seems reluctant, Miranda goes into her third try: "It'll take only a few minutes, and I'm sure you'll find it worth your while." In most cases, one of these attempts works.

MAKING THE PROSPECT LISTEN

Every Prospect Is a Multifaceted Individual

Experienced salespeople know that every prospect is different. Each has his or her own unique temperament and personality.

Attempts have been made to catalog various "types" of prospects and customers to establish specific strategies and techniques that the salesperson can use on them. None of these "systems" is completely practical for the simple reason that they don't make allowances for individual differences. Although someone might be correctly described as a specific "type," there will be times when this same individual behaves quite differently. Most customers and prospects are a composite of several personality types and may display varying temperaments during the course of a single interview.

What, then, should you do as you encounter changing personality traits?

The following sections tell you what signals indicate your prospect's mood at any particular moment and suggests practical strategies for meeting and handling each of these situations successfully. Tips are provided for selling to the following personality types:

- Talkative
- Silent
- Fast talking
- Deliberate
- Impulsive
- Vacillating
- Trusting
- Suspicious
- Opinionated

REMEMBER One individual might display any or all of these temperaments at different times.

Steer the talkative prospect back to "sales"

Some people are just plain talkative by nature. The best technique is to give them a reasonable length of time to "talk themselves out." They may finally say, "Let's see now. You wanted to tell me about your new line of spring novelties?" If they don't "come around" in a reasonable amount of time, however, you will have to find some means of steering the conversation back to business. Here are some suggestions:

Pick up on a comment the prospect has made and tie it in with the purpose of your call.

☐ EXAMPLE

"Your views about the economy are certainly interesting, Mr. Jones. The point you made about people spending more money at this time of year ties right in with a preseason discount I can give you."

At the first available opportunity, agree with the prospect and lead right into your message.

☐ EXAMPLE

"I certainly agree with you—we need rain desperately. Incidentally, one of the things I want to be sure to tell you about is that our new line of spring novelties . . . ."

EXCEPTION If the talkative prospect doesn't engage in "small talk" but begins what sounds like a long discourse on why he or she won't buy, take stronger measures and put them into action sooner. If you let the prospect talk as long as he or she wants on the subject of how bad business has been lately, or dwell on some other reason for not buying, he or she will end up convinced that this is a bad time to place an order. You must get into the conversation yourself to counterbalance the negative picture the prospect is trying to paint.

Ask the silent prospect leading questions

The silent prospect is the most perplexing type for many salespeople. Small wonder! He or she sits there, indicating neither agreement nor disagreement, and you have no idea whether he or she is even listening.

The best remedy for this situation is to try to draw the prospect out by asking questions that demand a response: "I think that's an important advantage, don't you, Mr. Barclay?" or "Do any of your competitors do much volume in this line?"

Usually the response, even though it may only be a nod or a monosyllable, will indicate fairly clearly how the prospect's mind is working. A single word can reveal as much about how well or how poorly you are faring as a longer response.

Pace yourself to match the "fast talker"

A fast-talking person likes *action*. He or she wants to be told the highlights or essence of your story, not the details—and to be told quickly, not in a slow or deliberate way.

The rule here is simple: Pace your manner and delivery to match the prospect's tempo. Get straight to the point.

Give the deliberate prospect the "full treatment"

This type of prospect wants to have every question answered to his or her full satisfaction and likes to know every detail about your product and how it works.

There is no use in trying to hurry this prospect. Since you will only succeed in irritating him or her by trying to speed up the conversation, be prepared to provide all the facts and details he or she might want.

Deal quickly with the impulsive prospect

The impulsive person is apt to interrupt your sales presentation before you've had a chance to state all your points. He or she might say, "Okay, I'll take it" or "No, I'm not interested."

The impulsive prospect is just as likely to change his or her mind after announcing a decision. On the other hand, it's often possible to get this type of person to change his or her decision by stating one more fact for consideration.

It is best to deal quickly with the impulsive type and seize any opening for a favorable decision.

Be firm with the vacillating prospect

The vacillating prospect literally doesn't know his or her own mind and will usually accept help in arriving at a decision if assistance is offered properly. It is often a mistake to move quickly with such a person. He or she responds best to guidance that is at once authoritative and deliberate. Points need to be repeated frequently, and small facts explained. It's best not to give the prospect who vacillates a choice, but to focus gradually his or her attention on a single course of action. When the ground has been fully covered, you might find it necessary to force the sale to a close. This can be accomplished by taking a firm position.

> ☐ EXAMPLE
>
> "Mr. Waycross, we've gone over the whole proposition pretty thoroughly, and I'm certain you'll be pleased if you decide on this particular contract. I know you don't want to rush into a matter of this sort, but really I don't see how you could go wrong. Here, if you'll just initial this form, I'll get started immediately to see that you get our service."

Exercise caution with the trusting prospect

It's not often that you run across a trusting prospect, but when you do, it's best to handle him or her with caution.

The person who has absolute faith in you will take everything you say as "gospel" and will almost always do what you recommend. Be careful to avoid misunderstandings, and be sure that you tell "the whole truth and nothing but the truth."

If this person discovers, or even *believes*, that he or she has been misled, it's unlikely that he or she will ever trust you again. But when treated squarely, such prospects usually turn into solid customers and are often an excellent source of "free advertising" for you and your product.

Allay the fears of the suspicious prospect

The distrustful person suspects the world in general and is often convinced that every salesperson he or she meets is trying to "pull a fast one." Such individuals jump at every opportunity to turn what you say or do into "proof" of why they shouldn't trust you or buy from you.

The best way to persuade the suspicious prospect to buy is to "soft-pedal" yourself and your product. Make no extravagant claims; "tone down" your presentation to avoid giving him or her a chance to find fault with it.

If you couple this strategy with courtesy and deference, the prospect will soon get the idea that you are not out to "hoodwink" him or her but that you are sincerely interested in providing a valuable product or service.

If you get the chance, you might even try some "homegrown" psychology on this individual: let him or her "win" some minor point of contention; give this person the feeling that he or she is "hard to fool." These tactics can result in a sale.

Guide the opinionated prospect to your way of thinking

Just as some people don't know their own minds, others are overconfident. Unlike the impulsive thinker (who often reverses decisions in an instant), the person with strong opinions must be "guided" into changing his or her mind. A skillful salesperson can often get the strong-minded prospect to "come around."

Conform to Your Customer's Buying Habits

The wise salesperson adjusts his or her approach to customers' buying habits, knowing that any other course of action invites unnecessary trouble.

For example, you don't encourage a prospect to listen if you start chatting with him when he prefers that you get right down to business. Nor do you establish rapport with a customer who likes to chat for a while by jumping right into your sales story. Similarly, if a customer is growing lukewarm because you are calling too often, or because you are not calling often enough, it's a signal that you should change your calling schedule.

Find out how your customers like to buy, adjust your ways to theirs, and you'll have less trouble getting them to listen. These are some of the things about your prospects and customers that you should know:

- Is there a special time this customer prefers to be called on?
- Does she buy small quantities frequently or place large orders at longer intervals?
- What grades, sizes, colors, models, and so on, does he use?
- What are her hobbies or other interests that you should remember to mention?
- Does he like salespeople to leave as soon as their business is done or to stay and chat for a while?
- Does she like the salesperson to drop in or to telephone in advance for an appointment?
- Is this customer particularly impressed by what certain other customers, whom he knows and respects, decide to buy?
- Does she have any idiosyncrasies that should be remembered? For example, does she have strong political opinions that should not be argued? Is she hard of hearing? Does she often cancel orders she has placed? Does she like to do most of the talking?
- What competitive sources does he buy from?

Any alert salesperson should be able to add other items to this list.

Use the Prospect's Name to Make Him or Her Want to Listen

A simple technique for making a prospect want to listen is to address him or her by name. Make sure you use the correct name and that you don't mis-pronounce it.

Some people have trouble remembering names. Here are some proven techniques for making a name stay with you:

1. As soon as you're introduced to a prospect, repeat his or her name. For example, you might say, "Hello, Mrs. Johnson, I'm glad you were able to spare me a few minutes of your time."

2. Try to use the name several times in your first conversation with a new prospect. Preface questions with it, and use it to end statements.

3. Every time you use a person's name, look him or her in the eye.

4. When you're talking to a person, try to pick up peculiarities in his or her speech that you can identify with the name.

5. Get into the habit of jotting down the names of people you meet during the business day. Then, at night, run down your list and see how many you can connect with faces.

Listen and Your Prospect Will Listen to You

The prospect will have every right to resent you if you try to monopolize the interview. He or she must be given a chance to talk and ask questions.

Be sure that your sales talk includes ample listening time. Being a listener gives you these advantages:

- You won't talk too much. You will spoil the effectiveness of your presentation if you prolong it by unnecessary chatter.

- Your prospect's questions and comments, even objections, will tell you where you have hit the target and where you have missed, and why.

PUTTING YOUR FINGER ON THE PROSPECT'S REASON TO BUY

Every Buyer Has a Buying Motive

No sale is ever made unless the buyer has a specific buying motive. This infallible rule—that behind every sale lies *a reason to buy*—can be a miracle key to guide you to more profitable selling.

Motives vary from prospect to prospect. One has a different motive from another for buying the identical product. The same prospect may have different motives at different times for buying the same product.

When you accurately put your finger on your prospect's primary reason to buy, you have found the "heart" of the sale. The prospect's motive—or desire to buy—*wants* to be satisfied. Your sales talk can then aim to satisfy this desire to buy and lead your prospect into selling himself or herself.

The Ten Most Common Buying Motives

There are ten common buying motives that account for most sales:

1. Desire for wealth (profit, economy, saving, etc.)
2. Desire for health
3. Desire for admiration from others (pride, prestige)
4. Desire for gratification of some appetite
5. Desire for amusement
6. Desire for safety and security of self or dependents
7. Desire for utility or use value
8. Desire for self-improvement
9. Desire for saving of time, trouble, or worry
10. Desire for comfort

A specific product usually appeals to only one, or a few, of these ten reasons to buy. Once you know which buying motive (or motives) your product satisfies, you can formulate a successful presentation based on those aspects of your product or service that are most likely to appeal to these motives. (Chapter Five offers tips on how to develop your presentation.)

Three Techniques to Help You Find a Prospect's Primary Buying Motive

As previously mentioned, one buying motive is usually dominant in your prospect's mind. If it should be different from the one around which you have built your prepared presentation, your job is to pinpoint this customer's particular buying motive and adjust your sales talk accordingly. The following sections describe three ways to find out which buying motive is strongest in your prospect's mind.

Ask a direct question to bring out the prime buying motive

When you know that you're on the wrong track, try using the direct question method to find your prospect's motives for buying. When you discover the prime motive and begin to show the prospect how your product will satisfy it, he or she will be in a receptive mood to listen.

■ IDEA IN ACTION

Frank Meltzer had done some preliminary checking before his call on a prospect whom he was trying to interest in a certain type of envelope. The envelope was just the kind that Frank thought would appeal to this economy-minded prospect. Yet the prospect showed little interest in Frank's offer.

Realizing that he was making no headway and that he was appealing to the wrong buying motive, Frank stopped selling for a moment and tried a direct question.

"Ms. Schwartz, is it possible that you've already found a low-priced envelope that suits your needs as well as the one I just showed you?"

"Well, what we actually want is a *better* envelope. You see, within the last two months we've changed the emphasis of our service and now aim at the higher-priced mailing business. Frankly, that envelope you showed me looked pretty low-grade."

Relieved, Frank brought out samples of his best material, envelopes used by other quality houses in the prospect's line, and soon Ms. Schwartz was showing real interest.

A direct question enabled Frank to switch successfully from an appeal to the *economy* motive to an appeal to *prestige*. Continued appeal to his prospect's new buying motive enabled Frank to close the sale.

Use trial and error to find your prospect's major buying motive

The alert salesperson knows how and when to use a trial-and-error approach to determine a prospect's strongest buying motive. He or she uses judgment in the selection of sales points to present and then carefully observes the *actual result* when they are put into practice.

When a sales point tests out well in actual practice, the top salesperson capitalizes it. He or she knows that a sales point that "clicks" is a precious possession, for it indicates the buying motive that is uppermost in the prospect's mind. It can be used again and again—right up until the sale is made.

Similarly, the successful salesperson *drops* a sales point, no matter how good it seems in his or her own judgment, if *actual practice* proves it to be ineffective. If a sales point tests out poorly when given a fair trial during an interview, there is no point in continuing to emphasize it. Prior judgment of a sales point's effectiveness should never cause you to keep plugging it if it fails to achieve the desired impact.

> **IMPORTANT** The trial-and-error technique is a continuing process. Changing conditions often trigger changes in buying motives. Excellent sales points may suddenly become obsolete, or your own company may launch new products that appeal to different buying motives.

These changes mean that the successful salesperson must keep abreast of his or her prospects' buying motivations and know the new sales points that will appeal most strongly to them.

Use your imagination to "think out" a prospect's strongest buying motive

Star salespeople put their imagination to work and try to figure out what a prospect's strongest buying motive will be *before they meet him or her*. As in other phases of their selling, these "stars" perform the creative work that is always the mark of the outstanding salesperson.

■ IDEA IN ACTION

Stephanie Shearer sells life insurance and an annuity program. During one month she sells large policies to three individuals whom other salespeople have tried in vain to sign up.

In the first case she emphasizes the *investment* aspect of her proposal. She does this because she knows that this particular prospect is investment-minded; he has considerable holdings of securities that are worth more than he paid for them.

Stephanie reasons that a well-to-do businessperson with a successful record in the stock market won't be nearly as impressed by the *protection* argument as by the investment approach *(desire for profit)*.

Stephanie's second big sale is made to someone in quite different circumstances. This prospect recently lost his partner in an automobile accident. Stephanie reasons—and rightly so—that this is an individual who will listen when she speaks of unexpected tragedy and the need for full protection for one's family *(desire for safety)*.

The third big sale is made on still different grounds. The prospect in this instance is inclined to be impressed with his own importance. "Mr. Logan," Stephanie says at just the right moment in the interview, "there is one thing you may want to consider in connection with this matter. If you let me write up the policy as I've described it to you, you will automatically become a member of a very exclusive group. Here are the names of a few others who are already members." She repeats the names of half a dozen of the country's most successful businesspeople. Mr. Logan's face lights up with intense interest as Stephanie mentions these names.

"Now, only a few people in America—fewer than 200, to be exact—have ever bought a policy in this amount. You belong in that group, Mr. Logan, and since you already understand the sound investment and security reasons for buying, I thought I should call this additional fact to your attention" *(desire for prestige)*.

Stephanie Shearer made a sale in each of these three cases by using her *imagination*. Before she even approached her prospects, she figured out what their strongest buying motive would be and then designed an approach that would appeal to it.

A Different Approach to the Same Buying Motive Can Win the Sale

There are various ways to appeal to a particular buying motive. When one approach doesn't work, use another—but don't stray too far from the motive if it's the dominant one.

■ IDEA IN ACTION

Bart Merrill sells mill and factory supplies. One of his customers turns him down one day on a rather large order, saying, "There's another company that has just quoted us a little better price on the same item, and I'm sure you understand that we've got to buy where we get the most for our money."

Bart realizes, of course, that the buying motive in this instance is *economy*—a form of the *desire for wealth*. He realizes that on price alone he cannot win this order. But, having been up against similar situations before, Bart has a ready answer.

"Mr. Jones," he replies, "I know you've got to buy where your dollar will get you the most, and that's exactly why I think you should place the order with us."

"How do you figure *that*? Your price is a little *higher* than the other quotation," his customer says.

"I know it is," continues Bart, "but let's look at it this way. Not too long ago there was a shortage on certain items that you regularly use. You may remember that you were rather anxious about it and asked me whether we could fill your needs."

"Yes," Mr. Jones says, "I recall that situation."

"Well," continues Bart, "I told you then not to worry—that we would take care of you. I explained that we're a reliable organization, one that buys right and sells right. We don't try to buy at cut prices, nor do we sell at cut prices.

"The result is that when an emergency crops up, we're likely to get preferred consideration from *our* sources, and this enables us to take better care of our customers.

"Now, Mr. Jones, if on that occasion you had been dealing with a less reliable company, you would have had to pay them or someone else a premium price for the scarce merchandise you needed so badly. On that one item alone you saved enough money, by dealing with us, to balance out the savings on *ten* orders like the one you're about to place."

Bart got the order. He found a different way to meet his customer's primary buying motive *(economy)* in spite of the higher price.

How to Meet an "Unusual" Reason to Buy

You can "tie in" your sales talk with a prospect's buying motive even if it differs from the motive that usually spurs people to buy your product. When it becomes clear that the sale can't be made solely on the basis of your "set" presentation, you should be prepared to use your "reserve" sales points to make the sale.

□ EXAMPLE

A commercial real estate salesperson gives a presentation that stresses business *security*. She meets one prospect who is interested in real estate as a means of avoiding taxes. The salesperson then proceeds to stress the tax shelter *(economy)* aspects of real estate that she now knows will interest her prospect the most.

How to Convert Buying Motives into Sales

Once you have found the buying motive that is uppermost in your prospect's mind, you can change the desire to buy into a *decision* to buy.

▪ IDEA IN ACTION

Sandra Vogel sells juvenile furniture to retailers. Her house builds a quality line that naturally sells at prices a little above average.

Sandra knows her customers well. Hence, to a certain class of retailer, she emphasizes the *prestige* value of handling her products, rather than the volume or profit that will ensue. She does this for an excellent reason—the fact that in this particular class of trade there is an active desire to build prestige.

Yet on her next call Sandra might emphasize *profit*. She will point out that while her products won't achieve the volume that less expensive articles enjoy, there is an unusually attractive profit, both dollarwise and percentagewise. Again, Sandra does this for a very sound reason. She has learned that this second type of retailer is primarily interested in increasing profit-building sales.

Into a third category fall those retailers to whom Sandra emphasizes reliability (*desire to save trouble*). These are retailers who would rather forgo part of the profit they might earn in exchange for fewer returns, complaints, and adjustments.

Sandra designs her presentation so that a different point is emphasized for each class of customer. She is successful because she realizes the importance of this and proceeds accordingly.

Your Appeal Must Change with the Times

You must always be alert to changes in business conditions that may change a prospect's buying motives.

▪ IDEA IN ACTION

For several years a salesperson used a standardized approach to gain attention. He would request interviews with top executives and win them by promising to show them a way to increase their sales by 10%. The phrase "increase your sales by 10%" worked like magic—and he had no trouble getting all the interviews he could handle.

But there came a time when the magic words lost their effectiveness. He would make his usual telephone calls, but get no interviews. Something was wrong. It was time to discover why his prospects were no longer interested in increasing their sales and to change his tactics.

The salesperson tackled the problem by thinking up three new appeals. He made a dozen calls using each and discovered that one was much stronger than the others. This one really worked. It got him the interviews that the old "increase your sales" phrase used to get him.

Instead of saying he had something that would help his prospects increase sales by 10%, he now told them of a plan that would cut their selling costs. This change, as minor as it seemed, got him in because it appealed to executives whose primary goal now was to cut selling expenses.

How To Address Different Buying Motives While Following Your Prepared Presentation

In Chapter Five, we point out that a *great* presentation must be prepared and memorized if you want to reach high-bracket selling. We show you how to develop and give such a presentation. The fact that different buying motives exist and that you must emphasize different points to different prospects does not necessarily conflict with having a standard presentation that you've memorized.

Your standard presentation is based on the selling points that you want to make, regardless of a particular prospect's buying motives. For example, it may be built around speed, accuracy, versatility, ease of operation, or savings. Once you have mastered that presentation, you acquire flexibility. You can switch emphasis from one sales point to another, as your prospect's needs and buying motives demand.

MAKING CALLBACKS PAY OFF

Make Several Callbacks If Your Selling Situation Requires It

Just as there are situations that require making a sale on a single call (door-to-door selling, for example), there are also situations in which several callbacks must be made before you can expect to make a sale.

If you are in a multicall line, don't make the mistake of stopping your calls too soon. One extra call might be all that is needed to put you in the group of salespeople who place the bulk of the orders.

□ EXAMPLE

A large company that sells supplies to builders informs its salespeople that 80% of its business is placed after the fifth call. Despite this known fact, 88% of the salespeople stop calling after one, two, or three calls. According to these figures, a majority of the company's salespeople waste their valuable time by making one to three unproductive calls.

Since it often takes several calls to sell a prospect, you must be especially thorough in qualifying your prospects as to their potential buying ability. Here are some of the situations in which it's usually necessary to make several calls before you get an order:

- **Selling to a group.** Group selling makes it necessary for you to see more people; you often have to sell them individually before you get a crack at selling them together. Be prepared to call back a reasonable number of times until the sale is made. (See Chapter Two for tips that can help you make every call count when you sell to a group.)

- **Selling intangibles.** In selling intangibles (insurance, stocks and bonds, or services) callbacks are usually more frequent than in selling a hard goods line. You sell an idea; often the idea is unfamiliar to the prospect. Your job is to "educate" the prospect, and in many cases he or she will need time to "think it over."

- **Conforming to a prospect's policy.** Some companies are hard to win quickly because it's their policy to make salespeople "prove" themselves. Such companies usually expect to become long-term buyers and want to know exactly what kind of salesperson they will be dealing with. Once they are convinced of his or her reliability and worth—and it may take several calls to convince them—they close. When the salesperson has earned the confidence of such a prospect, he or she usually has a loyal customer and a steady source of orders.

- **Selling in a buyer's market.** When a "buyer's market" develops, most salespeople have to increase the number of calls they make on a customer or prospect before they can get the order.

Three Key Queries Before Making a Callback

The time to decide whether you are going to call back on a prospect is immediately after you have had an unsuccessful interview. When making this decision, consider the value of your selling time and weigh carefully the probable outcome of another call.

Your answers to the first two questions that follow will help you to weed out the prospects on whom callbacks would be futile. The third question is necessary for taking action.

1. **Is this account worth another callback?** To answer this question, ask yourself if there is something in the situation that makes a callback worthwhile. (For example, the fact that it routinely takes several calls to make a sale in your particular line may be enough to justify another call.) Do you feel that you are still making headway? Has your prospect just given your proposition full consideration? Did he or she show interest? What was his or her reaction when you suggested another call?

2. **If I call back, what strategy can I use that will get me somewhere?** Have you exhausted all the approaches that could possibly appeal to this prospect? Have you any ammunition left, or would another call be a rehash of previous calls?

What creative idea can you develop to bring to this prospect before the next call?

3. **When is the best time to call back?** Your knowledge of each situation will enable you to determine whether to call back in a week, a month, or some other specific amount of time.

Remind the Prospect of Your Previous Visit on a Callback

When you call back, begin by reminding the prospect of your previous interview. Take time to review the points that you made during the last meeting, especially those that he or she liked best. If possible, get the prospect to respond favorably again to each point. This technique creates continuity between interviews and gets the callback off on the right foot.

> **TIP** Rely on good records to tell you what happened during that last interview and to help you decide what you want to accomplish this time. See Chapter Ten for samples of records that will help you remember.

A "Last-Ditch" Attempt After Several Calls May Make the Sale

A good salesperson makes it a rule to call on big prospects regularly. He or she insists upon "staying with" the prospect because the potential sales are worth it. But even a persistent salesperson will occasionally decide to give up when he or she discovers some fact that destroys his or her confidence in the prospect. Before giving up, however, he or she will make one last attempt and will "sell dangerously." The force of such desperation will often break the bottleneck.

▪ IDEA IN ACTION

Ralph Foster, who sells business systems, had called once a month for four years on a large organization that used forms supplied by competitors. On these calls, Ralph was always able to see the purchasing agent, but he never succeeded in getting her to look at his product. The purchasing agent had promised him, however, that the next time the company needed to replenish certain forms, she would let Ralph know about it.

Through a friend Ralph learned that the prospect subsequently bought a large quantity of forms from a competitor. Ralph felt that there was no longer any use in calling on the prospect; the purchasing agent had not kept her word. But, being a good salesperson, Ralph decided to make his parting call a telling one.

Getting the interview was no trouble, for Ralph had been a welcome caller for years. But this time, when he approached the prospect, he said: "Ms. Adams, I promise you that I'll never step in here again if you'll look at our forms just once." The prospect looked, and Ralph left with a sizable order.

Colleagues Can Give You Ideas to Be Used in Callbacks

Contacting a fellow salesperson for help in solving a selling problem that was brought up in callback interviews is good practice. For example, a colleague who sells products to the same prospect for another division of your company may give you the very information you need to make a sale.

∎ IDEA IN ACTION

Glenda Faulke approached the president of a tool steel company to interest him in a new type of industrial grinding wheel. The president was satisfied with the grinding wheels he used. No order was received and further contact seemed pointless.

Glenda contacted the salesperson in her area who represented another division of the company. She learned from him that the prospect had another application for the same grinding wheel she had tried to sell. This different use for the same wheel in finishing certain grades of steel appealed to the president and Glenda made the sale.

Seek a Higher Authority After Repeated Calls

The person you contact first might balk at your repeated attempts to interest him or her in your proposition. By contacting someone higher up, you may be able to make a sale. But remember to maintain good relations with the first contact—he or she might be called in when a decision to buy is made.

■ IDEA IN ACTION

Bill Larson, a salesperson who specializes in filing equipment, failed to sell the manager of office services on his bid for a survey of the company's filing operations.

Bill then approached the vice president in charge of systems and was promptly assigned a company methods expert to assist him in the survey. Bill immediately contacted the manager of office services to inform him of this move and to build his goodwill. The manager smoothed the way to a multiple sale when he was called in to help make the purchasing decision.

Call Back After Changes in a Prospect's Organization

A reason for not buying will often disappear when a company undergoes a change in management, location, size, and so on. Here is how a salesperson's alertness to a change in management led to a sale.

■ IDEA IN ACTION

Donna Cooke had called on a large hospital for several years, trying repeatedly to sell them certain equipment that she knew would benefit the hospital. She had seen the administrator and every other person who might influence a purchase, but had not been able to make the sale. The hospital's lack of money and the reluctance of anyone to take the initiative were responsible for her failure.

Some time later, Donna noticed that the hospital had undergone a major change in board membership, which was soon followed by changes in administration. She immediately contacted the new administrator, who agreed to watch a demonstration. Donna made an important sale that justified her having "stayed with" the customer for several years.

CHAPTER FIVE

MAKING A GREAT PRESENTATION

*When your prospect lets you tell your story,
that's your big moment.*

It's astounding but true that 20% of this country's salespeople bring in 80% of the sales that are made. In other words, each top salesperson sells 16 times as much as an average salesperson does. Why? The answer lies in the way the top salespeople present their products and services to their prospects. They not only get interviews; they know how to use them to get orders.

Poor or average salespeople may see many prospects and spend a great deal of time explaining the benefits of what they sell, but they produce only a fraction of the sales that leading salespeople in their line achieve. This is because their presentations are mediocre or downright poor.

There is only one way to reach the top in selling: You must know how to give a great presentation. You can't be an effective closer until you have become a convincing presenter.

Without losing sight of the fact that selling is a continuous process—that every single step in the selling process is related to each of the other steps—this chapter covers the presentation without discussing closing techniques. Chapter Six covers closing techniques.

There are four basic steps involved in giving a great presentation:

1. **Preliminary preparation.** This includes gathering the facts about your product and service as well as your competition and deciding how to use the most telling ones.

2. **Outlining the talk.** In this step you blueprint your sales story.

3. **Putting it into words.** You work up each point of the outline, using *tested techniques* for achieving a surefire demonstration, making masterful use of all your selling tools, and handling price expertly. Also, make your words "sell."

4. **Learning how to give the sales story most effectively.** This means injecting your personality into selling. The know-how gives you complete and confident control of every selling interview.

WHAT IS A GREAT PRESENTATION?

Any explanation of a salable item or service by a salesperson could be called a sales presentation. *Your* objective, however, must be to develop a *great* presentation, one which will accomplish the following five tasks:

1. Hold the prospect's interest throughout.

2. Clearly and adequately explain, in a convincing manner, what is being sold and the benefits to be derived from it.

3. Establish definitely that the product or service being presented would satisfy one or more of the prospect's buying motives.

4. Overcome or answer to the satisfaction of the prospect all questions and objections to buying that he or she may have.

5. Make the prospect decide that he or she wants to buy.

IMPORTANT In each of these objectives, the emphasis is on the *prospect's* point of view—on how he or she stands to gain by making a purchase. The prospect is the final judge of the effectiveness of your presentation, so put yourself in this individual's shoes as you work it out.

REMEMBER A great presentation is one that satisfies your prospect's buying motives so convincingly and removes all buying obstacles so persuasively that he or she decides to place an order. The success of a sales interview thus depends to a large extent on how closely your presentation anticipates the prospects' motive(s) for buying. This, in turn, depends on how thoroughly you know your product or service, how much you have been able to learn about your prospect, and how well you fit the two together.

Components of a Great Presentation

A good presentation is a smooth and convincing sales talk that leads in a logical manner from the opening sentence to the close of the sale. It cannot be disjointed or confusing; it must be a well-forged unit.

Even the smoothest sales talk can be broken down into five definite steps. Each step must be accomplished before the presentation is complete:

1. Get the prospect's attention immediately after introducing yourself.
2. Arouse his or her interest by describing your product's benefits.
3. Stimulate his or her desire for these benefits.
4. Convince the prospect that the benefits described are true and that they can work for him or her.
5. Get the prospect to take action and sign the order.

These steps are meant to be taken in order, but in many cases two steps can be combined into one. The opening, or attention-getting stage, for example, might be accomplished by getting right into a discussion of significant benefits. Steps 1 and 2 would then be combined.

WARNING Although two or more steps in the presentation process can sometimes be combined, no step should ever be left out. Many otherwise skillful interviews have ended in failure because a single step has been omitted. Each step depends on the one before it, and skipping one undermines the effectiveness of the step that follows.

IMPORTANT Your presentation should be like a good golf swing: one continuous motion, not a jerky progression of steps. Each stage of the presentation has to lead smoothly into the next.

Determining the Length of a Presentation

A sales presentation should be as short as it can be and still be complete. The average salesperson spends only four hours a day in face-to-face selling, and it is easily demonstrated that this time has a definite dollar value (as discussed in Chapter One). Each minute of the interview should be regarded as selling time, and a real money-earning presentation wastes neither time nor words. It must, however, be *complete*. It must contain enough to accomplish every step of the sales process and do a convincing selling job. Brevity must never overshadow the purpose of the interview.

The actual length of a presentation in minutes will depend on what you sell, but it should normally be no more than 15 minutes and usually less. Some products can be effectively presented in a minute and a half, using in that time perhaps two hundred well-chosen words.

Remember: Some of the time consumed in an interview will be devoted to listening to what the prospect has to say, answering questions, or waiting out interruptions. When this time is added to an "overstuffed" presentation, the interview can stretch out to the point where a busy prospect starts looking at his or her watch, and then you're in trouble. The chapter also describes how a great presentation is built to show you how to combine clarity with brevity.

A Prepared Presentation Is a "Must"

Salespeople who are earning big money favor a carefully planned, word-for-word presentation. They depend on a memorized "script"; they do not extemporize. If they deviate at all from the memorized script, they do so to fit the needs of the moment. But they always get right back to the script and follow it exactly as they prepared it.

If you prepare your presentation as we instruct you to in this *Guide,* every word of it will count; it will be lean and hard—electric with power. It will be built from the prospect's point of view, it will be studded with supporting facts, and it will be so effectively dramatized that it will carry your prospect along to the final decision to buy. It will be a great presentation, one that you've memorized and can use in every interview.

Advantages of a prepared presentation

Here's what you gain by preparing your presentation and following it practically word for word:

- In the process of preparing you learn all about what you're selling and how it should be sold.

- You master your presentation completely so you won't forget or overlook vital points during the interview.

- You make the best use of your interview time. A planned and orderly presentation is the most efficient; it moves logically and convincingly from one point to the next.

- Choosing your words carefully means that they will have maximum impact and persuasiveness.

- Being well prepared gives you confidence.

- Prospects are impressed by salespeople who demonstrate that they have taken the trouble to prepare and organize their material.

- Mastering your presentation gives you flexibility. Flexibility means being able to switch your emphasis to appeal to a particular prospect's buying motives. Flexibility also means being able to meet unexpected problems and interruptions without losing control of the interview. If your presentation has been thoroughly prepared, it has anticipated what would otherwise be "unforeseen" problems. Unexpected changes of direction will thus be kept to a minimum.

- An organized presentation enables you to control the interview and guide the prospect smoothly toward the close.

"Canned" presentations can be great

Don't let anyone discourage you from using the presentation you have prepared because it is "canned." Some of the greatest presentations have been prepared ones. Let's examine some of the arguments that salespeople have used against prepared presentations and see how a compelling presentation undermines their objections.

- A "prepared" sales talk lacks spontaneity. Actors in long-running plays bring meaning to the lines they have said perhaps a thousand times. So do successful salespeople who stick to a memorized presentation that has proved its effectiveness many times over. Having found the best way to tell their story, they continue to use it in its best form. Even salespeople who are inclined to discredit standardized presentations admit that any kind of presentation, if given often enough, tends to settle into a fixed pattern.

- Interruptions can throw you off base when you're in the midst of a memorized sales talk. Any presentation can be disrupted by questions and interruptions, unless you know how to maintain control over the interview. A well-prepared presentation actually minimizes interruptions by making one point flow smoothly into the next.

- Since no two prospects are alike, a presentation must be flexible. Most salespeople call on prospects for whom their product or service is well suited, and whose wants and needs therefore tend to be more or less similar.

The best tribute to the effectiveness of the standardized presentation is its increasing use on a companywide basis. Your company may furnish you with such a presentation, recommending either that you use it verbatim or that you develop your own personalized version. This chapter is intended as a guide for the ambitious salesperson who lacks specific company help and who wishes to build a great sales talk. It is also intended for those who have the freedom to develop their own presentations, provided they use certain basic materials provided by the company.

Exceptional situations.

For some products and services, a memorized, standardized presentation may be impractical. For example, salespeople who deal in specialized products designed to meet individual customer needs must vary their selling talks from prospect to prospect. Nevertheless, they must go through the preliminary steps of studying their product, their competition, and their prospects' needs and buying motives. They must also go through the basic steps of selling, from getting attention to closing the sale. Although they do not have to write out a complete sales story, they must plan what they are going to say in each interview ahead of time.

> **SUGGESTION** Even if the use of a standardized presentation is not feasible in your situation, you will gain by standardizing the elements that are common to all of your interviews. You will thus reduce the time needed to prepare for each new interview, and you will arrive at the most effective way in which to present the most frequently covered points.

PRELIMINARY PREPARATION FOR DEVELOPING THE PRESENTATION

Know What You Have to Offer

The first thing to do in developing your presentation is to take inventory and determine exactly what you have to sell.

Chapter One described how exhaustive knowledge of your product or service is essential to success. Without complete knowledge of your product, you can't have a great presentation.

To be sure that you know your product thoroughly enough to begin planning your presentation, list every possible selling point. When this list is complete it will serve two purposes:

1. You will be able to choose the best and most effective points as a basis for your presentation.

2. The remaining features will provide additional support to be used during the interview when it is necessary to convince a stubborn prospect.

IMPORTANT The more you know about your product, the stronger your faith in its performance. The more faith, the more conviction you have in selling.

Tips on listing your selling points

You may feel that you already know all you have to about what you're selling, but remember: It's the salesperson who knows the *most* who reaches the top. To make sure you've listed every selling point, follow these tips:

- **Write down all the points you can think of.** Search your mind for every single feature that might be a selling point, including ones that you are aware of but aren't currently using in your presentation.

- **If you sell a tangible product, study it as if you had never seen it before.** If possible, take it apart. Try to get a look at it in action, where you can watch it and listen to it.

- **Ask other salespeople in your company** (choose *good* salespeople) what features they have the most success with.

- **Ask your customers for their opinions.** People who actually use a product can shed valuable light on its advantages and drawbacks.

- **Review carefully all company and product literature** for points that you may have forgotten or overlooked. In designing its products, your company tries to make them better than what its competitors are offering. It may also use market research to discover the features that customers are likely to want in such a product. Since they are in on the development of the product from the beginning, the engineers and sales promotion people have a thorough understanding of what the product can do. For this reason, the list of sales features that your company prepares is your best source of information for building a great presentation.

SUGGESTION In most cases, you will be able to expand the company list, based on your own knowledge of the product and its uses. Also, be sure the company list has not become outdated by changing conditions in the industry, by changes in the design of the product, or by changes in competitors' products.

List both product and company features

In your list, be sure to include not only the benefits that customers get from buying your product but also the ones they can expect from dealing with your company.

▪ IDEA IN ACTION

Rich Stewart sells an industrial humidifying unit. As the first step in developing his sales presentation, he draws up a list of sales features that he knows his product offers. His unit isn't the *best* on the market for every point on the list, but he puts down everything he can think of. Here is the list:

- Low initial cost
- Low installation cost
- Low maintenance cost
- Low operating cost
- Low depreciation rate
- Compact size
- Good appearance
- Quiet operation
- Low vibration
- More mobile unit than others
- Greater output range (from low to high, as needed) than others
- Extra safety features
- Unit rates preferred insurance premiums
- A wider range of models and sizes than competitors offer
- Quicker delivery date than competition can meet

Knowing that he represents a good company, Rich also lists these advantages of buying from his company:

- Superior reputation
- Local service office ensuring prompt, efficient, and low-cost servicing

- Favorable credit terms, discounts for prompt payments
- Unit covered by a more complete guarantee than others
- Similar units in operation in vicinity and throughout the country
- Salespeople who are local residents of good reputation
- Well-trained sales force that can make sound, on-the-spot recommendations

With a little work, Rich is able to add more product *and* company benefits to his list, and he ends up with a solid idea of just what he has to sell.

Turn Facts into Benefits

Your presentation must satisfy the prospect's buying motives (as discussed in Chapter Four). Buying motives are satisfied not by lists of impressive features, *but by the benefits that those features will give.* There is a clear distinction between the two. A person does not buy strength; he or she buys the durability that strength provides. Nor does a customer buy beauty, but rather the pleasure and pride that possession of a beautiful object entails. He or she does not buy speed, but will buy the time savings, the increased production, or the excitement that speed gives. Behind everything the prospect wants, there is an even more important underlying reason *why* he or she wants it.

> **NOTE** It is particularly important to emphasize benefits when economic conditions are uncertain and buyers are wary of making commitments. As you select the selling points from which to develop your presentation, visualize each point in terms of the benefits that it can bring.

∎ IDEA IN ACTION

Jack Anderson was hired to sell power tools to dealers. He made a list of all the sales features he could find for the line of tools, selected the best ones, and then built a presentation around these points. His sales manager listened to the presentation and said, "But what's in it for the dealer?"

A little surprised, Jack said, "I just told you: low cost, a complete line, a popular item . . ."

"Jack," replied the sales manager, "a list like that tells the dealer only what the product is. You've got to show *why* he or she should buy it and what benefits it will bring. Ask yourself 'So what?' on each point you cover, and then list the corresponding benefit to the dealer. You'll see a big difference."

Jack did as he was advised and soon realized that the second list was what the dealers really wanted to hear. Here is what the two lists looked like:

Advantages	*"So What?"*
Popular item	Big turnover, higher sales, *more profit*
Low cost	Greater customer acceptance, less money tied up in stock
Complete line	Could service a greater percentage of customers, be a one-stop source
Manufactured locally	No delivery problems, quick service and repair
Well advertised	Big demand, customer acceptance

Jack had immediate success from the new presentation that he developed from the "So what?" list.

TIP The best way to convey to a prospect the benefits he or she will gain by buying your product is to use a visual demonstration. A visual demonstration tells your prospect more than you can explain in twice the time, and usually much more clearly. This is because seeing is the most important of the five senses for comprehension. (A detailed guide to a successful demonstration is provided later in this chapter.)

Study Your Competition

After you have compiled a list of what you can offer, take a good look at your competition. Knowledge of competing products enables you to evaluate your list of selling features. You want to emphasize those benefits that are better than competitors can offer, or exclusive with your line. Studying competitors enables you to find out what those benefits are.

> **NOTE** Although your presentation should emphasize the superior or exclusive features of your product or service, it must not omit other important advantages just because they are shared by competitors. Your two biggest competitors, for instance, might offer low operating costs, just as you can. Don't neglect this feature in your presentation. It is still an important point, even though it is not unique.

You must be aware of all local factors that make competitive conditions in your area different from those elsewhere. This will have a direct bearing on the sales features to be emphasized and how you prepare to meet objections.

□ EXAMPLE

You are working for a national company, selling ferrous castings in an area where there are several local foundries. You face stiffer price and delivery competition than you would in other areas. So you select the sales features that emphasize quality and justify the price differential. You use your testimonials of satisfied customers who are located at some distance from your plant to underscore dependable delivery.

How to Select the Selling Points for Your Presentation

You must build your talk around the *best* selling points on your list. To select the most telling sales features, put yourself in the prospect's place. Look carefully at every point and ask, "Is this what would satisfy my buying motives if I were the prospect? Is this something I would especially look for in this type of product or service? Would this feature make my offer look any better than, or different from, other propositions the prospect might hear?" Remember that the buyer is the final judge and that he or she will buy only what promises to meet his or her particular needs.

Naturally the features that help most to make your product or service stand out are its *exclusive* features. Whatever they are, major or minor, you should emphasize features that competitors can't offer. Even a small point carries weight when it has distinctive, only-one-in-its-field authority.

TIP The better you know your competition, the better you can select and utilize the features that are yours alone.

Obviously, you can't cover every point on your list in the course of a normal sales interview. Your presentation would take too much time. The points that are not included in your prepared presentation are there to bolster your confidence and serve as reserve ammunition when the going gets rough.

THE OUTLINE IS THE BLUEPRINT

Make an Outline

The best way to organize your material into a logical, orderly, and convincing presentation is first to make an outline. Outlining organizes your thoughts and enables you to make the best use of the facts, benefits, and sales features that you want to present to your prospect. Through an outline you can see how all your material is going to fall into place. You thus get a clear idea of what the actual presentation will be like.

Whether the outline is simple or detailed will depend on what you sell and on your personal preference. For most salespeople, the work that goes into a detailed outline is fully compensated by the grasp it gives them of what they must say and how they will say it. A detailed outline also simplifies the actual writing process.

SUGGESTION Make your outline as complete as you feel it should be to help you develop the presentation. Two adaptable forms are shown in this section: a written form and a chart form.

The Basic Pattern for an Outline

These steps, which form a natural outline for almost any sale, provide a framework within which to develop your own presentation:

1. *Introduce* yourself.

2. Get the prospect's *attention* and keep it.

3. Get the prospect *interested* in your product.

4. Make the prospect *desire* your product.

5. *Convince* him or her with proof.

6. Get him or her to take *action* (close the sale).

By arranging the elements of your own sales story under the appropriate heading, you will see your outline fall easily into place.

> **WARNING** Take pains to make each step connect smoothly with the next. This will be of particular importance when you use the outline to put your presentation into words.
>
> **NOTE** There are three exceptions to this established selling sequence:

1. **Steps may be combined.** For example, once you have the prospect's attention, you usually get him or her interested by describing benefits. If you can claim outstanding benefits, you can use this to capture attention at the start. You would then be combining the *attention* step and the *interest* step. Most sales, however, are made by leading the prospect from one step to the next.

2. **Convincing is not always handled as a separate stage.** Some salespeople sprinkle facts, figures, testimonials, and other 'convincers' throughout their presentation, making it a continuing process.

3. **The sale should always be closed at the earliest opportunity.** Don't wait until the end of your presentation to sew up the order if the prospect is ready earlier. Trial closings should be placed at intervals in your presentation to 'feel out' the prospect's buying readiness (see Chapter Six for closing techniques).

Sample Outline for Selling a Product: Written Form

Exhibit 5.1 is an outline of a presentation to sell a newly developed envelope, specially designed to entice people to open it and read its contents. The new envelope for third-class mailers, called the Sim-Pull and manufactured by the Tension Envelope Corporation, features a tucked-in flap at the end which comes open when the tab that protrudes is pulled, thus providing easy access to the material inside the envelope. The company has supplied its salespeople with a list of sales features and has advised them that there will be trade ads and mailings to familiarize the public with the Sim-Pull. Some orders have already been received.

EXHIBIT 5.1

Sample Written Outline

- **Attention**
  - Want a new and sure way to get your third-class mailings read?
  - The Sim-Pull envelope (patent pending), exclusive with us, will do it [show how].

- **Interest**
  - Different—attracts attention
  - Intriguing tab, gets more *openings*, more *returns*
  - Quick and easy to open—message put to work sooner
  - Doesn't rob space from advertising or merchandising message
  - Economical—only a few cents more per thousand
  - Foolproof on mechanical insertion
  - Company service, reputation for quality

- **Desire**
  - [Expand on benefits and personalize them]

- **Conviction**
  - Acceptance has been immediate, orders coming in [give facts, use testimonials and other evidence]

- **Close**
  - Be the first in your industry, get maximum effect
  - [Briefly summarize benefits]
  - All this at only [quote price]
  - How many will you need for your next mailing?

Sample Outline for Sale Entailing a Survey: Chart Form

You can adapt the chart form shown in Exhibit 5.2 in preparing your outline. The outline presented was drawn up by the Carrier Corporation for a one-call sale of a home air-conditioning system. Words are kept to a minimum, yet the outline is sufficiently detailed to provide for each step in a sale that includes selling the idea of a survey, making the survey, and closing the sale.

Additional Points to Include in a Complete Outline

If you are making your outline a detailed one, you can sketch in the following elements to show where they will appear in the final presentation:

Repeat the Important Points

As you prepare your outline, remember that the primary benefits should be brought to the prospect's attention more than once during the presentation. Repetition strengthens the effect of your statements and gives emphasis to them. A person may understand a statement the first time it is made, but he or she seldom absorbs its full impact until it is heard more than once.

> **CAUTION** Try to rephrase the points that are repeated so that you won't sound monotonous. Avoid mentioning any one feature too often.

Provide for the demonstration when making your outline

Working up the outline for your presentation will help you decide where the demonstration belongs. If your demonstration is so complete that it will comprise most of the interview, then you will usually begin it without much delay. If you have only one or two demonstrable features, they will be shown at the appropriate time during the interview.

EXHIBIT 5.2

Sample Outline of Presentation in Chart Form

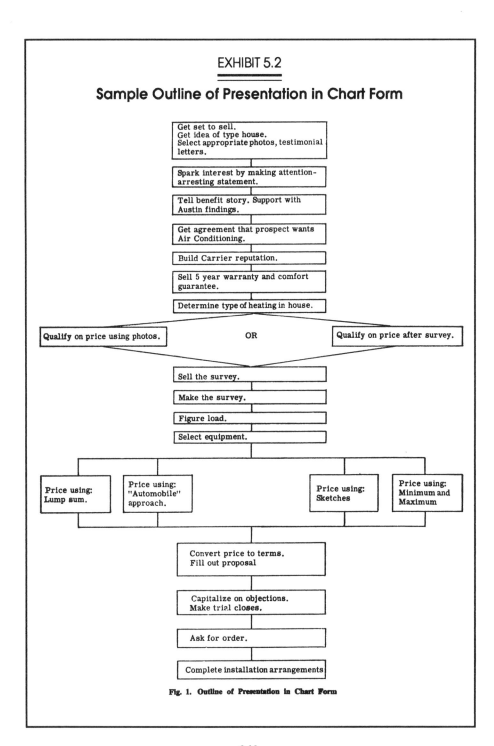

Get set to sell.
Get idea of type house.
Select appropriate photos, testimonial letters.

Spark interest by making attention-arresting statement.

Tell benefit story. Support with Austin findings.

Get agreement that prospect wants Air Conditioning.

Build Carrier reputation.

Sell 5 year warranty and comfort guarantee.

Determine type of heating in house.

Qualify on price using photos.   OR   Qualify on price after survey.

Sell the survey.

Make the survey.

Figure load.

Select equipment.

Price using: Lump sum.   Price using: "Automobile" approach.   Price using: Sketches   Price using: Minimum and Maximum

Convert price to terms.
Fill out proposal

Capitalize on objections.
Make trial closes.

Ask for order.

Complete installation arrangements

Fig. 1. Outline of Presentation in Chart Form

248

If the demonstration is a lengthy or involved one, fit it into the outline in steps. Then you can note along with each step the comments or benefits that accompany it. (The next section of this chapter offers detailed guidelines on preparing your demonstration.)

Plan in Your Outline to Use Sales Tools

How will you use the sales tools supplied by your company to help you make your presentation? These tools include samples, demonstrators or working models, videos, slides, photographs, presentation manuals, sales kits, catalogs or catalog pages, charts and graphs, descriptive literature, blow-ups of ads, and copies of publicity stories or testimonials. You can also develop certain sales tools on your own, to supplement or take the place of company material.

Notice that these tools all have the function of engaging the prospect's eyes: They are *visual* aids. (Guidance for getting the best results from each of these visual aids is provided later in this chapter, an example of a sales presentation built around the use of photos.)

Cover price when making your outline

Price is an important factor in any sale. It should be covered in your presentation and handled with the same confident, positive attitude that marks your presentation as a whole. If you avoid talking about price, you invite the prospect to wonder whether you're afraid to mention it because it is too high. (How to time the price quotation, how to quote with confidence, and how to minimize a price are discussed in detail later in this chapter.)

Provide for answering questions and objections as you go

A prospect's unanswered questions and objections are obstacles that can block the sale. Anticipate them and build the answers into your presentation. This eliminates problems before the prospect can bring them up and deprives him or her of reasons for not buying.

Here's how to get the right responses to questions and objections worked into your outline:

1. **Make a list.** List all the reasons you can think of why a prospect—any prospect—might decide against placing an order. Think of every question that might be asked about what you sell.

2. **Write down the means you have to overcome each objection.** Opposite each possible question, write out the complete answer or answers. See Chapter Seven on Making Objections Work *for* You.)

3. **Select from the list the most important points and the ones you are most likely to encounter.**

4. **As you outline your presentation, work in the answers to all the important questions and objections you have selected.** Put each answer or positive supporting fact into the appropriate section in the outline.

Include trial closings

In a complete outline you can work in trial closings and give your presentation closing strength. In every interview you should try for the order as soon as possible, and as often after that as necessary. Trial closings should fit naturally into your planned presentation, usually after strong points and at the end of your demonstration. You must also be prepared to insert trial closings during your "live performance" whenever they are feasible. (See Chapter Six for closing techniques.)

□ EXAMPLE

Evans Corporation supplies its salespeople with a presentation for the Evans Instant Pager, a paging service for small businesses. Built around a demonstration, the presentation is a short one that is loaded with selling power. One reason is that after each main point, a trial closing is attempted. If no affirmative response is forthcoming, the salesperson goes on with further demonstration and selling.

This sample sales presentation is scripted at the end of this chapter. In this sales story the first trial closing comes after the salesperson has sold the *quality* of the pager and the service; the second, after he or she has convinced the prospect of *performance;* the third, after he or she has developed the theme of *dependability.* The final close is made on the point of *value.*

GUIDES FOR A SURE-FIRE DEMONSTRATION

Seven-Point Guide to a Successful Demonstration

The demonstration is the part of your presentation that makes use of the product, a part of the product, or some other tangible item to show a benefit to be gained by buying the product. The demonstration may also show how the product works. The prospect's needs are the keynote to the demonstration. How the product fits those needs is the meat of the demonstration.

Each demonstration must be made to fit the particular product. No demonstration can be made successfully without careful planning and rehearsal.

Here are your seven guidelines to follow when planning the demonstration:

1. **Tell what you are going to show.** Before you start the demonstration, tell your prospect what you are going to show him or her. In this way you build interest and at the same time give the prospect clues as to what to look for.

2. **Start the demonstration at the most advantageous time.** If your demonstration is complicated, you will first want to create enough interest to warrant the time spent on it. If, on the other hand, you're relying on the demonstration to *create* interest, you should begin it as soon as possible.

   Many salespeople feel that the more time they spend building up to the demonstration, the more time the prospect has to say "No," and so they begin demonstrating almost immediately. Their introductory statement may be extremely brief, perhaps something like, "Mr. Smith, I'd like to show you something that will help you in your business."

NOTE This technique is especially applicable if you are withholding mention of your product or company name at first, to avoid premature sales resistance. The prospect in such a situation may say "What are you trying to sell?" You can then answer, "Let me show you," and begin your demonstration.

3. **Guard against being too technical.** An involved demonstration can be as confusing as a wordy explanation. Your purpose is to show *what* the product can do for the prospect, and details on *how* may be unnecessary.

4. **Get the prospect into the act.** Try to get the prospect to take an active part in the demonstration. Automobile salespeople always include a test drive by the prospect, because they know that the car will sell itself if the potential buyer has a chance to drive it.

    Sometimes you can get the prospect in on the act by asking questions that require him or her to observe what is happening. For example, "Can you see, Ms. Johnson, what will happen when the liquid level reaches that float?"

You can do even better if you can also bring into the act someone who is important to the prospect. Thus, if a prospect's child is to benefit by the purchase, bring in the child; if employees are to use the product, ask one of them to participate in the demonstration. If it's simplicity of operation that you want to emphasize, get someone into the act whose performance will prove that the product is easy to use.

■ IDEA IN ACTION

The demonstration of a piece of office equipment was to be made to a superintendent of schools. The salesperson prepared his demonstration in advance, paying particular attention to the customer's needs and requirements.

First, he arranged for a field demonstration at a nearby school district where similar equipment was being used. This choice had two advantages: (1) It eliminated the superintendent's objection to visiting the company's headquarters, which would have taken her away from her office for too long a time, and (2) the prospect was able to see the machine operating in a familiar setting.

Second, the salesperson arranged for the demonstration to be conducted by a 13-year-old student at the school. This idea also had two advantages: (1) It demonstrated the simplicity of the machine, which was of prime importance to the school district, and (2) it brought the prospect as well as someone of importance to her—a student—into the act. The superintendent herself ran half the demonstration.

5. **Ask questions.** As the demonstration proceeds, ask questions to be sure that the prospect understands, and to encourage thinking about how the product fits in with his or her needs. As you plan your demonstration, allow time for questions between steps.

6. **Keep it short.** The demonstration should not be a complete one *if it will take too long.* For example, a salesperson selling a laptop computer limited his demonstration to 8 minutes—one for each pound the machine weighed. He gave a convincing rundown of what the machine could do, but purposely left out some details of how it was done. If the prospect showed sufficient interest, the salesperson went into greater detail *after* the demonstration. Here the demonstration served its true purpose: It illustrated customer benefits.

7. **Make your demonstration dramatic.** A demonstration is an act, and it should be a dramatic one. Even a common everyday product can be dramatized. What can be more prosaic, for example, than a loaf of bread? Yet even this product can be dramatized—as shown by the bakery route salesperson who tells her customer that she is going to cut the loaf right down the middle to prove that its texture is smooth and even. She asks the customer to watch her do this, and to get the full dramatic value out of the demonstration she doesn't begin until she has asked, "Are you ready?"

Dramatizing a demonstration helps in these ways:

▪ It makes more of an impression on the prospect, and he or she is likely to remember the points longer.

▪ It adds importance to your product or service.

▪ It helps distinguish your product or service (and your presentation) from others the prospect will be exposed to.

- It helps to create and sustain interest at a high level.

   WARNING Don't make the dramatic element in your presentation so intriguing that the prospect forgets what you are trying to prove by it. To use the example of the loaf of bread one more time, it would be a mistake to brandish a large, shiny, and obviously very sharp knife when cutting into the bread. You're there to sell the *bread*, not the knife!

The Best Demonstration Is an In-Use Demonstration

You gain two great advantages by arranging to demonstrate your product in a satisfied user's office or plant:

1.   The prospect sees the product in true operational surroundings, which makes it easier to visualize what a similar installation or operation at his or her own place of business would involve. This kind of a demonstration also gives the prospect more confidence in you; it shows that you have faith in your product.

2.   Your satisfied customer will often give you the benefit of an on-the-spot testimonial.

MASTERFUL USE OF SALES TOOLS IN A PRESENTATION

Tips for Using Samples

Whether you carry a complete sample of the product you sell or a part of the product (swatches, for example), allowing the prospect to see the sample whets his or her appetite for the product. It also enables you to be far more convincing about the product benefits than if you simply talk about them.

   Here are some tips on how to get the best results from displaying the samples in your presentation:

- If you have a choice of samples, select only those that are suited to your prospect's needs.

- Don't show too many.
- Use perfect samples that are clean and in good condition.
- Don't let the prospect play around with a sample if it will distract him or her from what you are saying.
- Attach to each sample any information (such as style number, cost, color variations, etc.) that will help the buyer select and identify his or her choice.
- Follow up promptly any buyer with whom you have left a sample.

Tips for Using Working Models

A demonstrator or working model is a vivid way to explain the operation of your product. Such a device is not always available to salespeople as a sample. If it *is* available, use it but keep in mind the seven tips to a successful demonstration:

1. Tell the prospect what you are going to show him or her.
2. Start the demonstration at the most advantageous time.
3. Guard against being too technical.
4. Get the prospect into the act.
5. Ask questions as you go.
6. Keep your demonstration short.
7. Make it dramatic if you can.

Tips for Using Photographic Sales Aids

Videos, slides, and photographs are being used more and more as sales aids. Industrial photography and the making of industrial films is big business now, and your company may make some or all of these aids available to you.

Videos are especially valuable when it comes to describing complicated subjects. You must plan your showings with care, however, to make sure that all the people who should see the video are able to be present.

These tips will help you make the most of videos and slides in your presentation:

- **Be sure that the equipment is in perfect working order before you start.** Nothing will be more annoying to your prospects than waiting around while you try to fix something.

- **Point out to your prospects beforehand what to look for.** If the film is old and includes an outdated process or product, tell them so and explain why the basic information is still valid.

- **Act as though you are showing the video for the first time,** no matter how often you have seen it.

- **Summarize at the end and ask for questions.**

Photographs amplify your words. As you speak, the prospect sees, and your message makes more of an impact. Observe these points on the use of photographs:

- **Point out or tell the prospect what to look for.**

- **Make sure your photographs are clear.** They don't necessarily have to be dry-mounted, professional-looking glossies. Sometimes a snapshot can achieve just as much. (Tips on taking your own photos are provided in the section "You Can Devise Your Own Sales Tools.")

Tips for Using a Presentation Manual

Presentation manuals come in a variety of forms, from small booklets to large easel set-ups. They are usually intended as a step-by-step guide for the presentation. By going through the manual page by page with the prospect, you can be sure of a thorough, orderly, and time-saving coverage of the important sales points. At the same time you are keeping the prospect's eyes busy, letting him or her see each point as you explain it.

To get the most benefit from a presentation manual, observe these tips:

- **Practice using the manual.** That way you don't stumble through the presentation.

- **Maintain control of the manual and the interview.** Don't let the prospect leaf through the manual. Cover each point in turn; don't let him or her get ahead of you.

- **Check to make sure the prospect understands one point before you proceed to the next.**

- **Don't read the words printed in the manual;** tell your prospect about the product or service in your own words.

- **Make every effort to personalize the presentation.** Look for opportunities to point out how what is illustrated in the manual can be applied or related to the prospect's business.

Tips for Using Sales Kits

Perhaps your company is one of the many that have made up sales kits for their salespeople. These kits contain everything you need—samples, literature, visual aids, sometimes even the printed text—for a complete presentation. They are organized so that the sale can follow an orderly pattern. Sales kits are usually developed by the sales department or outside consultants, and if they are utilized properly, they can ensure a thorough and convincing presentation.

These tips will help you get the most from a sales kit:

- **A kit is designed to do a certain job in a certain way.** Don't defeat the purpose by using it halfheartedly.

- **Practice using it.** Some kits, for example, require removing and replacing samples or booklets that are kept in special pockets. You should be able to accomplish all such maneuvers without a hitch.

- **Keep the kit looking attractive.** Clean up samples, replace worn or creased literature, and replenish give-away supplies frequently.

Tips for Using a Catalog in Your Presentation

Almost all product salespeople have catalogs or catalog pages that can serve as visual aids during the presentation. Catalogs have pictures, charts, and other eye-catching items that can supplement your spoken sales talk. A catalog also indicates the range and completeness of your line. It acts as a "silent salesperson" in your absence; the prospect can refer to it later for additional information about your product.

If your catalog is issued in loose-leaf form, a page or two can make an excellent visual reference point for a presentation. These pages can easily be removed and left with the prospect. You can gradually build up his or her supply of catalog sheets by leaving different pages on subsequent calls. Or you may be able to capitalize on something the prospect likes in your catalog by leaving a copy of that particular page for him or her to peruse.

Here are a few pointers that will help you get the maximum sales value from your catalog:

- Know the catalog well. If you fumble when looking for something in it, the prospect will not think of it as a quick reference source.

- Bring out the catalog only after you have acquainted the prospect with the product so that he or she knows what to look for.

- Emphasize the special features of your catalog—a better than average index, more engineering information, more up-to-date material. Make the catalog appear outstanding to the prospect, so that it won't be buried on a shelf or in a drawer.

- Hand the catalog to an interested prospect and go over it with him or her.

- Keep your own copy of the catalog and those you give to customers as up to date as possible.

Avoid these mistakes in catalog usage:

- Don't base your entire presentation on the catalog. Use it instead as a supplement and as a reference source for answers to questions that come up during the interview.

- Don't try to show too much of the catalog at one sitting.

- Don't hand out catalogs indiscriminately. They are often expensive items and should be distributed only where they will do some good.

Tips on Showing Facts Through Charts and Graphs

Charts and graphs of performance data, market research findings, survey results, and so on, bring statistical information to life. One good chart can reveal more in a few seconds than can pages of figures and analyses.

Even the best charts and graphs need a little help from the salesperson. Here are some suggestions:

- When you present a chart or graph, tell briefly what it shows or make some other explanatory comment.

- Rehearse your use of graphic illustrations until you can handle even large ones without awkwardness, and can place them where the prospect can easily see them.

- Time the effect in advance; it will take a person longer to absorb one kind of graphic information than another.

Tips for Using Descriptive Literature and Similar Aids

Most companies provide supplementary visual material, such as descriptive literature, new product bulletins, blowups of company ads, or reprints of publicity stories. Any of these items can come in handy during a presentation, especially during second and subsequent interviews.

For instance, you can exhibit advertisements to dealers to show how your company helps them by creating a market for the product. You can use a colorful brochure describing a new product as the basis for a presentation aimed at prospects you haven't been able to sell. You can use publicity stories as proof that, although your product may be a new one, it has already proved its usefulness.

Just how you utilize this kind of material will depend on how many other visual aids you have and where in your presentation visual support is needed.

Tips for Using Testimonials

Testimonials furnished to salespeople by their sales managers take the form of letters from satisfied customers, case histories, lists of names of prominent users, photographs of the product in use, and so on.

Such testimonials are invaluable wherever proof of quality or service will help the sale. They erase doubts in the prospect's mind, provide moral support, and justify his or her decision to buy. This reassurance is especially important if your service or product is not wellknown or is new to the prospect. If your dealings with prospects require the disclosure of personal information, testimonials help overcome any reluctance they may feel about taking a stranger into their confidence.

The following tips should be observed:

- Be sure that the testimonial comes from someone whose opinion the prospect will value.

- Show testimonials from users whose business and circumstances match as closely as possible those of the prospect. Local ones are best.

- Give the prospect time to read the testimonial at his or her own speed to get the maximum effect.

  CAUTION There are two inherent dangers in the use of testimonials that are easy to fall into and which you must avoid: (1) You can easily antagonize the prospect if you are not careful to present the testimonial as supporting evidence and not as superior judgment, and (2) you can belittle the prospect unless you make it clear that you consider his or her case an individual one and not just like that of the person whose testimony is cited.

You Can Devise Your Own Sales Tools

Some of the selling aids that you can develop on your own are

- Written proposals
- Photographs that show previous successful installations or help in other ways to illustrate your points
- Testimonials from your own customers
- Copies of the latest product change information or other technical updates
- News clippings

These sales tools are discussed in the following paragraphs.

Use written proposals to build interest in a first interview

A prospect will be more inclined to listen to a salesperson who has obviously spent a lot of time preparing for the call. The more concrete the evidence of this preparation, the better the chances of gaining an interested listener.

One way to show your preparedness is to have in your hand a written proposal, custom built to apply your product to the prospect's problems or needs. Such a written proposal can be used profitably, in some instances, the first time you call on a prospect. It is particularly helpful in cases where a double-barreled selling job is required: first, selling the prospect on the idea of letting you gather specific facts about his or her situation, and second, selling your product or service after the facts have been gathered.

■ IDEA IN ACTION

Henrietta Lowell, a salesperson for the ABC Regulator Company, has learned that a large office building in her territory plans to overhaul its heating system and add air conditioning.

Using a photograph of the building as a cover, she assembles a booklet showing the advantages of centralized temperature control. In it she places several pages designed especially for this particular building, referring to it by name. She combines these custom-built pages with selected standard pages that fit this particular application. She also includes a list of other large buildings that are already using the type of control system she is recommending. She adds photographs and sketches that show probable control locations. The finished booklet is a professional-looking document with a clear plastic cover.

Henrietta practices using the proposal until she knows its contents thoroughly and can give a good presentation based on it. Then she calls on the prospect with the booklet and the descriptive literature on the controls it recommends. Impressed with her preparation, the prospect listens attentively to her page-by-page presentation.

In any line of selling that entails a fact-finding survey to establish the customer's needs, a written proposal is usually required.

The proposal is a tool by which the salesperson can present his or her recommendations and make a sale. It provides an opportunity to present information designed exclusively for the prospect—information that will naturally be of great interest to him or her. It enables the salesperson to sit down with this individual and give him or her a thorough idea of what the proposal will accomplish.

☐ EXAMPLES

- Industrial salespeople must often survey the customer's operations, plant, and problems before they can determine what their product will do for the customer. They follow up the survey with a written proposal and then sell from this proposal.

- A salesperson who sells duplicating equipment must study the prospect's operations before he or she can recommend equipment that will benefit the prospect.

- Someone who sells a transportation service must make a study of the prospect's shipping practices.

- A life insurance salesperson must secure facts about an applicant's birth, family, current coverage, and insurance needs before he or she can make recommendations for insurance coverage.

Since each proposal is tailor-made to fit a particular prospect's needs, the written proposal requires creative thinking. Both the contents and the appearance of the proposal should reflect the effort the salesperson has put into the survey.

What the proposal should include. Bear in mind that the proposal is based on the study you have made of the prospect's problems. Since it is tailored to the individual, there is no set format. However, an example will suffice to show the nature of the contents. A proposal worked up by someone who sells duplicating equipment would cover the following items:

- A *transmittal letter* showing that the report submitted is based upon a recent study of the prospect's operations and that it is designed to meet the prospect's objectives. (Exhibit 5.3 shows a sample.)

EXHIBIT 5.3

Sample Transmittal Letter

The ABC Company
120 Broadway
New York, NY

(Date)

Dear _____ (prospect's name):

This report is the result of our recent study of one phase of your paperwork procedures. The facts concerning your present method have been carefully gathered and analyzed; a proposed new method, designed to meet the objectives you have specified, is presented in detail. For clarity in presentation, our complete report is divided into four sections:

- Objectives
- A comparison of present and proposed procedures
- Summary of advantages
- Equipment recommendations

Based upon our extensive experience in business paperwork procedures, we believe the recommended method and equipment will accomplish or exceed the objectives outlined here.

We would like to express our wholehearted gratitude to Mr. John Smith, Chief of your Special Services Section, for the splendid cooperation extended to us during our recent survey.

We hope you will find this report both interesting and rewarding, just as we did when preparing it for you.

Very truly yours,

(signature of salesperson)

XYZ CORPORATION

- The *objectives* that have been set up to meet the prospect's needs.

- The *prospect's present method* of performing the work.

- The *recommendations* for accomplishing the objectives.

- A *summary* of proven benefits, each of which is presented as dramatically as possible.

Physical appearance of the proposal. The proposal should reflect the quality of the effort that went into the survey. A carelessly prepared report will hurt the possibilities of a sale; a professionally prepared report will augment the salesperson's prestige and help make the sale.

The following ideas will enhance the appearance of the proposal:

Include a title page which shows that the proposal has been prepared especially for the prospect. Exhibit 5.4 shows an example.

EXHIBIT 5.4
===

Sample Proposal Title Page

A Proposal

Prepared for

[NAME OF THE PROSPECT]

By

[NAME OF THE COMPANY MAKING]

PROPOSAL

Presented by

[NAME OF THE SALESPERSON]

Use illustrations of the product or equipment which is recommended in the proposal, and any other related pictures, diagrams, and charts.

Be generous in your use of space. Devote a separate page to each aspect of the proposal. For example, place all of the objectives on one page, spreading them out so that each is given importance.

Allow plenty of white space in the typewritten portions. Allow for adequate margins at the top, bottom, and sides; spacing between paragraphs and topics; and arrangement of tabular matter, such as costs of proposed operation, cost comparisons, and the like.

Consider eye appeal in setting up various portions of the report. For example, a summary of advantages can be staggered on the page; the recommendations can be placed in boxes, and so on.

Photographs can be a useful sales tool

Even if you are an amateur, you can make profitable use of a camera in your selling work. Prospects are often more convinced by a snapshot than by a glossy professional job, just because it is more believable. Similarly, a picture of a nearby plant, office, or home situation means more to the average Seattle prospect, for example, than does one taken elsewhere. A picture of places or people that your prospect knows personally has the greatest convincing power of all. For these reasons it pays to be your own photographer.

■ IDEA IN ACTION

Frank Casale sells for a company that specializes in home roofing and siding. Before he calls on a prospect, he takes a picture of the prospect's house with his camera.

When he makes his call, he begins by handing the prospect a picture taken with the same camera, showing a beautifully reconditioned home. Quite often it's a home in the prospect's neighborhood. As soon as the prospect acknowledges the attractive appearance of the house in the photograph, Frank hands him the picture of his own home. A surprising number of prospects admit that their house looks very poor by comparison. Frank then finds it easy to interest them in making improvements.

Here are some other ways in which you can use a camera as a sales tool:

- To show previous installations

- To illustrate successive or key stages in the development of your product

- To show "before" and "after" situations

- To illustrate what could happen without your product or service

- To facilitate discussion in one place of areas or operations that would otherwise require a walking tour of the plant

- To indicate trouble spots or proposed installation locations when submitting a written proposal

Because the use of a camera requires imagination to make it a versatile sales tool, more is said about it in "Ideas for Creative Selling" (in Chapter Three).

Ask your customers for testimonials

You can easily build up your own kit of testimonials by asking your best customers to give you a written letter expressing appreciation of your product. Or you can ask permission to quote your customer verbally.

Testimonials from your own customers are often more convincing than are those you get from your company because they have a personal touch and local flavor. They carry the names of people whom your prospects are likely to know and respect. They are also personal endorsements of your abilities and help you gain your prospects' confidence.

You use your own testimonials in much the same way that you do your company's. Just make sure you avoid antagonizing or belittling your prospect.

> **CAUTION** If you quote your customer verbally, don't exaggerate or misquote to make the recommendation sound more convincing. Your prospect may be better informed than you realize. Furthermore, what you say may get back to your customer, in which case it could undermine your relationship.

> **SUGGESTION** If your product can be seen in action, try to get a photograph of an installation to back up a testimonial.

Introduce new evidence with published reports or surveys

A copy of a test result or laboratory report can be a very convincing sales tool. It is especially useful in incorporating the latest, up-to-the-minute information into your presentation. You gain the double advantage of credibility and timeliness.

Keep your eyes open for material that will lend itself to this treatment. Sometimes excerpts from company bulletins or engineering announcements can also serve a purpose.

> **NOTE** Photocopying material can also serve the purpose of reducing information into more compact form. Parts of testimonial letters, for instance, can be reproduced and gathered onto one page. Significant sections of documents or articles can be extracted and reproduced.

Clippings from newspapers and trade publications update your presentation

News clippings are sales tools that you can easily add to your presentation. Items of interest might include product news, company expansion or merger announcements, personnel changes, performance figures, survey results, and so on.

Clippings can help at any stage of your sales talk. When taken from current issues, they make your presentation timely and vital. They show prospects that you stay abreast of changes and improvements in your business. Result: Prospects have confidence in what you say and they regard you as a source of information.

HOW TO HANDLE PRICE IN A PRESENTATION

Value Must Justify Price

Your job is to convince your prospects of the true value of your product or service. People will buy the most expensive items if they are convinced that they're getting their money's worth. If you sell a quality product that is priced higher than that of the competition, take every opportunity to describe its features in a way that justifies the high price. Sell the difference that makes your product worth the added cost.

When to Bring in Price

There is no hard-and-fast rule about when to quote price in an interview. Most salespeople feel that it is best to mention price *after* they have clearly demonstrated the value of the product or service. There are many, however, who make a point of mentioning the price several times during their presentation.

Salespeople whose products or services carry a hefty price tag often prefer to make this clear early in the game rather than risk shocking their prospect at the end. Having stated the price and conceded that the amount seems large, they proceed to show that the benefits make it worth every dollar. In cases where low price is a strong selling factor, salespeople frequently bring it into play early, along with the other sales features.

The timing, therefore, is up to you. Plan to quote price when you think the time will be right. But *plan it*—don't try to wing it.

How to Put Off the Impatient Prospect

There will always be prospects who ask about price before you're fully ready to tell them. In this situation you should postpone quoting, if you can do so without giving the impression that you're stalling. Here are sample phrases used by salespeople to avoid discussing price prematurely:

"I'll be happy to tell you the price in a moment. May I wait until then?"

"The price will depend on quantity, the style you choose, and so on. It might be better if I tell you first about one or two more features."

"You'll like the price, so let me save it for last. Meanwhile, I'd like to show you what else this system can do for you."

When a prospect will not be put off, tell him or her the price, then pick up where you left off and begin selling again. Don't get involved in a full-scale price discussion until you've told your complete sales story.

Quote Price with Confidence

Regardless of when in the interview you inform the prospect of the price, quote what you feel is the best price and quote it with assurance. You must believe that it is a fair price for which your customers receive full value, and the prospect must sense this confidence. Unless you are satisfied that your price is fair and fully justifiable, you will lack the confidence to make that price stick.

If you have any doubts about why your product or service is priced as it is, get rid of them by finding out all the reasons. Remember that your company is entitled to a profit. If you reduce your price, the prospect naturally assumes that is was too high in the first place. So quote your best price and stick to it.

> **CAUTION** If yours is not a fixed-price item, or if pricing is complex and fast changing, be fully prepared to figure and quote the price without hesitation. Readiness to state the price might be essential to maintaining the momentum of a promising interview.

Techniques for Minimizing Price

Several techniques can be used in quoting price to make the amount more appealing to a prospect:

- Use minimizing words such as "only" ("It costs only $28.00"), "low" ("The price is a low $28.00"), "mere" ("It will cost you a mere $28.00"), and so on. Such phrases suggest that the price is very reasonable.
- Tie the price in with a brief summary of benefits, or a statement suggesting substantial value for the money. Here are some examples:
  - "The price for all this economy, versatility, speed of operation, long life, and attractive appearance is only $43.50."

- "The price is $29.95, and that includes the machine, free installation, and a full year's guarantee."

■ Suggest possible prices that are higher than the actual price, which will then sound low by comparison. Example: "Wouldn't you expect to pay $200 for that kind of protection, Mrs. Jones, or at least $150? Well, all it will cost you is $85."

■ Break a large price down into smaller units of cost. A large lump-sum price looks less forbidding if it is broken down into cost per month, week, day, or individual use.

☐ EXAMPLE

One company's premium mattress costs more than those of many competitors. Salespeople point out that based on the mattress's anticipated long life, the cost is only about 2 cents per night. Stated this way, the dollar difference between the premium mattress and other mattresses is hardly noticeable.

■ Offset a large initial price by emphasizing savings. Emphasize savings advantages in as many ways as you can, and always in terms of dollars and cents. Express them not only as a lump-sum figure but as daily or weekly savings, or savings of so much per unit of production. Emphasize such savings as lower labor costs, reduction of overtime, elimination of errors, lower repair and maintenance costs, and so on.

When you make the prospect think in terms of how much he or she will save, it's easier to overcome resistance to high price.

☐ EXAMPLE

"Mr. Jones, although Transite at first glance looks much more expensive than multiple duct tile, the actual material cost difference is usually no more than 4 cents per duct foot. That's because you save on three points:

1. There are fewer items to inventory. That means lower warehousing and inventory costs.

2. There is less handling of material from plant to job, which means lower handling costs.

3. There is less duct breakage, so you'll save on material costs.

"Savings on installation costs with Transite will more than offset the initial price difference. The difference in labor costs between Transite and tile can reach 20 cents per duct foot and is usually at least 5 cents per duct foot. And the installation is faster. Look at the many ways you save on even a straight-line installation:

- There is no joint material to make. The couplings are all made up and come with the sections.

- The joint material is easier to place. Simply connect the coupling to the section.

- Sections are lighter and easier to handle than tile.

- Ducts are easier to position. Struggling with heavy sections for hairline alignment is eliminated.

- Closing of joints is easier. No tying or wrapping—just tap the section in.

- There are fewer lengths to install because they're longer.

- Only a small crew is required because Transite is easy to handle.

- Tie-ins at manholes are easier to make.

- Rodding costs are lower.

In this way you build advantage on advantage. Each of your statements is a convincing one because it is supported by facts and illustrations, supplied by the company, that nail it down.

Quote Quantity Prices to "Up" the Sale

If your prices vary with quantity, apply the technique used by a successful forms salesperson. She quotes three prices: the first for the quantity mentioned by the prospect, the second for a larger quantity, and the third for a still larger quantity. Quite often the prospect will decide to order the middle quantity quoted to take advantage of the price saving.

Know How to Handle Price Objections

Every salesperson runs into price objections of one kind or another, or meets buyers who try to bargain. To find out how to handle these problems, turn to Chapter Seven. There you will find full details and examples of how successful salespeople make their prices stick.

HOW TO MAKE YOUR PRESENTATION "GREAT"

The presentation that you develop from the outline must be more than a bunch of descriptive words. It must have certain qualities and embody features that make a presentation great. To give your sales talk a real selling edge, sharpen it in these proven ways:

- Use the "you" approach.
- Dramatize it.
- Use vivid words and good language.
- Tell stories to make your points clear.
- Ask questions as you go along.
- Appeal to the senses.
- Use examples.
- Use parallel situations.

Each of these techniques is discussed in the following sections.

Use the "You" Approach

Vanity is a human characteristic that must be considered in any dealings with people, and it is especially important in selling. You must be sure that your presentation is geared to the natural vanity of the prospect and that it satisfies his or her desire to be treated with respect as an individual. A benefit may lack persuasive appeal if it is not clear that it is intended for the prospect and that you fully expect him or her to profit by it.

There are positive ways to inject the "you" emphasis into your sales talk:

- Use the words "you" and "your" frequently.

- Capitalize on opportunities to personalize the interview. Complimentary references to the prospect's responsible position, reputation, or even a family picture that you spot on his or her desk are good examples here.

- Indicate by common courtesy and a willingness to serve that you respect your prospect's importance as a potential buyer, no matter what his or her present buying potential is.

- When the prospect talks, listen. All interviews should allow some time for the prospect to make comments.

Dramatize Your Presentation

What lifts your presentation above the ordinary more than any other factor is its dramatic force. Without such force, yours is just another sales story—the kind that doesn't make much of an impression. But if you make what you do and say dramatic, yours is the story the prospect will remember when comparing your product with others before making a decision.

Here are some ways to add dramatic flavor to your sales talk:

- Use dramatic words. Choose words that will have an impact on the prospect, words with power and color, for example, "glide with silky-smooth power" or "the rich colors, the easy-chair comfort of the interior." (See the next section for techniques on how to add power with vivid-picture language.)

- Use dramatic comparisons and illustrations. Note how these remarks dramatize speed, strength, and economy:
  - "Less time than it takes to dial a local phone call"
  - "A football quarterback could stand on it and not harm it"
  - "No more expensive than burning a light bulb."

- Use a dramatic demonstration. A refrigerator salesperson, demonstrating the quiet operation of his company's refrigerators, would strike a match and ask the prospect to listen. The silence of that tiny flame spoke more eloquently than words for how little noise the refrigerator made.

■ Be dramatic in your manner when making important points. Put emphasis on your words when you want them to have impact. Use pauses to build suspense. Use your body to dramatize those statements that need force—by pointing, leaning forward, and so on. Here is where rehearsal of your presentation really pays off. ("How to give your great presentation" is discussed later in this chapter.)

WARNING The word "dramatic" does not mean unrestrained. If you conduct your interview like a three-ring circus, it will have impact, all right, but the message will be lost.

Importance of Language

No matter how many visual aids and demonstrations you use in a presentation, your chief communication with the prospect will be through the spoken word. Correct language is the clearest and most expressive way to get your message across. Ungrammatical sentences are confusing, often waste words, and make a bad impression.

SUGGESTION An added benefit of writing up your presentation is that it gives you time to polish your language. Get someone who really knows grammar to read over what you've written and point out any grammatical errors. You can also consult a basic grammar text when you're in doubt.

The words you select for telling your sales story must obviously be chosen with care, since they have important work to do and a limited time in which to do it. You should avoid using long or complicated words and concentrate on simple, direct ones. Long words, however descriptive or meaningful, are often hard to take in at a normal speaking pace, so their value is lost. The words in your presentation must be vivid and expressive. They must summon up images in the prospect's mind, so that he or she has a clear understanding of the benefits you are describing. Your words must also carry conviction, since persuasion is your goal.

Three steps to increase your word power

Using vivid-picture language is one technique for making your presentation lean, sharp, and electric. You can add power to your presentation by finding the right selling words to *describe, explain,* or *demonstrate* your product or service.

You must take the time to develop a vocabulary of selling words that make what you are selling come alive in your prospect's imagination. You don't add power with words like "good," "fine," "nice," and other weak adjectives. Your selling vocabulary must be made up of strong, vivid words—picture-building words. Without them you cannot effectively transfer to your prospect the image of the sale that you have in your own mind's eye.

Here is a three-step method by which you can revitalize your selling talk and then illustrate how this method should be applied:

Step 1. From your list of product features, select a strong selling feature that calls for a description of a specific attribute of your product.

Step 2. Write down all the colorful, vivid, vital words you can think of that give the feature meaning and that help the prospect visualize that feature and how he or she will benefit from it.

> **OBSERVATION** You won't use all the words that you gather in writing any one paragraph, but they will be there for you to use throughout your presentation.

> **SUGGESTION** Have a good dictionary and thesaurus handy to help you get started. Study your company's advertising and see what power words have been used by the copywriters. Make use of the words and phrases they've chosen for describing your product.

Step 3. Write a paragraph expressing what you want to convey to your prospect, choosing words from your list.

> **REMEMBER** You must combine the words from your list with some of the other techniques that make your presentation lean, sharp, and electric: the "you" emphasis, questions, dramatization, story-telling, specific statements, appeal to the senses, examples, and parallel situations. Make your sentences *short*. Don't let them get too complex.

> In the paragraphs that follow, we illustrate how to apply the three-step method to increase your word power.

Using word power to explain a product

The product. The product is oil. You want to explain the main benefit to the prospect, which in this case is the lubrication of the machine parts to which it is applied, and to impress the prospect with the quality, duration, and vitality of the product.

Power words. "Lubricate," "film," "regularity," "smooth," "density," "viscosity," "thickness," "friction," "efficiency," "slippery," "lengthens," "wearing," and "qualities."

What to say. "Mr. Prospect: Oil-e-O is not only a good oil. It is an oil that *lubricates* every minute part of your machine. It forms a *slippery film* between moving surfaces. It makes every wheel turn *smoothly* and easily with clocklike *regularity*. The low *density* of this oil determines its *thickness* and makes it just right for your particular use.

"Every molecule of this oil is geared to give the full lubricating value to your entire machine. It reduces *friction* and increases the *efficiency* of every operation. It adds many years of *wear* to your machine.

"Mr. Prospect, there is no oil like Oil-e-O for general lubrication, for efficiency, and for *long-wearing qualities.* Order now."

Using word power to demonstrate a product feature

Product feature. The product is Tupperware. The feature to be demonstrated to a group assembled at a home party is the patented seal. The benefits that the prospect is buying are the freshness the sealing affords, the elimination of kitchen accidents and messes, and the ease of sealing the container.

Power words. "Air-tight," "liquid-tight," "vacuum-tight," "snuggles," "grips," "saves food flavors," "original flavor and richness stays in," "easy to handle," "it's virtually canned," "protects the food."

What to say. "We call these Wonder Bowls—after you've used them, you'll call them 'wonderful.' They come in sets of three, and each bowl has its own seal. To seal Tupperware, all you have to do is *snuggle* the rim of the Bowl into the groove of the seal, starting from the back with your thumbs and sliding them along until the seal has *gripped* the edges of the bowl all around . . . now the bowl is covered, ready to seal. Press hard in the middle of the seal with one hand and at the same time, lift one edge just enough to let the air out. Now, if you listen you will hear the air come out. There! Did you hear it? Now you have a sealed container that is absolutely *air-tight* and *liquid-tight* . . . one that not only *protects the food* but eliminates accidents and messes in the kitchen because the seal will keep the bowls from spilling, even if dropped. The contents are *virtually canned.*

"Accept no substitutes; there is NO substitute for quality!

"Use your Wonder Bowls for making Jell-O and puddings and for leftover potatoes, rice, macaroni, and other foods that are hard to keep moist. You'll be delighted with the results . . . the *original flavor and richness stay in.* Tossed salads will stay crisp even with dressing added. I'm going to pass around some of the bowls and let each of you APPLY THE SEAL.—I want you to see how *easy it is to handle.*"

> **COMMENT** The salesperson applies the seal while describing the technique verbally. When she is about to say, "There! Did you hear it?" she glances up, pauses if necessary, but makes the people she is talking to actually listen. She holds the bowl up and turns it around slowly, handling it as though it were a jewel. Then she drops it—lets it slip from her fingers without letting her listeners know what is going to happen. The element of surprise adds to the dramatization.

How to increase your word power

The three-step method described should be only the beginning of your efforts to make every word in your presentation count. The following suggestions will help you increase your word power:

- List in alphabetical order the vivid words you have selected. Keep this word file active by adding to it every word or phrase you come across in your reading or conversation that has power for your selling purposes. Work these new words into your presentation from time to time.

- Be sure you understand the meaning of every word you use in your sales talk and that you pronounce it correctly. Use a dictionary if you're unsure.

- Guard against using high-flown language. You don't magnify your word power with high-sounding phrases. It is the familiar, down-to-earth, compelling words that have power to carry your prospect along with you.

- Eliminate from your vocabulary all grammatical errors and distracting speech mannerisms. Cut out the "well's," "so's," "um's," and trite sayings like "Let's face it," or belittling phrases like "Do you get my point?" They are not only a waste of time, but they can actually weaken your presentation by detracting from the power words you do use.

- Use the jargon of the industry to which you are selling. Most businesses have their own special jargon. The smart salesperson gets to know some of the terminology used by a prospect in his or her business and works it into the presentation.

Test what you are going to say for "word strategy"

Word strategy means phrasing your remarks in such a way that they achieve the desired effect. Let's say, for example, that you want to get in to see a prospect. How should you phrase your request to get the desired response? If you say, "Can I see Mrs. Jones?" the receptionist is likely to say, "Of course you can't. She's much too busy." But if you say, "Do you think you can get me in to see Mr. Smith?" the answer will probably be, "Well, what do you wish to see him about?"

Take the case of a salesperson who wants to give a demonstration. By asking "May I give you a demonstration?" or "May I leave the machine with you on trial?" he or she puts the prospect on the defensive. But asking "May I show you?" or "Won't you use this?" avoids the overused words "demonstration" and "trial" and gets the affirmative response the salesperson is seeking.

Your sales will soar as your word strategy improves.

Use the Power of Story-telling

There are three reasons why successful salespeople use stories in their work:

1. People enjoy hearing stories. A well-told story is interesting and entertaining as well as instructive.

2. Stories put the imagination to work. Explanations and factual statements satisfy reason, but a story brings the listener's imagination into play. Imagination is the magic power that lets the prospect visualize instead of merely comprehending. Most sales depend upon the prospect's ability to visualize— in other words, to turn words into pictures.

3. Stories can be used at any stage of the interview. They can accomplish anything from getting attention to motivating the prospect to sign the order.

The best stories are ones illustrating the benefits that others have received from your product or service. Such stories enable the prospect to picture himself or herself in the same circumstances and visualize the benefits your product would bring. If your story tells about someone the prospect knows, its persuasive effect is greatly increased.

CAUTION When you use a story for the purpose of illustrating how someone else has benefited, make sure that it is a *believable* story. An anecdote that arouses doubt or disbelief will work against you. There must be no doubt in the prospect's mind that what you say happened *did* happen, and that the same benefit could be his or hers.

Ask Questions as You Go Along

There are a number of reasons why you should ask the prospect questions as you proceed with your presentation:

- A question serves as a brief summary or restatement after each point has been made.

- By asking a question you can be sure that the prospect understands one point before you proceed to the next.

- The answers to your questions help you judge the progress you are making toward closing the sale.

- If the prospect can be conditioned to saying "yes" in response to questions during the presentation, it may reduce his or her resistance to making a commitment at the close. The more often the prospect agrees with you, the more unreasonable an arbitrary turn-down will seem at the end.

Here are some examples of the kind of question that you should ask your prospect:

"A savings of $250 each year on cleaning bills would be nice to have, wouldn't it?"

Wouldn't a 10% increase in production from such a small investment be a real gain?"

As parents, isn't the safety this would provide for your children something that you want?"

Appeal to the Senses

People can absorb information by seeing it, hearing it, touching it, tasting it, or smelling it. Of these five senses, *seeing, hearing,* and *touching* are most important to the majority of salespeople. The more senses that a salesperson can engage, the stronger the impact of his or her message on the prospect, and the greater the chance of making a sale.

Of the three—seeing, hearing, and touching—seeing is by far the most effective. We understand what we see quicker than any other way, we remember it longer, and it makes a stronger impression on us. It's also true that we tend to *believe* what we see, even though we might doubt the same information if we received it through our other senses.

Make use of this knowledge in your presentation. Try to engage all the prospect's senses with your sales message rather than rely on speech to do the whole job. Pay special attention to the eyes. Here are some tips on what to do:

- If you sell a product, key your presentation as much as possible to a demonstration, or a sample or model, so that the prospect can *see, touch,* and *hear* about your product at the same time.

- If you sell a service, arm yourself with photographs, letters of recommendation, testimonials, copies of lab reports, printed statistics—anything the prospect can *look* at as evidence of what he or she is hearing.

- Make full use of company-supplied visual aids, such as films or slides, flip charts, visual portfolios, catalogs, scale models, mock-ups, cut-away sections, and so on. These are designed to help put the prospect's eyes to work for you.

WARNING Two senses transmitting the same information reinforce each other and create a strong impression. But two senses trying to take in different information can create confusion. You must coordinate your demonstration and the use of visual aids with your words, so that the prospect gets one strong impression, not scattered and confusing ones. If the prospect is allowed to handle a sample or model longer than necessary, or browse at random through a catalog as you talk, his or her attention will be divided. It's up to you to control the presentation in such a way that this doesn't happen.

Use Plenty of Examples

Examples are often necessary to clarify your statements. Even if the prospect understands your point, an example gives it emphasis and helps him or her visualize it.

■ IDEA IN ACTION

Eliza Cooper sells insurance. She has found that the benefits she offers don't really register until she gives an example of the circumstances under which these benefits might be needed. After she describes each feature, therefore, she states a pertinent example. Her presentation abounds with phrases such as these:

"Say, for example, that a deliveryperson trips over a rug in the hall . . ."

"Suppose someone upstairs had a fire and the water from the hoses dripped down . . ."

"That means that if for some reason you became sick and were temporarily unable to make premium payments . . ."

"If, for example, you choose instead to withdraw all the money at that time to buy a home . . ."

Each example is one with which the prospect can identify, and Eliza, like many salespeople, says that her use of such examples is one of the biggest reasons for her success.

Explain with Parallels

To make a point vivid and easy to understand, use parallel situations, especially if the point is a technical one. This is one of the best ways of simplifying an explanation.

Here are some examples of the use of parallel situations to clarify a point:

"This 'hold' feature acts like a memory. The machine will 'remember' a figure and then recall it and add it to a later total when you need it."

"These guide slots work just like tumblers in a lock; nothing can happen until you line up the two parts perfectly."

"These shelf units can be stacked one above the other, just like building blocks."

PUTTING THE PRESENTATION INTO WORDS

Develop the Presentation from the Outline

When your outline is completed, the next step is to write out the presentation just as you intend to give it. Take the information you have already decided upon, in the shape or form that your outline gives it, and put it into your own words. In doing so, you must include as many as possible of the techniques explained (e.g., dramatizing, using the "you" approach, using vivid language) to give your story selling power.

First Introduce Yourself

Almost all interviews begin with the salesperson introducing himself or herself and stating what company he or she represents.

Since this is the natural beginning, it should be the first thing you write in your presentation.

The first few seconds of an interview are so important that they warrant a little extra thought. You want to show the prospect that you know his or her name and at the same time to impress his or her name on your own memory. A good technique for achieving both objectives is to state the prospect's name as a question, as follows:

Salesperson:	Mr. Brady?
Prospect:	That's right.
Salesperson:	Mr. Brady, I'm Alicia Franklin.

Normally, the next step is to explain what company you represent, although in some specialty selling this is not done if mentioning the company or product might create a negative response.

If you want to impress your own name on the prospect, repeat it right away, like this:

Salesperson:	Mr. Brady, my name is Franklin—Alicia Franklin.

The prospect thus hears your name twice and is likely to remember it.

Get the Prospect's Attention in First Sentence

As soon as you have properly introduced yourself, you must get the immediate and complete attention of the prospect. Just because you are standing there does not mean that you have the prospect's undivided attention. Your first sentence must be one that will make him or her an attentive listener.

The following types of opening remarks have all been used as attention-getters by successful salespeople. Select one that is best suited to your product or service, your personality, and the prospects with whom you deal.

- State an emphatic benefit.
- Promise to solve one of the prospect's problems.
- Ask the prospect a thought-provoking question.
- Use an unusual or dramatic opening.
- Tell a story that will lead into your subject.
- Begin with an exhibit.
- Use a news item of related interest.

Each of these openers is described in the following paragraphs.

> **NOTE** Some of those openers are similar to those you use in writing letters that get interviews (as described in Chapter Four), where the goal is the same: to get immediate attention. Both your words and your manner should tell the prospect that something important has brought you to his or her office. *Never* use the cliched "Just happened to be in the neighborhood" opening. It indicates that you don't have much regard for your own time or for the prospect and his or her business—and it certainly doesn't do much to grab his or her attention.

Use an emphatic benefit as your opener

The prospect wants to hear benefits that satisfy his or her buying motives. If you can offer a substantial benefit that will be sure to interest the prospect, use it as your opening remark.

A statement of benefit as an opening must meet these four tests:

1. The benefit should be one that the prospect wants.
2. The claim must be thoroughly substantiated by your presentation.
3. It must be a benefit that you are sure you can deliver in full.
4. It should be specific. A dollars-and-cents offer is far more effective than a sweeping generality as a means of getting attention.

Here are some examples:

"Mr. Carlysle, what I stopped in to tell you about is a new type of truck rental service that will save you up to 15% on your present delivery costs."

"Mrs. Worth, we have a new process that can cut operating time in your lithography department by one-third."

"Ms. Upton, my reason for calling today is that we are offering a special this month that enables you to have your word processor and other office machines completely reconditioned at 25% less than the usual charge."

Tell the prospect that you can solve a problem for him or her

If you are in a position to solve a prospect's specific problem, you have an ideal opening. This, too, is a statement of benefit, but it's usually more personal and specific. A prospect who is wrestling with a problem is eager to listen when someone offers to help solve it.

☐ EXAMPLE

"Mrs. Prospect, it took me 4 minutes to reach your office from the street, and the return trip would double that. Multiply 8 minutes by the number of your employees who go to the corner drugstore for coffee every morning; then add the time they spend waiting for it and drinking it. The nonproductive time consumed by this daily ritual is considerable, as I'm sure you realize. Our on-the-spot coffee service recovers that lost time and puts it back to work for you."

Ask your prospect a thought-provoking question

A method that has been used successfully by many salespeople is the question opening. You can frequently get a prospect's attention by asking a question that is stimulating or thought-provoking, related to your presentation, and not confusing or obscure.

These examples show questions that have worked in getting a prospect's attention:

"Can you afford to gamble with important mail?"

"Ms. Prospect, if your family is like mine, you probably carry some sort of health insurance. It probably costs you a few thousand dollars a year and doesn't do one thing to improve or protect your health, does it?"

CAUTION Avoid the kind of question that implies some failing on the prospect's part. Consider the unfavorable reaction you would probably receive to these questions: "Have bad relations between management and employees got you down?" "Do you realize that your maintenance costs are probably much too high?"

Use an unusual or dramatic opening

One of the best places to use the dramatic element in your presentation is at the beginning. Something out of the ordinary will usually succeed in getting the prospect's attention.

Lead into your presentation with a pertinent story

An interesting, well-told story or anecdote has universal appeal. You can use this appeal to win your prospect's attention if you begin the interview with a story that will lead directly into the subject of your visit. Many top-bracket salespeople consider this kind of opener their best.

NOTE It is not necessary to be a great raconteur to make effective use of the anecdote or story opening. But it *is* necessary to choose a story that is suitable as a lead-in. The most charming story is wasted breath if, when it is over, you haven't really begun your presentation at all.

☐ EXAMPLE

"Mr. Prospect, there's a statue in Italy near the entrance to a tunnel under the Alps. The statue honors the Italian engineer who supervised his country's part in the construction. Just before the tunnel sections were scheduled to meet in the middle, the Italian supervisor, listening to the muffled sounds of the Swiss crew approaching from the opposite direction, became convinced that the sections would not line up correctly. In despair over his failure, he shot himself, never to know that the two tunnels were soon to meet in perfect alignment."

"If only he'd had our company's Sounding and Underground Measurement Unit, he would have known ahead of time that nothing was wrong."

Start your presentation with an exhibit

One way to get attention is to catch the prospect's eye with an exhibit or visual attraction of some kind. Some companies provide their salespeople with scale or cutout models, blowups, and other visual aids, which in many cases can get the interview going. Salespeople who have access to these aids, or who sell a product that stirs curiosity by its appearance, can often get under way by simply saying something like: "Ms. Prospect, this is the new _____ , the fastest-growing home appliance on the market."

Remember that the eyes are a person's most effective point of registration. Your prospect's eyes work for you if you have something interesting on which they can focus.

> **NOTE** Not all visual aids are suitable as initial eye-catchers. Some are designed more as explanatory aids and are not much help in getting attention.

Use an interesting news item as an opener

News of something that has happened in the industry, or of something out of the ordinary that has a bearing on the interview, can help you get your prospect's attention. The more directly the news affects your prospect personally, the more likely it is to capture his or her interest. The effectiveness of this method is increased if you present an actual article or newspaper clipping for the prospect to look at.

> **NOTE** News isn't news for long, so you must change this kind of opener at frequent intervals to avoid letting it get stale.

These examples illustrate how news can serve to launch the interview:

"Mrs. Prospect, perhaps you saw the amazing results of *Fortune* magazine's recent survey of the petrochemical industry and its future. Let's look at this figure in particular, the one that concerns you most . . . ."

"Mr. Prospect, it isn't often that a new product is exciting enough to warrant a cover story in two leading trade magazines in the same month. But our new machine is that exciting, and here are the articles . . . ."

Build Your Prospect's Interest by Stating Benefits

Your goal in the opening is not only to get your prospect's attention but to turn that attention into favorable interest. Do so by telling your prospect what benefits he or she will gain from the purchase of your product or service. This is why you should "boil down" your list of selling features until they take shape as benefits to the buyer (as described earlier in this chapter). Now you can put that analysis to profitable use.

> **IMPORTANT** In developing your presentation, choose the benefit that suits your largest class of prospects.

> ▪ IDEA IN ACTION

Hill International makes a machine that imprints paper at speeds up to 1,000 per minute. The sales presentation emphasized the product's features—in this case speed, accuracy, versatility, and ease of operation—in terms of *benefits* (savings and convenience) as follows:

> "By comparison [with manual imprinting], the new machine will imprint up to ten times faster, with improved convenience and accuracy plus big time and payroll savings."

> "The machine enables you to keep skilled workers at their proper jobs and costs less per day than an average worker's pay for just one hour."

> "It cuts waste on misprinted labels, lets your company meet production requirements exactly, and provides a quality control coding that is easily legible to dealers and salespeople."

"Over 100 case studies and testimonials prove the savings that this machine has provided in payroll, time, materials, and morale."

Notice how much more meaning these benefit statements have for the prospect than simple claims of speed or accuracy. They show what speed or accuracy means to his or her business. Notice, too, that wherever possible the benefits are geared to the needs and interests of the particular prospect.

Turn the Prospect's Interest Into Desire

Making the prospect *want* what you offer—in other words, creating *desire* for your product—narrows the important gap between interest and a signed order. While interest is primarily a mental reaction, desire is an emotional one that incites the prospect to take action.

People want (1) whatever answers a strong need and (2) whatever gratifies a personal buying motive, such as comfort or amusement. You must, therefore, focus on the need that your product or service satisfies, and you must personalize your offering in every way possible.

Here are means by which to accomplish these goals:

- Build up the prospect's need, pointing it out if necessary.
- Show in what way your product or service is the best answer to that need.
- Point out the prospect's personal stake in the matter.
- Emphasize the *satisfaction* that the benefits will bring.
- Add glamour or fascination to your product.

The following sections provide details on each of these approaches.

Build up the prospect's need for your product or service

You must remind most prospects how important their need is to trigger a desire for what you are offering. In some cases you have to point out a need of which the prospect is unaware before your story can strike a responsive chord.

No matter how obvious you feel the need for your product or service may be, restate that need to amplify the prospect's awareness of it. Only then will he or she begin actively to want the benefits you promise.

□ EXAMPLE

International Minerals and Chemical Corporation makes and sells fertilizer, something every farmer needs. To build desire for Rainbow Plant Food, the salesperson prefaces each benefit by pointing out why the farmer needs it, using a visual presentation based on slides.

(The complete presentation is given at the end of this chapter. Notice how the farmer is first reminded of his or her needs and then told why Rainbow is the right answer. The result is to make the farmer *want* Rainbow Plant Food.)

If for some reason the average prospect doesn't realize that he or she needs your product or service, you may have to point out that need to make him or her want what you're selling.

□ EXAMPLE

The Hill International imprinting machine is designed to cut the "concealed" cost of imprinting paper items by hand. The Hill International salesperson must point out its importance. Here are examples of how a presentation can highlight these concealed costs:

"There are many concealed costs when employees mark by hand or use an inefficient hand-fed machine. But you can begin to appreciate what that cost is when you consider employees' wages, time lost away from other work, spoiled materials, and inaccurate counting or marking . . . ."

The prospect is first made to appreciate his or her need so that the benefits of automatic imprinting can be more fully appreciated. Once the prospect starts thinking about these hidden costs, the benefits of the Hill machine suddenly become clear.

How to show that your product is the best one for your prospect's needs

Create desire for your product by presenting it as the best one for your prospect's needs. Make it stand out in his or her mind as the answer to a specific need. This is especially important when you have close competition.

To do this, make full use of exclusive product or service features—whatever your product or service can do that others can't. Even a minor point seems important when it is presented as unusual or unique.

Knowing all about your product and its market, and where your prospect fits into that picture, helps you to portray your product as the ideal one. You know what features to emphasize, what changes or new ideas in the industry you can capitalize on, and what will make your offer sound up-to-date. If you run a close race with competitors, the more you know about them and their product, the better equipped you'll be to portray your product appear as the best one.

Point out that the prospect has a personal stake in the sale

You may sell to buyers for large corporations or people who otherwise have little personal connection with the materials or services they are purchasing. If this is the case, you can give your sales talk special appeal by pointing out how the prospect is personally involved.

Purchasing agents, for example, usually try to do the best job they can, regardless of the nature of their purchases or their personal feelings about the things they buy. You can make them want your product by connecting it favorably with their success and good judgment. If they are having frequent trouble with returns, short shipments, and incorrect billings, emphasize how buying your product or service will alleviate the situation.

> **CAUTION** This is not to suggest that a purchasing agent or anyone else will buy flattery in place of a good product. The point is to combat the impersonality of some purchasing situations by highlighting the aspects of the sale that concern the prospect as an individual. The following examples illustrate

how this personalizing can be done after you've been specific about the benefits.

"Ms. Prospect, you have a responsible job and I know you're intent on doing it well. That's why I'm sure you will be enthusiastic about this service. It takes a large burden off the shoulders of your office staff. Equally important, it assures you of putting your money where it will do the most good."

"Isn't it important to know that placing your orders with us will assure you full-order deliveries every time, thanks to our large stock?"

"Mr. Prospect, my product not only does its job better than others, as I've just shown you; it also tells the people who use it that their purchasing agent knows his stuff."

In each case, the idea is to promote personal enthusiasm for your product or service by searching out ways in which the prospect will benefit as an individual.

Make your benefits sound personally satisfying to the prospect

Elaborate on the happiness, the enjoyment, the pride, the admiration or whatever other personal satisfaction you can offer your prospects. If it will make their job easier, urge them to picture the physical comfort and pleasure that less work will mean to them. If it will help them make more money, stimulate thoughts of how that extra money will provide enjoyment or supply their wants and needs. If you can get them to envision personal satisfaction, you will succeed in making them want to buy.

□ EXAMPLE

Let's say that you sell home air conditioning. One of the main benefits is comfort. To make the prospect really want that comfort, you build up its advantages in his or her imagination. You remind the prospect how uncomfortable hot, muggy summer days can be and the misery of sweltering, sleepless nights. You describe clothing that sticks to their skin, frayed nerves, and the prospect of another steaming night spent tossing and turning. Then, when you describe the cool, dry indoor air and the extra hours of sleep each night that come with air conditioning, the prospect has an active desire for it.

As you write out your presentation, try to picture each benefit as bringing personal satisfaction to the prospect, no matter what the product or service is. It's this kind of touch that makes *your* proposition sound more desirable to prospects than others they hear.

Add glamour to your product

A touch of the romantic or glamorous gives your product a special appeal. If there is an intriguing angle you can weave into your story, use it to create desire.

■ IDEA IN ACTION

Brown & White, maker of advertising products, has an item called the Touch Rest Desk Pen. This is a desk set in which the pen is held at an easy-to-reach angle by a ceramic magnet in the base.

When a Brown & White salesperson recommends this pen to a prospect as a remembrance gift to customers, here's what he or she does. After pointing out how attractive and how useful the pen is, the salesperson capitalizes on the fascination of the ceramic magnet. He or she describes how it is formed by baking and how strong its holding power is. The salesperson shows how shaping can concentrate the magnetic field in a certain area, and how the hole in the magnet in the Touch Rest base serves this purpose.

Then he or she plays up the novelty of a magnetic pen holder and its value as a conversation piece. By building up the intriguing aspects of this practical product, the salesperson makes the prospect *want* that pen as a remembrance gift.

The result? Out of 800 products that the company offers, the Touch Rest Desk Pen frequently appears on the weekly list of its top twenty order-getters.

Make Your Presentation Convincing

A prospect isn't sold until he or she is convinced. Conviction is "a firm belief founded on evidence," says the dictionary. That firm belief is what a prospect must feel before he or she makes the decision to become a customer. Your presentation must, therefore, do far more than convey information; it must create conviction in the prospect's mind.

The most essential ingredient in the formula for a convincing sales presentation is evidence. Evidence can take a number of different forms, among them the following: (1) a demonstration; (2) visual aids, especially testimonials; and (3) facts and figures.

Almost as important as the evidence is the manner in which you present it and your attitude during the interview. To carry conviction, you must:

- Have enthusiasm.
- Be confident.
- Speak forcefully.
- Be sincere and willing to serve.
- Show loyalty to your company and product.
- Make only those promises that you can keep.
- Be thorough.
- Speak on the prospect's level.

There is no substitute for the facts

The most fabulous sales story in the world wouldn't sell anything if the benefits weren't backed up with proof. Making a prospect believe in your product or service depends on how well you support your statements with facts. Even a demonstration isn't fully convincing without the facts that supplement and explain it.

Include plenty of hard-hitting facts in your presentation if you want it to be convincing. See that these facts meet the following tests:

Facts must be truthful. If your prospect detects exaggeration or half-truths in the facts you present, or thinks they are misleading, you stand to lose the battle. Once his or her confidence in either you or your product wavers, conviction becomes impossible. Stick to the truth, and prospects will believe what you say.

Facts must be specific. No one decides to invest a sum of money in a product or service because it is "a lot faster" or "more efficient than other machines on the market." Most prospects will demand to know how much faster or how much more efficient. Tell your prospect exactly what your product can do for him or her, and then back it up with specific facts, testimonials, and so on. Never rely on generalities when you can talk in terms of dollars and cents, hours and minutes, percentages, numbers, or other specific means of description.

Facts must be easily understood. Avoid technical language, unless a technical approach is absolutely essential to your product or service. Complexity creates more confusion than conviction, and once a prospect gets confused, he or she is likely to lose interest. Remember that the prospect may be hearing these facts for the first time, and that presenting them as simply and clearly as possible will promote understanding and underscore your sales message more effectively.

TIP Don't overlook the persuasive power of understatement. Whereas people react unfavorably to exaggeration, they tend to believe what seems understated.

Get the facts from your company

Most salespeople can turn to their company for facts and figures to back up statements that are made to convince a prospect. The company is usually in the best position to secure data from laboratories, sales offices, outside sources, and so on. The experienced salesperson can often add facts acquired in his or her selling efforts.

■ IDEA IN ACTION

Salespeople who sell Emerson's single-duct conduit have an 18-page bulletin of facts to draw from. This booklet thoroughly analyzes the material, installation, and upkeep costs of the ducts. It compares the costs of using the single-duct conduit with the cost of a multiple-tile-duct installation. Costs are broken down to the penny, based on cost data from actual installations, and illustrations and charts make each cost factor clear. From this material, salespeople can develop a hard-hitting presentation aimed at telephone company buyers and contractors, based on the claim that Emerson carries the lowest-cost material when all cost factors are considered. The company bulletin gives the facts to prove it, and Emerson sales reps use these facts effectively as sales aids.

A thorough presentation is more likely to convince

A presentation that tells a complete story is more likely to be convincing than a sketchy one. The suspicion that you have left things out or are slighting important points will make a prospect wary. You should be thorough, even to the extent of discussing your product's disadvantages if their omission would suggest a deliberate cover-up. When a prospect sees you lay all your cards on the table, he or she knows that you have confidence in what you are selling. This in turn gives the prospect confidence that your statements are valid.

> **NOTE** Your presentation can tell a complete story even though it omits some of the selling points that you are holding in reserve. You must be selective in choosing which selling points to cover if you want to keep your presentation within time limits.

Talk to the prospect on his or her own level

Prospects prefer to do business with salespeople who can speak their own language. If your speech is too formal or high flown for the prospect to understand easily, he or she will miss part of your message and resent your attitude. If, on the other hand, your prospect's education and experience lead him or her to expect a more refined or technical presentation than you are able to provide, you will fail to earn the respect that is necessary for conviction. Aim your presentation at the level of the average prospect upon whom you will call.

The following statement is used by a pharmaceutical company salesperson to sell an injected tranquilizer to doctors: "This product has proven its effectiveness in alleviating symptoms of

anxiety, tension, psychomotor excitement, and other manifesta-
tions of emotional stress. It is also a highly effective antiemetic
agent for the symptomatic control of nausea and vomiting due to
a wide variety of causes."

To a doctor, this language is perfectly understandable. It
would be utterly unsuited to anyone else.

Gather your forces before you make the final assault

When you have won all but the final battle, the close, reinforce your
advantage by summarizing. Repetition enhances the effect that
your sales points had when first made.

Summarizing is one method of bringing the sale to a close. In
this respect it is a definite closing technique.

A summary can be as simple as this one: "So, it's all there . . .
a plant food designed for your soil . . . the right ingredients to help
throughout the growing season and a product kept ahead of the
times by International's staff of 300 scientists and agronomists.
Quality? Sure . . . we've been delivering it for 50 years. Reliable?
You bet. International has the mines and the plants and the people
to furnish what you need right when you need it."

MAKE A FIRM BID FOR THE ORDER

A Good Presentation Leads into a Good Close

Your presentation must include as an integral part a final close, the
attempt to get the order after the story has been told. Because this
is so important, it is treated separately, in the next chapter.

Closing the sale will hold no terrors if you know just how to
go about it and remember that the prospect expects you to do so.
Study the closing techniques in Chapter Six. and give careful
thought to which one will suit your situation best. Then write a
close for your own presentation, revising it until you're sure it's a
strong one.

The trial closings you include at intervals throughout your
presentation are tentative, but there must be nothing tentative

about your final effort to get the order. The decision to buy is the logical conclusion to any sales interview. Don't rest until your closing words are action words that move the prospect toward the dotted line.

HOW TO GIVE YOUR GREAT PRESENTATION

Control of the Presentation

Each interview with a prospect is a performance in front of a new and critical audience. Its success hinges not only on the material (the presentation) but also on your skill in putting your story across. If you hope to attain your sales and earnings goals, this is where you have to excel.

The secret of a winning performance is a simple one: *You, not your prospect, must be in charge.* You must subtly but effectively dominate the interview and make the prospect like it. You must exert gentle control throughout, always leading politely but firmly in the direction of a sale.

This section describes five moves that will put you in charge of the interview:

1. Start off on the right foot.
2. Give a smooth-flowing talk.
3. Act worthy of your prospect's confidence and business.
4. Hit hardest those points he or she likes best.
5. Dominate the "give and take."

A Good Personal Impression Gets You Off on the Right Foot

Selling is a very personal business. In most cases it involves one individual dealing face to face with another, and personal likes and dislikes can affect the relationship. You must recognize that your prospects are free to let their personal feelings toward you influence their actions—while you, the salesperson, must control your personal feelings toward them. Even an exceptional proposition may fall on deaf ears if the prospect decides that he or she doesn't like you or takes exception to your manner or dress.

Here are some of the measures you must take to win your prospects' good opinion:

Make the first impression a good one. The first few seconds can make or break a sale. A prospect starts to size you up the minute you walk in the door, just as you are judging him or her. By the time you have approached, shaken hands, and said your first sentence, the average person will have formed an opinion of you. With some people this first judgment will be tentative, but with others it can be lasting. Make that first impression work for you; don't begin the interview with one strike against you.

Do everything you can to avoid having your appearance act as a detriment to the sale. The soundness of this precept is explained and illustrated in Chapter Eight, on Making a Positive Impression.

Get the prospect's name straight and refer to him or her by name during the introduction and throughout the interview. Mispronouncing someone's name is always annoying—so get it straight the first time.

Have a natural and confident manner. As you approach the prospect, be in a positive and friendly frame of mind, confident that both of you will benefit from the interview.

Smile to establish rapport. A smile helps you put your prospect and yourself at ease. As long as it is sincere, your smile can win goodwill.

Be courteous. Ignoring the basic rules of courtesy invites the same lack of respect that it shows. Always respect your prospect's personal tastes and feelings.

Mix diplomacy with authority. You're expected to know your business, but an overbearing attitude will work against you. Make a point of being open-minded and objective about nonbusiness subjects that crop up. You can demonstrate that you honor the prospect's opinion with these techniques:

- **Ask for his or her advice.** Somewhere in your presentation you can arrange to ask the prospect what he or she thinks of a point you have made, or of a certain condition in your industry. The answer may give you important clues to his or her buying motives.

- **Agree with or show respect for what the prospect says.** It's flattering to the speaker to find that his or her remarks are accepted or respected.

- **Repeat the prospect's words.** Be alert for the opportunity to take advantage of something he or she has said as a way to further your own cause.

Give a Smooth-Flowing Talk

If you can control your presentation, you can control the interview. Since it determines both the direction and the general content of the interview, the presentation gives you the initiative and the advantage of knowing what comes next.

To gain maximum control, the presentation must be smooth flowing, with all the jerkiness and rough spots worked out of it, both in the writing and in the telling. It must be lean and hard, yet complete.

Make sure your presentation, as written, doesn't meander, drag, or pull in several directions. Ask other people to read it or hear it and tell you whether it flows and progresses in logical sequence. If it doesn't flow smoothly, work on it until it does.

Learn the final version of your presentation by heart. Rehearse it until you can handle yourself, the words, and any visual aids without a hitch.

Be Worthy of Your Prospect's Order

Your prospect's buying decision will be greatly influenced by the kind of impression you make. It isn't enough that he or she like you personally; you must come across as a strong, competent, reliable salesperson. Once the prospect decides that you are that kind of salesperson, you have gained another element of control over the interview.

Follow these hints to get your prospect to respond favorably to you:

Act with confidence. Success depends to a large extent on having and inspiring confidence, not only in your product or service but also in your company, your statements, and your own ability and judgment. Looking, acting, and sounding confident gains your prospect's confidence; without this confidence, the odds are decidedly against you. The following guidelines will help you feel and act confident.

- **Be well prepared.** Nothing helps your confidence like knowing what you are going to say and do during the interview.

- **Speak forcefully.** Convey confidence by speaking with authority and with emphasis. Avoid tentative or noncommittal statements. Speak as though you firmly believe and want your prospect to believe what you say.

  CAUTION Don't confuse confidence with boastfulness or arrogance. You don't want to bulldoze or overwhelm the prospect. Your objective is to draw him or her along with the strength of your own assurance.

- **Don't knock your competition.** Besides being in questionable taste, slamming your competition often reveals fear or lack of confidence. You gain stature with most buyers by welcoming comparison and by tending to emphasize your strong points rather than your competitors' weak ones.

- **Show loyalty to your company and your product.** A surprising number of salespeople are quick to make apologies when a prospect maligns the company. A loyal defense is the only logical response in such a situation. If you show a lack of respect for, or confidence in, the company behind you, so will your prospect.

Keep your enthusiasm high. People prefer salespeople who are enthusiastic. You can never afford merely to "go through the motions" when you're trying to sell. You have to be enthusiastic. Enthusiasm puts life into your presentation; it distinguishes you as someone who enjoys his or her work. Buyers value this quality in a salesperson and are often influenced by it. (See Chapter Eight for valuable advice on developing and maintaining enthusiasm.)

Be sincere. Stick to the facts, be sincere in presenting them and in promoting your product's benefits, and your presentation will acquire strength. A new prospect doesn't know you and may be completely ignorant of your product or your company. A sincere approach will help break down the barriers between you and win his or her confidence.

Be alert and eager to serve. Unless your selling situation is the single-call, no-repeat kind, your prospects usually judge from your first call what your attitude will be after the order is placed. Buyers like to deal with salespeople who will follow up on orders, offer helpful advice, and are there when they're needed.

Hit Hardest the Points the Prospect Likes Best

Emphasize the points to which your prospect responds best. If he or she seems to brighten when you mention product appearance, act as though appearance is an especially important feature. Your presentation will then jibe more closely with his or her strongest buying motives.

You've got to be on the lookout for reactions that will reveal what your prospect favors. Asking questions at intervals, to be sure that he or she understands points as they are made, will help smoke out your prospect's response. Some close-mouthed prospects will give little indication of their feelings, but most will give signs of agreement or disagreement that will be your cue.

Use the following techniques to emphasize particular sales points and benefits within the framework of your planned presentation:

Use your voice to add emphasis. Changing the pitch, volume, or excitement in your voice will add punch to statements that your prospect seems to like.

Use pauses and changes of tempo. If you see that a point has hit home, don't be in a hurry to move on. A pause gives a good point time to sink in. Slowing down as you cover a feature emphasizes it and gives it more time to register.

Repeat a point to give it greater force. If a sales feature gets a good response from a prospect, repeat it—either verbatim or in slightly different form. Sometimes a question ("Isn't that an important savings, Mrs. Prospect—18% less on freight bills?") is an effective way to repeat a point that merits extra emphasis.

Add fuel when you see a spark. If the prospect shows real enthusiasm for a particular benefit, make the most of it by elaborating. This kind of flexibility is often needed and is entirely compatible with a prepared presentation.

Make the summary hit the high spots. In summarizing sales points, emphasize those statements or benefits that seemed to impress your prospect the most when he or she first heard them.

Dominate the "Give and Take" of the Interview

If your presentation is both thorough and sound, interruptions by the prospect to ask questions will be minimized. Once your basic product or service story is told, however, the interview frequently takes the form of "give and take." You should try for a final close as soon as you have presented your case, but many times the prospect will have questions or objections, or will perhaps try to end the interview without making a decision.

You usually can't rely on a prepared format at this stage, since the interview can turn in almost any direction. But you still have to maintain control over the intended direction of the interview, which is toward a closed sale. You must dominate every exchange, meet and master each new development, turn every attempted detour into a supporting argument. And you should manage all this with the same easy confidence, the same lack of apparent pressure, the same pleasant manner that characterizes your presentation.

Profit by these three tips on how to keep the upper hand:

Don't lose the initiative when your prepared presentation ends. If the momentum you have built up with your sales story doesn't quite get the prospect to sign, then you must keep the ball rolling. There is a danger that you will find yourself on the defensive once the prospect begins asking questions and looking for loopholes. Obviously, the defensive position is not where you belong.

There are at least two ways to keep the initiative, and attitude is a prime factor in their success:

1. **Keep pressing for a close.** Don't back off and slow down just when you have some more selling to do. Instead of waiting for the prospect to come up with new and better reasons for *not* buying, go over the reasons why he or she *should* buy. Act as though you fully expect the order, just as you have all along.

2. **Welcome questions and objections and treat them as stepping-stones to the sale.** The art of handling objections in this way is demonstrated in Chapter Seven.

Know and use auxiliary selling points. Complete knowledge of your product or service helps here as it does elsewhere in the interview. If you have secondary selling points and facts (the ones you left out of your presentation) at your fingertips, you can contend with questions that might otherwise rattle your composure.

Control yourself and you'll control the "give and take." Control means being able to use tact when a discussion threatens to become a difference of opinion. You must avoid showing hostility of any kind, or rising to the bait when a prospect makes a provocative remark. You are there to please, not to antagonize, and self-control is essential. Remember the old selling motto: "Win the argument and lose the sale."

Who Ends the Interview?

Rather than wait for the prospect to close the interview, it's best if you bring it to a close. When a prospect hints that you had better be going, you have already stayed too long. Give your sales story, get the order, and then *leave.* This is especially important with first calls on new prospects.

> **TIP** Friendly conversation with old customers, after you get the order, is natural and valuable. Yet even here you must learn to terminate the visit or you will find your productive time slipping away.

EXAMPLES OF SUCCESSFUL SALES PRESENTATIONS

Example 1

A two-call presentation to sell the need for fire protection, make a survey, and then sell the equipment indicated by the survey.

FIRST INTERVIEW
Gets attention

Salesperson: Mr. Prospect, my name is John Collins. I'm with Augustine Industries Incorporated.

Prospect: Hello, John.

Salesperson: May I sit down, Mr. Prospect?

Prospect: Please do.

Salesperson: Mr. Prospect, this appointment was arranged specifically to discuss fire protection for your business records. Have you ever thought about being unemployed?

Prospect: No, I can't say I have. Business is so good, that thought has never entered my mind. We've been so busy that we haven't had time to think of anything but business.

Creates interest; starts the prospect thinking

Salesperson: It's wonderful to hear that your business is doing so well, but just consider this a moment. A fire tonight could put you among the unemployed tomorrow. The fact is, Mr. Prospect, that many businesses whose records are destroyed by fire never reopen their doors. I'm sure you wouldn't want to be one of them.

Objection

Prospect: No, I wouldn't. But we don't have anything to worry about, because our building is fireproof, and the records are in these steel file cabinets. That's all the protection we'll ever need.

Agrees with objection, but

Salesperson: Well, sir, your first statement about the building is correct; it is fire resistant. What is stored in the building, however, is not.

Answers objection with question

Salesperson: Don't you agree that it's possible for your stock downstairs to burn? Papers, paneling on the walls, floor covering? These can all burn and produce enough heat to burn your records. It takes only 350°F to burn paper and any one of these can produce that much heat, don't you agree?

Obtains agreement before proceeding

Prospect: I'll go along with you on that, but how about the files?

Salesperson: A steel file cabinet will protect your records from flame but not from heat, and heat is what burns. Records housed in steel containers will last approximately 4 minutes. In fact, Mr. Prospect, many of our cooking utensils are made from steel because of its excellent heat-conducting qualities.

Demonstrates point

Salesperson: Allow me to demonstrate this point. If you will place your hand on top of this file, I will light a match under the top cover, and you tell me when it gets hot. *[Waits.]* Do you agree that heat burns and not flame, and that steel conducts heat?

Gets agreement before continuing

Prospect: Yes, but I'm not completely convinced.

Salesperson: Well, sir, then you wouldn't mind if I took one of these ledger cards with me, would you?

Prospect: Of course I would. It would take some time to get the information that's on that card.

Demonstrates; makes him smell fire

Salesperson: *If* you can get it at all. Is it worth taking the chance? I have here a ledger card that was burned around the edges where all your important information is. What use, other than scrap paper, can you make of this? You see, fire can also burn your source documents, and then you would never be able to reconstruct your ledger cards.

False objection

Prospect: I can always depend upon my customers to furnish me with the information.

Shows why protection is needed. Creates more interest

Salesperson: Then why keep these records at all? You're wasting time and money, if your customers will provide this service for you.

No doubt your customers are fine people, and would probably come to your assistance, but there is always the chance that they won't. Business is business. Don't let yourself and your business be a statistic.

If for no other reason but to prove to your insurance company the current value of your inventory or accounts receivable, you need record protection. Remember, the burden of proof is on the insured. What do you think you'll prove with a burned card like this?

Prospect is interested

Prospect: That's a good point. I'll have to think about that some more. What exactly are you proposing to do?

Salesperson shows that he or she has proper service and equipment to do job; sells the company

Salesperson: Mr. Prospect, our company is in an excellent position to assist you in planning your record protection needs. Our high-quality products are designed to house all types of business records. Our 50 years of experience and know-how leaves us no reason to recommend anything but the best system and product, because we make all types.

Prospect: That's fine, but what is it that you have to offer?

Closes for survey

Salesperson: We would like to survey your records and present a proposal showing exactly what you will need to protect your records. [Pinpoints date.] Can we arrange an appointment for this Friday?

Prospect: Friday is a bad day. Next week would be better.

Salesperson: How about Monday afternoon at 2:00?

Prospect: That's O.K.

Names a satisfied user

Salesperson: Fine, we'll see you Monday afternoon. By the way, Mr. Prospect, Ms. Johnson of the XYZ Company has just purchased our complete proposal for the very same equipment we discussed today. We also did a survey for her. How about visiting XYZ to see what she purchased? At the same time we can show you the different products available.

Prospect: Good. Do you think we can go on Wednesday?

Arranges to show product in use

Salesperson: I'm sure it will be satisfactory. I'll call Ms. Johnson for the appointment and then confirm it with you. By that time the survey and report should be completed. Let's make it for 10:30 at

XYZ Company and 10:00 here. We can review the proposal before going.

Prospect: Fine.

SECOND INTERVIEW

Goes over proposal, making sure each point is understood clearly; gets agreement on each point

Salesperson: Mr. Prospect, before going over to the XYZ Company, let's go over the proposal so that all points will be clear in your mind.

The letter of transmittal explains briefly what the proposal consists of and how we will proceed to carry out its recommendations.

Talks positively, as though he or she already has the order

Salesperson: Part I gives a detailed breakdown of your records and how you are presently housing them.

Avoids negative phrases such as, "I think," "I believe," "It may be"

Salesperson: Part II contains the proposed equipment and shows what protection you will have. Part III is a summary of benefits you will receive when you purchase our equipment. Part IV is a users' list, which includes the XYZ Company. Part V has the actual quotation on the equipment.

Price objection

Prospect: What? Those prices are out of this world!

Answers objection with a question

Salesperson: Mr. Prospect, the total price may seem high to you. However, when you compare the price you will have to pay should your records burn, which price will be higher? What you've paid for the equipment, or what your loss will cost you?

Prospect:	My loss, of course, but that's assuming my records burn.
Salesperson:	True, but can you be sure that they won't? In fact, how can you be sure you won't have a fire tonight?
Prospect:	Well, I guess you're right; nothing is sure.

Trial close; asks for order

Salesperson:	There is only one way to be sure. Mr. Prospect, and that is to purchase our fire protective equipment. Why don't we go ahead and order it now?

Buying signal

Prospect:	Not so fast, I haven't even seen the equipment yet.
Salesperson:	Fine, then let's go over to XYZ Co. It's about time for our appointment.

(AT XYZ COMPANY)

Salesperson:	Mr. Prospect, I'd like to introduce Ms. Johnson, controller for the XYZ Co. Ms. Johnson, can you tell us the major reason why you placed your records in fire protective equipment?
Ms. Johnson:	Yes, the salesperson came in and made a complete study and showed us why it would cost more to reproduce our records after a fire than to be safe and place them in fire protective equipment. We didn't take his word, mind you; we had to see for ourselves. So we made our own little study. Sure enough, everything the salesperson said was true. At least I can go home at night now not worrying about whether I'll have a job to go to tomorrow.
Prospect:	Yes, I'm beginning to see your reasoning.
Salesperson:	Ms. Johnson, would you mind if I demonstrated your equipment to Mr. Prospect?
Ms. Johnson:	No, go right ahead.

Covers product feature by feature. Answers objections before they are voiced

Salesperson: Mr. Prospect, this piece of equipment is called a "Safe File Deluxe." It is the unit we recommended to protect your open orders. Notice the sturdiness of this unit, how well built it is. Doesn't it look as though it will go through any fire?

Prospect: Yes, how is it made?

Shows inside of drawer

Salesperson: It is made of a monolithic (one-piece) construction, precast and predried. One-piece construction means that the sides, top, bottom, back, and even the drawer separators are all cast as one unit before the steel frame is placed over it. We precast it to remove all possible imperfections in the insulation, such as cracks, air holes, and so on. It is predried to less than 1/2 of 1% free moisture. The steel frame that is placed over the insulation would rust if the free moisture were not removed.

Gets prospect to say "Yes"

Salesperson: You don't have to worry about rust with our unit. Isn't that a wonderful feature?

Prospect: Yes.

Gets prospect in on demonstration

Salesperson: While I have the drawer open, take a look at the gear-actuated full progressive suspension. Due to the weight of the drawer we use gears instead of the normal-type suspension. This provides maintenance-free operation and ease of drawer pull. Try the drawer. Open and close it a few times. Doesn't it operate smoothly?

Prospect: Yes, it does.

Salesperson: Mr. Prospect, this Safe File Deluxe bears three labels of certification.

1. The government's A-1 rating which means that it will withstand.

   a. Severe fire (reaching 1700°F) for at least 1 hour without interior temperature reaching 350°F

   b. Sudden heating without producing an explosion

   c. Impact due to falling 30 feet after being heated for 1/2 hour and reheating for 1/2 hour in the inverted position after impact without destroying the usability of papers or records stored inside

2. The Safe Industries Consolidated Association Approval, with the same specifications.

3. The Safe Cabinet Lab 1 hour label, which is the label of our own laboratories, where research and development of these units are constantly being performed.

Gets agreement

Salesperson: Doesn't this give you a feeling of complete protection, knowing there are such organizations behind this product?

Buying signal

Prospect: Yes, I never realized there was so much entailed in marketing such a product. How about the locking device?

Gets prospect to try lock

Salesperson: I'm glad you mentioned that, Mr. Prospect. Most people seem to take it for granted. It is a plunger-type lock and can be made to control one drawer individually or all drawers simply by flicking this lever on the side of the drawer. Here, try it . . . . What do you think of this little added feature?

Buying signal

Prospect: Very interesting. I could use that for my personal drawer.

Salesperson: Yes, sir, and this is one of the additional features, which is standard on the files we are recommending. If you should desire a combination lock, that, too, can be placed on the file.

Prospect: That's nice to know, but I don't think I'll need that much protection.

Salesperson: Do you have any questions on what was covered thus far?

Prospect: No, everything is quite clear. About how long would it take to get this equipment?

Trial close

Salesperson: If we place the order today, we will have your equipment in two weeks. Shall we enter the order?

Answers "procrastination" objection

Prospect: No, let me think it over a little while.

Salesperson: I'm glad to see you're cautious in making decisions, Mr. Prospect, but fire, unfortunately, is not. You can't afford to wait or think about this problem.

Summarizes, getting agreement again; gets prospect to keep saying "Yes"

Salesperson: You agreed that our one-piece monolithic construction, precast and predried, was an excellent feature, right? Certainly you concurred that the unit is well constructed. You also agreed on the excellence of our gear actuated suspension, didn't you?

Prospect: Yes

Salesperson: You were quite pleased to hear about the organizations backing our equipment. And our locking device solves your problem of how to lock your personal drawer without affecting the operation of the other drawers, correct?

Prospect: That's true . . .

Asks for the order

Salesperson:	Since you agree on all these points and since you concur that fire protection is needed for your records, why wait? Why take the chance? Let's place this order today and minimize your waiting time. Each moment wasted can mean the life of your business.

Helps prospect make a decision

Salesperson:	By the way, Mr. Prospect, shall we specify our slate blue color to match the decor of your office?
Prospect:	Yes, that's an excellent suggestion.
Salesperson:	Fine. Thank you very much, Mr. Prospect. I'll get to work on this immediately.

Example 2

A presentation to purchasing agents or shop supervisors to sell a grinding wheel that requires a semitechnical explanation.

Opening

Salesperson:	Good morning, Wes, how are you today?
Customer:	Hi, Lou. I'm fine. What's new?

Gets attention by handing customer a piece of abrasive

Salesperson:	I've something interesting to show you.
Customer:	What is this?
Salesperson:	That's a piece of green silicon carbide abrasive—we call it 39 CRYSTOLON. It's the abrasive used to make our wheels for roughing out carbide tools.
Customer:	It really sparkles, doesn't it?

Creates interest in explaining how specimen is made

Salesperson:	Yes. I thought you would be interested in knowing a little about it. This is made by

charging an electric furnace with silica sand and coke. When the electric current is turned on, the heat starts a reaction between the silica in the sand and the carbon in the coke, and the result is silicon carbide, just like that piece you're looking at.

Customer: Then you crush it up and make wheels out of it?

Hands customer hardness chart

Salesperson: That's right. But, Wes, we're faced with quite a problem in making wheels to do a good job grinding carbide tools. Here, look at this chart. This chart shows the relative hardness of various materials. This hardness test is used for very hard materials. You see, hardened tool steel comes out about 740. Here are your bonded cemented carbides that run between 1900 and 2000, and here is ALUNDUM, aluminum oxide abrasive, at 2050.

Uses chart to explain degree of hardness

Salesperson: Now some of the hard particles of tungsten carbide in the tool bit go to 2480. There is CRYSTOLON abrasive also at 2480, Norbide at 2800, and diamond at 8000, or higher.

You can see the problem now. In the case of green grit plate-mounted wheels, you have to grind the carbide with an abrasive that is no harder, or at best only slightly harder, than the carbide itself. It is like whittling on a piece of wood with a wooden knife.

Makes sure customer understands

Salesperson: Do you see what I mean?

Customer: Yes, but what about the Norbide?

Salesperson: Well, the Norbide is hard enough all right—in fact, it does a good job when used for lapping. But it doesn't have the necessary strength or toughness to be used as an abrasive in a wheel. This is why green grit wheels are usually very soft.

Customer: They sure wear down fast.

Uses simple imagery to clarify

Salesperson: If you think of a grain on one of those wheels, you can see that it wouldn't have to hit the carbide many times before becoming dull. If the wheel were made hard, to give you long wheel life, those grains would be held in the wheel too long and you would be grinding with dull grains. A wheel like this would grind very slowly and heat up the carbide and maybe crack it. Even if it didn't crack, the heat would probably damage it so that the edge wouldn't stand up in use. That would be bad, as you know. So the wheels have to be made soft to allow those grains to break out of the wheel as soon as they start to dull.

Creates interest in new product

Salesperson: In the past, wheel manufacturers have gone to open structure wheels—wide grain spacing—to try and get longer wheel life. But that didn't seem to be the answer because the grains still became dull just as fast and the wheel still had to be just as soft to get rid of the dull grains, before they could damage the carbides.

We've tried something new and now have a wheel that will last longer, cut faster, and still not heat up the carbide.

Explains with parallelism

Customer: What's that?

Salesperson: You know, if you have a hacksaw and are cutting something soft like aluminum, you use a blade with wide tooth spacing. But if you used that blade on a very hard material, it wouldn't cut very well. As a matter of fact, the teeth would probably strip off the blade, so you go to a blade with a close tooth spacing— lots of teeth, each taking a small chip—and this blade cuts quite fast. Isn't that right?

Gets agreement before continuing

Customer: Yes.

Points out benefits resulting from product improvement

Salesperson: Well, we've done the same thing with our plate-mounted CRYSTOLON wheels: packed more abrasive grains into the wheel.

Each time the wheel turns around there are more grains cutting the carbide. This makes the wheel cut faster. And, of course, any savings you can make in time are valuable, considering what labor and overhead costs are today.

Each grain still gets dull just as fast as before, but since there are more grains in the wheel, the wheel lasts longer. So you don't buy as many wheels to grind the same number of tools.

Shows sample wheel

Salesperson: We call this dense structure wheel a #4 structure wheel. Plate-mounted wheels are 14" × 4" with a 1 1/2" rim, and the marking would be 39C60-K4VK.

More benefits

Salesperson: This wheel not only saves you money because it lasts longer, but it also produces savings because it cuts faster. You can see for yourself.

Objection

Customer: It seems logical enough, but we're having pretty good luck with our present wheel.

Answers objection with a question

Salesperson: Yes, but you wouldn't mind having a wheel that would last longer, would you?

Customer: No.

Closes

Salesperson: Here, I'll write down the marking of this wheel and you can requisition one to test. Mark your requisition "test orders," and we will bill you at your normal quantity discount. Will you order one of these to try?

Customer: Okay.

Example 3

A presentation to farmers, built around the use of photgraphs, to sell a premium fertilizer, emphasizing dependability of the supplier.

Reminds prospect of pre-interview mailing

Salesperson: Hello, Mr. Farmer, I'm Ted Moore. I'm with International Minerals & Chemical Corporation. Remember the postcard I sent you last week? I mentioned that I'd like to talk fertilizer with you.

I know your time is valuable. And, of course, there wouldn't be much point in my taking up your time if I had only an ordinary fertilizer to offer.

But we have a premium plant food and I would like to tell you about it . . . . And also give you a brief sketch of our company and explain why it pays to do business with us. As I mentioned on the postcard, I'll need only a few minutes. I'd like to show you some photographs that will help you see what makes our food plant superior.

Photo 1—Bag of Rainbow. Mentions farmer's need

The first photo shows you the product . . . Rainbow Plant Food. It's a premium fertilizer . . . made for people who want to farm better . . . for farmers who want better than ordinary results.

Photo 2—Gas pump. Explains need with parallelism

The point I'd like to make with the next slide is that Rainbow is a modern fertilizer . . . the kind of plant food that goes with today's farming. Just as you need a high-octane gas for a high-compression engine, you also need a better fertilizer to give you yield and crop growth advantages.

Photo 3—Two piles of fertilizer

The next photo brings up a question: "How can you tell if a premium fertilizer is really more than ordinary and worth the little bit extra it costs?" Unless you spend a lot of time studying fertilizers, it's hard to know exactly what you should be getting in a fertilizer.

Photo 4—Tailor-made for crops and soils

As the next photo suggests, the plant food you buy should contain what your soil needs. Sounds simple, doesn't it? But not when you think about it. Soils vary all over the country . . . rainfall varies . . . cropping practices vary . . . as a result, some areas are more deficient in certain elements than others.

Yet a good many fertilizers are made the same for Illinois, California, New York, or any other state . . . just as though all soil needed exactly the same fertilizer. Of course, that's not the case with International Rainbow. All our fertilizers are tailor-made for your soil.

Photo 5—Help at the right time

The point I'd like to make with the next photo is that you need a fertilizer that helps out at exactly the right time. For example, some nitrogen sources give your crops a fast spurt early in the season and then fizzle out. Other sources may not go to work until later in the summer . . . they work fine in August but don't help a bit in May.

You and I can't tell just by looking at a handful of fertilizer what kind of nitrogen it contains or when it will be available to plants. But the point is that one source usually isn't enough. You generally need more than one nitrogen source in the fertilizer you buy, to provide for your crops throughout the growing season. That's another reason why Rainbow is better.

Photo 6—Builds up company reliability

You'll notice the word "dependable" on the next photo. And that's what you want . . . a dependable fertilizer from a dependable company that keeps ahead of the times. Everything else you buy is being improved. Tractors are better . . . combines are better . . . and your fertilizer should be better. There is no good reason why you should settle for a fertilizer that hasn't been improved for 20 years. Our company recognizes that fact and therefore keeps up with new discoveries . . . keeps Rainbow Plant Food up to date. That's the kind you need.

Photo 7—New IMC administrative building

The next slide shows you our headquarters . . . International Minerals & Chemical Corporation. It's a progressive company with a 50-year reputation for standing behind its fertilizer and other products.

Photo 8—Print of recent ad

You've probably seen our plant food ads. The one you see on the next slide recently appeared in leading farm magazines. You'll see more of our ads because International Minerals & Chemicals Corporation has been a major factor in the fertilizer business for more than 50 years.

We're basic producers of fertilizer ingredients. For instance, we have our own deposits in Florida, where phosphate is mined and refined. The point I'd like to make is that we don't depend on just anybody's source of phosphorous. With our own deposits we're assured of a constant, uniform supply.

Photo 9—Super Scooper; dependability of source

The next slide shows how it's mined. The large dragline you see is called the Super Scooper . . . it digs a freight car full at one bite.

Photo 10—Clam Loader; more on dependability of company; freight savings

We also have our own potash deposits in New Mexico. The photo you're looking at shows a hard-working machine that loads 14 tons per minute. It's just one of the machines that helps to make the mining of potash an efficient operation.

Photo 11—Noralyn facilities; brings the prospect into the picture; salesperson states facts and explains what those facts mean to the prospect

This fall we're also opening up new potash mines in Canada. This mine will be important to Midwestern farmers because it means a potash source closer to the farm with important freight savings.

Of course, you're wondering what all this means to you. Well, it means this . . . more efficient production of fertilizer. It also means better quality because we have better control over what goes into the fertilizer we sell you and can keep an up-to-the-minute check on quality all along the way.

Photo 12—Quality control

At every step in the process of making fertilizer or processing the ingredients, we run careful tests and quality checks. Our quality control program is concerned with more than the rigid specifications set by the government. We have our own research and agricultural specialists who keep an eagle eye on Rainbow and demand the finest ingredients and top performance from them.

Photo 13—Formulation check. Turns facts into benefits

In addition, samples of all the production in our plants are sent to the Plant Food Division's main control laboratory and checked for quality and proper ratio. This means that you can depend upon the formulation you buy and that the Rainbow Plant Food you buy will give you the results we say it will.

Photo 14—Storage facilities; moves from product to service advantages

We also have modern storage facilities where the plant food is carefully cured under ideal conditions. This means two things to you . . . you get plant food that's in top-notch physical condition, free-flowing and easy to spread . . . and you can get quick service . . . you get the kind of plant food you want, when you want it.

Photo 15—U.S. map with Rainbow plants

The next slide shows the locations of our plants . . . 24 plants in the Midwest, South and East. You'll notice there's one near here . . . over at [*names nearest plant*]. Even though we're a large nationwide fertilizer manufacturer, our service is local . . . we're close to you so that we can serve you better and faster.

Photo 16—Loading slide; names plant again; more facts turned into benefits

The next photo shows the loading facilities we have at *[names nearest plant]* . . . plenty of help so that your truck gets loaded fast if you pick up your fertilizer. Or, if you buy through a dealer, it means that the dealer can guarantee delivery because he knows he can depend on our faster service.

Photo 17—Agricultural experiment station

The point I would like to make with the next photo is our interest in plant food research. For instance, we have contributed about a million dollars for agricultural college and experiment station research projects. We help them carry out the soils and plant research that shows how to get better crops and bigger yields. Right now we are working with 20 agricultural colleges on 26 separate plant nutrition projects. Here in *[name of state]* we're working with *[name of local university]* on a research project. Other projects which we have recently supported here are *[cite specific relevant projects]* .

Photo 18—Green house

And in our own laboratories, IMC scientists check results and work constantly to develop even better plant foods . . . better methods of making raw materials work in the soil . . . keeping Rainbow Plant Food ahead of the times, tailor-made for your farm to give you better returns on fertilizer and farm investments.

Photo 19—Rainbow billboard; summarizes

So, it's all there . . . a plant food designed for your soil . . . the right ingredients to help throughout the growing season and a product kept ahead of the times by International's staff of 300 scientists and agronomists. Quality? Sure. We've been delivering it for 50 years. Reliable? You bet. International has the mines and the plants and the people to furnish what you need *when* you need it.

You may have heard the old saying: "Fertilizer doesn't cost . . . it pays." Well, that's certainly true of Rainbow Plant Food. Rainbow turns each acre into a profit maker.

Assumptive closing

Mr. Farmer, you have been very attentive to this demonstration. I know that you've been visualizing the better crops you will get with Rainbow Plant Food. I'm sure you'll want it delivered to you by *[date]*, in time for your next spreading.

CHAPTER SIX

POWER–CLOSING TECHNIQUES

*Closing is the most important thing in selling:
you can't sell if you can't close.*

Many salespeople do a good job with every step of the selling process until they get to the close. Then they falter, and all their work is lost.

In terms of time, the close may represent only 5% of the entire presentation. But because they don't know what to do during that all-important 5% period of time, they often waste the 95% that is spent on the preliminary steps.

You have to be a strong closer to make top-level income at selling. But it's something that's relatively simple to master—and that will repay you with high-bracket earnings for the rest of your selling days.

This chapter gives you the closing techniques that top-earning salespeople use. These techniques will work just as well for you. What's more, they'll free you from all anxiety about the close.

They have been known to work even for salespeople who approach the closing with dread.

This chapter explains and illustrates these four techniques that will make you a strong closer:

1. *Close early, close often, close late*

2. *Twelve tested ways to get the signed order*

3. *There must be a "hook" to close*

4. *Ideas for working out your own closing techniques*

The all-important "hook" is explained in detail. You'll see why no sale has ever been lost because there are two hooks, but why hundreds of sales have been lost because there was *none*.

CLOSE EARLY, CLOSE OFTEN, AND CLOSE LATE

The Multiple-Close Technique: The Key to More Closings

The multiple-close technique is something you must master if you want to move up fast in selling. It requires making a series of trial closes, each time attempting to determine whether or not the prospect is ready at that moment to buy.

In the multiple-close technique, a negative reply to a trial close is not regarded as final. It merely indicates that the prospect is not ready to buy at that point. A top-flight salesperson makes, if necessary, from four to eight attempts to close during the course of a presentation.

This is the key to "closing power." You must try and try again to close.

When to Attempt to Close

Since the multiple-closing technique calls for several attempts to close, the safe rule to follow is *close early, close often, close late*. Begin as soon as possible with trial closes. Your own good judgment, based on the surrounding circumstances, will tell you when and how to make the necessary trial closes.

Trial closings come naturally and effectively at these times:

- After strong points in your presentation
- After overcoming an obstacle presented by the prospect
- When your demonstration ends
- When the prospect indicates that he or she is ready to buy

Before demonstrating how to make a strong closing at each of these times, let's see first *why* it's never too early to try for a close and how expert closers handle a "No" and follow it by another trial close.

It's Never Too Early to Try for a Close

Many salespeople postpone the first attempt to close until the interview has almost run its course or at least until they have made their full demonstration. This is almost always a serious error. More frequently than most salespeople realize, the prospect—if he or she can be sold at all—can be sold well before the presentation has been made in its entirety.

Since it is sound practice to get the order at the earliest time it is obtainable, delay in trying to close indicates poor selling skills. Interruptions can occur that may cost you the sale. And continuing to "sell" after the prospect has decided to buy can result in talking yourself out of the order.

Salespeople who defer their first trial close usually do so because they *fear* a turn-down. They have missed the whole point of the multiple-close technique, which is designed to eliminate fear of a turn-down.

The Proper Attitude Toward "No" in Trial Closings

A turn-down on a trial close doesn't mean that the sale can't be made on the *next* try or on the one following that. By using the multiple-close technique, you know that you lose nothing by making an unsuccessful attempt, since you are prepared to carry on with sales points that you have kept in reserve for the next try.

▪ IDEA IN ACTION

Jake Williams sells a home insulation service. He has told his story to his prospect, Mr. Jensen, and quoted the cost of insulating his home. Jake decides that now is the time to make his first trial close.

"Sounds like a pretty profitable thing to do, doesn't it, Mr. Jensen?" says Jake.

Jake knows that there is only an off chance that this first trial close will win him the order. Of course, if it *does,* he is ready to write it up immediately.

"Well," replies his prospect, "I'm not so sure. Even if it cuts down our heating bills as much as you say, it would take several years to pay for itself. No, I don't think I'd want to invest that amount of money."

Jake, a skillful closer, does not permit this reply to throw him off base. He knew in advance that the odds were against a "Yes" at this point—so his response to his prospect's reply is to continue with his sales talk. But this time he focuses on the extra *convenience* his product offers.

"There are some mighty important conveniences that you will enjoy from the very day your insulation is installed. First is the wonderful relief from that 'oven' feeling when the sun's been baking down on your roof all day. Second, you won't have to spend as much time next fall cutting, splitting, and stacking wood for that woodstove you've been complaining about. The heat that it generates will stay in the house instead of disappearing through the roof and walls.

"These two things alone make insulating worthwhile, don't you think?"

Jake knows that if Mr. Jensen replies favorably to this second trial close, the sale can be closed then and there. He also knows that the odds are against an early trial close evoking a "Yes"—that it may be the fourth or sixth rather than the first or second trial that will do the trick. Jake knows, finally, that even when a second trial close evokes a "No," he has lost nothing by the attempt. He is prepared to go right on with his sales talk, should Mr. Jensen turn him down on this second attempt.

"How long did you say I can have to pay for this job?" is Jensen's reply to Jake's second trial close.

This response indicates to Jake that Jensen is just about ready to buy. So he says, "Three years, Mr. Jensen, and I think you'll find that the modest monthly payments will be a small price for all the benefits you'll get from insulation. If you'll just okay this form, I'll see that the job is started without delay."

"All right," says his prospect, "it'll be a relief to get a good night's sleep when it gets really hot in another six weeks or so!"

Try for a Close After Strong Points in Your Presentation

At certain times in your presentation, you summarize what you have been saying in one briefly stated strong point. After you deliver this "punch line"—or a series of them—try for a close.

■ IDEA IN ACTION

Ruth Cavanaugh sells automobiles. She has told her prospect, Mrs. Damron, the highlights of the presentation about the car she is trying to sell her and decides to make her first trial close.

"You'll want the car for the weekend, won't you, Mrs. Damron?"

"Well, first I've got to decide to buy it!" comes the response.

"Yes," Ruth says, "and let me tell you why most of our customers say they'd never own another make car." (Here Ruth continues with her presentation. She climaxes her talk with a convincing fact about the car's pickup and economy, then tries for another close.)

"What color will you want, Mrs. Damron—the metallic blue or the gray that's been so popular this year?"

"Well, of course, I haven't decided yet whether or not I'm going to buy. But if I do, I'll want my daughter's opinion on the color," says Mrs. Damron.

Ruth replies, "Of course you will—especially since she'll be doing so much of the driving. But something you'll both appreciate is the extended warranty." (After briefly explaining the specifics of the warranty extension, Ruth launches into her third trial close.)

"Let me tell you about a friend of mine. He bought another make car—a popular make—that didn't have this extra protection." (Here Ruth goes into a close that stresses her friend's regret.)

"So you see, Mrs. Damron, why I think you'd be wise to select a car with the peace of mind that our extended warranty brings."

Noting that her prospect is silent and apparently hesitating, Ruth picks up her order book and says, "Suppose I fill out this form—"

"No," says Mrs. Damron, "I'll have to think it over. It's a good car all right—and a good buy—but there's no point in rushing into a deal like this. I'll come back tomorrow, after I've had a chance to consult with my daughter."

"Okay, Mrs. Damron, that's fine. But let me just go over the high points so you'll have a clear picture of what we offer . . ." (Here Ruth summarizes the strong points in her presentation.)

"Now," she concludes, "let's see what all this adds up to—comfort, appearance, safety, economy, easy terms, a nice trade-in allowance plus the extra peace of mind our warranty offers—just about all you can ask for, isn't it?

"Yes," replies Mrs. Damron after this series of "punch" lines, "I guess you're right. How soon can I pick it up?"

Try for a Close After Overcoming an Obstacle

When you have successfully overcome an obstacle presented by your prospect, you have just gained a point; the "balance" of the sale has tipped in your direction. You can best capitalize this advantage with a trial close.

An objection raised by a prospect is the most common obstacle.

There is a very close relationship between the ability to close and the ability to overcome objections. Indeed, the relationship between the two is so close that it is difficult to deal with either one apart from the other. This is true largely because most buyers are inclined to voice their objections at the moment when the salesperson attempts to get them to commit—unless, of course, they are ready to buy. A prospect or buyer who has no remaining objections can logically do nothing *except* buy. By the same token, a lost order always represents a situation in which there remained one (or more) objections which the salesperson was unable to overcome.

Seen in this light, overcoming objections is, in a practical sense, synonymous with closing the sale.

■ IDEA IN ACTION

Dick Larsen represents a new company selling industrial dyes. He knows that the biggest barrier to a sale will be the "present supplier" objection. Dick prepares not only to overcome this objection, but to capitalize on it to make a sale.

When he is met with the brush-off, "We've bought from the same source for 20 years—I see no reason to change," Dick hands his prospect a portfolio of testimonial letters. He says, "Let me show you some companies you know and respect who *have* changed to our brand."

He uses the testimonials to overcome his prospect's objection and to lead in to a close at the same time.

"You see," Dick tells his prospect, "these other companies that are comparable to yours have found it profitable to adopt our product." His prospect is impressed. Dick attempts a trial close.

"Would you like to order your usual quantities, or would you prefer to take advantage of the 5% discount we're offering this month on bulk sales?"

After a brief explanation of the savings possible with the discount, Dick's prospect signs up for an order larger than he normally places.

Whatever the obstacle may be, the technique is the same: Overcome the obstacle and try for a close immediately.

Try for a Close When the Demonstration Ends

After a demonstration has been made, the time is usually ripe to try for the order. If the demonstration has been good, you have created a desire for ownership, and the close is frequently nothing more than a routine agreement on price, delivery instructions, and so on.

■ IDEA IN ACTION

Bella Corazzi represents an internal communications system company. She has just made the last move of her demonstration and is stating her final strong point. "So you see, Mr. Hilton, use of our system permits you to contact key people in your organization instantly and eliminates the time-consuming walk from your office to theirs."

Bella's very next words begin her close.

"I appreciate your undivided attention, Mr. Hilton. If you'll be kind enough to give me the number of stations you require and the location of the individuals who will be using this system, I'll quickly estimate the total time and cost of installation."

Bella has little difficulty getting an affirmative response to this natural and logical close.

Try for a Close on a Buying Signal

Stay alert, and you will often detect signals from your prospect indicating that he or she is seriously considering buying. You must try to close as soon as you recognize the buying signal. It may be a comment, a question, a note of interest or enthusiasm in the prospect's voice, a gesture, or a facial expression. If you read the signal right, you'll probably close the sale.

■ IDEA IN ACTION

Robert Sanders, a real estate salesperson, is showing his prospect a newly listed home. The prospect looks at the heating equipment and the utility room with nothing more than polite attention. However, when he sees the workshop area, his voice indicates a high level of interest and enthusiasm.

"I've always wanted a shop for woodworking," he says. Bob builds up the prospect's interest on this point and tries for a close. Although the prospect has not seen enough for him to commit himself, Bob's early trial close has focused the prospect's mind on something he likes about the house and has laid the groundwork for a close.

A while later the talk turns to financing, and Bob explains the down payment and monthly terms. He watches his prospect closely. The prospect rubs his chin thoughtfully and smiles; Bob sees that the conditions appeal to him. So Bob tries a second time, but again is unable to close.

Later, the prospect asks, "Did you say I could have this roof fixed for about fifteen hundred dollars?" "Why, yes," Bob responds, "you can have it fixed for that amount." This question indicates to Bob his prospect's keen desire to buy. "But you can do it yourself for a lot less than that. You're evidently pretty handy at fixing things up, and with summer coming on, this is the time to do it."

Bob moves into a close and this time makes the sale. Constant awareness of his prospect's attitude—as indicated by what he says and how he acts—tips Bob off as to when he should try to close.

IMPORTANT The way a prospect phrases an objection is often the signal to try to close. When such a signal is flashed, you must stop "selling." (Chapter Seven provides a complete explanation of how to recognize an objection that means "Yes, I'll buy.")

The multiple-close technique raises the question: "Isn't persistence a form of pressure that many people resent?" The fact is that all effective selling involves the use of pressure, since it takes pressure to change a person's mind. (Chapter One covers how to use low-pressure techniques effectively.)

Offer Something Special to get an Immediate Order

Are you in a business that sells by direct mail as well as through salespeople like yourself? If so, you might whip up an immediate closing by using some of the techniques your company uses successfully in getting orders through the mail.

▪ IDEA IN ACTION

A large publisher sells some of its products through direct mail and some through salespeople. To get direct mail orders, this company offers premium booklets which are valuable in themselves.

Alva Strong sells an information service for this company. She keeps track of all the booklets that are bringing in mail orders. When Alva tries for a close, she throws in a selection of booklets to get her prospect to give her the order *now*.

She glamorizes these booklets because she knows that each one was prepared by a specialist in the subject covered. She doesn't treat them lightly. After all, haven't they brought in thousands of orders by mail?

TWELVE TESTED TECHNIQUES THAT CLOSE SALES

Here are 12 tested closing techniques you can use to close sales effectively. All of them will be of value to you at one time or another if you use the multiple-close technique.

The skilled salesperson masters all 12, knowing just the right one to use for each trial close. He or she may even try the *same* technique several times in a row and then swing into another type when it becomes obvious that more power is needed.

Begin by mastering three or four of the closes that feel most comfortable to you. As you gain proficiency in them, incorporate others into your selling. Remember, the ability to use all these closing techniques—and any others that you may develop—is what distinguishes you from the average salesperson.

In 3 of the 12 closing techniques, the salesperson assumes that the prospect has decided to make the purchase. The difference lies in the manner in which this assumption is expressed, as illustrated in the first 3 techniques described.

Technique 1:
Assume That the Prospect is Ready
to Buy (Assumptive Close)

You go into an assumptive close by making a statement indicating that you *assume* the prospect is ready to buy. If the prospect goes along with this statement, the sale is safely closed; if he or she balks, you resume selling until you're ready to make another trial close.

■ IDEA IN ACTION

Paul Jackman works for a large pharmaceutical company. He has spent about 15 minutes explaining a new drug to his prospect. The prospect mentions that a gross lot costs $50 more than the type he has been ordering, but also shows a preference for the new drug.

Paul realizes that the time has come to try to close the sale. He stops his sales talk and says, "I'm sure you'll be satisfied with it. Suppose I write up an order for one gross."

Paul, a seasoned salesperson, knows that his prospect may back away from this assumptive close by saying something like, "No, I haven't really decided yet." Paul also knows that if this occurs, he must go further into his presentation until he reaches the proper place for a second trial close.

Although most prospects will respond to an assumptive close by either expressing agreement or backing off, some will do nothing to indicate their response. When Paul's prospect is silent, he knows that he could take advantage of the situation to force a decision on the spot. But he also knows that this technique can backfire. So he decides to interpret his prospect's lack of response as an indication that he is still undecided. Paul shifts the focus of his presentation to the new drug's effectiveness by pulling out an impressive file of newspaper and magazine clippings. When he sees that the prospect is swayed by these testimonials, he moves in for another trial close. This time, he makes the sale.

The assumptive close should never *seem* like a closing maneuver, but rather like the salesperson's recognition of a decision that has already been made by the prospect. When this effect is achieved, even if the prospect responds by backing off, he or she simply feels that the salesperson's confidence in the product's value has led him or her to overestimate the prospect's enthusiasm for it. In any case, no harm is done. Backing off simply means that the customer is not yet ready to buy and therefore needs to be exposed to an additional presentation to provide the basis for another trial close.

When a prospect meets an assumptive close with *silence,* the salesperson must decide whether (1) to take the chance of continuing to assume that the sale is closed or (2) to follow the safer course and assume that the customer has not yet decided either way. The first alternative is dangerously close to high-pressure selling, which is normally not good selling. Furthermore, it tends to force an immediate decision, and since the silent response does indicate indecision, there is a relatively high chance of losing the sale altogether. Therefore, while the salesperson would obviously prefer a "Yes" response to an assumptive close, he or she should be almost as well satisfied with silence at this point. Silence indicates two things: (1) indecision and (2) enough interest on the prospect's part to justify the expectation that a little more "selling" will very likely lead to the sale.

IMPORTANT Every salesperson should master the assumptive closing technique because it is so safe and effective. It suits all personalities and is appropriate for all types of prospects and products.

Technique 2:
Act as if the Prospect Will Buy
(Physical Action Close)

Closely related to the assumptive technique is another closing technique known as "physical action." Here the salesperson assumes that the sale is closed but expresses this assumption with a physical action rather than verbally.

Here are some ways to use the physical action technique:

- Begin to write out the order.

- Hand the order form and pen to the prospect for his or her signature.

- Pick up the telephone and say, "I'll phone the order in now, to save time."

- Hand the item to the prospect and say, "I guess you want to take it with you."

The physical action close does not have the appearance of pressure—provided it is executed in a manner that leads the prospect to think that the salesperson has merely overestimated the degree of the prospect's own enthusiasm or decision on the matter. If placed with some skill in the course of the interview where such a "mistake" might seem logical, it is never offensive.

> **CAUTION** If the prospect wishes to back off from a physical action close, he or she will have to say something to stop the salesperson's act, for example, "No, don't write it up yet; I'm not sure I want this." A "backing off" response to a physical action close is likely to weaken the salesperson's case, which is rarely true of a similar response to an assumptive close.

Technique 3:
Get the Prospect to Decide
on a Minor Point (Choice Close)

This closing technique is an attempt to get a decision from the prospect on some detail of the salesperson's offer by having him or her make a choice. A decision on the choice is obtained in such a way as to imply or involve a decision *on the sale itself.* For example,

Real Estate Salesperson:	Shall we prepare the lease as of May 1 or June 1?
Office Equipment Salesperson:	Now that you've heard the facts, do you think our electronic typewriter or word processor would best suit your needs?

The minor point technique can be applied mildly or forcefully to suit individual circumstances.

For instance, it is "milder" to say, "Would you prefer this in blue or gray?" than to say, "Do you want this in blue or gray?" The milder form is also the safer one and normally evokes the order if it is obtainable at that point just as successfully as the bolder form. This is a technique that you can "season to taste" for almost all occasions.

Technique 4:
Offer the Prospect Something
for Deciding to Buy Now
(Concession Close)

In some types of selling it is possible to get the prospect to decide to place his or her order immediately by offering "something special" for an immediate decision. The concession close has its place in the realm of selling. There are "close-out" and various other situations where negotiation, rather than a fixed quotation, is used to determine the price, terms, and conditions of the offer.

■ IDEA IN ACTION

Yolanda Smith, a real estate agent, has finished showing the house her prospect is interested in. She has attempted several trial closes during the course of her presentation; each time the prospect has argued for a lower price. Her last close almost worked, and she sees that the prospect needs only a little "nudge" to help him make a decision.

"If you'll close right now, I'll drop the price of the house $1,000. Is it a deal?" Yolanda asks.

"Okay, I'll take it," the prospect agrees, convinced by this price concession.

Technique 5:
Induce the Prospect to Close
(Inducement Close)

This technique involves offering something "extra" that is available to *anyone* who takes advantage of it. The offer of something "extra" tends to overcome hesitation and delay. It has helped close many a sale. For example,

Salesperson (wholesale drugs):	We have a special introductory offer on this new product. The regular price is $54 a dozen, but we can take your order now at $48 per dozen.
Salesperson (furniture manufacturer):	On any order you place with me now for fall merchandise, we will give you a 10% advertising allowance to help you start the season with a good advertising campaign.

Technique 6:
Give the Prospect a Reason to Buy
Now (Last Chance Close)

When you can honestly state a condition that will or may arise in the near future that would make buying more favorable now than later, you are in a position to use the "last-chance" close.

Manufacturer's Representative:	We are closing out this model and have only 18 left to sell. They will no doubt all be sold within a week, and then you can buy only the new model at the regular price."

Salesperson (life insurance):	Your last birthday was almost six months ago—that means you'll have to place your application before next Thursday or pay a higher annual premium.
Salesperson (photographic supplies):	There's a 7% increase in price on this item effective the first of next month. This is your last opportunity to stock up at our present low prices.

This "last chance" close relies on an appeal to fear—fear that an offer that is available now will (or may) be lost if there is delay in acceptance. Since fear of losing something of value is a strong buying motive, this closing technique has a lot of power.

> **CAUTION** This technique can be used only when a factual situation exists or the possibility that such a situation will arise exists. On the other hand, the alert salesperson can often find such an opportunity where others see none.

Technique 7:
The Right Kind of "Story" Will Help Close the Sale (Narrative Close)

Each of us relies heavily on the experiences of others in practically every decision we make. We all try to duplicate the success of others and to avoid their failures. This is what gives the narrative method of closing its force.

One facet of the narrative technique sets it apart from others: When you use it skillfully, you can, without referring to the prospect directly, point out how unwise he or she is to hesitate. For example,

Salesperson (real estate):	Another couple was looking at a similar lakefront property with the same idea of building a summer home. They found just the spot they had been looking for, too, but because they hesitated a little too long, they lost out to another buyer.

Salesperson	There's a woman not far from here who just
(children's	ordered a dozen additional prints of her young
photographs):	children's photograph, on top of the six that
	we offer at this special price. She liked the
	photo so much that she sent one to relatives
	and old friends, many of whom had never seen
	the children.

In each of these illustrations the salesperson is suggesting, indirectly but nevertheless effectively, that the *prospect* is being foolish to postpone the decision to buy. To say so directly would be tactless; to make the nameless person in the narrative the "villain" gets the message across in a more tactful way.

CAUTION This technique must be used with sufficient skill to make the narrative "ring true." If your listener feels that you're telling a trumped-up story, the net effect is unfavorable rather than advantageous.

NOTE You don't have to "name names" when you use this technique. In fact, it is probably easier for the prospect to identify with the narrative when no names are mentioned.

Technique 8:
Use the Names of Other Buyers
to Persuade Your Prospect to Buy
(Testimonial Close)

The testimonial technique is based on the "follow the leader" instinct. If certain persons who are respected by the prospect or great numbers of persons whose names he or she may not know have decided it is advantageous to say "Yes" to a proposition, the prospect is inclined to go along with it, too.

■ IDEA IN ACTION

A salesperson selling dresses to leading department stores might tell the buyers in her territory how successful her line has proved to be in a leading department store chain. She may or may not substantiate her claim by showing copies of orders, reorders, correspondence, or other material. The point is that she mentions *names*. These names should, of course, have some special meaning to those to whom they are mentioned.

The testimonial technique often relies on the sheer weight of numbers. For example, a salesperson may leaf through his or her order book, showing (with carbon copies) the name of buyer after buyer who has chosen the company's product.

Technique 9:
Summarize Your Strong Points to
Convince the Prospect to Buy
(Summary Close)

Many salespeople get excellent results in closing by summarizing all the reasons for buying their product.

■ IDEA IN ACTION

"Let's look at it this way, Ms. Tepper," says stockbroker Joe Mercer to a hesitant prospect. "This investment is a very sound one—I'm sure you realize that. Second, it assures you a higher rate of return than most others of its class. Finally, there is an excellent possibility of appreciation in value—you may end up realizing substantially more than the amount of your initial investment when you do sell. And it's so marketable that you can sell any time you wish.

"In view of these facts, Ms. Tepper, is there any reason to hesitate?"

The sales points here gather impact as each one reinforces the other. Safety, high return, possibility of appreciation in value, liquidity—all these are brought up in the prospect's mind at the same time.

The salesperson's enthusiasm must be discernible as he quickly reviews the list of reasons to buy. When both logic and enthusiasm are joined in such a close, there is every likelihood that the order will be forthcoming.

Technique 10:
Ask Your Prospect Why
He or She Doesn't Buy
("Why Not" Close)

When they are unable to close by other means, many successful salespeople stop further "selling" and simply ask the prospect why he or she won't buy. Saying, "I know you have a reason for hesitating, and I'm sure it's a good one. Would you mind telling me what it is?" is one way to find out why the prospect won't buy. The experienced salesperson changes the wording to meet individual circumstances, but the query itself is basically the same.

Few prospects fail to respond to such a question, because it implies that the salesperson is at a loss to understand what is going on in the prospect's mind. The prospect knows that under these circumstances he or she must appear to be a bit slow, or stubborn, or even unreasonable. To justify his or her position, the prospect will feel obliged to explain. The "why not?" closing question is advantageous for these reasons:

- It puts the prospect on the defensive, since his or her reasons must have substance.

- It enables the salesperson to learn exactly what obstacles must be overcome if he or she is to win the sale. If the obstacle *can* be overcome, it is likely that the sale will be closed.

- In stating his or her reasons, the prospect is acknowledging a willingness to buy if the obstacle could be overcome.

- When the prospect gives an explanation, the salesperson wins another opportunity to restate his or her case more persuasively.

   NOTE Not every reply to this question will be complete or accurate. For example, a person who does not have the authority to commit to a purchase may not want to admit it. It follows that the sale is not always automatically won even if the *stated* obstacle can be eliminated.

How to "move" the prospect who hesitates

This is a subtler version of the "why not" close. Prospects who indicate that they want to buy but hesitate to make a final decision can often be "drawn out" by asking questions that demand definite answers. When they are forced to respond, they will often indicate by their answer exactly what is making them so indecisive.

> ▪ IDEA IN ACTION
>
> Margaret Simmons sells an industrial machine. She proceeds to give her presentation to her prospect, makes several trial closes, but realizes that none of them is going to work. The prospect is held back by an unseen obstacle. Margaret immediately begins to force the issue by asking definite-response questions.
>
> "This machine fits your purchasing budget, doesn't it?" The prospect's response indicates that this is not the problem.
>
> "Its performance will meet your production standards, won't it?" she asks. This time the prospect expresses some concern about the machine's production capacity. Margaret immediately reiterates pertinent facts from her presentation. She points out that her machine's precision minimizes rejects and actually gives a higher rate of acceptable pieces than competitors' models, even though the competitors quote a higher piece-per-hour figure than she does.
>
> The prospect is satisfied. Margaret then moves into a close and makes the sale.
>
> **IMPORTANT** Make your questions specific. In many cases, the prospect may not know exactly why he or she is hesitating. The blunt question, "What's holding you back?" can easily antagonize or embarrass the prospect, who often needs your help to find out what the answer is.

Technique 11:
How to Close a "Tough" Prospect
(the "Hat Trick" Close)

This close is used by aggressive salespeople to handle "tough" selling assignments successfully. Use it when all other methods of closing have failed.

■ IDEA IN ACTION

Ray Remington's job is to sign up companies to lease their company cars rather than buy them outright. He tells a convincing story of the advantages of leasing, but since acceptance of his offer often involves a change in the prospect's policy or practice, he frequently finds it difficult to close. "I want to think it over" is the usual reply when he tries to close the sale.

When Ray feels that he has "stayed with" his prospect as long as he should, he picks up his briefcase, reaches for his hat, and thanks the prospect for his time and courtesy. The prospect, seeing that the attempt to "sell him" is being terminated, relaxes.

Then Ray goes into his "hat trick" close. In what seems like an entirely casual afterthought he asks, "Mr. Trombino, do you mind if I ask one more question before I leave?"

The prospect is glad to oblige. He probably thinks that Remington is going to ask if he can check back in a month or so.

So he says, "Not at all, Mr. Remington."

Then Ray gets in his "extra lick."

"Do you know, Mr. Trombino, that if my figures are correct—and I'm sure they are—it costs your company at least $450 for every week you delay taking on our service?"

This is a point that hasn't been specifically stated before. Making such a point at this moment, when the prospect's guard is down, gives the salesperson one more opportunity to win the sale.

Most salespeople can use this device in one form or another. All that is required is that you indicate that you've "given up the fight." Then do the unexpected by making one more strong appeal for the sale.

CAUTION It's important to reserve a strong sales point to use in this close. If you use a weak point, or one that has already been mentioned in the interview, it might cause the prospect to feel even more justified in deciding not to buy.

Technique 12:
Ask the Prospect for the Order (the
"Ask for the Order" Close)

Some orders are obtained by the simplest of all closes: *asking* the prospect to buy.

The closing techniques discussed thus far also represent different ways of asking for the order. But they ask indirectly, using logic, or facts, or some other appeal; they don't come right out and say, "Will you give me the order?"

Many salespeople prefer not to use this close, feeling that it is an appeal to sympathy or a request for a favor. Some, on the other hand, have great faith in it. They feel its frankness and sincerity get them business they might not otherwise obtain.

Whether this close should be used or not depends on the salesperson's temperament, the type of product sold, and the prospect—How is he or she likely to react to such a frank request?

THERE MUST BE A "HOOK" TO CLOSE

"I'll think it over"—"I'll let you know"—"I want to discuss the matter"—these words cause many sales to founder. Once you realize that they really mean, "Give me one reason why I should decide now," you gain power to close more sales.

The "hook"—the reason to *buy now*—is perhaps the most important word in the entire sales vocabulary. It closes every sale that is made, whether or not you're aware of it. It can be supplied either by the prospect or the salesperson. In some cases, the reason may hinge solely on the question, "Is there any advantage in waiting?"

The following paragraphs explain how the hook works.

The Prospect Frequently
has a Reason to Buy Now

Many prospects supply their own reasons for wanting to buy now; they may even make a point of telling the salesperson what it is, relieving him or her of the burden of having to come up with a convincing reason.

☐ EXAMPLE

A retail merchant looks at the samples displayed by a traveling salesperson. The merchant realizes that the salesperson is in town only for a day or two and that if he wants to stock the line, he will have to place his order *without delay.*

☐ EXAMPLE

The prospect is interested in planning a trip and securing reservations. Because her vacation begins in two weeks, she is eager to make arrangements *immediately.*

☐ EXAMPLE

The prospects, a couple, have just bought a new home. They want to purchase new kitchen units *now,* before they move in.

IMPORTANT The fact that a sale can often be closed without offering a hook leads many salespeople to believe that a hook is not essential. Don't be fooled by this assumption. If you have not supplied a hook, then the prospect has done it for you. In some cases, the reason may not be divulged—but it is present nevertheless.

Most Often the Salesperson Must Supply the Hook

Since you cannot depend on the prospect to supply a reason to buy, you must be prepared to deliver one yourself. The alert salesperson can always find some reason why the decision should be made now rather than at a later date. The hook need not be important; often a relatively unimportant reason will suffice. For example,

---

| *Salesperson (television):* | Some of the best shows are on the air Friday evenings. If you decide now, we can promise to have your set installed by 5 o'clock Friday afternoon. |

Salesperson	Mr. Albright, other stores in this neighborhood
(air	will probably have their air conditioning in
conditioning):	operation in about six weeks, when the
	weather begins to get warm. If you're going to
	install a unit, why not order it now, when we
	can be sure of installation before other orders
	can cause delays?

Sometimes It Pays to Ask the Prospect If There Is Any Reason to Delay

If nothing else, you can always ask the hesitant prospect, "After all, is there really any reason to postpone a decision?"

Two responses are possible. If the prospect says, "No, I guess not," he or she creates an opportunity for you to swing into a close. If the answer is, "Well, I'm hesitating because of . . .," you have a chance to overcome the obstacle and then try another close.

In either case, the sale is much nearer to completion once you have focused attention—your own as well as the prospect's—on the question of whether there is, in fact, any advantage in waiting or whether now is as logical a time as any to decide.

IDEAS FOR WORKING OUT YOUR OWN CLOSING TECHNIQUES

Your Own Closing Technique Increases Your Selling Power

Most products and services have some unique aspects around which successful closes can be built. Sometimes the salesperson's own special situation lends itself to an individual closing technique. In the next few paragraphs you will see how some outstanding salespeople have evolved closing techniques that work for them—and that may work for you. At any rate, they will guide you in thinking about comparable situations in your own field and in developing special closing techniques adapted to your experience.

IMPORTANT Whether you develop your own special closing methods, you can't afford to bypass the closing techniques that have been presented in the preceding sections.

Demonstration with Prospect's Own Records Closes Sale

Closing immediately upon demonstrating to a prospect how a definite loss could be eliminated by using the product was the technique one salesperson found worked best for him. What made this the right time to close was the fact that he proved his point conclusively by *using the customer's own cost records.*

■ IDEA IN ACTION

Stuart Long sells a guide that indexes domestic and foreign shipping and postal rates. These rates are commonly used by the shipping departments of many different types of companies to determine the most economical method of shipment.

In attempting to sell one prospect, Stuart was told, "I don't believe you have anything to offer that we can use. We have our shipping problems down pat."

Stuart then asked to see some of the company's shipping receipts. Checking a number of these, he showed the prospect how $250 could have been saved if the company had employed his guide.

Proving Quality and Justifying Price Leads into Close

Learning from experience that a unique fact about her product broke down price resistance by emphasizing quality, a soap salesperson used this fact over and over again to lead into a close.

■ IDEA IN ACTION

Loretta Sands, a soap salesperson, has just made a trial close. "It sounds good," says her prospect, "but your price is too high."

Loretta knows the fact that will break down this resistance to price.

"Are you buying soap or water?" she asks the prospect. She then proceeds to quote facts (and show them in print) proving that her soap contains 60% more soap and 60% less water than other soaps.

The prospect is convinced that the price is justified and places an order.

Giving the Prospect a "Ready-Made" Idea Clinches the Sale

If you give the prospect an idea that makes it easier to get full value from what he or she buys, the sale can be closed.

■ IDEA IN ACTION

John Tulley sells gift items. He shows his prospect an insulated travel mug and succeeds in raising her interest in the product as a perfect "client gift." The prospect hesitates until John shows her how to make these gifts pay off.

"Here's a terrific idea," says John. "With each travel mug you send to your customers, you include this distribution letter. It will 'wrap up' your customers' gift item effectively, and save you the trouble of creating your own greeting."

John shows her a sample distribution letter—a catchy, friendly note intended to build customer goodwill. The prospect is delighted with the idea and makes a sizable purchase.

Strengthen "Easy" Sales as Much as You Can

The prospect who decides to buy a costly product before hearing your full story has probably done some previous shopping around. Nevertheless, there is a danger of cancellation unless you take pains to "nail it down." One way to strengthen a "quick" sale is to congratulate your customer.

■ IDEA IN ACTION

Chris Summers sells a popular line of pleasure boats. She briefly tells one prospect about the many advantages of owning a particular model, then leads into her first trial close. To her surprise, the prospect says, "I'll take it."

Chris begins to write up the order. However, she wants to "cement" the sale as tightly as possible to ensure against a later cancellation. So she says, "Let me congratulate you on a decision that I'm sure you'll be happy with for many years to come. No other craft will serve your family purposes as safely and comfortably as this one, or be so inexpensive to maintain. Happy sailing, and catch some big ones for me!"

The customer is made to feel that he has bought something worthwhile, and he leaves feeling more "sold" than at the time he said he would buy.

TIP Many salespeople use this technique after *every* sale. A psychological pat on the back in the form of congratulations for making a wise decision makes any customer feel good.

CHAPTER SEVEN

MAKING OBJECTIONS WORK FOR YOU

You can capitalize on almost any objection that is thrown your way.

A strong sales presentation anticipates objections and nips them in the bud or answers them before they arise. But even though you have attempted to forestall them, they might turn up at any moment. You must be ready to do more than answer them; you must make these objections work for you, just as top-flight salespeople do.

Years of study have been devoted to the subject of dealing with objections by the country's leading sales consultants. They have discovered what should—and shouldn't—be done to make each objection a stepping stone to a successful closing.

You can profit by what these experienced and successful salespeople have learned. By applying the techniques they've developed, you can make your income exceed even your most optimistic goal.

The first section of this chapter gives you the four basic rules to apply in answering any objection. The chapter then provides general guidelines for handling objections as well as tips on the right attitude for handling objections.

The rest of the chapter is an "Answer Guide to Specific Objections," which furnishes a foundation on which you can build convincing answers to a variety of objections you may encounter in selling your product or service. Adapt the language, ideas, and tone of the "live examples" to your particular needs.

> **NOTE** Objections will work for you only if you immediately follow up your response to them with an attempt to close. For power-closing techniques, see Chapter Six.

HOW TO USE THE OBJECTION TO MAKE THE SALE

The Four Basic Rules

Objections aren't hard to handle, once you have mastered four basic rules that will take any salesperson to the top. Those rules are

1. Deal with the objection as though it were merely an excuse, and try to evade it.
2. Capitalize on the objection.
3. Find the hidden objection.
4. Obey the buying signal.

Later in this chapter you will also find other powerful techniques to make objections work for you. But the "big four" that are explained in the following sections must be made an integral part of your selling skills.

Rule 1: Respond to the Objection as Though It Were Merely an Excuse

The proper *initial* response to any obstacle to selling is to *deal with it as though it were merely an excuse* and try to evade it. By applying this technique, you will quickly learn whether you are facing a true objection or one that is merely an excuse.

If the objection is real—a substantial obstacle in the prospect's mind—you must meet it head on. If the objection is merely an excuse, you will be able to bypass it and get on with your selling.

> **WARNING** Do not use the evasion tactic when a prospect objects to giving you an interview; use it only in a *selling* interview. Always remember that you must sell the interview before you can sell your product or service.

Why evasion is the right initial tactic

The evasion tactic involves nothing more than avoiding a discussion of the obstacle on its *merits*. For instance, if a buyer says, "We're not ready to buy any spring merchandise yet," the salesperson (who should assume that this is an excuse) may reply, "Well, I know it's early, but I'd like you to see our line now, so you'll be sure to remember it when you *are* ready to buy."

In handling the objection in this way, the salesperson has skillfully avoided discussing the merit of the claim that it's too early to buy.

If the objection is merely an excuse, it will be forgotten. Assuming that the line appeals to him or her, the buyer will probably place an order in spite of making an earlier statement to the contrary.

But if this statement is a *true objection*, the buyer will not permit the salesperson to use the evasion tactic. He or she will say, "I'm sorry, but we make it a firm rule here never to buy spring merchandise until November 1. So we'd both be wasting our time if I were to look over your line now."

Since nothing is lost by treating the obstacle initially as if it were an excuse, the evasion tactic is the proper one to begin with in every case. If the obstacle is in fact an excuse, this tactic will dispose of it. If it is a true objection, the prospect's response will make this clear. The objection must then be met squarely on its merits.

> **NOTE** Overlooking the objection until the prospect has raised it a second time saves you from making "too much, too soon" of every objection. This is a fault of many experienced sales-people, but not of top producers.

TIP Evasion is often useful toward the end of your presentation. For example, suppose that you are quite confident that your prospect is ready to buy and then he or she proffers a lame excuse—one that you recognize as a substitute for a pause before signing the order. You ignore the excuse, change the subject to something quite apart from the sale, and hand him or her the order to sign.

How to evade an objection with "Yes, but . . ."

The alert salesperson can easily swing the conversation from an excuse to some other point of discussion. The "Yes, but . . ." method is probably used more than any other. The following example explains how.

■ IDEA IN ACTION

Norma Kendall sells textbooks to colleges. She is talking with the head of the geology department, who says, "Ms. Kendall, we like the text you publish, but the instructors' guide is rather sketchy. I'm afraid we'll have to pass it up."

Norma feels that this is probably just an excuse, without real substance in the professor's mind. She replies accordingly by using the "Yes, but" tactic in an effort to swing the conversation to another point.

"Yes," Norma says, "but when you consider that our new edition is the only text that deals with such recent discoveries as . . ." (here she gives the facts), "it seems to me to have advantages that you cannot duplicate."

"I guess you're right, Ms. Kendall," says the professor, "but I don't think the index is as complete as it might be."

In reply to the professor's criticism of the index, Norma decides to use another tried and true evasive tactic. "I'll get back to that in just a moment," she replies. "But first I'd like to show you these unique charts."

"I realize that the charts are valuable, Ms. Kendall," comes the reply, "but in my opinion no text is better than its index."

Her prospect's reply shows that the matter of adequate indexing is not merely an excuse, but a true objection. Norma therefore proceeds to discuss it on its merits.

Here the "Yes, but" technique has been successfully employed in a situation where a mere excuse is proffered. Since what is needed is to change the focus of the conversation without going into the merits of the excuse itself, the "Yes, but" tactic is a very useful tool.

Direct approach may be necessary to identify a stall

In some situations you may have to use the direct approach to discover whether the prospect is sincere in raising an objection or is using the objection as a stall.

☐ EXAMPLE

Your prospect says that your credit terms are too tough. You want to find out whether he really means it or is using this objection as an excuse. So you ask him to suggest acceptable terms. If he is sincere, he will frankly state the credit terms he considers equitable. If he is merely using the credit terms as an excuse, he will probably be caught off guard and state a proposition that cannot possibly be met.

CAUTION Sometimes when you try to pin your prospect down to acceptable terms, his or her floundering will reveal the need for ˜more selling.˜ You must look at the entire situation before deciding whether or not the person is sincere.

Rule 2: Capitalize on the Objection

Every salesperson who is a big earner employs the technique of *capitalizing on objections.* If you have not yet developed this technique, now is the time to start. Here's the formula: Answer the objection in such a way that you make your case even stronger than if the objection had never been raised.

▪ IDEA IN ACTION

Wilbur Gorman sells banquet arrangements for conventions. The hotel he represents is located in downtown Chicago.

"No, Mr. Gorman," a prospect says to him, "we will have over 500 members attending our annual convention, and it's just too much trouble for them to find parking in the down-town district."

Wilbur has the facts that enable him to refute this objection. He uses them, but he also uses the objection itself as an opportunity to get in some extra "plugs" for his own hotel, *which he would not otherwise have a chance to mention.*

"Mrs. Raymond," Wilbur says, "you needn't worry about parking. All your guests need to do is to leave their cars with our doorman—he'll see that each one is properly parked and available again on 10 minutes' notice."

Having thus completely refuted the objection, Wilbur proceeds to *capitalize* on it. "You see, Mrs. Raymond, our exceptional service is what has led many organizations like yours to return to our hotel again and again. Here's a list . . ." The opportunity to show this impressive list of "repeaters" arose *because of* the objection. Instead of being weaker because of the objection, his case is actually stronger than it would be if the objection had never been raised.

Wilbur, like other good salespeople who have learned how to capitalize on objections, is constantly on the alert for such opportunities. A few minutes later, therefore, when Mrs. Raymond says, "Well, we'll have to think about it; our convention is ten months off, and there's no hurry," Wilbur again uses the capitalizing tactic as he refutes the "stall."

"Really," he says, "it would be wise for you to make your reservation just as quickly as possible. Here is our reservation chart for May—let's see . . . the organizations that have already made firm reservations with us for that month include . . .," and he lists more than a dozen organizations.

Apply the capitalizing technique to all kinds of objections

Once you get the knack of capitalizing on objections, you can learn to apply the technique to almost *any* objection. Strong salespeople constantly seize the opportunity to strengthen their selling talks while they answer objections.

A few short illustrations will show you how they do it.

Prospect:	We can't afford to go in for that sort of thing right now.
Salesperson:	Actually, the dollars you will save are the most attractive feature of our service. (Gives details and proof.) If it's money that you base your decision on, I frankly don't see how you can afford to pass us up.
Prospect:	I must discuss the matter with several of my associates.
Salesperson:	Let me summarize the advantages of our offer so that you won't forget anything when you talk to them. (A chance to repeat the main points.)
Prospect:	We buy just as cheaply from the ABC Company.
Salesperson:	I'm sure you do. But there must be some reason, don't you think, why we do the largest volume in our field? (A strong plug.)

It takes only a few well-planned statements to equip yourself with this income-building technique. Develop the capitalizing remark you will use to follow up each objection you are likely to encounter. Memorize it from your "Answer Book" (which you'll be creating later in this chapter) and try out the technique the very next time you have to answer an objection. You'll find that it removes your fear of objections. You will no longer be put on the defensive but will be in a strong offensive position with a new selling point.

Rule 3: Find the Hidden Objection

If the prospect has an objection in mind that he or she has not brought up, it is as much of a barrier to the sale as if it had been expressed. And since such an obstacle must be met if it is to be overcome, the best approach is to get it out in the open.

☐ EXAMPLE

"Ms. Prospect, are you hesitating because you think prices may drop?"

"Well, yes! That what's bothering me!"

"O.K., now here's why we're quite certain prices will not go down this year."

Or, "O.K., here's how we will protect you," and so forth.

You must keep pressing for the unmentioned objection until you uncover it. Only then can you meet it squarely and close the sale.

▪ IDEA IN ACTION

Belinda Coleman sells real estate. She has been talking with a prospect, Mr. Lu, about a house that seems to suit his needs. But although Belinda feels that she has overcome every obstacle that has been raised, she is unable to close the sale.

Belinda knows that it is always an unresolved obstacle that keeps a prospect from buying, so she reasons, correctly as it turns out, that there must be a hidden objection. And whatever it is, she knows that she has to get it out in the open.

"Mr. Lu," she probes, "are you hesitating because the house is so old?"

"No, that doesn't bother me," he replies.

"The price is right, isn't it?" she continues.

"Yes, I suppose I can't do any better for the money."

"Would you mind telling me, Mr. Lu, whether there's anything about the offer that doesn't seem just right?"

"Well, Ms. Coleman, I'm wondering what the neighbors are *really* like—good neighbors are so important!"

Belinda's problems are over. She is able to reassure her prospect about the neighbors, since she herself has previously handled several transactions on that block. This sale might never have been made if Belinda had not probed for the hidden obstacle.

Rule 4: Recognize when the Objection Means "Yes, I'll Buy"

Sometimes a prospect will make a statement in the form of an objection, while in fact it is a signal to buy. Such a situation is technically called a "buying signal." You must be quick to recognize this type of objection and try a close immediately. Phrases such as the following and others indicate that the objection really means "Yes, I'll buy."

"I suppose."

"I wish I could."

"It looks good."

"If I could."

"Maybe I will."

"I ought to."

"Perhaps I should."

The prospect's tone of voice, facial expressions, and actions are also clues to a buying signal. Notice the buying signals in the following remarks:

"Well, I don't suppose I really *should* spend quite that much money."

"I guess it would be smart for me to wait until my partner gets back next week."

■ IDEA IN ACTION

Harry Bryce sells motor boats. He is calling on a prospect who has listened to his presentation and has looked at photographs of various models of power craft.

The prospect is obviously tempted to make a decision in favor of one of the models, but has not expressed outright agreement during Harry's trial closes.

"I'm sure you'll be very happy with this boat, Mr. Dodge," Harry says. "If you give me the order now, I can guarantee delivery within 30 days."

"I suppose I really should think it over for a bit," says Mr. Dodge.

Harry is elated. He is a seasoned salesperson who recognizes a buying signal when it is expressed. He knows that this sale is now "in the bag," for even though his prospect's remark sounds like an objection, it really means, "I'll buy."

Had Mr. Dodge really meant that he wanted to wait, he would have said it differently. He would have said, "I want to think it over." The difference in wording should be noted with care. What Mr. Dodge actually said was *qualified* by the words "I suppose."

When a person says, "I *suppose* I should wait," he does not actually mean, "I definitely intend to wait."

The buying signal consists of more than *words*. Mr. Dodge's voice and facial expression also indicate that while he thinks he should wait, he'd rather not. Furthermore, he has not put away the photo of the craft that tempts him; instead, he holds it in his hand and keeps looking at it with evident interest and desire.

What to do when the buying signal is flashed

Why does the prospect raise what sounds like an objection at the moment when he has just about decided to buy? The answer lies in the realm of psychology. In the previous example, the prospect knows that it would be wise to consider the matter. He is tempted to disregard the voice of wisdom. However, before doing so he wants some *reassurance* that he is not doing the wrong thing.

Hence, what he really means is: "You don't think I'm making a mistake, do you?"

WHAT TO DO When a buying signal is flashed, you *must* . . .

- Instantly stop "selling," even if you're in the middle of a sentence or have several more points to make. No matter what you have planned to do, when you are given a buying signal, you must *stop selling*.

- Express, in a slow, matter-of-fact way, your reassurance that the prospect will not regret buying now. "I'm sure you'll never regret having settled this today," you might say. Such reassurance, spoken slowly and calmly, is all that is needed. You should follow up by writing up the order or acknowledging in some way that the decision *has been made*.

WARNING If you don't stop selling on a buying signal, you are almost sure to lose the sale. The buyer isn't asking you for more reasons to buy; he or she merely wants reassurance.

HOW TO HANDLE OBJECTIONS

Lower the Prospect's Selling Resistance with an Empathetic Remark

Before you try to answer an objection, put yourself in the prospect's shoes. This is called *empathy*. Say something that shows you understand how the prospect feels, and then go on to answer the objection. Your *empathetic* remark won't be an out-and-out agreement with the prospect, but it will have a softening effect and will make it easier to answer his objection. A few examples will show you the type of remark that does the trick:

Prospect:	I'll have to talk it over with my wife.
Salesperson:	I understand. After all, this decision is as important to her as it is to you.
	(An answer to this objection is provided later in this chapter.)
Prospect:	I buy only from local merchants.
Salesperson:	Most people prefer to do business with their neighbors.
Prospect:	I hate to change. We've been buying from Jones & Company a long time.
Salesperson:	Yes, we all hate to change. But sometimes a change can put you at an advantage.

RECOMMENDATION You may have to use this technique more than once in your presentation. Therefore, you must be prepared to vary your empathic remark. Make a list of, say, five such remarks to suit the objections you encounter most often in selling your product or service. Memorize the list, and you will be able to draw upon it automatically for the right response.

Convert the Objection into a Question

Think of every objection raised by a prospect as a question that you can answer. By doing so, you avoid the negative influence of the word "objection," and you build a positive attitude that inspires confidence.

If you can get your prospect to think that he or she is raising a question rather than posing an objection, you will put him or her in the right frame of mind to listen for your answer.

How to prove that objections can be turned into questions

Here are some simple objections and the questions that they imply.

- *Objection:* Your price is too high!
- *Question:* Will I get my money's worth for the price asked?
- *Objection:* Your company is too small!
- *Question:* Will this salesperson's company give me the kind of service I get from the bigger suppliers?
- *Objection:* I can do without it!
- *Question:* What will I gain by taking on this additional expenditure?

How to build a positive attitude

For each objection you encounter in your selling, find the question the objection implies and note it in the "Answer Book" we recommend later in this chapter. Learn these answers by heart. You will thus train yourself in the technique of treating objections as questions.

How to condition your prospect to think he or she has a question and not an objection

The prospect will begin to think that he or she has a question and not an objection if you're able to lead him or her to that attitude.
Here's how to do it

1. Agree that he or she has posed a "question."

Prospect:	Your company is too small for our account.
Salesperson:	That does raise a question. I'm sure you're wondering whether our company can give you the kind of service you get from the bigger companies. As a matter of fact, because we *are* smaller, our company can actually provide you with *better* service. Instead of being relegated to the status of a small account in a large company, your account would be one of our largest. As such, you can expect the kind of personal attention that a larger company just can't give you.

---

2. Get the prospect to agree that the objection is really a question.

Prospect:	Your price is too high.
Salesperson:	What you are really asking me, aren't you, is whether you're going to get your money's worth from these batteries.
Prospect:	Yes.

NOTE By saying "Yes," the prospect has invited the salesperson to convince him or her that these batteries will outlast those available elsewhere for less money.

3. If the prospect does not agree, get him or her to tell you what the question is.

Prospect:	We tried something like that a while ago; it didn't work.
Salesperson:	You're really asking why my product will work if the other one didn't, aren't you?
Prospect:	No, that's not the question.
Salesperson:	Then what is the question?

Every time you answer the question you have made of the objection, you must go right into a close.

Make the Objection the Reason for Buying

This is a technique to be used when you face the prospect's strongest objection. After you have given him or her an empathic response that softens resistance, you take the very objection that has been raised and make it work for you as a reason to buy.

☐ EXAMPLE

A prospect tells you she cannot afford your product. You show her that if she uses your product, it will make her more money. In other words, she can't afford it now because she isn't using your product. Or you show her that if she uses your product it will reduce her costs of doing business. The very reason she has given for *not* buying becomes her reason for buying.

☐ EXAMPLE

A prospect says he doesn't need your product because what he is using now has lasted a long time and is still good. Show him that *because* it has lasted a long time, he should think about replacing it. Some products start having problems or require costly maintenance as they near the end of their useful life.

☐ EXAMPLE

The prospect says, "We can't use your machines now. We're replacing about a third of our truck fleet."

You reply, "I can't think of a better reason why you should install our machines right now. I'll show you how you can recoup a sizable portion of your investment with the new profits you're bound to make by stepping up your production over the next six months. Here's the way I figure it . . . ."

Get the Prospect to Answer His or Her Own Objections by Asking "Why"

Getting the prospect to answer his or her own objection is a technique employed by many successful salespeople. Sometimes you can get the prospect to explain away the objection by saying, "I wonder if you'd mind telling me why." Other times you must raise the question more subtly.

Asking "Why?" gets the prospect talking. While you can't use this strategy repeatedly with the same prospect, you can start off by asking, "Why do you hesitate?" "Why do you believe it is too costly?" or "Why do you want to wait until fall?" As you follow up the reply, you must vary the question until you have overcome the objection by asking—not telling.

Here is an example of how skillful questioning can be used to overcome a prospect's objection to tying himself down to monthly payments over a period of years.

■ IDEA IN ACTION

Knowing that her prospect was anxious to buy an annuity to protect his family but objected to the "long haul" of future payments, the salesperson said: "Are you paying for a car?"

"Yes," the prospect replied.

"Well," said the salesperson, "for most of us buying automobiles involves an endless sequence of payments. But we never seem to get tired of them or let them bother us too much, do we?"

"I guess we don't seem to."

"That's right, and it just goes to prove that usually we'll carry out a contracted obligation, doesn't it?"

"Yes, I guess so."

"Now in this case you already have the obligation. What I'm offering you is merely a contract to carry it out. You're fortunate that you can buy security for your family the same way you buy a car."

"How much insurance are you proposing?" the prospect asked. "You know I recently bought a policy from another company. My application was originally for $50,000, but I cut it down to $25,000 because I was afraid I wouldn't be able to handle the premiums."

"Does the size of the premium make any difference as long as it buys security for your wife and son and you can put aside the deposit?"

"When you put it that way, I guess it doesn't."

The application was signed on the spot.

Think Creatively to Get Around an Objection

In some lines of selling you can get around an objection with a concrete suggestion that gets the prospect thinking along entirely different lines. In other words, you let the prospect have his or her own way, but then go on to show how he or she can gain by following your constructive idea. The big-money salespeople in many fields are constantly getting around objections through creative thinking. (See Chapter Three for creative ideas that increase sales.)

Mention an Obstacle That Doesn't Exist in the Buyer's Mind

By getting the prospect to agree that a given point (or series of points) is, in fact, not an obstacle, the sale can often be expedited.

The purpose of raising the objection that you know is not a real objection in the buyer's mind is to get him or her to express the advantages of what you are selling. Repetition of the points that are not obstacles pave the way for making the sale.

When you raise the objection yourself, you should be confident that the prospect is going to agree that he or she has no such objection. But even if the prospect doesn't agree, you can easily answer the objection because you have selected one that does not create a serious problem. The following example demonstrates three keys to meeting objections successfully:

- Get the prospect to repeat what he or she likes about your product.

- Capitalize on the objection that you yourself have purposely raised.

- Smoke out the hidden objection by raising nonexistent objections.

■ IDEA IN ACTION

Bill Graham works for a popular automobile dealer. He has just given his sales talk to prospective buyers, Mr. and Mrs. Smith, and has taken them for a demonstration ride. Back in the showroom, he attempts to close the sale but realizes that something is preventing them from making the final commitment.

Bill begins to raise "objections" by reiterating the sales points he has made, hoping to smoke out the hidden obstacle to the sale.

"Did you both feel the acceleration in that six-cylinder engine?" Mr. and Mrs. Smith agree. (Bill is strengthening his sales talk by getting them to agree.)

"And did you like the greater control that power-steering gives you?" They agree that it's a nice feature.

"By the way, did I mention how much easier it is to park in crowded city conditions with power steering?" (Now he is capitalizing on an objection he has already raised.)

Bill keeps trying. "And think how much fun driving a brand-new convertible is going to be with vacation time just around the corner." Here the couple hesitate. Bill knows they like the convertible, but he sees an opportunity in their hesitation.

"How many children did you say you have, Mr. Smith?"

"Two—a boy and a girl," he replies.

"And Tommy's going into first grade next year," adds Mrs. Smith. (Bill has found the hidden objection.) Immediately he says, "Why, then, you'll want the safety-designed sedan with the steel reinforced roof for greater protection. It has safety grip handles and child-proof door locks. Let me show it to you."

The sale will be closed because Bill was skillful enough to raise objections he knew he could use to his own advantage.

How to Answer Objections That Have No Real Basis in Fact

Whether it relates to the price or quality of your product, your company, or anything else, an objection that has no real basis in fact is the easiest to answer. All it requires is that you refute the objection by introducing facts and/or an explanation that undermines the substance of the objection.

□ EXAMPLE

Wendy Bruno sells time for a television broadcasting station. Her prospect turns down her offer on the grounds that her rate is higher than that of a competing station. Bruno easily overcomes this objection by proving that, because of a larger audience, the cost *per person* in the audience is actually lower than the cost *per person* reached by her competitor.

Direct denial

Sometimes a direct denial is the only way to meet an objection that has no basis in fact. For example, if a customer says that some of the parts of your machine are made of aluminum when actually they are made out of stainless steel, you can be emphatic about setting him or her straight without causing offense.

Counterattack with facts

When you run into a prospect who is inclined to keep raising objections about the construction of your product or other features, revealing that he or she does not have the facts, the best approach might be to let him or her continue talking. Don't interrupt, don't object; don't argue; just listen. When he or she has finished, come back with a strong counterattack of *facts*, supported by *proof.*

> **TIP** A prospect who makes assertions about your product or service that you know run contrary to fact is actually showing his or her interest in your product. The misinformation may have come from a competitor, and the prospect's attitude may be, "I'm not going to let this salesperson put anything over on *me.*" Recognize the need for answering and closing in the present interview before the competitor takes the sale away from you.

Minimize Objection When Facts Can't Be Refuted

In some cases, all you can do is to *minimize* the objection. Although this is less effective than *complete refutation,* it often serves to overcome objections. In the following example, the salesperson minimizes an objection that can't be refuted by fighting fear with faith.

■ IDEA IN ACTION

A young man, hesitating to buy an insurance policy, told the representative, "The economy is just too unstable right now. I could lose my job six months from now and then I'd have to let the policy lapse because I couldn't afford the premiums."

The agent said, "Well, *something* must be left to hope. You only have one premium to pay today, and for every future premium you'll have a whole year in which to pay it. When you consider the peace of mind that this policy will bring for you and how it will provide for your family in the unfortunate event of your death, the commitment doesn't seem like such a big one."

Delay the Answer to a Sincere Objection

The key to answering objections is *first* to evade any obstacle raised by the prospect so that you can find out whether the objection is real or just an excuse (see Rule 1 at the beginning of this chapter). You must discover quickly whether the objection is sincere and answer immediately if it is. Otherwise, your prospect will continue to think about the objection until you answer and thus miss what you are saying. He or she may even jump to the conclusion that you have no answer and thus begin to lose confidence in you. But sometimes delaying the answer can be the best strategy and, if handled skillfully, can help you win the sale.

Here's your guide to delaying the answer to a sincere objection:

Momentary delay

It's usually safe to delay the answer to a sincere objection if you're in the midst of your presentation and know that you're going to answer the objection momentarily. Tell your prospect that you'll cover that point in a moment. Then make sure you *do* cover it. The purpose of delaying the answer briefly is to avoid breaking your own train of thought.

Prolonged delay

Suppose the prospect interrupts you with an objection in the middle of your presentation, and you don't expect to cover this point right away. You want to delay the answer because it can be covered most effectively as you logically proceed with your sales story. You feel that if you break in immediately to answer it, you will disturb the logic of your sales story and may lose control of the interview. In this case, frame your response along these lines:

- You agree that the prospect has raised an interesting point.
- You intend to discuss it in connection with another feature that he or she will be interested in.
- With the prospect's permission, you'd first like to be sure that he or she is thoroughly familiar with the features that are most vital to him or her.

Don't pause or wait for this permission; go right on from where you left off.

Delay in answering price objection

Suppose that early in the interview your prospect interrupts you with a price objection before you've had a chance to cover the product's merits. Are you going to answer the price objection immediately or put it off until you have covered the real selling points of the product or service? You know that you can prove the value of the product if you can only get the prospect to listen to the sales story. Frame your response along these lines:

- You agree that price is important.

- You're certain that if the product doesn't provide the benefits it has given to hundreds of users (profit making, cost cutting, time saving, etc.), the prospect won't want it at any price.

- Turn the focus of the presentation to the prospect's specific needs. Then proceed immediately to explain and demonstrate the value of the product to the prospect.

Delay to find the answer

You must, of course, delay answering an objection when you don't have an adequate answer. Tell the prospect frankly that you don't know the answer, but that you will get the necessary information as soon as possible and report back to him or her. Then be sure to carry through on your promise.

> **CAUTION** Don't make the mistake of making up an answer if you don't know what it is. The fabrication won't fool your prospects; it will only antagonize them and lower their opinion of you.

Mere Excuses May Be a Sign to Summarize

A prospect who offers excuses after you have completed your presentation may be interested, but may not have had time to think over everything you've said. He or she is stalling for time to weigh your offer and reach a decision.

This is a signal that your presentation must be made more clear cut. What is probably needed is a good summary of your proposition, emphasizing the benefits the buyer will gain, restating the facts, and reviewing the evidence. Testimonials and names of your product's users carry extra weight at such times.

When Every Sales Effort Has Failed, Ask for the Hidden Objection

After every sales effort has failed and you can think of no reason why the prospect does not buy, you might still get a chance to close the sale if you ask the prospect directly why he or she has not bought.

■ IDEA IN ACTION

You have called on a prospect several times. Every call has strengthened your conviction that he or she stands to profit by your offer. You decide to use a direct question to get at the hidden objection. So you say,

"Mr. Stonewall, I have been calling on you for some time. I haven't sold you—but I think I can do you a service by selling you. You need my product. You're a difficult person to sell, because you never openly state your objections. Will you do me a favor?

"If I'm not going to get this account, I'd like to know the reason why, because it will teach me a valuable lesson. On the other hand, if you're not buying because of some objection you've failed to state plainly, will you tell it to me now and give me a sporting chance to answer it?"

Look for the Hidden Obstacle When You Lose a Sale to a Competitor

The technique of asking the prospect why he or she will not buy can be used profitably when you have lost a sale to a competitor. In finding out why the competitor beat you, you may discover much more than a hidden objection. Here's an example of what you might find out.

■ IDEA IN ACTION

Margaret Daly was selling an electronically operated paper cutting machine. She had been working with a prospect whose plant could use two such machines. Margaret expected to earn a sizable commission on the sale.

Everything went well with her presentation. She had the purchasing agent's full attention during two interview calls. When the prospect asked for a written proposal with full specifications, Margaret felt quite sure that she would get the order on her third callback.

But she didn't—because the order had been placed with a competitor! Margaret was determined to find out why she lost the order. She wanted to know what her competitor had done that she didn't do, since she knew that the competitor did not have a superior product and could not offer any price advantage. The selling points of her product and the competitor's were the same—safety and speed. The construction differences in the two competing machines were really immaterial.

Here's what she discovered in a talk with the purchasing agent after she'd lost the sale. *There was no hidden objection.* But the competitor's salesperson had used two important strategies that won him the order: (1) He had asked to meet the plant superintendent after he had made his presentation to the purchasing agent, and (2) he had explained to the plant superintendent, an engineer, the technical ways in which the company had engineered the machine to acquire greater speed and safety (the machine was not actually superior in these respects).

By probing for the obstacle that lost the sale, Margaret learned how to overcome the competition. She immediately improved her presentation and her strategy. In all future selling, she made it a point to "sell" the plant manager as well as the purchasing agent. She gave more attention in her presentation to speed and safety. In the future, the purchasing agent would always be able to convince the factory people that the speed and safety of the machines were the best that could be had.

IMPORTANT Always find out why your competition got the business when you lose out. Get the reasons out in the open where you can work on overcoming them.

Techniques for Handling a Trade-in

Trade-in allowances have a strong appeal to customers in some fields—such as automobiles, industrial machines, household appliances, and other items. If the product that is traded in can be repaired or reconditioned, or sold as is, the trade-in allowance can be used to spur a sale; if it has little value, the problem is to keep the prospect's disappointment from hurting the sale.

Sell the new product first

Even when a trade-in allowance helps close a sale—and certainly when the trade-in value is insignificant—it is important to sell the new product first on its merits. Get the prospect's mind off the trade-in by assuring him or her that he or she will receive a fair price on the article that is traded in, and then proceed with your sales presentation.

For example, in selling automobiles, the salesperson first finds out whether the prospect has a car to be traded in, gets the keys to the car, and turns the car over to the appraiser on location. Having thus gotten the old car out of the way, he or she goes about selling the new car with even greater emphasis on the values it represents.

How to handle the trade-in allowance

After you have sold the customer on the merits of the replacement, use the trade-in allowance as an inducement to buy. Don't make the mistake of taking a quick look at the trade-in and offending your customer with derogatory remarks about its condition. Instead, try to get the prospect to tell you what he or she expects to receive for it. Before mentioning a specific figure, explain what must be done to make the article salable, if indeed it can be resold. Build up your customer's confidence in your fairness by being businesslike and dignified in your discussion of the trade-in allowance.

> **TIP** It always helps to let the customer see that you have a basis on which to make your appraisal of the old item's value. Have some record to which you can refer for trade-in values. For example, your record may be a sheet showing appraisal value fixed by model numbers, year of acquisition, and so on. If your company does not supply you with such an appraisal sheet, you can prepare one for yourself on the basis of your experience, what you know about the original cost of the product, how your company disposes of traded-in products, the market for used products, cost of parts to be replaced, and the cost of a general overhauling.

How to answer the objection that a better trade-in allowance can be obtained elsewhere

Your prospect may have been offered a better trade-in allowance by one of your competitors; if so, he or she will probably tell you so. You must then explain why your allowance is just as good, if not better, than the higher offer. You might mention that your product is superior, that it will have a bigger trade-in value eventually than the competing product, that it will last longer, or that it will be more economical to maintain. In other words, you are really answering a price objection.

How to overcome the trade-in obstacle

A trade-in allowance might present an obstacle in selling to an industrial user whose controller makes a careful economy study to justify a replacement. The trade-in allowance can be the decisive figure in calculations affecting the capital recovery period (the length of time in which the investment must be recovered). When your prospect refuses to buy because the trade-in allowance is a problem, and you can't offer him or her a larger allowance, all is not lost. You can still win the sale by showing how your equipment will bring substantial savings in operating costs. The higher the savings, the shorter the recovery period.

Show economy of regular short-term trade-ins

You may be able to convince your prospect that it is more economical to replace the equipment every few years than it is to hold onto old equipment until it *has* to be replaced. To do this, you must have the facts and figures that apply to your product. In some cases, the key factor that induces owners to replace old equipment is the "expensive pair of hands" that uses the equipment—in other words, the high cost of labor as compared to the low cost of the investment in new equipment. A new machine that speeds up production and efficiency can actually pay for itself in terms of reduced labor costs over a specified period of time.

HAVE THE RIGHT ATTITUDE TO ANSWER OBJECTIONS

No More Fear of Objections

Your attitude toward the objections raised by prospects and customers is the key to your confidence in making objections work for you. The first essential is to eliminate any fear of them. After you have mastered the techniques for handling objections explained in this section, you will have no reason to fear them.

Your prospects and customers don't expect you to take "No" for an answer. They meet many salespeople and are accustomed to stating their objections. But these prospects and customers do buy! And when they do, it's not because their objections have been answered, but because the salesperson has made them want the product or service for the benefits it offers.

So if you have confidence in your product and your company, and master the selling strategies and techniques for handling objections, you won't take "No" for an answer. And the people you approach to sell will admire you for it.

Look Upon Objections as Misconceptions

Prospects often make negative statements—not because they don't want to buy or want to get rid of the salesperson, but because they lack information or have misconceptions about the product.

If you regard the prospect's negative statements as arising from misunderstanding or misconceptions, you avoid becoming argumentative. This attitude also encourages you to give the prospect the information needed to change his or her viewpoint.

Answer Objections Without Arguing

When objections are raised, the skillful salesperson knows how to express his or her opinion without being blunt or brusque. He or she does not argue or invite an argument, knowing that to win an argument is often the way to lose a sale. A skilled salesperson is trained to soothe, rather than to ruffle, the other person's feelings—especially at those points where a difference of opinion must be resolved.

■ IDEA IN ACTION

Elmer Holsman sells a well-known home encyclopedia. This is not an easy selling assignment, since an order represents a commitment of over $2,000. The sale is usually made to both husband and wife, and each interview is likely to bring its full share of resistance.

"You have a nice set of books there," says Mr. Jones, "but our own encyclopedia is only 10 years old, and we're quite satisfied with it."

Elmer doesn't agree with that conclusion. Were he a less tactful salesperson, he would express this disagreement along the following lines:

"Now, Mr. Jones, you seem to think that because the paper and the binding of your old set are almost as good as new that you've got a good source of information. Actually, your books are quite out of date, and you can prove this to yourself by looking at the headlines in this evening's newspaper and then trying to track down more information about places and events in the news in your ten-year-old encyclopedia!"

But Elmer knows better than to talk that way. So he frames his rebuttal more tactfully.

"Mr. Jones," says Elmer, "I know exactly how you feel. You have a very fine encyclopedia, and I can see it's in excellent condition.

"You may wonder, Mr. Jones, why many people who have a set just like your own decide to replace it with the edition you and I have been talking about. The answer is really quite simple. These people tell me that in the majority of cases when they turn to their encyclopedia, it isn't just for casual reading but because something specific has come up and they want up-to-date information.

"I'm quite certain, Mr. Jones, that if someone were to offer to trade you a 20-year-old encyclopedia for your *own* set, giving you, say, an additional hundred dollars, you'd turn it down. The extra 10 years that *your* set covers makes quite a difference, doesn't it?

"But let's look at it this way," Elmer continues, turning to Mrs. Jones. "I think you told me, Mrs. Jones, that you have a daughter 14 years old and a son who is almost 12."

"That's right," Mrs. Jones replied.

"Well, as you of course know, schools today emphasize discussion and study of *current events.* I'm sure that both of your children frequently look things up in the encyclopedia. If they don't find what they need, it means not only that their classmates have better reports, but that they may actually lose interest in doing research, which will become more and more important as they get further on in school."

Instead of challenging his prospects to prove whether their present encyclopedia would help them understand today's headlines, the salesperson portrayed years of benefit to the family's two children.

Be Tactful in Meeting Objections

In a sales interview it is normal for the salesperson to emphasize reasons why the buyer should buy, and for the buyer to emphasize reasons why he or she hesitates to buy or should not buy.

If the sale is to be made, the salesperson must succeed in convincing the buyer that each of his or her objections is overruled by some reason or fact. The process of answering objections presents many opportunities for the salesperson to reply forcefully and still avoid overstepping the bounds of tact.

REMEMBER Tactlessness can kill a sale. You must be prepared to answer each objection with a sound, smooth rebuttal.

■ IDEA IN ACTION

Ralph Blount sells a moving and storage service. His calls are based on leads that have come in by telephone.

Ralph works on straight commission, and each sale he succeeds in making means an important addition to his weekly check.

This, plus the fact that his is a highly competitive business, has been responsible for Ralph's gradual adopting an unfortunate mannerism. The tension under which he works under has put him on the defensive, and his response to it is a gruff sort of aggressiveness that is displayed in tactless remarks.

"We can do the whole moving job for you for $1,500, lady," Ralph says.

"Isn't that a little high for such a short move?" counters his prospect.

"Well, you might get somebody else to do it for a little less, but don't blame us if some of the stuff gets broken."

This response is tactless and does not make the sale. Ralph should be equipped to answer the objection to price. If he were so prepared, he would not be put on the defensive by the combination of high stakes plus stiff competition.

A salesperson who is habitually tactless is usually unsure of his or her ability to handle the job. In an effort to hide this fact, he or she resorts to a "tough" manner—as if to say, "I don't have to depend on your business!" Of course, these are exactly the two points about which such an individual actually *is* worried. He or she may lack self-confidence and at the same time be very eager to close the sale.

Protect Your Prospect's Ego

Don't argue; be tactful! If both these commands are obeyed, there is little danger of losing ground by offending your prospect's ego.

But in some situations, you must be particularly careful to *protect* the listener's ego—even to build it up.

Take the case of the prospect who made a bad purchase in the past and is now objecting to buying your product because it reminds her of the one she was stuck with. You find out from her what happened and you see that she made a mistake in judgment. Any reference by you to her poor judgment or any attempt to tell her how she might have avoided the mistake will do you no good. Reminding the prospect of her shortcomings is the surest way to lose a sale, no matter how right or logical you may be.

Under such circumstances, you should win the customer's goodwill by building up her confidence and pride. One way would be to tell her an interesting story of how some well-known person experienced adversity through an error of judgment and used the lesson of this very mistake to build an extraordinarily successful business. Then go on to point out what the prospect now knows about buying a product such as yours.

Consider the Prospect's Temperament in Answering Objections

Every good salesperson is sensitive to the prospect's temperament and mood and takes all circumstances into account when answering his or her objections. Here's an example of how you might respond to one type of temperamental prospect: the opinionated person.

A prospect who is this sure of himself considers it a disgrace to reverse an opinion once he has expressed it. In answering the objections he raises, you must be careful never to put him in the position of having to modify his opinion because of something you said. Instead, you must make it appear that he has changed his mind because of his own superior judgment. The following case illustrates how a skillful salesperson accomplishes this.

■ IDEA IN ACTION

Bob Reynolds, a real estate broker specializing in office space, learns that the Smith Company is seeking new quarters in a suburb of Chicago. Bob knows about an office building at 100 Main Street that seems entirely suitable and calls on Ms. Edgecomb of the Smith Company to try to arrange a lease.

After listening to Bob's proposal, Edgecomb turns it down in no uncertain terms.

"We wouldn't think of going into that section of town," she says. "Why, nobody in our line of work is located within several blocks of that address! No, sir, not a chance! Let me know if something really good turns up."

Bob could easily disprove his prospect's contention then and there. But as a smart salesperson he knows that a more tactful approach is needed. So he says, "Well, you know exactly what you want, Ms. Edgecomb, and my job is to try to find it for you. It would be very helpful if you would tell me the types of companies that would occupy offices in a building that you *would* consider."

Edgecomb replies, a bit pompously, "Well, you know—first-class legal firms, or architects, or insurance companies—*dignified* firms."

Bob proceeds with care at this point. "Isn't it a coincidence," he says with a disarming smile, "that you should mention an insurance company! I know you're not interested in 100 Main Street, Ms. Edgecomb, but when you mentioned an insurance company—well, let me make sure now—I have a list of all the tenants at 100 Main, and if I'm not mistaken . . ."

Bob takes the tenant list from his briefcase and reads off a name here and there. "Wilcox & Bannigan, the big law firm; Corrigan & Corrigan, the architects who get most of the big deals—oh yes, here it is, Star State Insurance Company!

"I thought they were at 100 Main. Well, I'll go over some tenant lists for other buildings and call you when I've found something interesting."

"Does Star State have *offices* there or only a small agency?" Edgecomb inquires cautiously.

"Well, they have the entire sixth floor," Bob replies. "Here, Ms. Edgecomb, let me leave this tenant list with you—it tells you who's there, what space they occupy, and so on."

When Bob telephones in a day or two to suggest another building, he is not at all surprised to hear, "You know, I happened to be driving down Main St. yesterday, and I went over to 100. That building has changed a lot in the past couple of years, hasn't it? I might just take a quick look at the premises you mentioned."

Bob has handled an opinionated prospect in just the right way.

Don't Waste Time on Hopeless Objections

You were advised in Chapter Four to make advance preparations before meeting the prospect, and to get as much information about him or her as you can. That's usually your assurance that you're approaching a live prospect. But sometimes the prospect is not really a prospect for your product—perhaps for a reason that you cannot overcome. In this case, leave the prospect immediately, but in a friendly way. Don't waste any more of your time.

☐ EXAMPLE

You are selling stainless steel valves that are designed for corrosive, hard-to-handle fluids. Your prospect is a chemical company. In your interview you discover that the prospect uses only dry chemicals. He has no need for valves. This is a hopeless objection—one you cannot answer.

Such an experience should caution you to find out about the prospect's manufacturing process in advance, if possible.

CAUTION Be absolutely sure that the objection is hopeless.

MAKE UP A PERSONAL "ANSWER BOOK"

How are you going to benefit immediately and permanently by the techniques explained in this section for making objections work for you?

Do you remember your old school books with their "drills" at the end of each lesson? They were put there because drill is a necessary part of instruction in any branch of knowledge.

We strongly recommend, therefore, that you put together your own "Answer Book" to develop facility in answering objections the way top notch salespeople do.

WHAT TO DO

Get a loose-leaf binder and list on a separate sheet each objection you are likely to meet in your particular selling job.

On each sheet, write the question the objection implies and how you will get the prospect to agree that he or she has really raised a question.

Write in the answer to the question, which is really the answer to the objection.

Then write: "I am glad you brought that up, Mr./Ms. Prospect. It gives me the opportunity to tell you some very important things that make my case stronger." Vary this remark from page to page so that you have a number of different ways of leading into your strategy for capitalizing on the objection.

Write down the "capitalizing" statement that strengthens your presentation, gives you a chance to bring in testimonials, lets you summarize the reasons why the prospect should use your product, and so on.

Now study your "Answer Book" until you know it by heart.

The "Answer Book" can become your most valuable tool for increasing your earnings. Add more pages as you run into unexpected forms of resistance. Don't hesitate to change a page when you've found through experience a better way to overcome an objection. Keep up the drill by reviewing your "Answer Book" regularly.

SUGGESTION To be sure that you cover each of the points mentioned, prepare the blank pages of your "Answer Book" with these headings:

1. *Objection*
2. *Question implied by objection*
3. *Answer to question or objection*
4. *Lead-in to capitalizing*

5. *Capitalizing statement*

> **COMMENT** The "Answer Book" is desirable even though you have already worked into your presentation the objections you're accustomed to meeting and your answers to them. Why? Because you may run into other objections that you feel should be anticipated. When this happens, you'll want to change your presentation to cover the omission. At such times your "Answer Book" becomes a reference source for developing the most effective strategy for handling the objection.

ANSWER GUIDE TO 25 SPECIFIC OBJECTIONS

How to Use the Answer Guide

To help you convert objections into sales, two special aids are given here: (1) the objections you're most likely to run into and how you can build the strongest answers to overcome them and (2) real-life examples of proven answers to the most important objections.

Use the aids in this section as follows: Look through the paragraph immediately following the objection and select the items that apply to your product or service. The ones you select will have to be fully developed to make the most of them for your particular product. Then read over the examples to find ideas and language to strengthen your response. Test your answer against the four rules at the beginning of this chapter to be sure you have made the best use of the guidance given there.

Objection 1:
"Your price is too high."

To build a strong answer to price objection, offer the following reasons:

- The price is justified by the quality of the materials; superior workmanship, design, or construction; durability; built-in conveniences; and so on.

- Price is relative. Your price is actually lower than your competitor's when economies of operation, quality, and service are considered.

- Your company could produce a lower-priced product, but experience shows that it would not give the same high degree of satisfaction.

- An inexpensive product costs more in terms of complaints, mishaps, breakdowns, and so on.

- When selling to a dealer, higher-priced products are prestige-builders for the dealer. There's also more profit in it for the dealer: Your company's nationwide advertising helps the dealer sell your product, and an inexpensive product costs more in loss of customers and in customer dissatisfaction.

- High-grade performance is what the customer is buying. It is the result of years of experience and specialized "know-how."

- Your company produces at the lowest possible cost and sells at a fair price.

- If a less expensive method of production were developed, your company would be the first to apply it.

(Chapter Five also provides suggestions for how to handle the issue of price in a presentation.

Real-life example: Capitalize on the objection by showing your volume of sales

---

Prospect:	Your price is too high.
Salesperson:	Yes, we're the highest-priced in our field, yet we do $6 million of business a year at these prices. We couldn't do that if our values weren't exceptional, could we?

Real-life example: Capitalize on what your competitor can't; beat price with proof

---

Salesperson: Here's a list of our users in this city who are now operating pumps that have pumped more than 2 million gallons of gasoline with practically no repair costs. These pumps are still in splendid condition. I suggest that you take this list of names and addresses and go see these pumps. Give them a careful inspection. Then ask the other company if they can furnish you with such a list. They won't be able to do it. Their pumps simply will not stand up.

Real-life example: Be ready with exclusive features when prospect wants to shop for better price

Ken Morgan sells electric motors and related supplies and equipment to large industrial plants.

"Mr. Morgan," says one of his customers, "what size transformer do you suggest we install in our new heat treating department?"

Ken reaches for the catalog issued by the ABC Transformer Company. "Here are the capacities of all the units we manufacture. Now let's see . . . Model 69B seems as though it would fit your needs."

"How much does it weigh?"

Ken replies, "I'll tell you in a second. Weight and other specifications for model 69B—here they are, on page 54."

"Fine," says the customer. "That gives me the picture on the ABC product. But they're higher-priced than some other manufacturers', aren't they? Guess I'll have to look around before deciding."

But Ken is prepared for this, too. "Mr. Young," he replies, "ABC has several exclusive features that I think you ought to consider." Here he produces a circular furnished by the manufacturer. It not only pictures a typical unit, but it also lists two special features that Ken has referred to. Furthermore, there is a copy of the guarantee that backs up every one of the units and a list of big company users.

The customer examines this with some care. He is obviously impressed. Finally he says, "Well, Mr. Morgan, I guess this is the transformer we should buy, even if it does cost a bit more."

Real-life example: Plead guilty to high price and sell the prospect anyway

---

Salesperson:	Yes, my price is too high—if you're thinking of the $20 customer. Our product, frankly, isn't manufactured for that market. For the $100 customer who walks into your store, this lamp is the biggest value you could possibly offer. In fact, wherever this item has been set up alongside the $20 item, it has actually sold better than when displayed without any competition. The comparison is so striking that customers don't hesitate to pay the difference. Why should you? Incidentally, the $100 market must be growing like wildfire, because last month alone we doubled our volume of the same month a year ago.

Real-life example: Answer "Your price is too high" with showmanship

Let's say you're a printer. Your estimate is in and the customer has made comparisons with two or more of your competitors. "You're asking too much money," your prospect says. What's more, he can prove it in writing by referring to the bids sent in by your competitors.

Salesperson:	Mr. Jones, here are the names, addresses, and telephone numbers of 25 other printers right here in the city who can beat any price of ours by 10 to 25%. The chances are that most of them could even lick the price you have and give it

to you at a lower figure. What's more, any one of them will tack a bigger profit on your job than we could, in spite of the fact that we have one of the most efficiently run plants in the city.

Here's an example of how it's done. (Takes out a printed circular and a typewritten comparison sheet.) A couple of months ago I lost a job to one of those 25 low-priced printers. I was curious to know exactly what they put into the job so I got this circular when it was finished and had someone from our shop analyze it and compare the results with the figures I had submitted. Here's what he found.

According to specifications, both of us figured on an 80-pound coated stock. The big difference was that we counted on using a *folding* coated paper. Notice how this circular cracks almost the minute you open it. Look at the halftones—good plates, but weak and unimpressive because they had maybe an hour of make-ready for every two we knew were necessary to bring out the details and highlights. Look at the sloppy registration between each of the four colors in this picture. Did you know, Mr. Jones, that on a four-color job we run every sheet of stock through the presses before printing the first color, just to take the static electricity out of the paper and make sure of hairline register? We do. You can go through the rest of this comparison sheet and see for yourself how a printer has to cut corners to come up with a price like the ones you've been given.

Well, Mr. Jones, there's only one reason why you print a folder to begin with: to get results. A job that won't do its best work when distributed is too expensive no matter how low the printing price.

A printed piece that brings you business is a

> bargain at any fair price. That's the kind of job
> we were figuring on.

Real-life example: Use prospect's own slogans to meet price objection

An advertising agency client found herself on the point of okaying a fairly big job when she suddenly wavered, venturing that the price seemed rather high.

Salesperson: Very well, I can cut corners here and there and probably get the work done at a lower price. But I like to feel, as you do (and here he casually pointed to the slogan on the agency's own calendar), that "quality is remembered long after price is forgotten." Two or three months from now, the important thing will be not whether this job could have been done for $40 or $50 less, but whether I put everything into it that would bring you the most business possible. Don't you agree?

SUGGESTION Examine your customer's advertising and sales literature carefully; chances are you'll find words or phrases that can be used to counteract the price objection.

Real-life example: Make your higher price an asset

If your price is a selling liability, make it an asset. Here's how a salesperson for standard-brand products (oil burners, in his case) gets around the price objection.

"In our line of business, we're forced to meet the competition of numerous oil burner companies that have rushed into the market with a hastily made burner. They depend on price alone for their sales.

"When a buyer or prospect comes to us, one who has been considering the cheap burners, I don't try to conceal the fact that ours is higher in price. Instead, I make it a selling point. First, I explain the heater and give a demonstration. Then I concentrate on our company's reputation, financial responsibility, and standing in the oil burner industry.

"There are a lot of oil burner companies that are making burners in one corner of their plant. There are other companies who have organized hastily and are turning out an inferior product to meet a price. Now remember, if you buy the wrong burner you're making an expensive mistake. Even a cheap burner is too expensive if you end up throwing it out after a couple of years.

"Here's a list of users who bought cheap burners and had to throw them out. They've spent their money, and today they haven't got the money *or* the burner. You'll probably buy our make sooner or later. Why not get it now and save the extra expense of having to throw out a burner that won't heat your house? Remember, it's heat and comfort and economy of operation that you're buying, not just a machine to put in your basement and forget about."

Real-life example: Prospect's own products are not the cheapest

Prospect:	No, I simply won't pay any such price. Why, I can beat that by 15%.
Salesperson:	Ms. Prospect, I'm under the impression that your products aren't the cheapest, either. Am I wrong?

Nine times out of ten, this approach will do the job. Ninety percent of the people you call on—whether they're manufacturers, doctors, merchants, or others—do not want to be known as the cheapest provider of their product or service. They know that price is meaningless when it is considered apart from quality. All you have to do is to tell them in the fewest possible words that *you* know they know it!

Objection 2:
"I can get a similar product for a considerably lower price."

To build a strong answer to this objection, use these reasons:

- The two products may look the same, but they are very different in quality and performance. Supply the facts that prove there's a difference.

- Underscore the special advantages offered by your company—a guarantee, better service, easier terms, reputation for reliability, and so on.

- Answer price objection generally, as discussed in the previous section.

Real-life example: Lose the argument, win the sale

Prospect:	Why, I can get these goods from so-and-so for $5 a gross less than you're quoting me.
Salesperson:	Probably so. I wouldn't argue that point with you for a minute. So-and-so is much better qualified than I am to tell you exactly what his goods are worth. But I do know what *my* goods are worth, and I know that at the price I've quoted, they'll be a better buy than anything else you can get, no matter what the price. Of course, you can get more expensive goods than ours and you can get stuff a lot cheaper, but for your purpose, ours is the best buy because . . .

Real-life example: Compete on merit, not price

Prospect:	I can buy the same line for a good deal less from Company X.

Salesperson: My firm knows that line, but we don't make it. If we did, our price would no doubt be as low as theirs. On the other hand, if Company X made our line, their prices would probably be as high as ours. You've got to figure that my product—and only my product—pays you the profit you have a right to make. We don't compete on price. If we did, there would be no bottom. But we do compete on the merits of our products, and I think you'll agree there isn't much competition there. If price were *your* customers' only concern when purchasing your products, then the lowest-priced product would be your best-selling product. And that isn't true, is it?

Objection 3:
The prospect wants a lower price or extra discount.

Here's how to deal with a bargainer:

- Tell the prospect that you don't cut prices, nor does the company. Then sell him or her on the merits and quality of your product.

- Use the fair play argument. The prospect would not cut the price of the product he or she sells, so why should you be expected to do so?

- Point out that if you reduced your price, your prospect would feel that you are reducing prices for other customers— perhaps giving them an even better deal.

  TIP Sticking to your price and terms is bound to gain your prospect's respect. You may not get the order the day you refuse to lower your price, but the next time you call on the prospect, there'll be no play for a cut or special treatment, and the order will be won on merit.

Real-life example: Stand pat on price

A produce firm was in the market for two tractors. Mark Burton submitted his price, and so did his competition. Not long after, Mark was told by the prospect that his competition had submitted a new price on the tractors. Since the new competitive price was considerably lower than the first quotation, the prospect wanted to give Mark the same opportunity to lower his bid.

Here's how Mark handled the situation: He reminded the firm that in the beginning he had been asked to offer his best price. "That's exactly what I've given you," Mark said. "Consequently, even if I could cut the price now, I wouldn't—you'd no longer have any faith in me or the company. After all," Mark went on, "you can't expect to do business with someone you don't trust—and how can you trust someone who doesn't keep his word?"

Mark concluded by reminding the prospect once again that he had submitted his best price initially and that he would stand on that price. Apparently his explanation struck a responsive chord, because the prospect gave Mark an order.

Real-life example: Play on the prospect's vanity and hold to your price

---

Prospect: No sale unless I get an extra 5%.

Salesperson: I know I haven't been selling half as long as you've been buying these goods. I know that I'd be no match for most of the merchants I call on. They know the market at least as well as I do. I also know that you're a darned good judge of values yourself, and you would know in a minute if I added a single nickel to the rock-bottom price for which these goods can be sold. I figure prices down to the last penny in the first place and let it go at that.

Real-life example: How to handle the discount hog

The sales manager for a successful office machine manufacturer explains how one of her salespeople handled a customer who always thought the price was too high.

"Sometimes," she explains, "the reason for the price problem is that the buyer thinks he should be able to get a special price or discount. Back when this company first started selling its calculating machines, buyers were not accustomed to having printed prices mean exactly what they said. Everybody wanted a special 'deal.'

"One of our salespeople, encountering this objection, went around to a dozen or more of his leading customers and got them to give him the canceled checks they'd used in purchasing their calculating machines. Then he used one of our machines to total up these checks while the prospect watched over his shoulder. Thus, in one demonstration, the salesperson not only showed how fast and easy it was to use the machine, but also proved to the prospect that a dozen or more of the biggest businesses in town had bought our machines and that they'd all paid full price."

Real-life example: How to handle the dealer who wants a shipment on consignment

---

Salesperson: I wish I could do that—but I can't. The only way we can keep our costs down to a level that allows you a 40% profit is by operating on a sound business basis. We're in the manufacturing—not the banking—business, and we've got to get our money promptly enough to be able to take advantage of purchasing opportunities. If we distributed our goods on consignment, we'd be paying interest to the bank for working capital—and in the long run, you and your customers would have to absorb those higher costs.

I'll tell you what I'll do, though. I'll send you a case on our regular 30-day terms. Then, if

> within two or three months you still have more
> than half the lot unsold, I'll get the home office
> to exchange the stock for any other items in our
> line. I can have the goods here by Friday.

Company policy may require you to refuse all requests for
consignment. However, the policy may be worth reconsidering. A
farmer who raises and sells seed consistently refused to deliver
seeds on consignment. He weakened on one occasion and left a
consignment of seeds with a customer. In a short time he had
reorders; in fact, a surprisingly large amount of seed was sold by this
customer. Here's the explanation the customer gave him: "Your seeds
are out on the floor where I can see them, so I sell them."

Objection 4:
"Your credit terms are too tough."

Here's how to meet the objection against credit terms:

- Judge whether the prospect is sincere or merely using the
  credit terms as an excuse.
- Defend your credit terms as being standard in the trade.
- Ask the prospect to suggest acceptable terms.

Real-life example: Ask what terms are acceptable

> *Prospect:* Your company's credit terms are too tough.
>
> *Salesperson:* Actually, our terms are on a par with the rest
> of the industry. However, if you tell me exactly
> what terms you feel would better suit your
> situation, I'm sure that my company will con-
> sider any reasonable proposition.

Objection 5:
"We have a lower bid from
your competitor."

Here's how to meet the "lower-bid" or "better-deal" objection:

- Ask to see the specifications on which the competitor made his or her bid. You want to be sure that there has been no misunderstanding as far as requirements are concerned and that the competitor's bid is on the same quantity and quality of material as yours.

- Ask for the details of the proposition; then, point by point, clarify why your deal is as good as, if not better than, the competitor's.

- Resell on the basis of quality, performance, low cost of maintenance, service, your firm's reputation for giving customer satisfaction, and so on.

- Use reasons given in Objection 1 to answer price objection generally.

- Assure the prospect that you can give him or her as good a deal as the competitor because you've been doing it for years.

Objection 6:
"I can't afford it."

Here's how to overcome the "I can't afford it" objection:

- Use the objection as the reason for buying, if what you are offering has money-saving advantages.

- If you can legitimately do so, present a proposition that makes it possible for the prospect to buy—for example, offering easy terms, partial payments, a trade-in allowance, and so on.

  REMEMBER You can't earn big commissions by selling to people who really can't afford to buy your product. A salesperson who is aiming to get into high-bracket income will bypass the financially unstable prospect and concentrate on full-potential prospects.

Real-life example: It's the reason for buying

Prospect: I can't afford it.

> *Salesperson:*   Mrs. Jones, I'm glad you mentioned that, be-
> cause one of the big features of our equipment
> is the money it saves you from the very first
> minute you install it.

Real-life example: Itemization of daily expenses proves a convincing argument when prospect "can't afford it"

Quite often a prospect who "can't afford" to make a purchase hasn't analyzed his or her assets correctly. The following argument presented by a life insurance salesperson shows the prospect how her income is being spent and the advantage of putting aside something for herself.

> *Salesperson:*   Ms. Prospect, when you're paying your bills
> every month, does it ever seem as if you're
> working for everyone but yourself? Now these
> figures are not absolute, but they're probably
> pretty close. Let's assume that you've received
> your pay for the month and that you're writing
> out checks to pay your bills:
>
> - Eight days' pay is going for groceries.
> - Eight days' pay is going for rent and utilities.
> - Three days' pay is going to doctors, dentists, and other professionals.
> - Four days' pay is going for clothing.
> - Four days' pay is going for movies, eating out, and luxuries.
> - Three days' pay is going for the car.
>
>   "If you add these up, you'll find that 30 days'
>   income is spent the minute you earn it. If
>   you're lucky and the month has 31 days, you
>   may be able to save this extra day's income for
>   yourself.
>
>   Now my thought is this: Instead of work-
>   ing for all these other people, pay the one

who is making all of this possible. Pay yourself first.

There must be a figure—even a small amount—that you feel you should be putting away each week for yourself."

Real-life example: Ask for a time payment proposition

Prospect:	I can't afford one now.
Salesperson:	Well, what sort of a time payment proposition would you like? Because your old machine loses trade-in value as it deteriorates, you might be able to save some money by buying now on satisfactory terms.

Real-life example: Get a delivery date

Prospect:	I don't have enough money right now.
Salesperson:	That doesn't matter. Tell me exactly when you expect to be ready for it and I'll put the order through for any date you say. All you have to do now is let me have a small deposit and tell me which of these two colors you prefer.

Objection 7: "My budget doesn't leave room for the expenditure."

To build a strong answer to the "no room in the budget" objection, use these reasons to convince your prospect:

- The prospect is always ready to save money; delay in savings is the same as adding to costs. Show specifically how the savings are made, and total them up to show that they come to more than the expenditure.

- The prospect is always ready to make more profits on sales, and delay means a loss of profits. Show specifically how profits can mount through faster turnover or larger mark-ups.

Real-life example: Figure the savings

Danielle White, who sells office equipment, called on a firm that was at the tail end of its budget year. Consequently, they were hesitant to make any further capital expenditures. Danielle's customer was using two units of a particular model, which kept up with their demands for two weeks of the month. However, the other two weeks would be hectic, involving three hours a night overtime on the part of two operators. In making a survey, Danielle found that a net saving of $1,250 could be realized if production were increased to eliminate overtime costs. A demonstration of the machine she recommended, with a selling proposal, closed the deal.

In spite of a so-called "shortage of funds," a company can usually find the money if the salesperson has a sound proposition and follows the appropriate steps in making the sale.

Objection 8:
"I'll think it over."

Here are some ways to get the procrastinator to act now:

- Ask "why" the prospect needs to think it over. It may bring out a hidden objection or resolve the prospect's uncertainties.

- Point out the advantages of making an immediate decision. Make the prospect feel the penalty of postponement. Perhaps he or she will be entitled to a special discount by making the purchase now, or the delivery will be made in time to meet the initial demand that the company's nationwide campaign is sure to trigger, or prices may be slated to go up. At any rate, quicker enjoyment of the product's benefits will be gained by an immediate decision.

- Ignore the remark and proceed with your strong selling points, dramatizing savings and other gains.

- Indicate that your prospect now knows all he or she has to know about the value of the product and that you're right there to answer any specific questions.

- When you sense that the prospect is sincere and not just looking for an "out," say that you understand how important a decision this is and summarize your product's benefits. Then make an appointment immediately for a callback. Leave the prospect with something to remember you by. You might want to arrange to come back with someone; bringing a "specialist" to the next interview might give you the psychological edge you need to make the sale.

- If the prospect says that he or she wants to "think it over," ask what you can do for him or her to make the decision easier. The prospect might be looking for a special inducement.

- Suggest that you'll put off seeing someone else to whom you were going to make a similar offer. The rivalry might stimulate the prospect to decide now.

- If possible, leave the product with your prospect for a trial period, or make use of your guarantee.

NOTE When the economy is just beginning to turn around after a recession, buyers in industries that are slow to feel the recovery will tend to put off buying until their own business has turned the corner. They need reassurance that the recovery is real. You can give them this reassurance by quoting current economic data published in recognized business periodicals.

The procrastinator who puts off a buying decision because he or she doesn't like the way things look in Washington, Europe, or somewhere else in the world has to be shown that the future is by nature unpredictable. For example, in 1928 and 1929 optimism ran high, and few people predicted a depression. In 1931 and 1932, the situation was just the opposite. And the postwar decline that was predicted after World War II turned out to be a boom.

Real-life example: Make prospect see why he or she can decide now

Here is a typical sequence in which a prospect begins by agreeing that the product—in this case, an insurance policy—sounds worthwhile, but ends with "I'll think it over. Call back in a week."

Salesperson:	There are only two things to think about: (1) Do you need it? and (2) Can you pay for it? Am I right?
Prospect:	I guess so.
Salesperson:	Don't you know just as well *now* as you will next week whether or not you need it?
Prospect:	Yes.
Salesperson:	And don't you know just as well *now* as you would a week from now whether or not you can pay for it?

The prospect, in most cases, admits he or she does—and the case is closed.

Real-life example: The power of the "why" over the procrastinator

The hardest question for a wavering prospect to answer is *why*. The prospect often finds it difficult to put his or her objection into suitable words. A vague or hidden objection is often so intangible it can't be framed in words. For example:

Prospect:	I'll think it over.
Salesperson:	Why?
Prospect:	Well . . . I . . . it just seems best.

COMMENT By repeating the question "Why?" you gradually bring all the prospect's objections out into the open where they can be answered. But sometimes the prospect still won't buy. *One key objection* still worries the prospect. What is it? Cost? Weight? Construction? Practicality? Features? Keep asking "Why?"!

Salesperson:	Is that your only reason for not buying?
Prospect:	Yes, that's my only reason for not buying.

COMMENT The prospect has revealed that there is only *one* objection! If you can answer this key objection, the sale will soon be yours. When you do answer the objection, be sure to say: "You told me that your only reason for not buying was such-and-such. I guess this means that you're ready to have me schedule a delivery."

Real-life example: Show what it costs to delay decision

Prospect:	I'll think it over.
Salesperson:	The last time I was here I sold Company B, across the street, one of our machines. That was three months ago. This morning they told me that it had saved them over $3,000 since they started using it. At that rate, every month you spend thinking it over costs you $1,000.

Real-life example: Ask the prospect if he or she wishes to delay his or her own sales

---

Prospect:	I'll wait and see how the election turns out.
Salesperson:	Well, Mr. Richards, if that's your only reason for not buying now, let me ask you a question: Are your own customers waiting to see how the elections turn out before sending you any more business? No, they're not! In fact, last week's nationwide business index shows a slight increase over the week before. Are you laying off your sales force until you see how the elections turn out? Of course not! If you did, you might as well close up shop for the next six months and take a vacation. Besides, with steel prices going up the way they are, you'll end up paying a lot more for this equipment after the election. Why not save money and start realizing profits right now?

Real-life example: Get the prospect to listen a little longer

Prospect:	I'll let you know later.
Salesperson:	Mr. Prospect, I'm glad you want to think this over. You don't buy this kind of service very often, and I can see that you are very careful when it comes to making decisions. That's the kind of customers we like; they appreciate our careful workmanship. Now if you'll give me a few more minutes of your time, I'll show you how you can make your work a lot easier right away, and then you won't have to bother letting me know later.

COMMENT With a little persuasiveness you may be able to get your prospect to listen while you point out an advantage that will make him or her act immediately.

Real-life example: Get action—now— from a prospect who is "in no hurry"

Prospect:	I like the idea of a retirement income policy, but I'm in no hurry. I have five months to go before my "insurance age" changes.
Salesperson:	It's very easy to put off taking the policy for five months, but that means your first retirement check will also come five months later. Do you really want to wait five months longer for that income? You might have to rely on someone else for a time—which is exactly what you're buying this policy to forestall. Why not make sure of enjoying your retirement five months earlier?

Real-life example: Leave the prospect something to remember you by

If you're convinced the sale won't jell right then and there, here's one way to keep the door wide open:

Salesperson: All right. While you're thinking it over, perhaps you'd like to see the whole picture. I have a booklet here that will help you study the proposition at your leisure. I've got only two left and I need them while I'm waiting for the new ones to come in, but I can lend you one of them and drop by later to pick it up. Here you are!

Objection 9:
"I'm too busy."

Here's how to meet the "too busy" objection:

- Use the objection as the reason for seeing the prospect now, if what you are offering has time-saving advantages.

- Get the prospect to agree that he or she is never too busy to make a profit if what you are offering will save money or increase profits.

- Ask for 10 minutes of the prospect's time, take out your watch to show that you won't exceed 10 minutes, and stop when the 10 minutes are up. If your prospect seems interested, ask for a little more time. If not, leave as you said you would, but try to arrange an appointment for another time that will be more convenient.

  REMEMBER If your prospect was too busy to see you on your first call, and too busy again on your callback, you might want to weigh the value of your own time or use a different strategy.

If you see that your prospect is obviously in a hurry to break away, don't waste the call. Make it count by fixing a definite appointment: "Suppose I come back at 2:30 tomorrow afternoon— or would 10 o'clock Friday morning suit you better?" Not only do you thus avoid an outright dismissal, but you return on your next visit in the position of an invited caller.

Real-life example: "Eleven minutes" does the trick

A top salesperson of appliances explains how he handles prospects who are "too busy":

"I've discovered that the best way to calm down a rushed buyer is to pin him or her down to a few minutes. I might say, 'You've got eleven minutes, haven't you?

"The prospect will mutter something about nobody ever sticking to time limits, but will concede that he or she probably has that much time.

" 'Well,' I say as I take out my watch, 'that's all the time I want from you. I'll lay out my watch where we can both see it, and please forgive me if I talk fast.'

"I lay out my watch and I time my talk. If the dealer gets interested in my proposition, I ask his or her permission before I take more time. It is always granted with a grin."

Real-life example: Get order for "specially priced" items now

Prospect:	I can't spare the time right now.
Salesperson:	All right, I'll come back to see you on my next trip. But I'm here today with a chance for you to take your pick from a list of specials at mark-downs which can save you from 20 to 40%. Some of the more important items that are on my list include . . . .

Objection 10:
"I'm not interested."

Here are some ideas to get the prospect interested:

■ Find the reason for lack of interest and overcome that reason. Has the prospect tried such a product before? Does he or she have a binding contract?

- Give an example of a customer who said he or she wasn't interested at first, but bought after recognizing the opportunity to profit through use of the product.

REMEMBER If a prospect claims not to be interested after you've given most of your presentation and doesn't give you a concrete reason, it's time to do some self-questioning about why you failed to arouse the necessary interest. (See Chapter One for guidelines on how to review and improve your sales approach.)

Real-life example: Answering the prospect who has tried once before

Prospect:	We tried something like it a while ago. It didn't work. We're not interested.
Salesperson:	Mr. Prospect, have you ever eaten a dinner that didn't agree with you—gave you indigestion? Of course you have! But you didn't give up eating just because that dinner didn't click. You say you've tried my plan before, but it didn't work. Isn't it possible that the plan itself is as good as you thought it was when you decided to try it last year—that the only reason it flopped was the method used to implement it? I've got a method that's been tested over and over—and it works!"

Real-life example: Build interest by example

Prospect:	I'm not interested.
Salesperson:	A couple of hours ago I called on another very busy executive, and she wasn't interested either—until I had the chance to show her how she could save $5,000 a month that she's been literally throwing away for years. I don't know exactly how much you may be losing on returned goods every month, but

I'll bet I can show you in the next 8 minutes how to save at least $60,000 a year, and maybe a whole lot more. Here's an example of what I mean—.

Objection 11:
"I'm all stocked up."

Here are some tried and true ways to help a dealer move your line when he or she is stocked up:

- Get behind the company's efforts to secure dealer cooperation. Many companies use such dealer aids as lower prices for quantity purchases, discounts and rebates, premiums, coupons for a discount or free product, contests among consumers, samples, trade-ins, and so on.
- Get the dealer to feature a display of your product.
- Get dealer cooperation in window displays.
- Influence the dealer to advertise and feature your product. Manufacturers usually take the initiative in offering assistance to the dealer. They furnish dealers with advertising mats, dealer ads to tie in with the manufacturer's own ads, direct mail circulars to be used by the dealer, ideas and layouts for dealer signs and billboards, and the like. The salesperson helps carry out the manufacturer's efforts.
- If the dealer is stocked up, but not with your line, prove that your line moves regardless of overall stock condition and is a sure money-maker.
- Make the dealer see the profit possibilities that will result from your company's forthcoming special promotion campaign, if such advertising is actually planned.

  CAUTION If your prospect is really overstocked and is not merely using the objection as an excuse, don't overload him or her. Arrange to come back at a definite time when the stock is lower—and move on to a better prospect.

Real-life example: Get an order and display when the prospect is "stocked up"

When a merchant wearily tells you that he or she is "all stocked up," say that you have something outside you'd like him or her to see. Stand outside the merchant's window, select a position (one you picked out before you entered the store), and tell the merchant that your money-making display, which just fits that spot, will pay good rent for a space that at the moment isn't producing a nickel's worth of profit.

The moment you plant this idea, you're on your way to a sale. If the merchant rejects the spot you point to, ask him or her to select a better one. In either case, you not only get the order but the precious display space as well.

Real-life example: Remember the turnover factor

Prospect:	I can't make any money on your goods. The profit is too small.
Salesperson:	Yes, your *gross* profit is small, but you've forgotten the turnover factor. Consider your investment in that slow-moving line over there (you'll find some in every store). You double your money on that, but you do it only once a year. Our gross profit is only half that, but you turn our goods over four times a year. Thus you make a lot more on the same investment. You need a fast-moving line like ours to balance the slow turnover on the goods you have to keep on hand.

Real-life example: Get an order for later delivery

Prospect:	We've got too many gloves in stock *now*. I couldn't place an order with *anybody* today!

> *Salesperson:* If your inventory is heavy, I certainly wouldn't suggest that you add to it at this time. But here's what I *do* suggest: Place an order now for delivery in 30 days, when your inventory will be in need of some additional fresh styles.

Objection 12: "I can get a better guarantee from Blank Company."

Here's how to meet an objection to your guarantee:

- If your guarantee is for a shorter period than your competitor's, justify its duration by showing that (1) experience and factory research have proved that defects, if there are any, show up in the first six months, and (2) the guarantee terms you offer are simple and clear cut when compared with the complicated clauses in other guarantees, which are designed to give the manufacturer numerous "outs."

- If you don't have a written guarantee but the company stands firmly behind its product, offer a written guarantee if company policy permits you to do so.

Objection 13: "I've never heard of your firm."

To build a strong answer to the "unknown company" objection, offer your prospects the following considerations:

- Although your company is not as well known as others, it soon will be, because of the caliber of its management.

- Although your company is small, it can give your customer as good service as any larger, better-known company, and it can also provide more individual attention.

- You have become associated with the company because of your confidence in its management, the excellence of its product, and your conviction that the company is bound to grow.

- If your company is well established, but unknown to the prospect, use your testimonials.

Real-life example: Use testimonials

Salesperson: Our line, Ms. Dealer, has been handled for years by such fine stores as Carson's and Worth & Tempest. If our goods don't give permanent satisfaction, and if our service is not the best, do you suppose for a minute that firms like these would continue to sell our products?

Objection 14:
"Your product is too new."

To build a strong answer to this objection, tell your prospects:

- Newness means progress; every product that is commonplace today, like CD players and VCRs, was at one time considered "too new."

- Your new product has been thoroughly tested, as shown by your testimonials and list of users.

- Your company has made extensive efforts to advertise the product.

- Your product has superior quality (in other words, sell other product benefits to the customer).

- Popularity of well-known brands is not necessarily an indication of their superiority. Instead of putting its money into advertising, your company may have been putting it into research, development, and improvement of the product.

- Your company has earned a reputation for customer satisfaction that can't be beaten by producers of the better-known products.

Objection 15:
Criticism of your product

Here's how to overcome objection to the product itself:

- A demonstration of confidence in your factory's judgment will often work wonders if the design of a product is criticized or when the prospect says that a competitor puts out a better line.

- Use testimonials of other users, or show reorders, if a dealer-prospect says the product won't sell.

Real-life example: Make your confidence contagious when the product is criticized

Prospect:	Your product isn't built right.
Salesperson:	Well, I'm not a mechanic, and I don't know all about the whys and wherefores of these hinges, but I do know who makes them, and I know that if they weren't the best hinge for that particular purpose, we wouldn't be using them.

Real-life example: Be specific when a competitor's product is alleged superior

Prospect:	The other company puts out a better line.
Salesperson:	I believe our company puts out the best line in the country. If I thought there was a better one, I would be carrying it, and with my record, I'd have no trouble changing. Why, I can think of seven ways in which our products are better made and easier to sell than anything on the market. Take this camera, for example.

Real-life example: Appeal to the customer's pride

Prospect: There's no demand for your product.

Salesperson: Did you ever stop to think why you go to the post office for stamps? Funny question, isn't it? But, listen! You go to the post office for stamps because you know you can get them there! People go to certain stores for the same reason—not because they want the latest merchandise but because they're accustomed to finding the same old stock there. When 86 stores out of every 100 in this city find our canned goods one of their fastest-selling lines, there must be quite a demand—one that you could capitalize on right here in this store. Why not make me prove it? Give our line a 60-day trial. Suppose I send you our special deal, so that you can make 15% extra profit at the same time you try out our line.

Real-life example: Break down the style objection

Prospect: The styles are wrong. Our customers won't go for them.

Salesperson: Well, on this trip alone, I've heard those comments from three other good merchants—people who are almost as good a judge of merchandise as you are. And it just goes to show you that *nobody* can tell what kids these days will go for. Here—look at these repeat orders from Syracuse, Rochester, and Buffalo. And as you know, right here in your own town you've seen things that sell like hotcakes—things that most of us would never identify as the latest fashion trend. The point is that compared with the styles that kids today see pic-

tured in the magazines and elsewhere, these
styles are anything but extreme!

Real-life example: Use facts to overcome a criticism that once prevailed

---

Prospect:	I've heard that your machines are not very good and that you don't sell as much as other companies.
Salesperson:	You're basing what you say on facts that existed many years ago. If you haven't seen the new models we've brought out over the past six years, I can understand your making that statement, but today we have a machine that is second to none. Our customer acceptance is worldwide. In the past 14 years our sales have tripled, and today our company's sales of this machine are at its highest point.

Objection 16:
Your former salespeople didn't leave a good impression.

To counter this objection, sell yourself:

"I'm new in this territory myself, and I suppose I'll make some mistakes. But I know I won't build this territory by not satisfying people. So the first thing I want to do is apologize for my predecessor and hope you won't hold me responsible. I certainly want to make friends for my company."

Objection 17:
"I've heard that XYZ Co. had trouble with your product."

This kind of objection usually comes as a surprise. Here's how to overcome adverse rumors:

- In most cases you don't know of the trouble and can honestly say so.

- You can assure the prospect that the company has undoubtedly taken care of the complaint, if indeed there was one.

- You might point out that the prospect, like every other businessperson, has at some time had a misunderstanding with a customer. He or she certainly wouldn't think it fair if his or her customers acted on a rumor without having heard both sides of the story.

- To get the prospect in a good listening mood, you might offer to find out whether in fact there *was* trouble, what it was all about, and how it was resolved.

Once you have disposed of the adverse rumors, you can proceed to show the benefits to be derived from your product, to emphasize its quality and service, and to use your testimonials and list of well-known customers to build confidence in the company's reputation and product.

Objection 18:
"A closer supplier will give me faster delivery and service."

Here's how to overcome the "distance" objection:

- Present facts that assure the prospect that there will be no delay in delivery or service. For example, your company uses airfreight for delivery, it guarantees that a serviceperson will call within 24 hours of notice, and so on.

- Use testimonials of satisfied customers who are also some distance away from your company's headquarters.

Objection 19:
Friendships or other personal ties stand in the way

To break down the "personal ties" objection, remind your prospect:

- It's to the prospect's advantage to switch, because your product is superior, has certain benefits, and offers significant savings.

- It is often difficult to get as good quality service and attention from a friend or relative as from an outsider.

- The prospect may sometimes feel that he or she would rather not give relatives or friends information that must be shared to obtain the full benefit of the product or service. It's easier to discuss his or her needs with an outsider.

Personal ties are often deeply rooted. Yet few prospects' devotion to their friends goes deeper than their own selfish interests. It's good strategy to admit openly that you admire loyalty toward friends. But caution your prospect about letting this admirable trait prevent him or her from realizing the advantages that he or she will gain by doing business with you. Remember that most prospects who continue to favor a friend do so for the simple reason that no one has given them a practical reason why it would be advantageous to switch. Remind them that they're in business to make a profit for their *company*, not to support their friends.

Even a close friend doesn't expect someone to continue a business relationship when it is obviously to one party's disadvantage to do so. Your job, therefore, is to put your finger on one or more points of superiority, either of product or service, that enable you to offer an advantage the "friend" simply can't equal.

Your best bet is to make a play for an insignificant part of the prospect's business and then "go to town" on performance, letting the buyer see for himself or herself the contrast between your service and the other company's.

Real-life example: Breaking down the friendship objection

Prospect:	I have a couple of good friends in the business.
Salesperson:	If you were to find yourself short of income, would these friends of yours make up the shortage out of their own pockets? Of course not! Well, if I could give you some ideas that would guarantee security for your family and

yourself, is there any reason why *I* couldn't have your business?

Objection 20:
"We've been buying from Blank & Company for many years and are completely satisfied."

To build an answer to the "loyalty" objection, remind your prospect:

- The prospect's first duty is to himself or herself to make the best buy.

- It is important to diversify to assure a continuous supply at all times.

- The prospect's business is big enough to handle more than one line; sales figures will show how well your product stands up.

- No one can afford to stand still; progress requires change.

- Your product is newer and better suited to today's needs.

- Perhaps the prospect is complacent because, having stayed with one source of supply, he or she doesn't know how far ahead your company has moved as a producer in the field. A test order will prove that it pays to broaden the source.

- The prospect can gain a definite profit by buying your product.

- Your product has benefits that the other supplier may never have thought of emphasizing because they are so obvious.

- If your product is for resale, and it is widely known because of the firm's advertising policy, your prospect should be carrying it or customers will go elsewhere for it. Thus your prospect might lose not only the profits on your product but other business as well.

- You don't expect your prospect to drop his or her present source, but it is to his or her own advantage to spread the business around a little.

Real-life example: You have something attractive to show

Prospect:	We've been buying our equipment from the Smith Company for almost 20 years. We have confidence in them and their values, and we've learned how to use their product, so it's no use trying to talk us into changing.
Salesperson:	Mr. Prospect, you've put your finger on a major point! We know, of course, that you buy from Smith, and that they're a fine outfit, and that you're accustomed to their product. We know that we'd be wasting your time as well as our own if we didn't have a really outstanding product to show you. I'm sure you'll at least want to hear our story.

Real-life example: Edge in by showing extra profit

Prospect:	I don't care to make a change.
Salesperson:	And I don't expect you to discontinue your present connections, just because I happen to want your business. All I'm suggesting is that you might want to add $500 to your monthly profits with hardly any extra capital investment on your part. You'll find that my line supplements, rather than competes, with the line you're carrying now and brings you extra sales. Look at these reorders from a half dozen typical department stores—stores that routinely carry from three to five other lines.

Real-life example: When it pays to be blunt with the prospect who has a contract

If you're the kind of salesperson who can sense when to "break the rules," you'll want to save this one for the prospect who can't be budged because he or she already has a contract. Change the language to suit your style, but try this idea when you've exhausted your regular ammunition. Remember that few companies dare tie themselves up 100% with any supplier—that there's usually a door through which a small percentage of the goods of noncontracted suppliers can still gain admittance.

Salesperson: You're in an awkward position. Blank & Company's got you where they want you. They're shrewd, all right. I don't doubt they're giving you service, but how do you know that their service is top-notch? Have you got anything with which to compare it? No, you've shut the door to competition; you've turned them into the clover field. What's more, you've closed your eyes to competing products. You've served notice that you are not progressive enough to want to keep up on the latest improvements. If every company in America did just what you have done, there would never be any more improvements in the machines we make. Research departments would be thrown out the window. Twenty years from now, your company would be using the same machines it uses today.

All I ask is that you try letting my machines meet 10% of your requirements. That will cost you no more than you're currently paying Blank & Company, but you'll get more for your money—not only from me and my company, but also from Blank & Company. You will have two suppliers competing on service. You will have two kinds of products competing on the basis of quality and cost of operation. You will have the advantage of what I know to be my machine's superiority in certain types of work. You will have at your disposal everything my company's mechanical experts can show you about special applications of our product. Perhaps we will be able to help you solve some difficult problem.

One thing I can promise you: You will get service from us the likes of which you have never seen before, because we'll know that we have to prove ourselves.

Real-life example: We have standardized on another make

Prospect:	While I like your machine, we have standardized on another make for economy.
Salesperson:	Yes, standardizing is economical. But sometimes what was at one time genuine economy becomes false economy. Our machine is the best for the money that you can buy on the market today. It is designed for more efficiency and is easier for the operators to use than any other machine. So you really would be economizing if you standardized on our machine. We know that a complete turnover of your inventory of machines now would be impractical. But by purchasing a few of our machines and putting them side by side with your present equipment, you will be convinced that there is real economy in standardizing on our machine. You can make the change-over gradually.

Objection 21:
"We buy from a supplier who buys from us."

You run into this objection frequently with big-company prospects who favor their own customers. When you encounter this objection, use the following points in trying to overcome it:

- Find out whether the objection is real or just a stall. (See Rule 1 at the beginning of this chapter.)

- Sell the special benefits of your product. Your prospect may realize that he or she is losing a valuable benefit under the reciprocal arrangement.

- Show the prospect in dollars and cents how much he or she can save by buying your product. It gives your prospect a basis for determining how much it is costing him or her to carry through on the reciprocal arrangement.

- Use the reasons that help win orders from prospects who buy from friends or have other personal ties to a supplier (as described in Objection 19).

The purchasing agent might become your ally if he or she has found the reciprocal arrangement irksome. Suppose, for example, that he or she has had to put up with poor deliveries and poor quality that would not normally be tolerated. The purchasing agent might be glad to help you get to top management to present your case.

NOTE Some companies instruct their salespeople to report the facts and not try to cope with the reciprocity problem themselves. Management has its own ways of dealing with the problem. It is in a better position than salespeople are to weigh the seriousness of the situation and look into its legal aspects. Also, management might consider becoming a customer of the prospect. It can investigate whether it is using the prospect's products or service directly or indirectly. Top management might even know someone in the prospect organization who can help you make the sale.

Objection 22:
"I must take it up with my partner."

Here are some ideas to get the prospect to listen first by himself or herself:

- Point out to the prospect that the partner (or associate) will want his or her opinion. By learning about the merits of the product, he or she can form that opinion now.

- Arrange an appointment at which both parties will be present. One partner often has a stronger influence than the other one in some matters, either because of personality or background.

■ At the joint meeting, try to detect which of the partners will exert the most influence over the buying decision, and direct your strongest appeals to him or her.

Real-life example: You be the one to explain your product

Prospect:	I must take it up with my partner.
Salesperson:	Would you do me this favor—let *me* be the one to explain the machine to your partner? I probably know more about it than you do, and if I were there, I could answer questions on the spot and save time all around.

Real-life example: Why bother the board of directors?

The fear of assuming responsibility for a major decision often frightens a junior executive into passing the buck to the board of directors. With a bit of imagination, however, you can minimize the weight of this responsibility and make the junior feel that the purchase is a relatively routine matter. Here's how:

Prospect:	I'll take up your proposition with our board.
Salesperson:	You don't call your executive committee together when you need to hire a new security guard, do you?
Prospect:	No, I don't.
Salesperson:	And what do you pay a new guard?
Prospect:	$500 to $600 per week.
Salesperson:	Well, I'd like to act as a security guard over your company's bank account. I'll watch over every check you draw no matter where it goes or who may intercept it, and I'm going to charge you a lot less than $500 a week for my

services. Do you really need to get the board's approval to hire me?

When the prospect saw the matter in this light, he decided that he could safely make the decision on his own.

Objection 23:
"I'll have to talk it over
with my husband/wife."

Here's how to get immediate action when one spouse wants to talk over the proposal with the other:

- Point out to the husband or wife that he or she doesn't discuss every purchase with his or her spouse. There are expenditures for clothes and groceries that amount to much more a year than he or she will spend on your product.
- Arrange to meet husband and wife together at a convenient time.
- If you can't arrange to meet both people together, be sure that the one you are interviewing knows the important points that you want him or her to pass on to the other.

  WARNING If the sale involves a substantial sum, you may risk having the order canceled, or the product returned, if you induce one spouse to buy without consulting his or her partner. The best strategy in the face of this objection is to arrange for a call when both parties can be present.

Real-life example: Turn the purchase into a pleasant surprise

---

Prospect:	I'll have to talk it over with my wife.
Salesperson:	Mr. Jenkins, as a rule, I'd do the same thing myself. But when you buy a gift for your wife, you don't tell her about it beforehand. That's just what this oil burner is—a gift that will save her the hassle of always having to call a

repairperson, a gift that will keep her comfortable by assuring the right temperature throughout the house. Why not surprise your wife by letting us install the burner while she's at work?

Objection 24: "The machine we have is still good."

To overcome an objection against replacing equipment that is "still good," try these approaches:

- By keeping the old machine, the prospect is losing the advantages of all the improvements that have been made in such equipment—improvements that speed up production, reduce rework costs, increase safety, and so on.
- The prospect's competitors have already replaced their machinery with the newer types.
- The longer the prospect keeps the old equipment, the more costly it becomes. The cost of labor and replacement parts used for repairs and the time lost by factory employees when the machine is down eat up any potential profits.
- The older the present equipment becomes, the lower its trade-in value.
- It is wise for the prospect to maintain the value of his or her investment by trading it in for modern equipment before it becomes obsolete.

Real-life example: Economy as reason for replacement

A computer equipment salesperson uses the following reasons to convince a prospect that there is real economy in replacing an old machine with a new one.

- Increased production. New machines are faster and will increase production in many ways.
- Better-looking work. The new laser printers are quieter, take up less space, and turn out better-looking work.

- Less waste. New paper-feed mechanism means that paper doesn't get jammed or wrinkled as often. Mechanical defects or worn parts do not exist in new machines.

- More modern and businesslike appearance of office.

- The insignificant cost of supplying power to the new machine.

- Psychological effect upon operator. Most computer users are happier when they know they're working with state-of-the-art equipment.

Real-life example: New model is more efficient

Prospect:	We can get along all right with our present equipment.
Salesperson:	I'm sure you can, Mr. Blank, and I appreciate that you know more about office management than I ever will. But couldn't you say the same thing about an old car? It still runs, and it still gets you where you want to go. The reason for buying a new machine is not that the old one is bad, but that the new one is so much more efficient and productive.
	I've read that the English as a rule are very reluctant to scrap old machinery because it will still run, whereas Americans will scrap a relatively new machine if they find that an even newer model will save them time and money. The whole point is that we have a brand-new model computer that will do things your old one wouldn't.

Real-life example: "Sharp pencil selling" shows insignificant yearly cost of new computer

Facts and figures will appeal to the average businessperson to a far greater extent than will a long verbal presentation. It is a very potent means of turning the prospect's thoughts from the capital expenditure involved in buying a new computer to the much greater investment in the *expensive pair of hands* using the equipment. Turning the prospect's attention from the cost of the new equipment to the time and effort it will save can be a key factor in inducing him or her to replace old equipment with new.

The best way to bring this message home is to have all the appropriate facts and figures down on paper. You can work up these computations ahead of time, or if you're fully prepared to do so, you can jot them down as you talk to your prospect and leave them behind so that he or she can study them in more detail later.

Here are some of the figures you might want to compile:

- Trade-in information. How do trade-in values compare when machines are traded in after three, five, seven, or more years?

- Initial cost of the new machine, spread out over a three-, five-, or seven-year time period.

- Estimated service costs for each time period.

- Labor costs—how much the operator of this machine or equipment must be paid and how much he or she will have to increase production or efficiency to justify the cost of purchasing a new machine.

Let's suppose that a computer salesperson has just completed her demonstration. How might she use "sharp pencil selling" to close the sale?

Salesperson:	Now that you've seen this amazing new machine, Mr. Smith, is it a good time to discuss trading in the computer you bought five years ago?
Prospect:	Oh, I don't think so. My old computer probably has a few years left in it.
Salesperson:	I'm sure that's true, Mr. Smith—most good machines can be kept running, whether they're automobiles or computers. But do you realize that you're actually paying for a new computer right now, without getting the ben-

efit of it? Give me two minutes more, and I'll show you how.

First, I'm sure you'll agree the biggest cost is not the computer itself, but the *expensive pair of hands* that run it. [She starts figuring for him on a scratch pad.] Let's say you pay your secretary $25,000 a year. One-twelfth of that is $2,083 per month. This new model computer costs $3,600—a little less than you'd pay your secretary for two months.

As you know, computer equipment goes out of date quickly, but we'd be happy to offer you a trade-in allowance of $600 on your old machine. That brings the cost down to just $3,000. According to the surveys I've seen [here she pulls several sheets of information from her briefcase], the increased speed of our new processor has accounted for improvements in output and efficiency of anywhere from 15 to 25%.

Let's take 20% as an average figure. If your secretary were to improve his efficiency by this much, you'd be saving about $5,000 a year. That means that the new computer would pay for itself in about seven months.

So you see, each day you keep your old machine in operation, you're actually paying for a new one in the form of lowered efficiency and higher repair costs—without getting the new machine's value! And in another year or two, you won't get much of a trade-in on the computer your secretary is using now. In other words, Mr. Smith, if you think of a computer as a machine and figure what it costs to keep that machine running, you can make a very persuasive case for keeping that machine up to date. I'd certainly be glad to have you approve that reasoning.

Objection 25:
"I'll buy a cheap
secondhand machine."

To convince a prospect to buy a new machine instead of a secondhand one, use these approaches:

- Show by facts and figures that a secondhand machine will cost more in the long run.
- Minimize the savings. Compare initial cost of new equipment with salaries paid to operators.
- Emphasize quality performance from new equipment that will be lost.

Real-life example: Minimize the savings in purchasing used equipment

Salesperson:	I don't need to tell you that it will cost you more. When you buy a used machine, you buy something someone else has taken the good out of and then discarded. You'll have higher service costs and lower trade-in value—but most of all you won't get the quality of work you want. Did you ever stop to consider that a computer is just a tool and that its initial cost is less than you pay *in one or two months* for the hands that run it? It's actually cheaper to buy a new machine and get what you pay for!

CHAPTER EIGHT

SELLING AT CONCERT PITCH

*The "star" manages to tackle tough
territory, tough prospects, tough breaks,
and other obstacles.*

When an orchestra plays at "concert pitch," the hard preliminary work has already been done; the long rehearsals are over. Now, at the concert, the individual instruments fuse together into one harmonious flood of sound. Smoothly and powerfully, the orchestra carries the audience with it.

So it is with selling. When you are selling at concert pitch, you are carrying your prospect along with you from sales point to sales point. You are in charge of the interview—quietly and unobtrusively perhaps, but you're in the saddle all the way. The interview concludes with the prospect's decision to buy. And what's even more important, both you and the prospect have a sense of personal satisfaction: The prospect knows that he or she has made a good purchase, and you know that you've made the sale.

How you achieve this confident, concert pitch frame of mind, and maintain it as your day-to-day selling technique, depends in large part upon your own attitude. There is no question that you can do it. And it is certain that you must do it if you are to win your way into the big money in selling.

To be a really big earner you have to know how to manage not only the selling end of your business but how to manage *yourself*. This personal or subjective side of the sales equation is where many potentially outstanding salespeople fall down. This section shows you how learning to manage yourself can make a big difference in your annual income.

- It tells you how to keep yourself at concert pitch day after day, so that every day becomes one of your *good* days because you're enthusiastic, energetic, and clear-headed, and filled with the expectation of good things to come.

- It shows you how to handle the management of your personal time so you have more of it for the actual job of selling—the only time that really produces income.

- It shows you what you can do to make a better personal impression—how to put yourself across with your prospects and thus make sales more easily.

- It tells how to make the most of your personality.

HOW TO BUILD AND MAINTAIN ENTHUSIASM

The Power of Enthusiasm

Many top salespeople have testified to the power of enthusiasm in their sales careers. In fact, so much has been said in recent years about enthusiasm that perhaps now we tend to disparage the salesperson or sales manager who preaches "be enthusiastic." But to disparage enthusiasm is one of the costliest mistakes we can make. It plays a special role in selling. It is the key to success in this field.

There is a sound psychological basis for the power of enthusiasm in selling. Every salesperson is subject to forebodings and fears. He or she may fear the first call of the day or be afraid of the greeting he or she will receive from a tough prospect. Sometimes the salesperson is afraid to ask for the order, or for a big order.

One of the chief values of enthusiasm is that it replaces fear. Fear is negative and crippling, but when the emotional force of fear is used to generate enthusiasm, our fears disappear. We become filled with positive power.

Enthusiasm Stems from Genuine Selling Strength

Enthusiasm based on awareness of *selling strength* is genuine; enthusiasm based merely on the *hope* or *desire* to make the sale is synthetic. No intelligent salesperson will have difficulty in understanding this vital difference or in deciding which approach is more potent in making sales.

▪ IDEA IN ACTION

Herb Crowley is the top salesperson in his company. He is also known as the most enthusiastic one in the group. This quality enables him to sell many a prospect whom the other salespeople would dismiss, telling themselves that "He doesn't need our product!" or "She's sold on one of our competitors, and there's nothing we have to offer that will change her mind."

To the casual observer it seems that Herb converts these prospects into buyers by the sheer force of his enthusiastic presentation. But a little analysis shows that his enthusiasm rests on a very solid and real foundation: *knowledge of his product.*

For instance, Herb has thought out, more fully than anyone else in his group, the *application* of his product. Hence when a prospect says, "No, I don't need it," Herb has at the tip of his tongue just the right facts and just the right story to show that particular prospect exactly why he or she *does* need the product.

Similarly, when Herb runs into a prospect who is "all tied up" with a competing supplier, he is usually able to overcome this obstacle simply because he has "dug out" so many points of superiority offered by his *own* product.

Because of this extra knowledge, Herb feels that he can sell almost any prospect he calls on. It is this awareness of his own strength that causes him to proceed enthusiastically. He *expects* to get the order.

Knowledge Stimulates Enthusiasm

Learn more about yourself, your product, and your customers. The extra knowledge will give you greater confidence and security. Your enthusiasm will increase in direct proportion to your knowledge of your job.

WHAT TO DO

1. Schedule periodic classroom sessions with yourself. Do this in your non-selling time.

2. Test yourself with questions about your product, your customers, and yourself.

3. If you don't have the answers to the questions you raise, find them out as quickly as possible.

4. Use the personal assessment questionaires in Chapter Ten.

Think Enthusiastically

If you want to emanate enthusiasm, you must *think* enthusiastically as well as act enthusiastically. It means banishing the nagging worries and trivial concerns that drain your energies. True, you may at times have real worries and concerns, but even those, if handled intelligently, can be controlled.

Find Something to Admire in Everyone

Deliberately looking for and finding something to admire in everyone you approach makes it easier to meet that person enthusiastically. Liking the person makes you impress him or her, and your best efforts will carry their own enthusiasm. It is just as important for you to like the individual you are going to sell to as it is for him or her to like doing business with you.

Pleasing Your Customers Raises Your Own Enthusiasm

You will feel enthusiasm and achieve success only to the extent that you make a point of pleasing your customers.

WHAT TO DO

1. Make a written note of your customer's likes and dislikes, interests, and hobbies.

2. When you are with your customer, say something you know he or she will like to hear.

3. Send your customer cards for appropriate occasions.

4. Between calls, phone or write your customer.

5. Please your customer and raise your own enthusiasm by being

    - Prompt—no one likes to be kept waiting

    - Courteous—everyone wants respect

    - Honest —you will attract more customers

    - Dependable—build a reputation for reliability and your customers will respond with a high regard for you

Make a Habit of Associating with Successful People

You can increase your enthusiasm and in some measure increase your success if you make a habit of associating with people who have become successful.

When you seek out the successful person, listen to what he or she has to say. Ask for his or her opinions and advice. You will find that almost invariably successful people are positive thinkers who are more than willing to help you. It's important to keep your association with successful people a two-way street. Be willing to share your ideas with them; make others aware of your enthusiasm.

Keep Physically Fit

The mental benefits of regular physical exercise have been well documented. You won't emanate enthusiasm if you don't feel well physically. Give yourself plenty of rest, eat the right foods, and exercise on a regular basis. Your body will then perform willingly and with energy.

Keeping physically fit is one of the requisites for building and maintaining enthusiasm. If you stay in shape physically, you will find yourself able to make more calls, speak with a stronger, more convincing voice, and give more forceful presentations. You will also have enough "drive" at the end of each day to plan your next day's sales.

An Increased Income Goal
Will Increase Your Enthusiasm, Too

Free yourself from the limitation that an unchanged earnings outlook places on your enthusiasm. If you think of "balancing your budget" solely in terms of your present income and do not raise your goals from time to time, the self-imposed limitation will hinder your professional growth.

> **REMEMBER** Because of inflation, the earning power of a stationary income will become less and less as the years go by.

> **WHAT TO DO** Plan an income that has definite, periodic increases. Give yourself "raises" by setting yourself higher monthly or annual income goals. Having chosen a definite goal, focus all your energy and thought on its accomplishment.

It is necessary to keep increasing your goals if you are to reach the top of your field—and stay there. As soon as you set a higher earnings goal, you begin thinking of yourself as a bigger earner. And thinking of yourself as a big earner makes you act like one when you're with a prospect. You become strong, confident, and able. These are qualities that influence prospects to buy from you.

Believe in Your Ability to Reach Goals

Just as positive thinking will strengthen your enthusiasm, so will a belief in your own power to reach the earnings goal you have set. Belief helps to generate enthusiasm.

Have you ever looked objectively at salespeople who are known to be high producers? Nothing about these individuals even hints at defeat. They expect to win, and believing that they will win changes their whole attitude. A very successful salesperson describes his approach:

"Before entering a prospect's office, I would pause for an instant and think of the many things I had to be thankful for, work up a great big, honest-to-goodness smile, and then enter the room with the smile just vanishing from my face. It was easy then to turn on a big, happy smile. Seldom did it fail to get the same kind of smile in return from the person I met on the inside."

Planning Builds Enthusiasm

The salesperson who hasn't the least notion of what tomorrow holds has literally nothing to be excited about. Planning each day's work is therefore essential to building enthusiasm.

> **WHAT TO DO** Get a head start on the day's work by preparing for it the night before. You will rest easier and you'll eliminate the confusion and upset caused by last-minute preparation. (See the planning forms in Chapter Ten.)

A Job Behind You Gives Momentum

Momentum accelerates enthusiasm. You can get some momentum before your first call of the day by getting one of the necessary, but not-so-profitable jobs behind you before you tackle your main task of selling. Filling out a report completely and carefully gets some momentum going. Finding the information you promised to give a customer is another accomplishment that will give you the feeling of moving forward. Try to select a job that you can complete in the time available, or at least one on which you can make substantial progress.

Be Creative and You'll Be Enthusiastic

Nothing will create enthusiasm as quickly and as powerfully as creativity itself. The moment you are on the track of a new idea for getting your prospect to want your product, you feel a surge of enthusiasm. It grows as you perfect the language with which you will offer your new idea, and it reaches its climax when you present the idea.

So vital is this method of building enthusiasm, and so capable is every eager salesperson of finding new ideas, that an entire section of this *Guide* is devoted to creative selling (see Chapter Three).

Wholeheartedness Is a By-product of Enthusiasm

One test of your enthusiasm level is whether you are doing all parts of your job, even the routine ones, wholeheartedly. Take the nonselling duties of keeping records, making reports, planning work, and studying new products. If you are doing these tasks well, promptly, and willingly, you know that your enthusiasm has developed into a habit.

Expand Your Morale Through Company Training Programs

You can build your morale through constant participation in your company's training programs. If you don't believe in these programs or if you don't participate in them willingly and wholeheartedly, you are out of step with your organization and may be courting serious morale problems.

WHAT TO DO Make a habit of reading company manuals and bulletins. Attend sales meetings. Check the bulletin board when you are in the home office. Request personal supervision of your field work.

Strengthen Your Morale Through Good Company Relations

If you feel that your home office doesn't know what it's doing half the time, you have created a morale-destroying conflict between yourself and your employer. Your dissatisfaction will make it impossible to maintain enthusiasm and to perform to the best of your abilities. Others will pick up on your critical attitude, and as your fellow employees in the home office learn that it is hard to please you, they will stop cooperating with you.

■ IDEA IN ACTION

Leslie Smallwood has been a salesperson for 17 years. Out of habit more than anything else, she has become more and more critical of the home office. One day this conversation takes place between two clerks:

"Here's a wire from Sam Toomey asking us to rush out an order," says Fran, the shipping clerk.

"Well, I was just getting ready to fill this rush order Leslie Smallwood sent in," answers Tom, her helper. "We can't get them *both* out today. Which one shall we ship?"

"Well," answers Fran, "better ship Sam's. Sam doesn't mark *every* order 'rush,' but Leslie is so sure we don't know what we're doing that she'll squawk whether we fill her order today or tomorrow."

WHAT TO DO If you find yourself continually "griping," ask yourself, "Would I really be any happier with another company or have I for some reason allowed my own morale to slip to the point where I can no longer see straight on the issues that affect me and my job?"

Look for the things that are right about your company and your working conditions. This will help you change your attitude and restore your enthusiasm.

When you have a justified criticism, offer a constructive suggestion at the same time, but watch the tone of your communication to be sure it will not be interpreted as carping.

Use a No-Sale as the Basis for Renewed Enthusiasm

Pave the way for an enthusiastic return interview with your unsold customer by making him or her your friend.

WHAT TO DO

1. When you fail to close a sale, act as pleased as if you had made it.

2. Ask the buyer why he or she failed to buy from you. You will often get a surprisingly honest and helpful answer.

3. Let your customer know you appreciate his or her willingness to listen even though you don't always make a sale.

Create Enthusiasm by Changing Your Customer's "No" to "Yes"

You can create enthusiasm and increase your income at the same time if you make a habit of simply ignoring your customer's first "No." Remember that this first "No" is seldom a final decision and that if you stop at this point, you will frequently lose your customer's confidence and business.

> **WHAT TO DO** If you learn how to make objections work for you (as shown in Chapter Seven) and the technique of multiple closing (described in Chapter Six), you will learn how to turn your customer's "No" into an enthusiastic "Yes!"

Change Your Attitude If It's Glum

If you feel fear, apprehension, or anxiety about a particular selling job, remember that you can transform fear and anxiety into cheerfulness and confidence through proper direction of your thinking. It will take a conscious effort to substitute healthy emotions like courage and determination for the stress emotions you're feeling, but it can be done! Begin by repeating over and over to yourself: "I am going to keep my thinking and my attitude calm, I am going to do this job successfully."

Then make your actions conform to this advice. Don't fritter away your energy and time on trivial tasks that suddenly seem important. Direct your activities toward the fulfillment of your goals. Prepare your approach to the customer; review your presentation; decide to try multiple closings. You will find that your thinking and feelings have changed from fear to eagerness.

Overcome the Negative Influence of the Past

It is good to learn from past failures, mistakes, or disappointments, but it is disastrous to dwell upon them. Once you have discovered how to profit by the error, dismiss it from your mind. Mulling it over will simply cripple your energies, willpower, and chance for success.

If you find it hard to throw off the dejection, try these spirit-builders:

- Visit a friend or acquaintance who emanates enthusiasm and always makes you feel good. Stay away from people who are habitual failures, who talk negatively about their past, present, and future.

- Find a hobby that will absorb your interest. The new skills and information that you acquire through such hobbies as painting, photography, collections of various kinds, gardening, do-it-yourself repairs, and the like will make you feel more alive. There's nothing like the new experience of a hobby to keep you from obsessing about your troubles. Try it!

- Go where you're part of an audience. Seeing others in action will make you less aware of yourself and your worries. At competitive games you will observe the skill, determination, and enthusiasm of the players—all pointed reminders that selling requires the exercise of these same qualities.

How to Overcome the "Blues"

The "blues" deprive you of the energy and willpower you need for consistently successful selling. You will be better prepared to overcome them if you follow these guidelines:

- The expressions "Blue Monday" and "I get the blues when . . ." indicate that emotional "lows" occur at specific times. One remedy is to prepare in advance for the attack by getting absorbed in a demanding task. It will counter the effects of these periods and carry you back into the stream of enthusiastic selling.

- Your state of mind is influenced by your physical condition. Everyone has experienced the low feelings that often follow a loss of sleep, overwork, or dissipation. Extra sleep and proper care of your body help to drive the blues away.

- Dismiss negative thoughts and get into positive thinking.

- Realize that the blues are temporary. Reminding yourself that brighter days are sure to follow will keep you from dwelling on feelings of depression.

- Turn the causes of your depression into springboards to enthusiasm. If you get the blues over your low closing average, for example, you might try working on your closing techniques. Your improvement will make you more enthusiastic.

What to Do About the Negative Emotions that Drain Your Power

Anger, fear, and worry undermine enthusiasm. Even though you do everything you can think of to avoid these emotions and the situations that provoke them, they are bound to occur. How you react to them is very important.

Psychologists tell us that you intensify your emotions with certain bodily expressions. For example, if you are angry and clench your fists or grit your teeth, you become more disturbed. If you are frightened on a dark street and walk faster, you intensify the fear. But if you consciously react in the opposite way, you minimize the emotion. Therefore, you should try to relax when you experience a strong negative emotion.

Psychologists also tell us that anger often arises when you meet a situation for which you have no ready response. When you are thwarted and anger is imminent, restraint is the first imperative; the next step is to seek the proper way to deal with the situation.

Here is another recommended plan of action for achieving the proper perspective on a troublesome situation before it undermines your enthusiasm: Discuss what is disturbing you with someone in whom you have confidence. Simply talking about it to a good listener will often make you realize that it's not as important as you thought it was. If there's no one in whom you want to confide, write out the facts and the ways in which you might meet the problem. Putting the problem in writing will help you find the solution and restore some of the equanimity necessary to bring the emotion under control.

Talk Yourself into Being More Confident

This is a technique that is especially helpful when your business or outside concerns are sapping your energy, enthusiasm, and spirit. What you need at such moments is to change your outlook.

WHAT TO DO

1. Pick a meaningful self-command to raise your spirits—for example, "I can, I will, I must have confidence in myself."

2. Repeat the words to yourself every now and then, or say them out loud, until they become part of your attitude.

The locker room "pep talk" is built upon this idea. The principal difference, however, is that the ball team depends on the coach to raise their enthusiasm and the players depend on each other to "talk up" their strength. Most of the time you have no one to depend on but yourself. Fortunately, any salesperson who puts his or her mind to it has the capacity to be a self-motivator when a change of outlook is needed.

How to Overcome Fear
of the "Tough" Customer

If you decide in advance that a customer is "too tough to be sold," you are depriving yourself of a selling opportunity. But if you believe that even the "tough" customer can be won over with good selling techniques, you will overcome defeatism and pave the way for more sales. You'll be able to take on all the "hard-to-sell" people with confidence.

You will increase your chances to sell such a customer by following these simple steps:

1. **Win his or her attention.** The customer who has a reputation for being "tough" is most likely a demanding buyer. He or she will not be satisfied with a run-of-the-mill approach. This type of buyer demands your best. However, once you've sold this person, he or she will probably be sold "hard."

2. **Try to meet his or her standards.** The hard-to-sell customer probably got his or her reputation by setting high standards. Remember, this customer is in a better position to know what he or she wants than you are. If you can meet his or her demands, you have a good chance of making the sale.

3. **Establish confidence.** The tough buyer may be a cautious buyer. It's up to you to establish confidence by showing that you're willing to serve him or her.

4. **Remember to close.** Some salespeople are frightened off by a "hard" buyer and never get as far as the close. If you remember to try to close—not once but many times—you'll increase your chances of success.

A Good Laugh Will Banish Tension

Laughter can often relieve tension between you and your customer. If a sense of humor isn't your strong point, you can at least think about the situations that try your patience and be prepared with an appropriate remark or story that you know will provoke a laugh. A little practice in the telling will give you assurance.

Although a "good story" will never take the place of a good presentation, knowing when to make a humorous remark will often carry you over the rough spots that may arise in your interview.

☐ EXAMPLE

The salesperson was about to demonstrate the model he had just gone over point by point when his prospect suddenly said, "No." Anxious to avoid antagonizing his prospect but unwilling to stop his presentation, he overcame the situation by saying, "Do you mind if I plug it in anyway? *I* haven't seen the darn thing work for over two weeks." The customer laughed and the relaxed salesperson went on to make the sale.

Review, Analysis, and Planning Restore Enthusiasm

At the end of a day well spent in selling, your enthusiasm will decline to a relaxed level—like that of the artists who perform at concert pitch. But there are two wind-up activities that will restore it to a good tapping level for the next day: evaluating your own performance and planning for the next day. How to evaluate a day's work and how to plan for increased production are explained in Chapter One.

Evaluating your performance and planning the next day's activities achieves two basic aims:

1. It shows you how to make the most of your personality—how to capitalize on your unique strengths and how to correct the shortcomings that may be undermining your success.

2. It shows you how to prepare yourself for greater selling effectiveness—how to use your "personal" time for increasing knowledge and skills.

The next section provides some techniques that will help you to develop the frequently neglected "personal" side of selling—techniques that will go a long way toward moving you up into the higher-income brackets.

SELF-MANAGEMENT TECHNIQUES TO GAIN SELLING TIME

Figure Your Gain from Added Selling Time

Every hour added to your selling time increases your income. Selling time is the time you spend face-to-face with a customer. Take the value of each selling hour and see how much more you can earn by adding one, two, three, or more selling hours to your day.

> **WHAT TO DO** Divide the number of hours you spend in interviews each week into your weekly income. The answer is the value of your selling hour.

> ☐ EXAMPLE
>
> A salesperson spends an average of 20 hours in interviews and earns approximately $1,000 a week. Her selling time is worth $50 an hour. For each selling hour that she adds to her average of 20, she can earn $50 more a week.

> **REMEMBER** Almost every salesperson can increase his or her selling time if he or she makes the effort. The following paragraphs tell how.

Determine How Much Time You Spend in Each Selling Activity

A record of the time you spend on each of your selling activities will enable you to manage your time for best results and to attain your higher income goal quickly. It will show you which activities are cutting unnecessarily into your potential earnings and which activities deserve more of your time.

> **WHAT TO DO** Use a small note pad to record the exact number of minutes you spend performing each activity. Travel time, time spent waiting for customers, interview time, "break" time, and time spent in desk work are some of the activities you might list. You will have to refer to a watch to be accurate.

■ IDEA IN ACTION

Glenn Robinson kept a record of his time. Exhibit 8.1 shows the results after one week.

Glenn saw that he spent too much time traveling. He cut down on this activity by routing his calls more economically. He also cut down on time spent waiting for customers by using the preapproach methods that assure prompt reception (described in Chapter Four). Glenn noticed that he never spent less than 1 1/2 hours on "break" time. He decided to limit himself to 1 hour a day. Desk work was done at home in the evening, giving him approximately 4 1/2 additional hours each week to devote to calls.

As a result of this time management record, Glenn became aware of the extent to which he wasted potentially profitable hours. He increased his interview time by cutting down on the amount of time he was spending on unprofitable activities.

SUGGESTION You have to work harder when economic conditions are unfavorable. You'll want to devote more time each day to actual selling during these periods to make up for the extra calls it takes to get the order.

Increase Your Selling Hours by Scheduling Desk Work Last

If you have "things to take care of at the office," consider the advantages of setting aside the last hour of the day rather than the first hour for this purpose.

■ IDEA IN ACTION

Greta Wilkins represents a manufacturer of portable power tools. She never schedules appointments for 9 o'clock in the morning, but instead devotes an hour or so to take care of the morning mail and to clear away paperwork. Since her customers know that Greta is at her office during this time, however, they often call her for information, quotations, special services, and so on. She is conscientious and takes the time to fulfill these requests immediately.

EXHIBIT 8.1

Sample Time Report

Activity	Monday	Tuesday	Wednesday	Thursday	Friday	Total
Travel	1 1/2 hr	1 3/4 hr	2 hr	1 3/4 hr	1 1/4 hr	8 1/4 hr
Waiting for Customers	1 1/4 hr	30 min	1 1/4 hr	45 min	1 hr	4 3/4 hr
Interviews	2 hr	3 1/4 hr	2 3/4 hr	3 hr	2 1/2 hr	13 1/2 hr
"Breaks" (including lunch)	1 1/2 hr	2 hr	1 3/4 hr	1 1/2 hr	1 1/2 hr	8 1/4 hr
Desk Work	45 min	1 hr	50 min	1 1/4 hr	40 min	4 1/2 hr

Greta finds that she is not ready to begin selling until almost lunchtime and that her first appointment is often not until 1:30. When her sales begin to dip dangerously, she decides to make her first call at 9 in the morning and to stay out in the field until 4:30. Greta then finds that during this later hour she can take care of things at the office more efficiently and with fewer interruptions. Her sales increase because she has more than doubled her selling time by making this one simple change.

Do your nonselling jobs after normal selling hours. There are very few situations in which it makes sense to take time for desk work at the start of the day.

Where to Cut Time Wasters

You can increase your time spent in actual selling by plugging the leaks where waste occurs. Examine the following list of time wasters; then manage every minute of your time to pay off in dollars earned.

- **Waiting for customers.** You can cut down on time spent waiting for customers by setting up definite appointments.
- **Talking to customers who can't buy.** You may be wasting your time if you "take a chance" by calling on a customer about whom you know little or nothing. Even cold-calling requires some qualifying of customers. (See Chapter Two).
- **Talking to the wrong person.** Be sure that your customer is the person who is authorized to buy (also covered in Chapter Two).
- **Talking about the wrong product.** Be sure that you know which of your products will best fill your customer's needs before you give him or her an unnecessary rundown of your line.
- **Unnecessary travel time.** Schedule your calls to reduce travel time.
- **Miscalculating customers' potential.** Always keep in mind the dollar value of your time, and you won't be spending more time on customers than they're worth to you.

- **Talking too long.** Once you have finished the business of your interview, you should leave.

- **Too many "breaks."** Limit yourself to one or two breaks a day and be willing to sacrifice them if they interfere with your job of selling.

- **Too many calls on friends or others who are not prospects.**

    WARNING Let's assume that each of your selling hours is worth $40.00. Each 15 minutes wasted costs you $10.00. An 85 cent cup of coffee that causes you to waste 15 minutes costs you at least $10.85. The greater your earnings objective, the costlier that cup of coffee will be. Each time you are tempted to waste selling hours, ask yourself this question: Is the cause worth the cost?

(For more ideas on how to plan your time for bigger selling, see Chapter One.)

What to Do When Your Customer Keeps You Waiting

If you have to wait for a customer, mentally weigh the value of the sale you might make against the value of your time. Your selling time is too precious to spend waiting for business that is too small to be profitable.

If you decide that it is worth your while to wait, don't let yourself become irritated. Irritation destroys enthusiasm. Spend the time profitably: Review your presentation, think creatively about your job, or read something that has a bearing on your work.

Once you have decided not to wait, give a good reason for leaving and make an appointment for your return call.

How to Save Time in Handling Collections, Adjustments, and Complaints

Adjustments, complaints, and collections should be handled efficiently but with minimum disruption of your normal selling schedule and with the least possible waste of your selling time.

Make it a rule to get all the facts before you attempt to settle the matter in question. You should temper the time-honored maxim, "The customer is always right" with another sales rule: "Get the facts—all the facts—and then let your own good judgment, as well as your customer's, indicate the proper settlement."

You will lose valuable selling time if you start discussing the problem upon hearing the customer's side of the story. Furthermore, you are actually in danger of losing, rather than encouraging, customer respect and goodwill if you immediately accept the blame when a customer states that something has gone wrong.

You will save your time as well as that of your customer if you tactfully but firmly insist upon delaying the discussion until you possess all the pertinent facts.

How to Save Time Installing or Servicing a Product

Some engineered products must be installed either by the seller or under his or her supervision. Sometimes the salesperson is charged with such duties, while in other cases the company maintains a separate technical staff for this purpose.

The salesperson should always ask himself or herself, "Is it necessary for me to be there personally? If so, can the installation be scheduled so as to minimize the interruption in my selling activities?"

The buyer's interests and convenience are important considerations. But frequently a time can be arranged that is favorable to both customer and salesperson. It is up to the salesperson to suggest such a time wherever possible.

These guidelines apply to servicing a product as well. If your product requires periodic servicing, always arrange to perform this duty at a minimum cost to selling time.

Prepare a Work Schedule to Help You Use Your Time More Profitably

Every salesperson must prepare a work schedule that fits the product and the territory. This is generally referred to as "planning your work and working your plan."

Unless you schedule intelligently, you might find yourself working a full week but failing to reach your earnings goal; you will be spinning your wheels instead of making progress. Keep in mind that your selling hours are your most valuable asset.

■ IDEA IN ACTION

Frank Elbert, who sells business systems and forms, has planned his work schedule. He has full knowledge of his product and has analyzed the buying potential of each of the groups in his market. He has also made a decision to concentrate on prospects and customers who buy big.

Frank breaks his work schedule into two daily segments: The first section covers 8:30 A.M. to 12:00 P.M., the second 1:00 P.M. to 5:00 P.M. He keeps a four-week schedule in the planning stage at all times; the current week is fully scheduled with allowances for unexpected emergencies.

Frank knows that the morning hours are the best for creative selling. Both he and his prospects are more alert then. So he devotes his morning hours to the challenge of canvassing new businesses and selling new accounts. He works either from a list of firms with good potential or by preselecting a section of the city. In either case, he plans his calls in a relatively small geographical area to cut travel time. A good schedule for Frank is a morning spent in one building or a shopping center.

Frank devotes the afternoon section of his daily schedule to calls on customers for reorders or development work for new systems. He also handles details—such as proofs, subsequent credit handling, complaints, and the like—in the afternoon. As in the morning, all calls are scheduled ahead of time and in the smallest possible geographical area. Reorder calls are scheduled four weeks in advance. Frank plans his afternoon work around the necessary reorder calls.

In drawing up his work plan, Frank avoids activities that might result in a waste of time during selling hours. He tries to establish the availability of the person he wants to see prior to the call so that he doesn't waste time when he gets there.

Frank can't afford to spend selling time waiting in reception rooms. If he finds that it will be necessary to wait more than

10 minutes to see a customer, he arranges to call back at a set time. Waiting for longer than 10 minutes not only wastes valuable selling time but reduces the importance of the call in the mind of the person he is waiting to see.

Frank avoids parking in an area where he'll have to put money in a meter or move the car. He leaves his car where it can remain for several hours. Quite often he saves time by riding public transportation to the area to be worked and then spends the day in one area or building.

Make the Most of Rainy Days

A rainy day is a slow day for most businesses, but it has the opposite effect on a salesperson who is serious about becoming a top producer. Those are the days when competition for a prospect's time is lightest and when the hard-to-see customers are freer to listen.

Consider Your Prospects' Work Habits in Determining the Best Time to Call

Good timing is a primary factor in the success of a call. If you call at a time when the prospect is not in a mood to be interrupted, he or she will refuse to see you or will give you only cursory attention and limited time.

> **CAUTION** Don't try to solve the timing problem by making *general* rules, for example, that you won't make any calls before 9:30 to give the prospect time to read his or her mail, or after 11:30 because the prospect might have a luncheon appointment, or after 4 P.M. because the prospect may be preoccupied with end-of-the-day paperwork. Such rules cut drastically into your valuable selling time. Also, they ignore the fact that work habits vary with the individual.

WHAT TO DO

1. Make discreet inquiries to determine the best time to call on particular customers. Ask the telephone operator, the prospect's secretary, or, if evening selling is contemplated, a

member of his or her family when you will most likely find the prospect in.

2. Study your customers' and prospects work habits. Base the timing of your calls on what you discover by observing your customers over a period of time.

MAKING A POSITIVE IMPRESSION

How the Buyer Sizes You Up

Put yourself in the buyer's shoes and examine yourself for the impression you make. If you find yourself falling into one of the unfavorable categories outlined here, it's time to correct the impression you make through proper self-management.

- **The superior salesperson.** If you approach a buyer with a big-shot attitude, you will not be welcomed back. Use your knowledge to inform your customer, not to patronize him or her or to prove your superiority. Making your customer feel that you're looking down on him or her will only make it more tempting to buy from another salesperson.

- **The know-it-all.** If you claim to know everything, you will only irritate customers. Keep in mind that your prospect or customer often knows as much as you do about your product.

- **The know-nothing.** If you fail to inform yourself about your product and your customer's needs, you will remain an order-taker.

- **The talkative salesperson.** Monopolize the interview and you will often talk yourself right out of a sale.

- **The high-pressure salesperson.** If you try to pressure a customer into buying your product, you will only antagonize him or her.

- **The salesperson who misrepresents.** If you oversell or make false statements about your product, you are inviting complaints and destroying your chances for a repeat sale. In addition, you may open the door for a breach-of-contract suit against you and your company.

- **The salesperson who bribes.** Try to induce a buyer to purchase from you by promising a reward and you will soon find yourself on his or her "unwanted" list.

- **The "chummy" salesperson.** One way to damage customer relations is to abandon your professional status in favor of a personal friendship.

- **The poorly groomed salesperson.** Buyers appreciate the respect you show them by appearing suitably dressed.

What Is a Good Selling Appearance?

There's only one rule to follow here: "Nothing about your appearance should distract attention from the sale."

Once you understand this simple precept, you'll never be in doubt about whether your appearance is suitable or not. It acts as a sure guide to an issue that has sometimes been needlessly complicated. The point is illustrated now.

■ IDEA IN ACTION

Stanley McRickard has read in a number of books that a clean white shirt, a neatly patterned tie, and a suit of conservative cut and color are "musts" for the well-groomed salesperson. His entire wardrobe has been built along these lines.

After eight years of successful selling in New York and Pennsylvania, Stanley is offered a promotion. He accepts the offer to become manager at one of his company's branch offices in Miami, Florida.

Shortly after his arrival in Miami, Stanley sets out to introduce himself to some of the company's more important customers in Florida.

His first day's calls leave him feeling disappointed. His interviews have lacked the warmth and cordiality that he had expected from people to whom his company is well and favorably known.

The real reason for this dawns upon Stanley as he is eating dinner in a downtown restaurant that evening. He notices that although most of the patrons are successful-looking business and professional people, he is the only one present who has adhered to the "white shirt, dark tie, inconspicuous business suit" formula. The others are wearing sport shirts with colorful neckties and, in many cases, sports jackets that are not of the same color or pattern as their trousers.

The next morning, Stanley buys a new outfit that is more in keeping with local customs. Almost immediately he notices the difference in the way his customers receive him.

WHAT TO DO This incident underscores three significant points about attire:

1. Personal appearance is important.

2. Time, place, and custom are dominant in answering the question, "What shall I wear?"

3. Clothes that are conspicuous for any reason tend to distract attention from the salesperson and his or her presentation. They mark him or her as an outsider who accordingly is not granted the same acceptance and cordiality as others whose appearance is not a detriment to the sale.

Don't Offend Your Customer by Smoking

"No smoking" is the rule these days, and many companies restrict smoking to specific areas or outside the building. While some of the people you call on may smoke themselves or at least be tolerant of others who do, the vast majority will resent it if a salesperson walks into the office with a cigarette.

It is never a good idea to "light up" once you're in the buyer's office, except under the following conditions: (1) when the buyer suggests it, (2) when the buyer is smoking, or (3) when you're on such a friendly basis with the buyer that you're *absolutely certain* your smoking will not be construed as ill-mannered.

Shake Hands Meaningfully

A firm handshake is important in making a positive impression. Follow these directions to develop your technique:

- Offer your full hand, not just the tips of your fingers.
- When your hand contacts your customer's, apply pressure. This will vary with the size and estimated strength of your customer.
- Make a clean break after you have shaken your customer's hand.
- Avoid "pumping" your customer's hand.

Walk with Assurance

The salesperson who walks as if he or she had just closed a million-dollar sale will impress others favorably; the one who saunters along in a half-spirited manner will make an unfavorable impression. If you walk with assurance, you convey the message that you know what you're doing and are in control of any situation you encounter.

Practice Poise

There are times in the life of every salesperson when pressures increase to the boiling point. How do you respond to the situation? If you allow yourself to get "steamed up" about each of the irritants, your enthusiasm evaporates as the pressure rises. But if you manage to bear them with poise and assurance, you can still harness your enthusiasm and use it to help you over the rough periods.

The secret of maintaining poise in the face of mounting pressure—a run of bad breaks, a disappointing call, a new competitor who seems to be crowding you out—is to learn to control the minor irritations.

Undue Familiarity Might Damage Customer Relations

Always let the customer lead the way when it comes to dispensing with formalities.

If the customer begins to call you by your first name, it is usually perfectly acceptable to do the same with him or her. The only exceptions are when the customer is much older than you are or when his or her voice, manner, or some other circumstance indicates that he or she doesn't *intend* the relationship to be one of full equality.

Enthusiasm Doesn't Condone Brashness

Once you feel that you have "sold" your customer, don't run the risk of losing the sale by breaking the bounds of propriety. A customer who chooses to buy from you feels that your product will benefit him or her the most and that you will provide the best service. But even these reasons won't make a customer tolerate brashness.

■ IDEA IN ACTION

Brenda Johnson felt exuberant when she was asked back for a second interview at which she was sure she would close the sale. She was feeling so self-confident that she breezed past the receptionist and walked right into the conference room, where the company representatives were sitting around discussing the sale. They were put off by Brenda's breach of courtesy and began to have doubts about buying from her. The interview which had promised much was cut short, and Brenda found herself losing the sale to a more discreet competitor.

Keep Your Troubles to Yourself

Always keep your troubles to yourself. Customers may sympathize with you if you share your problems and complaints, but they rarely, if ever, react by buying from you as readily as they might have otherwise.

Misery may love company, but if you're a professional, you know that "The show must go on." Burdening your customers with your troubles could have a negative bearing on your sales results.

Why Good Speech Is Essential

How you speak immediately identifies you as someone worth listening to. It tells your prospect how well educated you are and how seriously you take your job. Faulty speech can be eliminated and good speech habits substituted if you develop your skills in the following areas:

Awareness

You're not usually aware of the quality of your speech until you find yourself in an environment where speech characteristics different from yours are dominant, or until someone points out your speech differences to you, or until you learn to look for them yourself. You must know what the differences are before you decide to do anything about them.

Listening

Hearing alone will not enable you to correct your speech patterns. You must compare your speech characteristics with those of others who speak well before you can make improvements. Learn to listen intently to yourself and to others, and the process of comparing and altering will become a habit.

Motivation

If you are properly motivated to change your speech, you will have won half the battle. Knowing that your speech habits are not what you'd like them to be is perhaps the strongest motivation for improving them.

Effective speech is the result of proper coordination of pronunciation, breathing, intonation, pitch, and rhythm. Fortunately, it isn't necessary to undertake a formal speech course to correct the majority of poor voice habits that affect sales. What is required above all else is that you become *voice conscious*. Most speech mannerisms are caused by carelessness. Record yourself conducting practice presentations, speeches, and other situations. When you make yourself more aware of your voice, proper tone, speed, diction, and inflection usually come without effort.

How to Use your Voice Effectively

The following guidelines will help you use your voice more effectively in your contacts with prospects and customers:

- **Don't rush.** Your customer should be able to hear every word that you have to say about your product.

- **Speak clearly.** You will inspire confidence when you give strength and importance to every word you say.

- **Speak economically.** Choose only those words that state simply and effectively what you have to say.

- **Speak with dignity.** Give your product the importance it deserves by speaking of it with the proper respect.

- **Use a conversational tone.** When you speak conversationally, you reduce the possibility of tension developing between you and your customer. A relaxed, conversational tone is also more persuasive.

- **Smile when you speak.** Smiling encourages your customer and indicates that you are willing to meet his or her needs.

- **Use expressive words.** Your speech will be improved if you find and use those words that best express the unique qualities of your product. (See Chapter Five for a more detailed discussion of the power of language.)

■ IDEA IN ACTION

Rita York is vice president of a wholesale grocery concern. It's part of her job to talk with salespeople who call on her company to present various nongrocery products and services—stationery, office machines, insurance, trucks, warehouse equipment, and so on. She talks with eight or ten salespeople each day.

The first person who called on her today was a "mumbler." "This guy must think he's talking to himself," York mused as she cocked her right hand behind her ear to try to catch the salesperson's message.

Did the salesperson catch the significance of this gesture? Of course not. He just continued in the same manner, making it difficult for his words to "register." But even more important was the fact that his method of speaking made it easy for York to interrupt. At the first opportunity she broke into the salesperson's remarks, saying, "No, Mr. Hogan, we're really not interested in new lighting fixtures for our office. If you'll leave me your card . . . ."

The quality of the salesperson's delivery *invited* interruption.

York's next visitor was a different type. He told his story in a grating voice that seemed to imply, "I dare you to disagree with me!"

This individual was selling truck tires. Ms. York happened to have tire replacement on her mind, so she was an excellent prospect for the well-known brand of tire this salesperson was presenting.

"Tell you what I'll do, Mr. Gregory," said Ms. York after listening to him for about 10 minutes, "I'll check your prices against what we've been paying, and if there's no great difference, we'll try out your product. Is that fair enough?"

It was, of course, a crucial moment in the interview. Gregory knew the right answer, and he used the right words. "That's fair enough, Ms. York, but I just want to point out one thing more. I don't know what make of tire you've been buying, but if it's comparable to our own in quality and performance, price won't be an obstacle!"

It was an important point—and well made, as far as *words* go. But the quality of his voice made the remark sound more like a *challenge.*

As Ms. York asked her secretary to get her the necessary information, she thought to herself, "This fellow doesn't sound as though he'd be too easy to get along with if something went wrong. He seems a little on the belligerent side. Maybe we'd better stick to Joe, our regular tire salesperson. He's so pleasant and easygoing."

It's Important to Learn Your Sales Talk Perfectly

The difference between a presentation that has been learned perfectly and one that you only *think* you know well can mean the difference between making and losing a sale. Because it is extremely difficult to be objective in evaluating your own presentation, you should make a point to practice it in front of someone who's qualified to tell you how it sounds. He or she should be able to pick out the places where more effective words might be used, where rambling sentences might be cut down to size, and where important sales points might be clarified or emphasized.

■ IDEA IN ACTION

Doug Curtis was called in by his sales manager to role-play the presentation the company had prepared a few months back. Doug sincerely thought he followed the presentation very well.

The sales manager, who listened critically, found these flaws in Doug's use of the presentation:

- He had used the word "good" 17 times. (This colorless and almost meaningless word didn't appear once in the written presentation.)

- He completely forgot to mention one important sales point.

- He didn't go into a close until he had finished his presentation, although the model presentation had three trial closes woven into it.

- It took him 4 long minutes to deliver an inadequate version of a presentation that, in its suggested form, could easily be covered in 90 seconds.

Role-playing Prepares You for the Actual Sale

Sales managers who use the personal coaching method often play the part of a customer while the trainee goes through the selling process. This role-playing prepares the salesperson for real selling situations in the field.

Whether or not you have had this type of coaching, you can use the technique to improve your skills. Take the time to rehearse imaginary sales. Practice what you will say and do when you are with your prospect or customer.

How to Train Your Memory

Part of your job is keeping a number of facts at your fingertips—facts about your product, how to present it, names of prospects and customers, your customer's needs and wants, special requests, answers to objections, and so forth. Use these memory enhancement techniques to train yourself to remember important pieces of information:

- **Raise your interest in the things you want to remember.** You will remember them more quickly and for a longer time.

- **"Act out" the things you want to remember.** Practice your presentation. This is particularly helpful if you must demonstrate your product and you can't afford to have anything go wrong.

- **Learn details and characteristics.** It's much easier to "peg" your memory to a specific detail than to a broad, ill-defined picture.

- **Get a clear image of what you want to remember.** Precise images will stay with you longer than blurred ones.

- **Refer often to material you must remember.** You refresh your memory with each review.

- **Save your memory for the most important aspects of your selling job.** It is important that you know your presentation, your demonstration, and answers to possible objections by heart. But you can rely on prospect files, follow-up records, and so on in planning other aspects of your work.

HOW TO MAKE THE MOST OF YOUR PERSONALITY

Your Personality Is a Composite of Many Factors

Your personality is a composite of many characteristics, all of which merge—in the prospect's mind—into one general impression. In learning how to manage your personality for maximum effectiveness in sales, you must examine one facet at a time—just as a mechanic checks the carburetor, the spark plugs, and so forth, when performing a tune-up. Only when you appreciate the fact that any one personality characteristic can act as a sales handicap will you be prepared to think constructively about your own personality.

There was a time when salespeople were judged primarily on the basis of their appearance, voice, manner, and attire. But today's customers look beyond the surface; they're more interested in character than personal appearance. If you make minor misrepresentations or promises you can't carry through on, it won't matter how good a first impression you made when you walked through the prospect's door.

Integrity Plays a Large Part in Success

When a buyer says, "We have full confidence in you," it means three things:

1. That you have full and accurate information about your product

2. That you use sound judgment in drawing conclusions or making recommendations

3. That you are honest and sincere in your statements and recommendations

Such confidence is absolutely essential for success in all types of selling. It gives you an obvious and important advantage.

All salespeople are confronted sooner or later with situations that test their integrity. Any suspicion that a salesperson has attempted some form of dubious practice puts the buyer immediately and permanently "on guard." The dubious practice need not involve outright dishonesty, either. Here are some examples:

- Attempting to "overload" the buyer by exaggerating resale possibilities

- Agreeing to a specified delivery date without being certain that it can be met

- Neglecting to point out a certain limitation in a piece of equipment, even though you know that the limitation might become a material factor in its performance

The only way to prove your integrity is to keep your business communications and transactions open and honest at all times.

Sincerity Will Pay Off

If your customer feels that you are sincerely interested in helping his or her business, you stand a better chance to make more sales. You can show your sincerity in a number of ways:

- Take the time and interest to ask your customer about his or her changing needs and wants.

- Answer the customer's calls for service immediately. Your attention will convince him or her that you are truly interested in establishing a long-term business relationship.

- Make regular service calls. It will assure the customer that you are honestly interested in knowing whether your product is performing as expected.

- Treat your customer and his or her business with respect. Everyone likes to be taken seriously.

- Listen to your customer's opinions about your product. You may be able to incorporate a new appeal into your sales talk or emphasize a point you hadn't considered very important.

- Take your customer's questions seriously. This will convey your interest in satisfying him or her.

Courtesy Advances Your Customer Relations

The salesperson with a reputation for courtesy is the one buyers welcome back with open arms. Show your courtesy by respecting your customer's time. Get through with your business as quickly as possible. Your customer will appreciate that you value his or her time as well as your own.

Have the courtesy to remember your customer's likes. If you do and say the things that you know will please him or her, you will always find your customer courteous in return.

Your courtesy is reflected in your attitude. Make a point of being pleasant with everyone you meet. Their good opinion of you will be your reward.

Courtesy can be shown in the way you speak. If your tone of voice indicates annoyance or boredom, you are sure to offend your customer. Show by the way you speak that you are sincere and willing to be of service. Remain silent and attentive to your customer when he or she speaks to you. (See Chapter Four for guidelines on handling the talkative prospect.)

Be as mindful of courtesy on your latest call as you were on your first.

Tact Turns Opposition into Agreement

The tactful salesperson meets his or her customers on their own ground. If you get in the habit of being tactful, you will be able to turn opposition into sales.

Think of how a tugboat works. It doesn't head out to sea and meet a larger ship head on. Instead, it eases alongside the larger ship and heads in the same direction. Before long, the tugboat has the big ship moving in the direction it wants it to go.

When you are able to "go along" with your customers, you will find yourself better able to guide them toward a sale.

Use Your Power of Charm

Charm is the power to influence your customer by pleasing him or her. You can have the kind of charm that sparks the personalities of top-ranking salespeople because it can be developed. Here are the essential ingredients:

- **Readiness to adapt.** Adapt yourself to the personality of your customer and to the requirements of his or her business and you'll get a warm response.

- **Interest in the customer.** Your eagerness to learn more about the customer and his or her needs will generate "charm power."

- **Quickness to praise.** Acknowledgment of your customer's accomplishments by a "pat on the back" will make you more charming to him or her.

- **Desire to be yourself.** "Being yourself" can be the most charming thing about you. However, acting naturally is not enough if you haven't developed habits that please.

You Can Improve Your Performance by Acquiring Patience

Patience is the ability to endure circumstances that would otherwise hinder you from performing at selling peak. You can cultivate patience by learning to control yourself in situations that normally tend to be aggravating.

Help yourself exercise patience while you wait for customers by taking along something to read—a trade journal, sales magazine, a card outlining the steps of your presentation, or even a good book.

Have the patience to learn and to enjoy the many details that are part of your selling job. Patience with company reports, files, prospect cards, and so on will pay off in more sales.

Develop the forbearance to remain calm in trying situations, whether they occur with a prospect or in your personal life. If you realize that most obstacles are temporary, you will be able to accept them patiently.

Overcome Your Prejudices

Because an open mind is important to every salesperson, the "blind spots" of prejudice are a real danger. Prejudice closes a person's mind to ideas that might otherwise be used to advantage. To banish prejudice, the following measures are recommended:

- **Remain open-minded toward people.** A salesperson who doesn't have an open mind reduces the number of potential prospects.

- **Be partial to new ideas.**

- **Do away with preconceived notions.** Decisions based on unsubstantiated ideas or feelings rather than facts will undermine your success in selling.

- **Be fair.** Injustice is the other half of prejudice. If preferences for people are distorted by prejudice, someone is going to be done an injustice. Fairness to all is one of the virtues needed for successful selling.

Resolve That Your Prospect Will Find You Friendly

If you make an immediate friendly impression, your prospect will be more willing to listen to you. The opposite impression may cause him or her to terminate the interview.

Control your gestures, your bearing, your facial expressions, and the tone of your voice; each is an advertisement of your eagerness to be friendly.

Understanding the "Unapproachable" Customer Makes It Easier to Like Him or Her

Understanding what makes a customer act cold and unfriendly is not always easy. Sometimes you can discover the reason by taking the initiative and making a real effort to be friendly yourself.

■ IDEA IN ACTION

Harry Bergdahl, like most salespeople, is on friendly terms with most of his customers. One exception is Francis Murison.

Mr. Murison is a reserved person and inclined to be cynical. Harry tries to cover up the fact that he doesn't particularly like this man, but at the same time he realizes that Murison doesn't feel very friendly toward *him* either.

"I think I'll ask Murison to lunch today," Harry says to himself. "Even if he doesn't accept my invitation, maybe the gesture will help."

Murison declines the invitation but explains to Harry that for 15 years he has always gone home for lunch, to be with his invalid wife. Murison then adds, "I guess I miss a lot by not going to lunch with some of you salespeople, but that's how it is."

Harry suddenly begins to understand this man and to like him better. He realizes that Murison wouldn't have taken him into his confidence if he hadn't appreciated the invitation. From this day on, Harry's orders from this customer are substantially larger than they were before.

Capitalize on Your Customer's Individuality

If your customer has developed an unusual interest or characteristic, you can often please him or her by showing that you've remembered it.

> ▪ IDEA IN ACTION
>
> Tina Worth observed that one of her customers always talked about gardening. Tina took this as a cue to do one of those little things, like remembering a hobby, that sincerely flatter the customer. She presented this customer with a cutting from an unusual plant that grew in her garden. The customer was so tickled at this recognition of his pet enjoyment that he placed an order for Tina's product.

You Must Be a Self-starter

It takes a determined, self-starting salesperson to win in today's highly competitive market. Self-starting power will put you far ahead of others who waste valuable selling time by postponing their work.

Here are some suggestions to help you build your self-starting power.

- **Begin immediately.** Don't waste your time waiting for a vague impulse or someone else to get you started. Right now is the time for you to begin.

- **Avoid putting off tasks you dislike.** If you procrastinate you will disrupt your schedule and lose valuable selling hours.

- **Finish the first task.** Get in the habit of finishing the first job you start. A completed job behind you will give you the necessary momentum to plunge into the day's work.

Selling is the easiest job in the world if you work it hard—but the *hardest* job in the world if you try to work it easy.

You Can Strengthen Your Character Through Self-reliance

When you rely on yourself, you learn to depend less on others. Your reward is more confidence in yourself and more conviction in your actions.

Self-reliance is a necessary virtue for salespeople. You are your own boss and have the ability to make or break your own fortune. If you don't learn to rely on yourself, on whom can you rely?

Check Your Habits

Your character reflects the sum total of all the habits you have acquired in your lifetime. Good habits can be formed and strengthened. Undesirable habits can be stopped once you learn to recognize them. Remember that habits are consciously acquired and can be consciously improved.

Check your habits by asking yourself these questions:

- What habits do I have that give me a good start on the selling day?

- Do I make a habit of putting my customer's welfare before my own?

- Have I acquired the habit of positive thought and action?

- Do I practice habits that keep me physically strong?

- Do I practice habits that refresh me spiritually and keep me mentally alert?

- Do I make a habit of small courtesies?

- Have I acquired the habit of preparing myself thoroughly before I call on my customers?

Through self-management you can develop and strengthen good habits that will make the best impression on your customer.

Personal Mannerisms Can Affect a Sale

A gesture that is used purposefully to emphasize a point or to add force to a demonstration can help make any sale. But a mannerism that diverts a prospect's attention from the business at hand or that irritates the prospect is a fault to be corrected.

■ IDEA IN ACTION

Herb Colby is a dynamic salesperson who burns up lots of nervous energy in his work. His industry and enthusiasm, combined with his mastery of selling techniques, have made him a high producer. Yet periodically he goes into a slump that he cannot account for.

The answer is simple. When the going gets tough, Herb resorts to mannerisms that distract attention from his presentation. As he makes an important point, he frequently pounds the desk with the palm of his hand. And when it's the prospect's turn to talk, Herb is apt to shake his head in disagreement when an unfavorable point is made.

Herb is completely unaware of these mannerisms. Consequently, he does not realize that whenever the presentation isn't going his way, he resorts to them even more frequently. It is this factor that accounts for his slumps.

Herb could easily train himself to avoid these attention-diverters, especially when he is under pressure. This would eliminate his periodic slumps and make his selling task easier.

> **TIP** A person who uses distracting mannerisms is almost always completely unaware of them. Watch your prospect's reactions to the way you act. Check yourself when you're giving a presentation, or ask a friend for his or her opinion if you want to be sure that your mannerisms are not undermining your effectiveness.

Most detrimental mannerisms can be detected by an honest checkup. To aid you, here is a list of the more common things to guard against:

- Strumming your fingers
- Chewing a pencil or pen
- Toying with eyeglasses, pencil, keys, coins, and so on
- Constant crossing and uncrossing of legs
- Nodding or shaking head unnecessarily
- Exaggerated slapping or pounding table with hand or fist
- Frequent interruption when prospect is talking
- Slumping in chair
- Looking bored while prospect is talking
- Exaggerated facial expressions
- Raising voice unreasonably when enthusiastic or excited

Punctuality Shows That You Are in Control of Your Job

If you fail to observe punctuality in your appointments, you can never enjoy the full confidence of your customers. Being meticulous about commitments indicates that you are "on top of your job." Lack of this quality is usually interpreted as a sign of unreliability.

When it comes to punctuality, most salespeople are put to the test every day of their lives. When a customer specifies a certain shipping date, requests certain information or a quotation by a given time, or makes an appointment, he or she is going to feel slighted if the salesperson doesn't carry through. "I guess my business just isn't important enough" is the usual conclusion.

A reputation for punctuality is easy to establish and maintain. Two things are required:

1. Follow through to make sure that anything you promise to do is actually performed on time.

2. Explain immediately by note or phone call whenever this proves impossible.

Don't Make Yourself Hard to Buy From

Sometimes a customer will tip you off as to what he or she wants to buy. When you get a "break" like this you must not try to sell the person something that *you* think he or she should buy. Take your cue from what the customer has said and redirect your selling efforts toward the product in which he or she has expressed an interest.

■ IDEA IN ACTION

Letty Morgan, who sells electric signs, was offered an unusually large order. She had been told by her customer that there was no particular preference for color, design, and so forth. The only thing he wanted was a type of sign that would suit his purpose, at a cost that would not exceed $15 per unit. He was willing to place an order for 10,000.

In spite of this guidance, Letty spent the first 5 minutes of the interview extolling the features of a sign which, she blithely announced, could be bought for a mere $18. "Price isn't everything, you know," she countered as the buyer said that he wasn't really interested in paying that much. Letty then took 3 or 4 minutes to deliver a gratuitous lecture on the importance of value in a deal of this sort. Every time the buyer reminded Letty of the price, she would go right on talking value and features—at prices that in each case were above $15.

Finally the buyer said, "Sorry, Ms. Morgan, but I guess you haven't got what we want."

"We do have a sign that might fill your requirements, but I still think you'd be better off with this other one," Letty persisted.

The customer was unmoved. He ended up placing an order for 2,000 of the $15 signs, even though he was originally interested in buying five times that many. Letty didn't lose the sale altogether, but she did ignore the cues her customer was giving her. In short, she made herself hard to buy from.

Initiative Must Be Used with Caution

Initiative, properly exercised, is a powerful force in selling. Improper use of initiative can be an equally powerful sales deterrent.

Here's a guideline that will help you decide whether to use your initiative in any given circumstance: *Avoid taking any steps that will make it embarrassing or otherwise difficult for the buyer to say "No."*

■ IDEA IN ACTION

Tom Slater sells photographic supplies to retailers. He calls on his accounts about once a month. One day he discovers that one of his customers, Ruth Spooner, has gone home with a bad cold.

"Do you think Mrs. Spooner would mind if I telephoned her?" he asks one of the clerks.

"Why, no," comes the reply.

"Well," continues Tom, "before I call, I'd like to check up on the stock to see what you need. Will you give me a hand?"

In due course Slater makes his call. "Hello, Mrs. Spooner," he says, "I'm sorry to hear you've got a bad cold. Hope you don't mind my calling you at home, since I'm in town today."

"No, not at all, Tom," Mrs. Spooner says. "But I'm afraid you'll have to pass us up this trip. I don't think I'm up to coming downtown on a raw day like this."

"Oh, I wouldn't think of asking you to do that, Mrs. Spooner. But I just went over the stock with Joe, and I've written up an order for the things you're low on. It comes to $1,081.63. Suppose I just leave it with Joe, and you can look it over when you get in and mail it to me if it's okay."

"There's no need to do that, Tom," Mrs. Spooner replies. "I'm sure the order's okay, so just go ahead and fill it. I'll see you on your next trip."

Later that same day, another salesperson stops in. When he finds out that Mrs. Spooner is home ill, he proceeds to sell some new items to the clerk and says, "Just sign this order and we'll rush them right out to you."

"Well, I don't think I'd better," says Joe. "Mrs. Spooner does all the buying herself."

"Oh, she'll be glad you took care of it, seeing that she isn't here!"

Joe reluctantly signs the order. When he explains what happened, Mrs. Spooner is annoyed at the tactics used. "I know we need the supplies, but I'm going to cancel the order just to teach that salesperson a lesson!"

Avoid Putting a Customer "On the Spot"

It's never good strategy to put the buyer on the spot. His or her only "out" under such circumstances is to turn down your proposition completely.

■ IDEA IN ACTION

Alice Scott is introducing a new make of electric broiler. Her company decides that the quickest way to launch this product is to run an initial advertising campaign directed toward the consuming public and to use the resulting leads and inquiries to convince local dealers that they should carry the line. Accordingly, the home office sends to Alice all the leads that come in from the various towns in her territory.

"Mr. Dealer," Alice says on her first call, "we're introducing a new electric broiler that we know you can sell. To prove its salability, we've advertised direct to the consumer. Here are some orders and leads that we want to turn over to you. You will, of course, get the full dealer's profit on these sales. We think this proves you can profitably stock and sell our line."

The dealer agrees and takes on the line, ordering a dozen units in addition to those already sold.

Alice then goes to the next town in her territory, one that's about three times as large as the first town. "This dealer should stock three dozen units," she says to herself. "I think I'll tell her that we'll give her the orders from her town *provided* she orders three dozen extra."

When the dealer hears this proposition, she says, "We aren't interested in carrying your line. You come in here with some leads and try to use them to pressure us to place a larger order than we normally would on a new item. We don't appreciate such tactics, and we aren't interested in your proposition."

Use the Right Word to Avert Unpleasant Situations

There are many times when the right word can turn a potentially unpleasant situation into an opportunity to cement customer relations.

■ IDEA IN ACTION

Salesperson Luis Rivera finds himself provoked by a customer who tries to blame him and his product for a business slump. Rivera says, "I understand that business isn't as good as it should be for you right now. All I can do is reassure you that you're not alone. Fortunately, slumps are only preludes to peaks in business. I think this idea I have for you will help you be among the first to regain your usual high volume."

Rivera's words of understanding make the customer's ill temper evaporate and set up a healthy atmosphere for a successful sales talk.

At his next interview, Rivera is ushered into the office of a buyer who doesn't even bother to acknowledge his presence, but continues to write at her desk. Rivera could show his impatience in a number of ways; he could even turn around and leave. But he quietly stands there until the customer is forced to recognize him and offer him a seat.

Rivera makes a point of saying "Thank you" warmly, indicating his willingness to overlook the customer's breech of courtesy.

Rivera's next customer speaks sarcastically about the performance of his product. Rivera neither accepts the blame nor argues with his customer. He praises his customer for his good judgment and for not hesitating to express his opinions. Rivera adds that he knows his product is a good one and that he is there to be of service. The customer's attitude soon softens, and by the time Rivera invites him to repeat or write down his complaints, most of them have disappeared.

Rivera's last appointment for the day proves to be the most exasperating. The customer who had assured him that she would be free at 4:30 has not yet returned to her office. Rivera doesn't let this affect him. He decides that the possibility of getting an order is good and that the dollar value of this customer warrants his waiting. He further reasons that this customer has always been prompt before and has rarely kept him waiting. Rivera's calmness in the face of exasperation pays off. The customer returns after 15 minutes, thanks Smith for waiting for her, and proceeds to place a larger order than he had expected.

A Display of Optimism Can Often Make a Sale

Optimism, like enthusiasm, tends to be contagious. Put your customer in an optimistic frame of mind, and you can often get him or her to buy.

■ IDEA IN ACTION

Stanley White, owner of a manufacturing business in Chicago, meets a neighbor on the morning train going to town. As they chat about the weather, politics, and business, the neighbor, Owen Banks, mentions that his own business is bad and that he understands his competitors have felt the effects of the recession as well. "If you ask me, Stan," he continues, "we're in for some tough going. Things have been pretty good in our industry for quite a while, and I guess the old business cycle is catching up with us."

Mr. White arrives at his office feeling depressed. "Maybe it would be wise to hold off on that advertising contract I was going to sign this morning," muses White as he digs into his morning mail.

At 11 o'clock a caller is announced—Hester McNulty, who sells space for an important national magazine.

"Hester," says Mr. White, "I'm going to ask you to wait about a week on that contract. Business seems to be slipping off, and I don't want to sign up for a campaign of this size at the wrong time. Let me think it over, and call me in a week or so."

"Okay, Mr. White," Hester says with an easy smile. "I know just how you feel. But if I thought this recession were going to last, I'd be the first one to say to all my accounts, 'Let's take it easy.'"

"You mean you don't think things are tightening up?" asks White.

"Well, let's look at it this way," Hester replies. "Yesterday, about 4 o'clock, I signed the biggest contract ever placed by the ABC Company, one of the country's biggest corporations—and they usually know what they're doing!"

"Yes," says White, "they're pretty smart operators!"

"But that's only part of the story," she continues. "Earlier this week Hugh Simmons, our West Coast representative, faxed us that he had just signed up the XYZ Corporation, which has never advertised with us before, but is now going to have a full page in each issue for 12 months.

"The way I interpret this, Mr. White, is that companies like the ones I've mentioned seem to have decided that they're not going to sit there and take it on the chin if sales fall off a bit. No matter what happens to the economy, they figure to win by keeping their names right in front of the buying public!"

Hester's optimism is infectious. Because of her display of optimism, she gets her order. It's unlikely that anything else would have persuaded her prospect to buy at this time.

Divulging Confidential Information
Can Cost You Sales

One rule can help you avoid the penalties that befall the gossip: Never expect the other person to keep a confidence that you yourself have seen fit to divulge.

Compliance with this rule forces you to be willing to be quoted on everything you say. It forces you to think twice before relaying information that has come to you in the form of hearsay or that discretion suggests *should* be kept confidential. This point is so obvious that it might be dismissed without discussion. But many salespeople *do* engage in gossip, often without realizing the costly consequences.

■ IDEA IN ACTION

Dick Reese is a salesperson for a lithography firm. He has developed the habit of passing on to his customers whatever "news" he thinks might be of interest.

In the beginning, Dick discreetly selected what he would tell. But over time, his stories began to include those beginning with "Confidentially, I heard only this morning that . . . "

Dick doesn't know how big a price he's paying for his indiscretion. "We're running a big promotion at a special price," muses one of Dick's customers, "but I'd better not give the order to Dick Reese. He'd probably run right over to our competitors and spill the whole story, just so he could bring them some news!"

Dick might not do any such thing. But people rarely give a gossip the benefit of the doubt.

An Effective Parting Remark Will
Often Gain a Second Interview

When you leave your customer on a high note, you pave the way for a welcome return. You can make sure your customer will want to see you again if you spend a few moments planning what to say as you leave. Here are some suggestions:

- If you sell your customer, thank him or her for the business.

- If you do not sell your customer, thank the person for his or her time.

- Promise to bring something your customer may have requested.

- Make a friendly parting remark about something that is important to your customer, such as family or a vacation.

REMEMBER The salesperson who has nothing gratifying to say when he or she leaves gives the customer less incentive to grant the person another interview.

Win or Lose, Leave the Customer Smiling

The expression "nothing succeeds like success" can sometimes be modified to read, "nothing succeeds like the *appearance* of success." The experienced salesperson never hints that a sale did not turn out as successfully as he or she may have wished.

∎ IDEA IN ACTION

A friend of a real estate salesperson dropped in to say hello. She found despondency written all over the salesperson's face. He immediately launched into the details of a big sale that had just fallen through.

At that moment, his phone rang. Suddenly he was a new man. His eyes sparkled, and his voice rang with cheerfulness. When he put down the phone, his friend suggested that maybe things weren't so bad after all. But the salesperson's face turned melancholy again. "That was Jim Burrows, the buyer whose deal fell through. I have to be a good loser in front of him. After all, he'll be back again, perhaps with an even bigger deal."

On leaving the office, the friend noticed a little motto tacked up on the wall: "Win or lose, leave 'em smiling."

Self-management Can Turn You into an Expert Closer

Any salesperson can transform himself or herself in a few weeks from a poor closer into a very good one. Here's an example of how it can be done.

■ IDEA IN ACTION

Kathryn Graye's trouble was that she was afraid to make a strong bid for an order. Time and again, when she had her prospect just about sold, she'd be hit with an objection like, "Well, maybe I'd better think it over for a day or two." Instead of trying to show the customer that there was nothing to be gained by waiting, Graye would simply leave.

Then Graye's sales suddenly soared. She'd looked at her record, seen that she'd gotten nowhere during the past year, and determined that closing was her biggest weakness. She thought it was probably time to quit. But this gave her an idea. She knew that if she were going to leave her territory in a week, she could push her customers for all she was worth during the next few days.

Graye decided to make one final call on each of her customers. Whether they bought or not, it was going to be the last time she'd see them. She felt no need to hesitate or accept the excuse "Next time." If a customer tried to brush her off, Graye pulled no punches to get an order. She used the strong closing techniques she should have used in the first place, as the jump in her sales record soon proved.

It's important to note that although Graye's new closing tactics seemed like "high pressure" to *her*, in fact they were nothing more than the tactics a strong closer uses all the time.

Only You Can Follow Through on Self-management

It is not enough merely to recognize an area of self-management that needs improvement. To get results, you must follow through.

■ IDEA IN ACTION

Salesperson Len Jones, in spite of his better than average ability, has been doing a below-average job. His sales manager calls Jones in to talk things over, and after a complete and frank discussion, Jones realizes that the trouble is due to his lack of planning. So he makes a firm resolve to overcome that weak spot.

He succeeds, and after two months Jones finds himself leading the other salespeople. Although he never would have found his error if he had been left to himself, neither his manager's analysis nor his own resolve to correct the error would have been enough if Jones hadn't followed through.

NOTE One or two efforts at self-management will not do the job. Regular and methodical self-management are necessary for any salesperson who is aiming high.

CHAPTER NINE

SALESPERSON'S PERSONAL MONEY KIT

The "personal money kit" gives you the "extras" top salespeople use to earn more—and to keep more of what they earn.

The high cost of selling will continue to escalate throughout the decade. And as companies search for ways to keep sales costs under control, an increasingly watchful eye will be cast on travel and entertainment (T&E) expenses.

T&E expenses have always been vulnerable to abuse. In fact, expenses for personal telephone calls, overstated auto mileage, and doctored meal receipts were the most common T&E violations cited by a recent Executive Advisory Panel sponsored by *Sales & Marketing Management*.

But keeping close track of T&E expenses isn't solely for the purpose of avoiding trouble with the IRS. Knowing how to handle travel and entertainment expenses, what's deductible and what's not, ways to cut costs without impinging on your productivity—

these are all things the salesperson of the 1990s needs to know. This chapter provides you with the information you need to keep T&E costs under control—and your deductions within tax law guidelines. The most important thing to keep in mind is that your expenses are deductible only when your employer doesn't reimburse you for them or pay for them in the first place.

The "personal money kit" provides the information you need on

- Entertainment expenses—how much can be deducted, what's deductible and under what circumstances, and gifting clients compared with entertaining them.

- The deductibility of business transportation and travel expenses, including recent law changes. It also discusses how you may be able to increase travel write-offs while reducing recordkeeping.

- The distinction that tax law draws between travel and transportation expenses. Here's where you'll find information on deductions for business cars, including personal use of such cars, and commuting expenses.

- The tough new rules on company-paid T&E expenses—and why company-paid versus employee-paid T&E can benefit both you and your company.

- How to make sure that your T&E deductions will stand up under scrutiny of the IRS as well as state and local tax watchdogs. Included is a line-by-line guide to IRS Form 2106: "Employee Business Expenses."

HOW TO HANDLE YOUR ENTERTAINMENT EXPENSES

How to Increase Write-offs of Entertainment Expenses

Deductible entertainment expenses include more than what you spend on amusement or recreation for yourself and your customers. For example, you may be able to claim valuable write-offs for the cost of taking customers to restaurants, nightclubs, cocktail lounges, theaters, country and athletic clubs, sporting events, and hunting and fishing excursions. You may also be able to deduct a good chunk of the cost of entertaining at home—or even at luxury resorts.

This section spotlights the key tax rules you must know to boost your entertainment write-offs. It explains a special deduction cap on your entertainment expenses as well as which expenses are exempt from the cap. It also shows you how to pass tough hurdles that can sidetrack your entertainment write-offs.

NOTE Section numbers in brackets refer to the Internal Revenue Code (IRC).

How Much Can You Deduct?

You can generally deduct 80% of the cost of your business entertainment expenses [IRC Sec. 274(n)(1)]. The 80% deduction cap applies not only to the actual cost of your entertainment activity but also to taxes, tips, and other related charges (e.g., nightclub cover charges, parking fee at the entertainment site). However, it does not apply to transportation to and from the location of the entertainment; that cost is fully deductible.

☐ EXAMPLE

You pay a $10 cab fare to meet a customer for dinner. The dinner bill comes to $80, plus $5 tax and a $15 tip. Result: Assuming that the expenses qualify as deductible, you can write off $90 (80% of the total restaurant charges, plus the $10 cab ride).

NOTE THESE EXCEPTIONS Certain types of expenses are *not* subject to the 80% limit and are deductible in full (IRC Sec. 274(n)(2)). These include the following:

- Items made available to the public as samples or promotional materials.

- Entertainment sold to customers. If you charge a customer the full fair market value for an entertainment-type activity, your expenses are fully deductible.

- Sporting activities. The cost of business entertainment at a sporting event is fully deductible if (1) the event's primary purpose is to benefit a charity, (2) the entire net proceeds go to the charity, and (3) the event uses volunteers to perform substantially all the work needed for the event. Golf tournaments for charity are a prime example of this kind of business entertainment activity.

■ Employer-provided recreation. This covers holiday parties, summer picnics, and similar recreational and social activities that your company throws for its employees or that your sales manager throws for the sales department. However, this item is deductible only by the company or a sales manager.

■ Amounts treated as compensation. If an employer reports entertainment reimbursements as compensation on an employee's Form W-2, the reimbursements are fully deductible by the employer. The employee then takes the reimbursements into income but may be able to claim a partial deduction for the offsetting entertainment expenses.

■ De minimis fringe benefits. These are items of minimal value that are provided by an employer and excluded from employees' incomes (e.g., subsidized company cafeteria, holiday gifts of turkeys) [IRC Sec. 132].

What Expenses Are Deductible?

To get a deduction for your entertainment expenses, you must pass the following two hurdles: The expenses must be (1) ordinary and necessary in your business and (2) directly related to or associated with your business.

Expenses that are "ordinary and necessary"

Entertainment expenses are ordinary and necessary in your business if you incur the expenses with an intent to obtain a specific business benefit, if the expenses are customary in your business, and if they aren't lavish or extravagant.

When you entertain both business guests and nonbusiness guests, you must allocate your expenses between the business portion and the personal portion. For example, if you entertain three customers and three social acquaintances at a restaurant, only

4/7 of the restaurant tab is considered an ordinary and necessary expense (the portion allocable to your meal and the meals of your three customers).

When your spouse and a customer or client's spouse attend the entertainment activity, their expenses may be considered ordinary and necessary if you have a clear business purpose for the entertainment.

□ EXAMPLE

Ralph Soden is in town to negotiate an equipment sale. His wife, Gail, accompanies him. Ralph invites Dan Brown, a prospective purchaser, to dinner at a restaurant. Because it would be impractical for Ralph to dine without his wife, Gail also comes to the restaurant. And because Gail is there, Ralph asks Brown's wife to come too. Result: Ralph's entire cost is considered an ordinary and necessary expense.

Expenses that are "directly related to business"

Entertainment is generally directly related to your business if, during the entertainment period, you hold active discussions or negotiations with an eye to a specific business benefit. To qualify an expense as directly related to business, you must meet three basic conditions:

1. There is more than a general expectation of deriving income or other business benefit from providing the entertainment. However, you are not required to show that new income or a specific benefit actually resulted from each and every expense. If the business discussion is fruitless, a deduction is still allowed.

2. You actively engaged in a discussion, negotiations, or a transaction during the entertainment. However, expenses may still be deductible if you expected to talk business but no business was actually discussed for reasons beyond your control.

3. The principal character of the combined entertainment/business activity is the active conduct of your business. While you don't have to talk business all the way through lunch, an incidental business discussion will not suffice.

An expense automatically qualifies as directly related to business if it occurs in a clear business setting and is designed to further your business. A clear business setting is one in which the recipient of the entertainment could reasonably conclude that you have no motive for providing the entertainment other than business. For example, if a salesperson operates a hospitality room at a convention to display products, that would be considered a clear business setting.

Entertainment is presumed to fail the "directly related" test if you hold it under circumstances where there is little or no possibility that business can be discussed. The IRS says these circumstances include hunting and fishing trips and outings on yachts and other pleasure boats.

Expenses that are "associated with business"

Entertainment is associated with your business if it meets the following criteria:

- There is a clear business purpose to the expenditure, such as soliciting business or improving an existing business relationship.

- It directly precedes or follows a substantial and bona fide business discussion, for example, when you meet a client at the office, tour the plant, and then have lunch.

Whether or not a discussion is substantial or bona fide depends on the facts and circumstances of each situation. Generally, you must show that you are engaged in a business discussion, conference meeting, or negotiation that has a business or income-producing goal. The meeting does not have to last any specific length of time, and it does not have to last longer than the entertainment that precedes or follows it. But you must show that the principal character of the combined business/entertainment activity is business.

☐ EXAMPLE

Gilbert Evans is a car salesperson. He refers car buyers to Andrew Moss, who installs antitheft alarms and other add-ons in the cars. One morning, Gilbert and Moss discuss some new products that Moss is planning to sell. Then Moss takes

Gilbert out to lunch at a restaurant. After that they go for a round of golf, and Moss pays the greens fees. Result: The meal and golfing are associated with Moss's business and therefore are deductible.

A business conference or convention qualifies as a substantial business discussion, assuming you can deduct the cost of attending the conference or convention. For example, if you entertain a customer following a convention session, you can deduct 80% of your cost, even though it's strictly for goodwill and no business is discussed.

When must business be discussed?

Generally speaking, a business discussion should directly precede or follow an entertainment activity if both occur on the same date. If they occur on different days, the entertaining may be considered associated with business if the facts and circumstances warrant it.

☐ EXAMPLE

Paula Morton, a customer of XYZ, and her husband fly in from out of town. Mark Pickford, a salesperson with XYZ, takes the Mortons to dinner. Afterward, they go to the theater. The following day Morton and Pickford spend several hours at XYZ's office negotiating a sales contract. Result: The cost of the dinner and theater tickets is considered associated with Pickford's business.

Entertainment at Home

You don't even have to leave your home to rack up big entertainment deductions. You can deduct 80% of your out-of-pocket costs for home entertainment that is "associated with" your business.

☐ EXAMPLE

Al Medlin, a major customer, and three of his employees are in town for a few days. After a sales presentation at your office, you invite the four of them and their spouses to a party at your home. You also invite Grace Boyle, one of your key associates, and her spouse. (Boyle assisted you in the presentation.) In addition, you invite three other couples—no business connection, just good friends. So, including you and your spouse, there will be 18 people at the party.

Result: Since the party directly follows a substantial business discussion, it qualifies as "associated with" entertainment. So you can write off 80% of your expenses, except for the expenses allocable to your nonbusiness guests. If you spend $750 on the party, you can treat $500 as "associated with" entertainment ($750 @ 12/18). So you can deduct $400—80% of $500.

Entertainment at Luxury Resorts

The tax court recently allowed a company to deduct the cost of entertaining its officers, directors, and business guests at company meetings at distant resort areas. The court said that the expenses were ordinary and necessary, even though none of its competitors held meetings at similar locations.

> **KEY POINT** The court also held that the expenses were directly related to business, despite the fact that those attending spent a large portion of their time vacationing (*United Title Insurance*, TC Memo 1988-38).

■ FACTS OF THE CASE

United Title Insurance Co. issued title insurance in North Carolina. Because of its conservative underwriting policy, it was selective in the attorneys, lenders, developers, and realtors with whom it did business. On the other hand, it was dependent on these same groups for business referrals. United held three business meetings in New Orleans, Las Vegas, and Puerto Rico. On these trips, United took its officers, directors, and selected guests in the real estate business, along with their spouses. The meetings were designed to educate the guests on United's philosophy and soundness and to allow United to find out about the background and character of the people with whom it might be dealing.

On a typical trip, the first day would be spent traveling to the location. On the morning of the second day, a formal business meeting would be held. The participants had free time that afternoon and during the third day. They would return to North Carolina on the fourth day.

The IRS disallowed all deductions for the trips. It claimed the expenses were not ordinary and necessary because other North Carolina title companies did not offer such trips and the trips were not directly related to business. They were mere social gatherings, designed to build goodwill.

The court held against the IRS on both counts. The court did knock out United's deductions for the expenses of the participants' spouses. Their presence on the trip was purely social and could not be justified as an ordinary and necessary business expense.

As for the participants themselves, the court said that the fact that the trips were unique among title companies did not mean they were not ordinary and necessary. United was a new, small company in a competitive business. Inviting selected individuals to participate in out-of-state meetings fit in with United's marketing strategy.

Regarding the directly related to business test, the court pointed out that bona fide business meetings were held on each trip and the guests actively participated.

This fact distinguished the case from other cases where deductions had been disallowed for meetings at resort locations. These other cases involved primarily social functions where there was some "shop talk."

The court also noted that there was a good business reason for United to hold the meetings at resort locations. The guests were engaged in demanding businesses of their own. Having the meetings in vacation areas increased the guests' willingness to attend and removed everyday distractions.

Special deduction limits

In general, you cannot deduct expenses with respect to a facility used for entertainment [IRC Sec. 274(a)]. An entertainment facility includes yachts, hunting lodges, fishing camps, swimming pools, automobiles, and other items of personal or real property owned, rented, or used in connection with business entertainment.

Disallowed deductions include those for depreciation, rents, repair expenses, utility charges, and a loss on the sale of the facility.

The disallowance rule does not apply to the expenses that could be deducted even if the facility were not used for business entertainment. So property taxes, mortgage interest, and casualty losses on an entertainment facility may be deductible. And you can also deduct expenses attributable to the business use of a facility for other than entertainment.

In addition, you can write off out-of-pocket entertainment expenses at a facility, as long as they are otherwise deductible. For example, if you take a customer fishing on your boat following a business discussion, you can deduct 80% of what you spend for gas, bait, and so forth.

How About Gifts?

Gifts to customers, clients, or even the public may be a deductible goodwill expense for you. You generally can deduct up to $25 per recipient per year of the amount you spend on business gifts [IRC Sec. 274(b)(1)].

> **KEY POINT** You get the $25 deduction in full; there is no 80% deduction cap as with entertainment.

☐ EXAMPLE

Sam Harrison sends out hams at Christmas to his customers. The cost of each ham is $40. Sam can deduct $25. If the hams cost $20, Sam could deduct the $20 in full.

In figuring the amount subject to the $25 limit, you do not have to include incidental costs, such as engraving, packaging, or mailing. On the other hand, you do have to count a gift to the spouse of a customer (unless you have independent business dealings with the spouse). So if you give the spouse a $25 gift, you cannot deduct any additional gifts to the customer for the year. By the same token, you and your spouse are treated as one taxpayer for purposes of the deduction limit. If you and your spouse each give a $25 gift to the same customer or client, your total deduction is limited to $25 [IRC Sec. 274(b)(2)]. If your spouse gives to separate clients, he or she gets a separate deduction.

NOTE THESE EXEMPTIONS Certain gifts are exempt from the $25 deduction cap. Here are some of them:

- An item costing $4 or less on which your name or company name is clearly and permanently imprinted and which is one of a number of identical items you distribute generally
- A sign, a display rack, or other promotional material to be used on the business premises of the recipient
- Amounts, other than gifts, that are excludable from the recipient's income (e.g., scholarships)

□ EXAMPLE

Alyssa Roth gives a $3 pen with her company's name on it and a $25 floral arrangement to each of her customers at year-end. Result: She can deduct $28 per customer. The pen is exempt from the gift deduction cap, so she has the full $25 available for the floral arrangement.

Business Gifts Versus Entertainment

Let's say a major customer is coming to town. You plan to take the customer to the ballpark. The deductibility of the tickets you buy depends on how they are used. For example, suppose you merely give the customer tickets to a game. That may be treated differently than if you accompany him or her.

KEY DISTINCTION Treated as a gift, your deduction is limited to $25 per recipient per year. As goodwill entertainment, there is no dollar limit on the deduction, but the game must precede or follow a "substantial business discussion." And your entertainment deduction is limited to 80% of your cost.

If you and the customer go to the park, you can deduct the ticket only as entertainment (i.e., the game must precede or follow a substantial business discussion). But if *you* don't go, you have a tax choice: (1) You can deduct the customer's ticket as a gift subject to the $25 limit, or (2) you can deduct it as business entertainment subject to the 80% limit (as long as you meet the business discussion test).

□ EXAMPLE

You and a customer discuss business at your office. After the discussion, you give the customer two tickets to a sporting event, but don't go along. If the tickets cost $15 apiece, you can deduct $25 as a gift or $24 (80% of $30) as entertainment. If they cost $20 apiece, you're better off treating them as entertainment—$25 as a gift deduction versus $32 (80% of $40) as an entertainment deduction.

HOW TO HANDLE YOUR TRAVEL EXPENSES

Business Travel Expenses

This section explores the deductibility of your business transportation and travel expenses. It spotlights recent changes in the law and shows how you may be able to increase your travel write-offs while cutting your recordkeeping headaches at the same time. Keep in mind that you can take these deductions only if you are not reimbursed by your employer. If you are only partially reimbursed, you can deduct the remaining amount.

You can deduct most business expenses that are ordinary and necessary. To get a deduction for travel expenses, however, you must satisfy an additional requirement: You must incur the expenses while you are away from home.

What's "away from home"?

To get a travel deduction, you must be away from your "tax home" long enough to require sleep or rest. Generally, this means that your trip spans two or more days.

What's your "tax home"?

Your tax home is the location of your business or employment, regardless of where you live. The entire city or general area in which the business or employment is located is your tax home.

☐ EXAMPLE

Laura Domans has her residence in Boston. But she works in New York. She stays in a New York hotel during the work-week and eats her meals in a local restaurant. She returns to Boston every weekend to be with her family.

Result: Domans cannot deduct any of her expenses of travel-ing to and from New York and while in New York because it is her tax home. Additionally, she cannot deduct the cost of traveling to and from Boston because these trips are not for a business reason.

If you have two places of business

If you have two or more regular work locations, your main place of work is considered your tax home. In determining which location is the main place of work, you have to take into account such factors as the total time spent at each location, the degree of business activity there, and the amount of income derived there.

You can deduct the cost of business travel from your primary work location to a secondary location, even if your family residence is in the area of the secondary location. You can also deduct a portion of your family living expenses to the extent they are attributable to your presence while conducting business at the secondary location.

☐ EXAMPLE

Jill Knight works three weeks a month in Detroit and one week in Chicago. Knight's family lives in Chicago. Knight can deduct her travel expenses to and from Chicago because she is away from home (Detroit) on business. And, for the same reason, she can also deduct her allocable portion of the family's meal and lodging expenses while she is in Chicago. She cannot, however, deduct her living expenses in Detroit; that is her tax home.

If you have no regular place of work

It is possible that you have no regular place of work (e.g., you're an outside salesperson). In that case, your principal residence is treated as your tax home if all the following tests are met:

- You do some work in the area of the principal residence and stay at the residence while working in the area;

- You have duplicate living expenses when away from the residence on business; and

- You have not abandoned the residence (e.g., your family lives there).

If you satisfy only one of the three tests, you have no real tax home. Your tax home is wherever you happen to be at the time, and no deductions for travel expenses are allowed. If you meet two of the three tests, then your principal residence may be considered your tax home, depending on the circumstances.

Temporary versus permanent place of work

Once your tax home has been established, travel expenses away from the tax home to a temporary work location are deductible. However, employment at the new work location must be of a definite, limited duration. If the employment is of an indefinite duration, the new work location becomes your new tax home and travel expenses are not deductible.

In determining whether a new work assignment is temporary, the IRS uses three general rules:

- Assignments of less than one year are usually considered temporary.

- Assignments of one to two years are presumed to be a permanent change of tax homes. But you can overcome that presumption if you show that you realistically expected the assignment to last for less than two years (after which you would return to the claimed tax home) and that the claimed tax home is your regular place of abode in a real sense (e.g., you maintain a residence there and vote there).

- If an assignment is expected to last two years or more (or in fact, lasts that long), then it is not considered temporary under any circumstances.

What Travel Expenses Are Deductible?

The travel deduction allows you to write off your transportation costs and living expenses at the travel destination. Let's take these up item by item:

Transportation

You can go by plane, train, car, boat, bus, or cab and deduct the fare and tips. Any direct and reasonable method is okay. You can also deduct baggage charges and the costs of transporting sample cases, display material, and the like.

Automobiles

If you drive your own car to and from a business travel destination, you can deduct a percentage of your car expenses for the year, including gas, oil, maintenance, repairs, and tires. You also can deduct a percentage of your car depreciation. The percentage you can deduct is based on the business miles you drive during the year divided by the total miles.

What's more, you can deduct in full car expenses that have a direct tie-in to your trip. These fully deductible expenses include tolls to and from the travel destination and parking fees at the destination.

Lodging

If it's a business trip, there's generally no problem deducting the expenses of staying at hotels and motels. Your lodging expenses can also include the cost of sample rooms, business telephone and fax charges, laundry, and similar expenses.

Meals

You can deduct 80% of the cost of meals (including taxes and tips) eaten at the travel destination. The good news here is you have a tax choice when it comes to taking the deduction. You can either write off 80% of your actual meal expenses (including taxes and tips). Or you can take a "standard meal deduction."

If you go the standard deduction route, you can get by with less recordkeeping. You need to keep track only of the time, place, and business purpose of the meals. You don't need to keep track of your meal expenses, and you don't need receipts. The standard deduction allows you to write off 80% of either $26 or $34 per day, depending on your travel destination. The cities eligible for the higher $34 amount are listed later in this chapter, under "Meals and Lodging Allowances." All other cities are eligible for $26.

Education expenses

You can deduct the cost of education that maintains or improves skills needed in your business or employment or that is required to retain your current job or pay rate. If you travel away from home overnight to obtain education that is deductible, then your travel expenses (including meals and lodging) are also deductible. However, travel itself is not deductible as a form of education.

Mixing Business with Pleasure

You can deduct the cost of getting to and from a travel destination if you make the trip primarily for business reasons. You get no deduction for this cost if you make the trip primarily for personal reasons (although you can claim a meals-and-lodging expense deduction for days spent on business).

Whether a trip is primarily related to business depends on the facts and circumstances of each situation. The amount of time spent on business activities compared with the time spent on personal activities is an important determining factor.

☐ EXAMPLE

Greg Harris flies from his Chicago home to Philadelphia to spend a week meeting with his company's customers. He then decides to stay on another two days to go sightseeing. Result: Harris's trip is primarily for business. So he can deduct 100% of his airfare as well as his living expenses during the one-week business portion of the trip. What he spends during the final two days is personal and nondeductible.

TAX-SAVING IDEA Harris switches his schedule around so that he meets with his Philadelphia customers during Wednesday, Thursday, and Friday of the first week and Monday and Tuesday of the second week. In addition to deducting his airfare and living expenses during the five business days, Harris can also deduct his living expenses during the weekend.

A special tax rule says that reasonably necessary standby days count as business days for purposes of claiming a travel deduction. Since the weekend falls in between his business meetings, he can deduct his living expenses during those two recreation days (although he can't deduct any recreation expenses).

The same tax break applies to legal holidays and other reasonably necessary standby days that fall between business days.

Your Spouse's Travel Expenses

Let's say your spouse tags along with you on a business trip. Your spouse is there just to keep you company—not for any business purpose.

Deduction Bargain

Assuming that your own expenses are deductible, you can still deduct the full amount it would cost you to go alone—even though you get a bargain rate for the two of you. In other words, you are not limited to deducting half the travel expenses of you and your spouse.

☐ EXAMPLE

Your airfare and hotel expenses of going alone come to $600; with your spouse along the total is $800. You can deduct the full $600—even though half the cost for the two of you is only $400.

☐ EXAMPLE

You drive your car to a convention and take your spouse along. Your round-trip auto expenses come to $450. You can deduct *all* of them. Reason: They'd be the same whether or not your spouse came along.

Can you deduct your spouse's expenses along with your own? It's difficult, but not impossible. If you can show that bringing your spouse along serves a bona fide business purpose, you get the deduction.

☐ EXAMPLE

When the president of Walt Disney Productions went on a three-month world tour to supervise the marketing of Disney films, his wife went along and devoted a good deal of her time in helping him in his work. Result: Her expenses were deductible. She took the trip because of her husband's business, which required her presence at film showings, social gatherings, and meetings with the press and public. Additionally, her presence enhanced Disney's image as a producer of family entertainment [*Disney*, 413 F.2d 783].

Weekend Trip Home

Suppose you are out of town on business for a few weeks. A weekend arrives and you'd rather be home with your family. What's more, there's a dollar savings in taking a quick round-trip home. The airfare is less than your weekend hotel bill and meals.

Travel expenses (including meals and lodging en route) from the area of your temporary workplace to your hometown and return are deductible if they are no more than it would have cost you for meals and lodging had you stayed at your temporary workplace. If they are more, your deduction is limited to the amount you would have spent at your temporary workplace.

☐ EXAMPLE

You live and work in Miami. You fly to New York for two weeks of business meetings. You fly home to spend the intervening weekend with your family. You leave New York on Friday evening and return to New York on Monday morning to complete your assignment. Your airfare from New York to Miami and back is $200. To stay in New York over the weekend would have cost $225. Result: Your weekend trip to Miami—your purely personal trip home—is fully deductible because the cost of the trip is below what it would have cost you to stay in New York.

If your round-trip flight to Miami cost $250, you can still deduct $225 of your fare, the amount a weekend stay in New York would have cost. The $25 balance of the airfare, however, is nondeductible.

CAUTION Be sure to check out of your hotel before you leave on the weekend trip and reregister when you return. This is important because you can't deduct the cost of both the room and the trip. If you pay for your hotel room over the weekend, the deduction for the trip home is limited to the amount you would have spent for meals only had you remained out of town.

IMPORTANT POINT Records are always necessary to get your T&E write-offs. But the records are even more important if you take trips home during your stay. The records are the proof you must have to show what it would have cost you not to go home—and, thus, how much of your trip home is deductible.

Sales Conventions

You probably receive flyers for trade shows, sales conventions, seminars, and the like. If you plan to attend one of these out-of-town sessions in the near future, don't forget about taxes. You can deduct all registration charges provided they qualify as an "ordinary and necessary" business expense. But what about the cost of getting to and from the convention (including meals and lodging en route if you take a multiday trip)?

The tax rules

The tax rules for the cost of traveling to and from the convention site vary, depending on whether the convention is held within the United States, outside the United States but within the "North American area," or elsewhere on the globe. Furthermore, there are special restrictions that apply to conventions held on cruise ships.

Domestic conventions. The simplest rules apply to conventions held in the United States. If you attend primarily for business reasons, the full transportation cost (and 80% of the cost of meals while traveling) is deductible.

Conventions in the North American area. Transportation expenses relating to conventions held within the North American area, but outside the United States, are deductible *only* if they meet two tests: (1) Your primary purpose for attending the convention must be business, and (2) you must not spend too much time during the trip on pleasure. If you fail the business versus pleasure test, you have to allocate your transportation cost to and from the convention. Only the business portion is deductible.

> **TAX-SAVING EXCEPTION** You can deduct the full cost—without having to make an allocation for the nonbusiness portion of the trip—if (1) you are outside of the United States for no more than one week and (2) at least 75% of your trip is devoted to business-related activities.

For these purposes, the North American area includes U.S. possessions, the Pacific Islands Trust Territory, Canada, Mexico, Jamaica, and certain Caribbean Basin countries that have agreements to swap tax information with the United States.

Conventions in other foreign countries. To qualify for a deduction for foreign conventions held outside the North American area, you must pass an additional test: You must be able to show that it is as reasonable for the convention to be held outside the North American area as within it. In other words, there's no deduction if there's more reason to have the convention held within, rather than outside, North America.

In making the determination of what is reasonable, the IRS looks at these three factors:

1. The purpose of the convention and the activities taking place at the convention

2. The purpose and activities of the sponsoring organization or groups

3. The residences of the active members of the sponsoring organization and the places at which other meetings of the sponsoring organization or groups have been held or will be held

Once you pass the "reasonableness" test, the size of your deduction is governed by the allocation rules for foreign business travel.

Conventions held aboard cruise ships. These are subject to the toughest rules of all. First, there is no deduction unless the convention is (1) held on a U.S. flagship and (2) all ports of call are within the United States or its possessions. In addition, unlike other conventions, there's an absolute dollar cap on your convention deductions. You can write off no more than $2,000 annually for the cost of attending cruise ship conventions.

> **NOTE** The deductible limit is applied on a per taxpayer basis. So, for example, if you and your spouse both work in a family-owned business and both attend a deductible cruise ship convention, up to $4,000 is deductible on a joint return. Of course, if there's no business reason for your spouse to attend, you can't deduct any of his or her other costs.

> **WHAT TO DO** To substantiate the purpose of your trip to your company, be sure to hold on to a program cataloging sessions related to your business. As a further precaution, check off the sessions you attended and take notes. If each session has a sign-in book, make sure you sign in. Then, if the sponsoring organization keeps this book after the sessions are concluded, you can request certified abstracts, photostats, or even the books themselves, should the need arise.

> **CAUTION** There is a special reporting requirement for cruise conventions. You must attach two written statements to your tax return. One is a statement signed by you that contains the number of days of the cruise, the number of hours of each day devoted to business activities, and a program of the activities. The other is a statement signed by a representative of the sponsoring organization that includes a schedule of the business activities of each day and the number of hours you attended.

Trips Abroad

When you meet with a customer or client outside the United States, you may have to allocate your costs between business and pleasure in much the same way as under the business convention rules just described. Only the costs allocated to business are deductible.

As with business conventions, not all trips abroad require an allocation. There is no allocation unless (1) you're outside the country for more than seven consecutive days, not counting the day you leave and (2) you spend 25% or more of the time—including the day you leave and the day you return—on nonbusiness matters.

> **KEY POINT** Even if you fail both these tests, you still needn't allocate if you didn't have much say in arranging the trip (i.e., you're not a managing executive or closely related to your employer) *or* getting a vacation wasn't a major reason for going.

HOW TO HANDLE YOUR TRANSPORTATION EXPENSES

Travel Versus Transportation Expenses

The tax law draws a distinction between your travel expenses and transportation expenses. Your deductible travel expenses include transportation and living expenses you incur when you are away from home overnight. On the other hand, suppose you make a number of sales presentations in the general vicinity of your office. These presentations require an hour or two of your time, so you have no need to stay away overnight. Can you get a deduction for your "local" expenses?

Deductible transportation

When you make a local trip, you can write off all your transportation costs. For example, you can claim a deduction for the miles you put on your own car driving to and from the destination. Similarly, you can deduct air, train, or cab fare if you prefer not to drive. What you can't deduct is any of the living expenses (e.g., meals you eat alone) you incur at your destination.

Business Cars

Your business car can be one of the biggest and best sources of tax write-offs when it comes to your transportation expenses. As a salesperson, you probably put a lot of miles on the car driving to and from your customers. These miles are considered deductible transportation.

There are two basic methods of handling your auto deductions if you use your car in business. You can keep a record of your actual expenses and deduct them. Or you can use a tax shortcut called the "automatic mileage deduction."

This method has two advantages: convenience and tax savings. First, with the automatic deduction, you do not need to keep track of your actual car expenses. You can get by with a record of your business mileage for each trip, where you traveled, when, and for what purpose.

TAX SAVINGS ADVANTAGE If you use the automatic mileage deduction for your 1992 federal income tax return, you can deduct 28 cents for every business mile you drive (the mileage deduction is increased annually for inflation—for 1991 the figure was 27 1/2 cents per mile).

This makes the automatic deduction an attractive alternative to the actual expense method for taxpayers who drive a substantial number of business miles. It is attractive because the 28 cents figure includes an amount for depreciation—which keeps adding up as you drive more miles.

On the other hand, your depreciation write-offs under the actual expense method are subject to strict dollar caps. Your deduction is the same whether you drive 5,000 or 50,000 miles.

☐ EXAMPLE

In early 1992, Seth Myers bought a $40,000 automobile to use for business driving. He put around 36,000 business miles on the car during the year driving to and from his sales prospects.

If he deducts actual expenses for 1992, his depreciation write-off is capped at approximately $2,760. Of course, he also can deduct his out-of-pocket expenses for insurance, maintenance, and gas—perhaps an additional $4,000. Total 1992 deduction: $6,760.

TAX-SAVING ALTERNATIVE Myers decides to ride along with the automatic deduction. Under the 1992 rules, his deduction comes to $10,080 (28 cents/36,000 miles), an increase of nearly 50% over the actual expense method.

What's more, the automatic deduction also allows Myers to keep his recordkeeping headache to an absolute minimum. He can forgo keeping track of his out-of-pocket expenses and can get by with a record of his business mileage, purpose, and date for each trip. And if Myers keeps a record of his parking fees and tolls, he can deduct these expenses in addition to the automatic mileage figure.

Which Auto Deduction Method is Best?

If you deduct actual auto expenses, you have to keep a record of your expenses. But in return, you can deduct every penny of the business-related portion of your out-of-pocket expenses. In addition, you get a depreciation deduction. You can write off up to 20% of your cost the first year, 32% the second, 19% the third, 11 1/2% the fourth, 11 1/2% the fifth, and 6% the sixth.

Your depreciation write-off generally is the same no matter when during the year you first use the car on business. However, three important limitations can cut back the amount of your deduction.

1. If your car is used for both business and personal driving, you get a depreciation deduction for only the business portion of your car use.

2. Additionally, if you use your car 50% or less for business driving, you must use straight-line depreciation (discussed shortly).

3. The tax law places dollar caps on the amount of depreciation you can claim on your business car. This means, for example, that you can write off 20% of a car in the year you buy it, but only up to a depreciation dollar cap.

The IRS establishes dollar caps for a business car, depending on the year the car is first used in your business. For example, if you buy a car and drive it on business in 1992, your 1992 depreciation deduction cannot exceed approximately $2,760. That's the first-year depreciation dollar cap for a car first driven on business during 1992.

If, on the other hand, you first drove the car on business during 1991, you would be subject to the 1991 dollar caps. These caps would place a $2,660 ceiling on your 1991 depreciation write-off (the first year of your write-off period) and a $4,300 ceiling for 1992 (the second year of your write-off period).

Because of all the depreciation limitations, the automatic mileage deduction (28 cents per mile in 1992) is an attractive alternative to writing off actual auto expenses. But individuals who don't do much business driving can still come out ahead by deducting actual expenses.

> **RULE OF THUMB** If you drive a substantial number of miles (20,000 or more per year), you should probably use the automatic mileage deduction. You will probably end up with a bigger tax benefit—but even if you don't, the modest savings of deducting actual expenses may not be worth the extra recordkeeping. If you don't do much driving (business or personal), then you may want to deduct your actual expenses. You don't want your deduction to be based on the number of miles you drive when you *don't* do much driving at all.

Can you deduct the automatic mileage deduction in one year and actual expenses the next? Yes. You can use the automatic mileage deduction in one year and then switch to deducting actual expenses when that provides you with the greater tax benefit. But there are two limitations here:

1. If you don't use the automatic mileage deduction in the first year you drive the car on business, you can't use it at all.

2. If you use the automatic mileage deduction in the first year, you must use straight-line depreciation when you deduct actual expenses.

What About Leased Cars?

If you lease a car for business, you can write off the portion of your lease payments allocable to business use (you cannot use the automatic mileage deduction). For example, if 80% of your total mileage is for business travel, you can deduct 80% of your lease payments.

If you lease, you are subject to a tax rule that approximates the effect of the depreciation dollar caps. You must add back a portion of your lease payment deduction to your income if the car you lease is a so-called luxury model.

Personal Use of Business Cars

You can be hit with a tax penalty of sorts if you don't put enough business miles on your car. If your business mileage doesn't exceed 50% of your total mileage, you can't use accelerated depreciation on your car (i.e., larger deductions in the early years of use). You can still write off your car over six years, but you must use straight-line depreciation. If you flunk the 50% test, your first-year write-off is 10%—not the usual 20% of the business portion of your car cost. For the next four years, you can deduct 20%, and in the final year, your deduction is 10%.

☐ EXAMPLE

You buy a new car for $12,000. You put 20,000 miles on your car for the year—8,000 on business and 12,000 on personal travel. You deduct your actual expenses. Result: Your cost for figuring depreciation is $4,800 (40% of $12,000). But since you didn't pass the 50% business use mark, you must use straight-line depreciation. So your first year's depreciation is only $480 (10% of $4,800).

Obviously, this is one place where a few extra business miles—or a few less personal miles—can make a big difference in your tax picture.

☐ EXAMPLE

In early December, you total up your mileage and find out that, up to then, you have a total of 17,000 miles on your car—8,000 business and 9,000 personal. But it so happens that you intend to go to a trade show in Orlando, Florida, in January. Fortunately, there is another one scheduled in December. So you rearrange your plans and go then. As long as you are going anyway, you decide to bring your family along.

They take in the sights at Disney World while you attend the seminar. Round-trip mileage: 1,500 miles.

PAYOFF Your trip to and from Orlando counts as business travel for purposes of the 50% test. (The fact that your family comes along won't make any difference; your business mileage is the same with or without them.) That puts you over the 50% mark for the year—and allows you to take accelerated depreciation.

Commuting Expenses

The cost of transportation between your family residence and place of business or employment is generally nondeductible. Since the cost stems from your personal choice to maintain your residence at a distance from your work, it is not considered a business expense. But thanks to the IRS, you may now be able to write off a good chunk of your commuting expenses.

TAX BREAK When you drive from your home to a customer's office or from a customer's office to your home, your transportation costs qualify as a deductible business expense. The IRS says that any time you drive from your home to a temporary workplace (or from a temporary workplace to your home), the miles you put on your car are business connected.

Obviously, a customer's office is a temporary workplace. But it's not the only place you can drive to nail down a tax-saving deduction. For example, suppose a supplier takes you out to a restaurant after work to discuss delivery schedules. Your trip from the restaurant to your home is deductible. Or suppose you sign up for a two-week seminar on new sales techniques. The trips between the seminar and your home are deductible.

The key word here is "temporary." As long as your destination is not a place to which you routinely drive (e.g., daily trips to deposit funds at your bank or to pursue a long-term course of study at college), you get a deduction.

Business to business

The drive between two places of work is not commuting. It is deductible business transportation. So if you drive from, say, your office to a customer's office—or from your regular job to a second job—the miles you put on your car are business connected and deductible.

Home office

If you maintain a secondary office in your home, you generally can't deduct the miles you drive between the home office and your principal office. That's because you would have made these trips anyway, and you cannot convert commuting trips into business trips simply by locating another office in the home. However, you *can* deduct these miles if your principal office is in your home and you make trips to secondary work locations.

HOW TO HANDLE THE TOUGH NEW RULES ON COMPANY-PAID T&E

As a salesperson, you may want to set things up so that your company pays for your business travel and entertainment expenses. Doing things this way provides two key tax breaks.

1. You don't have to report the company-paid expenses as income on your tax return. And you don't have to worry about deducting any of your T&E expenses. The company payments and expenses simply cancel each other out.

2. You avoid a tough two-part deduction limit on business expenses.

This section summarizes the new rules on company-paid travel and entertainment.

Tough Deduction Rules

Employees who pay their own way when it comes to business travel and entertainment do not get a full deduction for their expenses. First, they can write off only 80% of the cost of their business meals and entertainment. Second, their expenses are subject to a special 2% deduction floor. And third—thanks to a law change that took effect in 1991—their expenses can be further reduced by a new itemized deduction reduction.

If you're an employee, you must group your business travel and entertainment expenses with your "miscellaneous itemized deductions" (e.g., investment counseling fees, office-at-home expenses, safe-deposit box rental, and tax return preparation fees). Your miscellaneous expenses are deductible only to the extent they total more than 2% of your adjusted gross income.

On top of that, a tough crackdown on itemized deductions recently went into effect. The new limitation applies after you have reduced your itemized deductions by all other limitations that apply (such as the 2% deduction floor).

This is how it works. For your 1992 return, the total of your itemized deductions—except for medical expenses, investment interest, casualty and theft losses, and gambling losses—is reduced by 3% of your adjusted gross income over $105,250 for head of household ($52,625 for married taxpayers filing separately).

There is a silver lining: The crackdown can wipe out no more than 80% of your itemized deductions. Unfortunately, the combined effect of all these deduction limitations can wipe out most or all of the tax benefit you get from your business travel and entertainment expenses.

How Your Employer Can Help

If you receive a company-paid allowance or reimbursement, you are not out of pocket for your business travel and entertainment expenses. What's more, the reimbursement is 100% tax-free income for you. You do not have to contend with the 80% deduction limit for business meals and entertainment (your employer gets an 80% deduction in your place). You do not have to contend with the 2% deduction floor for your miscellaneous expenses. And you do not have to contend with the itemized deduction crackdown.

KEY REQUIREMENTS For the allowance or reimbursement to be tax-free, the employer absolutely must

- Require employees to substantiate their T & E expenses to the company.

- Require employees to return any allowances or reimbursements they do not spend on business.

If either requirement is not satisfied, the employer must report the entire reimbursement as income on the employee's Form W-2. The employee gets a deduction, but it is subject to the deduction limitations discussed earlier.

All New Rules for Company-Paid Travel and Entertainment

Recent tax law changes have introduced new substantiation requirements for employee reimbursements and other expense allowances. They are designed to prevent employers from paying expense allowances that are really disguised compensation. In effect, the law change requires employers to put their expense allowances on a sound footing—to make absolutely sure that expense account money is used solely for legitimate employee expenses.

> **TAX IMPACT** As a result of the recent law changes, the IRS has divided employee expense arrangements into two categories: "accountable plans" and "nonaccountable plans."

An allowance paid under an *accountable plan* is generally tax free to the employee. It is not subject to payroll taxes, nor is it reported on the employee's tax return. The employee reports only the employer's payment as income if expenses exceed the allowance and the employee wants to deduct the difference. In contrast, payments under a *nonaccountable plan* are considered taxable wages. The employer must withhold on the payments and report them on the employee's Form W-2.

What is an "accountable plan"?

What the IRS calls an accountable plan is what many—if not most—companies already have in place. It is an expense arrangement that meets three requirements:

Business connection

The allowance must be limited to job-related expenses that would be eligible for an employee deduction if the employee paid for them out of his or her own pocket. An advance payment qualifies only if it is for business expenses that the employee is reasonably expected to incur. For example, a "travel" advance to an employee who never travels is subject to withholding at the time it is paid, even if the employee later returns the entire amount.

Substantiation

An employee must provide the company with the same detailed expense records that would be required to substantiate a deduction on his or her own return.

> **WELL-KNOWN EXCEPTION** An employee using a so-called "automatic" allowance meets the substantiation requirement as to amount as long as the allowance is within IRS-approved limits. These allowances include a per diem allowance for meals and/or lodging for employees traveling away from home on business and a mileage allowance for employees who use their cars for business travel.

Return of unspent amounts

The company must require an employee to return any advance payments in excess of the substantiated amount. Suppose an employee is required to return excess amounts, but doesn't. The arrangement is still an accountable plan to the extent of the substantiated amount. Only the excess amount is taxable.

> **NOTE** Time is a factor. In the case of advance payments, an employee must substantiate the expenses and return unsubstantiated amounts within a reasonable period of time after incurring the expenses.

What's a "reasonable" period of time? That depends on the individual facts and circumstances. For example, an employee on a month-long, out-of-town assignment will have more time to substantiate expenses than will an employee on an overnight trip.

The IRS does provide two safe harbors regarding the timeliness requirement. An employee will automatically meet the timeliness requirement if he or she

- Gets an advance payment no more than 30 days before he or she incurs the expenses,

- Substantiates the expenses to the company no more than 60 days after he or she incurs the expenses, and

- Returns the unsubstantiated amount no more than 120 days after incurring the expenses.

The second safe harbor requires the company to provide statements (at least once a quarter) to employees that detail the advances that have not yet been substantiated. The employee has up to 120 days following the receipt of the statement to substantiate expenses or return the unsubstantiated amount.

Per Diem Travel Allowances

The IRS has given new flexibility to companies that use per diem allowances to reimburse employees for meals and lodging expenses. At the same time, travel allowances that are not per diems must comply with the tough new requirements on substantiation and return of unsubstantiated amounts.

Companies that do not currently use per diem allowances may want to switch. Per diems equal to or less than IRS-approved rates comply with the new accountable plan requirements practically automatically. All a company has to do is get records from employees of where they travel, when, and for what purpose. The employees do not have to substantiate the amount of dollars spent.

Companies can provide tax-free per diems for meals and lodging, just lodging, or just meals. These allowances can be based on what the federal government pays its own employees, or they can be based on so-called high-low rates (described shortly).

Meals and Lodging Allowances

A per diem allowance for meals, lodging, and other incidental expenses automatically meets the new substantiation requirements if it does not exceed the rate given federal employees. However, there are many different federal rates; the exact rate depends on where the employee travels. For example, the 1992 per diem rates ranged from $67 in low-cost places like Vicksburg, Mississippi, to $174 in high-cost places like New York City.

High-Low rate

The IRS has released high-low rates for 1992 (the rates will be slightly higher for later years). Companies can now provide tax-free allowances of up to $147 per day for combined meals and lodging expenses in any "high-cost locality." This high per diem rate applies to the county in which the cities listed are located (for starred [*] cities, the rate also applies to certain surrounding counties).

> Aspen, Colorado
>
> Atlantic City, New Jersey
>
> Bala Cynwyd, Pennsylvania
>
> Boston, Massachusetts
>
> Chicago, Illinois*
>
> Columbia, Maryland
>
> Death Valley, California
>
> Hilton Head, South Carolina
>
> Key West, Florida
>
> Keystone/Silverthorne, Colorado
>
> Los Angeles, California*
>
> Martha's Vineyard/Nantucket, Massachusetts
>
> New York, New York*
>
> Newark, New Jersey*
>
> Newport, Rhode Island
>
> Ocean City, Maryland
>
> Philadelphia, Pennsylvania
>
> San Francisco, California
>
> Vail, Colorado
>
> Washington, D.C.*
>
> White Plains, New York

For travel to anywhere else in the 48 contiguous states, companies can provide tax-free meals and lodging allowances of up to $93 per day for combined meals and lodging expenses.

A company can use the federal per diem rates for some employees and the high-low rates for others. But the same employee cannot be reimbursed for some travel cities by one method and some cities by the other method. A company can, however, reimburse the same employee at the high-low rate for travel in the contiguous states and at the federal rate for foreign travel.

Lodging-only rate

Companies can provide an allowance for lodging only. The domestic federal per diem lodging rate is the federal travel rate for the locality less the meal and incidental expense rate for that locality.

There is also a high-low option for lodging per diems: $113 a day for travel to any high-cost locality (see the list on page 511) and $67 for anyplace else in the contiguous states.

Meals-only rate

Similarly, companies can provide a tax-free, meals-only allowance that is tied to what federal employees receive. The allowance is $34 for meals in certain designated cities and $26 for the rest of the country.

Instead of pegging the meals-only allowance to what federal employees receive, companies can opt to use the high-low rates. They can provide a tax-free allowance of $34 per day for any "high-cost" cities (see the list on page 511) and $26 for the rest of the country.

> **NOTE** Although the rates appear to be the same for both the federal employee meals allowance and the high-low meals allowance, there is a key difference: The government specifies rates for nearly 500 different cities when it comes to the federal employee allowance. On the other hand, the government specifies rates for only 21 cities for the high-low allowance. These 21 cities all qualify for the higher $34 rate; everywhere else is assigned the $26 rate.

As with the other allowances, the same employee cannot use both the federal and the high-low rates in the same year. Some cities have a meal allowance of $34 for the federal employee rate and a $26 rate for the high-low method, and vice versa.

Employer-Designed Travel Allowances

Companies may now use travel allowances that are tailored to their individual travel circumstances. The allowances can be based on a flat rate or on a stated schedule set by the employer. For example, a company could provide a cents-per-mile meal allowance for employees who spend most of their travel time on the road.

The rate or schedule must be "reasonably calculated" not to exceed the employee's actual expenses. It must also be "consistently applied" and "in accordance with reasonable business practice."

> **NOTE** The automatic travel allowances cannot be used by employees who own more than a 10% interest in the company paying the allowance. Travel allowances for these owner-employees must meet the strict accountable plan rules, or the allowances are fully taxable.

Travel Allowances Above Government-Approved Maximums

If an employee receives a per diem allowance in excess of an IRS-approved rate, only the excess is taxable. If an employee receives a total per diem amount before the trip and it exceeds the approved rate, the company does not have to require the employee to return the excess. The plan is still treated as accountable as long as the employee is required to return any portion allowable to days not actually traveled.

□ EXAMPLE

Jane Hill is a salesperson for the L&M Co. She goes to New York City on business. She receives a $560 advance for her meals, based on a meal per diem of $40 per day for an expected 14-day stay. The federal per diem meal rate for New York is $34. Hill stays in New York City for only 12 days.

Result: L&M must require Hill to return $80 ($40 @ 2), the amount of the reimbursement attributable to the two days she was not traveling. L&M does not have to require her to return the $72 [($40 less $34) @ 12] excess for the 12 days she was actually in New York. However, Hill must pay income and payroll taxes on the $72 excess amount. What's more, if Hill does not return the $80 for the two extra days, that is also taxable to her.

Companies that pay a per diem allowance in excess of the approved rates can permit their employees to substantiate their actual expenses. That way, if the substantiated expenses exceed the approved rate, only the allowance in excess of the employee's actual expenses is taxable to the employee. For example, suppose Hill's actual meal expenses in New York City ran to $540. If she substantiates this amount to L&M, then only $20 (the $560 allowance less $540 expenses) is taxable—not $72.

Company-Paid Car Allowances

The automatic mileage allowance has long been a popular way for companies to reimburse employees for their business car expenses. That's because it keeps paperwork to a minimum. In 1992, employees can receive 28 cents per mile tax free for all their business driving. What's more, a company can now pay an advance allowance based on the estimated business miles the employee will drive during the year, and that advance will be partially or wholly tax free.

A mileage allowance is taxed to the employee as income unless it is provided under an accountable plan. This means that the allowance must meet the following requirements:

■ The allowance must be reasonably calculated not to exceed the amount of the employee's car expenses.

■ The employee must provide the company with a record of the miles traveled, when, and why.

■ The employee must return any portion of the allowance that relates to miles of travel not substantiated.

If the employee satisfies these three requirements, an allowance of up to 28 cents per business mile is tax free in 1992. If the allowance is more than 28 cents per mile, only the excess is taxable.

☐ EXAMPLE

Jim Williams, a salesperson for Bedrock Granite Co., uses his car to visit a number of customers. In 1992, Bedrock provides

Williams with an advance mileage allowance of $7,000 based on an anticipated 20,000 business miles at 35 cents per mile and requires Williams to return any unsubstantiated portion. Williams's allowance is 7 cents higher than the 1992 IRS-approved mileage rate of 28 cents. Williams substantiates 12,000 business miles for a total of $4,200 (12,000 miles @ 35 cents) and returns the $2,800 attributable to the 8,000 unsubstantiated miles.

The allowance arrangement qualifies as an accountable plan. Williams owes no tax on the portion of the allowance allocable to the approved $3,360 (12,000 miles at 28 cents). Only the remainder ($840) is subject to income and payroll taxes.

SPECIAL FIXED- AND VARIABLE-RATE ALLOWANCE The IRS has approved a new substantiation method that some companies have already been using for business car expenses. It's called a "fixed- and variable-rate" (FAVR) allowance or a "Runzheimer" plan (after the name of one firm that helps companies implement these arrangements). A FAVR allowance is tailor-made for each company, based on a reasonable estimate of employees' car expenses (Rev. Proc. 90-34).

A FAVR allowance is made up of two parts: (1) a flat periodic payment covering the employee's fixed costs for depreciation, insurance, registration, and license fees for his or her car and (2) a periodic payment for the employee's operating costs for gas, oil, tires, and routine maintenance and repairs that varies according to the number of miles put on the car.

The costs used in figuring the FAVR must be based on retail prices paid by consumers in the geographic locality and must be "reasonable and statistically defensible." However, a company does not have to set up a separate FAVR for each employee and his or her car. Instead, it can set up classes and place employees with comparable cars and comparable driving patterns in each class. The FAVR for each class will be based on the estimated fixed and operating costs for a hypothetical standard car for that class.

CAUTION The IRS imposes three restrictions on the use of the FAVR allowance that it does not impose on the standard mileage rate:

- The FAVR allowance is not available to officers and directors of a company or employees who own a 10% or more interest in the company.

- At all times, at least ten employees must be covered by an FAVR allowance.

- At least 50% or more of the employees covered by an FAVR allowance must be nonmanagement.

IMPORTANT FAVR allowance plans are too complicated for most companies to set up and administer by themselves; they will need outside help. According to one expert in the field, that could run into thousands of dollars.

HOW TO MAKE YOUR DEDUCTIONS STAND UP

You must be able to back up your deductions for travel, entertainment, and other business expenses with good records. The same rule applies if you want to receive tax-free company cash for your business expenses—you must have good records. Here's a look at the tax law's recordkeeping requirements.

Key Recordkeeping Rules

To claim a deduction for your T&E expenses, you should make a diary entry at or near the time of each expense. Exactly what you should record in the diary depends on the type of expense involved—travel away from home, automobile, or entertainment.

Travel away from home

You must be able to prove the amount of each separate travel expense, the date of departure and return for each trip, the number of days away from home, the travel destination, and the business purpose of the trip.

Business entertainment

To deduct your business entertainment expenses, you must record the amount of each expense, the date and place of the entertainment, the business reason or benefit expected to be gained from the entertainment, and the name and title of the person you entertained.

If the entertainment is associated with your business (i.e., it precedes or follows a substantial business discussion), an additional rule applies. You must also record information about the business discussion: the date and duration, the place, the nature of the discussion, and the parties involved.

Automobile

To claim an automobile deduction, you must record the amount of each expense, the business mileage for each trip (and total mileage for the year), the date each expense occurred, and the business purpose involved.

> **NOTE** Be sure to keep receipts. Not only must you keep a record of your business expense but you must also keep receipts for any lodging expenses and any other $25-or-over expenses. Exhibit 9.1 is a sample page from a Travel and Entertainment Deduction Diary. You may want to photocopy the page and use it to jot down your travel, entertainment, automobile, and related business expenses. That way you will have the records you need to prove your T&E deductions to the IRS.

Travel Allowances and Reimbursements

An employee who receives an allowance or reimbursement must substantiate the T&E expenses to the employer. And the substantiation must satisfy the tax law's tough accountable plan requirements. Otherwise, the employer must report its business expense payments to employees as taxable compensation.

Exhibit 9.2 is a sample Travel and Entertainment Expense Voucher. An employer that uses this type of voucher system can satisfy the accountable plan rules with a minimum of effort.

EXHIBIT 9.1

Sample T&E Deduction Record

			\multicolumn{6}{c}{**Travel & Entertainment Deduction Diary**}		
DATE	TYPE OF EXPENSE	PLACE	\multicolumn{2}{c}{AMOUNT}	MILEAGE	BUSINESS PURPOSE/RELATIONSHIP
			TRAVEL	MEALS/ENT.		
	TOTAL					

EXHIBIT 9.2

Sample Travel Expense Voucher

Name _____

Department _____

For Period Beginning _____ Ending _____

													Total
Date													
Destination From													
To													
Purpose of Business Trip:													
Transportation — Car Travel — Mileage													
Rate × Miles													
Car Rental													
Parking													
Tolls													
Air Fare													
Rail Fare													
Carfare & Bus													
Limousine/Taxi													
Tips													
Hotel — Room Charge													
Hotel Tips													
Meals (inc. Tips) — Personal Meals — Breakfast													
Lunch													
Dinner													
Business Meals (explain on reverse) — Breakfast													
Lunch													
Dinner													
Misc. — Postage													
Telephone/Telegrams													
Laundry													
Other, Attach Statement													
Total													
											Less Amount Advanced		
											Balance Due		

I certify that these travel expenses were incurred by me in the transaction of authorized company business

Signature _____

519

An employer using a T&E expense voucher system requires an employee who receives a business expense advance or reimbursement to fill out a voucher periodically and submit it to the company along with receipts. The employer can require the employee to complete a monthly voucher, for example, or a voucher within 30 days of incurring a reimbursable expense.

> **KEY POINT** Whatever due date the employer chooses for its vouchers, the date should be strict enough to satisfy the accountable plan's timeliness requirements. A properly filled-out voucher submitted to the employer in a timely manner will satisfy the accountable plan rules. That means reimbursements or advances paid to an employee pursuant to the voucher need not be reported on that employee's Form W-2.

Employee's Obligation

An employee who receives an IRS-approved allowance or reimbursement does not have to keep track of the amount of any travel or transportation expenses. Nor does the employee have to keep receipts. And the employee does not have to retain a copy of the records after substantiating expenses to the employer. As with most rules, however, there are exceptions.

- The first exception applies when an employee's actual expenses exceed the company-paid allowance or reimbursement and the employee wants to deduct the excess. This excess can be deducted only if the employee keeps complete records (including the amount of each expense) and the necessary receipts, as well as copies of everything.

- The second exception comes into play when the employee is related to the employer. Examples: A member of the family (e.g., son who is employed by his sole-proprietor father) or an employee who owns more than 10% of the company. A related employee must keep complete records and receipts and retain copies of everything, because the employee remains open to audit even after substantiating expenses to the employer.

There is one exception to the exception. A related employee who receives a mileage reimbursement of 28 cents a mile or less does *not* have to make diary entries of the amount of each expense or obtain any receipts. The employee need keep only a diary that lists time, place, mileage, and business purpose. In addition, after substantiating expenses, the related employee need not retain a copy of the auto use log.

The Official Worksheet

Filling out tax returns is tough and complicated. To make things easier, this section provides a sample filled-in tax form for deducting travel, entertainment, and other business expenses—Form 2106. The line-by-line discussion takes you through each step of the form.

Watch out for "red flags." Employees who use cars for business claim their deductions on Form 2106. The form requires you to supply special information about your driving habits and recordkeeping. Here's a rundown on the facts and figures the IRS wants on Form 2106—and some "red flags" for potential problem areas.

- **What is the distance of your average daily commute to and from work, and how much of your annual car mileage represents commuting?** Generally, your commuting expenses are personal and nondeductible. Here the government wants to determine how much nondeductible commuting mileage you have for the year.

  RED FLAG Obviously, reporting little or no commuting mileage may be a signal for an audit. The IRS will take a close look if you show a big discrepancy between (1) your total commuting mileage and (2) your average daily commute multiplied by the number of workdays during the year. On the other hand, you may have legitimate reasons for a discrepancy. For example, you may frequently stop to visit a customer or client on the way to work. From that point on, your trip is no longer commuting; it's deductible travel between two business locations.

- **What was your other personal mileage during the year?** Assuming you kept a record of your business and commuting mileage, you simply take your total miles driven during the year and subtract out your business and commuting miles.

- **Do you or your spouse have another car available for personal use?** If the answer is "no" and you report low personal mileage for your business car, you should be extra careful to make sure your records are accurate.

  RED FLAG A typical taxpayer will have some mileage for personal errands and other family driving. If you have no other car, then your personal driving has to be done in the business car. Little or no personal mileage is a signal to the IRS to take a closer look at your return.

- **If your company provides a car, can you use it for personal driving when you are not working?** The value of using a company-owned car for personal travel is taxed to you as compensation. You must pay tax on what it would cost to lease a similar car for personal use, and your employer must report this amount as income on your Form W-2.

  RED FLAG Again, a taxpayer who has the use of a company car during off-duty hours will do some personal driving in it—especially if no other car is available. The IRS may audit your return if the value of your personal use doesn't match your W-2 amount or if both figures seem unusually low.

- **Do you have evidence to support your deduction?** This is a Catch-22 question. If you answer "no," you forfeit your auto deductions. If you answer "yes" and are unable to come up with the evidence in an audit, you will have to pay back taxes, and you may also be hit with expensive penalties.

- **If you have evidence, is it written?** This is another Catch-22. The tax law doesn't absolutely require written evidence to support car deductions. But Congress has stated that it has "much more probative value" than other forms of evidence, especially when written at or near the time the deductible expenses are incurred.

  RED FLAG If you answer that you don't have written records, the government computer may flag your return so that a revenue agent can give the unwritten evidence a close examination in an audit.

Suppose you answer "yes"—you have written records—but you are audited anyway. If you cannot produce the records, you open yourself up to penalties.

NOTE Congress has stated that the IRS and courts have not been tough enough in assessing penalties for lack of records. The tax authorities probably have gotten this message loud and clear.

Line-by-Line Guide to IRS Form 2106

The form in Exhibit 9.3 appears as it would be completed by Catherine Altman, a salesperson for Acme Toy Co. She had to do a fair amount of local travel as part of her job. She used her own car, which she bought early this year for $23,500, for these trips. She also used the car to commute to and from work, a daily round-trip distance of 36 miles. Catherine paid car expenses out of her own pocket and was reimbursed by Acme at the rate of 28 cents per business mile driven. She also spent $325 on parking and tolls.

Catherine recorded the details of each business trip (i.e., time, place, mileage, and purpose) in her T&E diary (see Exhibit 9.1). She turned in an expense report and submitted receipts to get her reimbursements. She also kept detailed records of other auto-related expenses (e.g., insurance, repairs). Catherine's actual out-of-pocket vehicle expenses totaled $4,600. Catherine also kept track of her beginning and ending odometer readings. For the year, her total mileage was 25,000 miles, 15,000 of which were business related.

Complete Part II of Form 2106 first

Part II of Form 2106 is filled out first since the amounts calculated here are needed to complete Part I.

Catherine completes *Section A—General Information*, where the IRS asks for details of her pattern of vehicle use. On *line 12*, she enters the date she placed the car in service. Catherine enters 25,000 on *line 13* to show the total miles she drove the car during the year and 15,000 on *line 14* for her business miles. She divides line 14 by line 13 to get her *line 15* entry of 60%, the percentage of her total use that was business related.

EXHIBIT 9.3

Sample IRS Form 2106 for Deducting Travel, Entertainment, and Other Business Expenses

Form **2106**	**Employee Business Expenses**	OMB No. 1545-0139
Department of the Treasury Internal Revenue Service (T)	▶ See separate instructions. ▶ Attach to Form 1040.	Attachment Sequence No. **54**

Your name	Social security number	Occupation in which expenses were incurred
Catherine Altman	123 :45 : 6789	Manager

Part I   **Employee Business Expenses and Reimbursements**

STEP 1   Enter Your Expenses

			Column A Other Than Meals and Entertainment	Column B Meals and Entertainment
1	Vehicle expense from line 22 or line 29	1	4,416	
2	Parking fees, tolls, and local transportation, including train, bus, etc.	2	325	
3	Travel expense while away from home overnight, including lodging, airplane, car rental, etc. **Do not** include meals and entertainment	3	1,050	
4	Business expenses not included on lines 1 through 3. **Do not** include meals and entertainment	4		
5	Meals and entertainment expenses. (See instructions.)	5		1,250
6	**Total expenses.** In Column A, add lines 1 through 4 and enter the result. In Column B, enter the amount from line 5.	6	5,791	1,250

Note: *If you were not reimbursed for any expenses in Step 1, skip line 7 and enter the amount from line 6 on line 8.*

STEP 2   Enter Amounts Your Employer Gave You for Expenses Listed in STEP 1

7	Enter amounts your employer gave you that were **not** reported to you in Box 10 of Form W-2. Include any amount reported under code "L" in Box 17 of your Form W-2. (See instructions.) . . .	7	4,200	

STEP 3   Figure Expenses To Deduct on Schedule A (Form 1040)

8	Subtract line 7 from line 6	8	1,591	1,250
	Note: *If both columns of line 8 are zero, stop here. If Column A is less than zero, report the amount as income and enter -0- on line 10, Column A. See the instructions for how to report.*			
9	Enter 20% (.20) of line 8, Column B	9		250
10	Subtract line 9 from line 8	10	1,591	1,000
11	Add the amounts on line 10 of both columns and enter the total here. **Also enter the total on Schedule A (Form 1040), line 19.** (Qualified performing artists and individuals with disabilities, see the instructions for special rules on where to enter the total.) . . . . ▶	11		2,591

For Paperwork Reduction Act Notice, see instructions.   Cat. No. 11700N   Form **2106**

EXHIBIT 9.3

(continued)

Form 2106   Page **2**

Part II   Vehicle Expenses (See instructions to find out which sections to complete.)

Section A.—General Information		(a) Vehicle 1	(b) Vehicle 2
12	Enter the date vehicle was placed in service **12**	1 / 9 / 92	/ /
13	Total mileage vehicle was used during 1991 . . . . . . **13**	25,000 miles	miles
14	Miles included on line 13 that vehicle was used for business **14**	15,000 miles	miles
15	Percent of business use (divide line 14 by line 13) **15**	60 %	%
16	Average daily round trip commuting distance. **16**	36 miles	miles
17	Miles included on line 13 that vehicle was used for commuting **17**	8,388 miles	miles
18	Other personal mileage (add lines 14 and 17 and subtract the total from line 13) **18**	1,612 miles	miles

19   Do you (or your spouse) have another vehicle available for personal purposes? . .   ☒ Yes   ☐ No

20   If your employer provided you with a vehicle, is personal use during off duty hours permitted?   ☐ Yes   ☐ No   ☒ Not applicable

21a   Do you have evidence to support your deduction?   ☒ Yes   ☐ No   21b   If "Yes," is the evidence written?   ☒ Yes   ☐ No

Section B.—Standard Mileage Rate (Use this section only if you own the vehicle.)
22   Multiply line 14 by   28¢ (.28). Enter the result here and on line 1. (Rural mail carriers, see instructions.) **22**

Section C.—Actual Expenses		(a) Vehicle 1		(b) Vehicle 2
23	Gasoline, oil, repairs, vehicle insurance, etc. **23**	4,600	
24a	Vehicle rentals **24a**		
b	Inclusion amount **24b**		
c	Subtract line 24b from line 24a **24c**		
25	Value of employer-provided vehicle (applies only if 100% of annual lease value was included on Form W-2. See instructions.) **25**		
26	Add lines 23, 24c, and 25 . . **26**	4,600	
27	Multiply line 26 by the percentage on line 15 . . . **27**	2,760	
28	Enter amount from line 38 below **28**	1,656	
29	Add lines 27 and 28. Enter total here and on line 1. . . . . **29**	4,416	

Section D.—Depreciation of Vehicles (Use this section only if you own the vehicle.)		(a) Vehicle 1		(b) Vehicle 2
30	Enter cost or other basis. (See instructions.) **30**	23,500	
31	Enter amount of section 179 deduction. (See instructions.) . **31**		
32	Multiply line 30 by line 15. (See instructions if you elected the section 179 deduction.) . . . **32**	14,100	
33	Enter depreciation method and percentage. (See instructions.) **33**	200DB 20%	
34	Multiply line 32 by the percentage on line 33. (See instructions.) . **34**	2,820	
35	Add lines 31 and 34 . . . . **35**	2,820	
36	Enter the limitation amount from the table in the line 36 instructions **36**	2,760	
37	Multiply line 36 by the percentage on line 15 . . . **37**	1,656	
38	Enter the **smaller** of line 35 or line 37. Also enter the amount on line 28 above **38**	1,656	

Next, she enters her average daily round trip commute of 36 miles on *line 16* and her total commuting miles for the year on *line 17*. *Line 18* is where she enters the remaining miles driven that were neither business nor commuting related (i.e., personal miles). To get this amount, subtracts lines 14 (business miles) and 17 (commuting miles) from line 13 (total miles). *Line 18 result:* 1,612 miles.

> **POTENTIAL RED FLAG** *Line 19* asks whether Catherine has another vehicle available for personal purposes. If the answer to this question was "no" and the number of miles shown on line 18 (personal miles) was unreasonably low, the IRS may get suspicious that Catherine was classifying personal miles as business related.

Line 20 doesn't apply to Catherine (asks about employer-provided vehicles), so she checks the "Not applicable" box. And since Catherine keeps detailed, written records, she checks off "Yes" to both parts of *line 21*.

Catherine does not complete *Section B—Standard Mileage Rate*—because she wants to claim deductions using her actual expenses.

Since Catherine kept track of her actual expenses and they exceed the deduction she would get using the standard mileage rate, she goes on to complete *Section C—Actual Expenses and Section D—Depreciation of Vehicles*. This way, she gets to deduct (at least partially) the expenses in excess of her reimbursements from Acme.

On *line 23*, Catherine enters her total vehicle expenses (other than depreciation)—gasoline, oil, repairs, insurance, and so on. This comes to $4,600.

> **NOTE** Don't include parking and tolls here. They are treated separately, in step 1 of Part I.

Line 24 doesn't apply to Catherine because she doesn't lease her car. If she did, she would have to reduce the deduction she gets for her lease payments by an "inclusion" amount (done on *line 24b*).

Line 25 also doesn't apply to Catherine because the car she used for business was owned by her, not her employer.

To get the *line 26* entry, Catherine simply carries down the $4,600 from line 23 (since she has no line 24 or 25 entries). For *line 27*, she multiplies her actual expenses on Line 26 by the business-use percentage computed on Line 15 (60%). Result: $2,760. She adds to this the $1,656 of depreciation she computes in Section D to get her total vehicle expenses of $4,416 on *line 29*.

Catherine enters the cost of her car, $23,500, on *line 30*. She leaves *line 31* blank because she will not get a bigger write-off by claiming a "Section 179" expensing deduction.

Line 32 is used to figure the portion of Catherine's basis in the car that is business related and, therefore, eligible for depreciation. She multiplies line 30 (her cost basis) by line 15 (her business-use percentage of 60%) to get $14,100. On *line 33*, she writes "200 DB 20%" to indicate the applicable depreciation method (200% declining balance) and percentage of the car's business portion she can write off for the year.

NOTE If Catherine used the car 50% or less for business, she would have to use straight-line depreciation to compute her write-off.

Catherine computes her tentative depreciation deduction on *line 34*. She multiplies line 32—the portion of her basis attributable to business use—by the percentage on line 33 (20%) to get her tentative depreciation of $2,820. Since she is not claiming an expensing deduction, she also enters this amount on *line 35*.

Note the depreciation limitation. *Line 36* says to enter the depreciation limitation amount from the table in the instructions. The maximum first-year depreciation deduction for a car placed in service in 1992 is approximately $2,760. (See your tax return for the actual figure.) This amount then has to be reduced to reflect the fact that Catherine used the car partly for personal purposes. To do this, she multiplies line 36 by her 60% business use percentage (from line 15) and enters the result—$1,656—on *line 37*.

Now Catherine compares line 35 (modified accelerated cost recovery system depreciation computed on her business use basis in the car) with line 37 (the depreciation cap amount). She then can deduct the smaller of these two amounts—$1,656, in Catherine's case—on *line 38*. She also carries this amount up to line 28 to arrive at her Line 29 total.

Complete Part I of Form 2106

Now Catherine is ready to proceed to Part I of Form 2106 where she computes the deduction for her other business expenses. Part I of the form is divided into two columns:

1. Column A for "Other than Meals and Entertainment"

2. Column B for "Meals and Entertainment"

Why the distinction? You are allowed to deduct only 80% of the cost of business meal and entertainment expenses, whereas other types of expenses aren't subject to this limitation.

Catherine also made several out-of-town business trips during the year. Acme's policy is to give its employees an allowance for out-of-town travel. Catherine received $750 for each of two trips she took. Acme doesn't require employees to turn in any record of their actual expenses or return any unspent amounts. Result: This is a nonaccountable plan and amounts employees receive must be included in box 10 on their W-2s as wages. Fortunately, Catherine kept track of what she actually spent so that she could deduct it on her tax return. Catherine spent $800 on meals and entertainment and $1,050 on other items (e.g., plane fares, lodging) while out of town on business trips. Catherine also spent $450 on local business entertainment (e.g., meeting customers for drinks after work) for which Acme didn't reimburse her at all.

Step 1—Enter Your Expenses.

This is where Catherine accumulates all her employee business expenses.

On *line 1,* she carries over her vehicle expenses of $4,416 from Line 29 of Section C. *Line 2* is for parking and tolls; Catherine enters $325 for these. On *line 3,* she enters all the expenses incurred while traveling away from home overnight, except for meals and entertainment—$1,050.

Line 4 doesn't apply to Catherine, and her *line 5* amount, for meals and entertainment, is $1,250—$800 while on out-of-town trips and $450 for local entertainment. On *line 6,* Catherine adds up all the expenses entered in each column. Catherine's totals come to $5,791 for column A and $1,250 for column B.

Step 2—Enter Amounts Your Employer Gave You for Expenses Listed in Step 1

This part of the form is crucial to determining what portion of the expenses listed in step 1 get deducted as miscellaneous itemized deductions on Schedule A.

Catherine enters here, on *line 7*, the employer reimbursements that were not included as wages (box 10) on her W-2.

> **NOTE** Catherine *does not* list here reimbursements that were made under a nonaccountable plan (i.e., substantiation not required). Since the two $750 payments for her out-of-town business trips are included in taxable income, she does not have to reduce her potentially deductible expenses by them.

Catherine enters just the $4,200 she received as a mileage allowance (28 cents per mile @ 15,000 miles). This reduces the expenses she's allowed to deduct—which makes sense since she shouldn't be entitled to a deduction for a tax-free reimbursement.

Step 3—Figure Expenses to Deduct on Schedule A

On *line 8*, Catherine enters the difference between line 6 and line 7—total expenses reduced by tax-free reimbursements. This gives her $1,591 in column A and $1,250 in column B.

Next, Catherine has to apply the 80% limitation to the meals and entertainment expenses in column B. To do this, she enters 20% of line 8 on *line 9*—$250. She subtracts line 9 from line 8 to get her deductible meals and entertainment expenses of $1,000 on *line 10*.

Grand Total

On *line 11*, Catherine combines the column A and column B amounts on line 10—for a total of $2,591. Catherine carries this amount to Schedule A of Form 1040 and claims it as a miscellaneous itemized deduction.

CHAPTER TEN

HELPFUL PERSONAL RECORDS TO REACH HIGH–BRACKET GOALS

Information on prospects can help you maximize your earnings.

HOW TO GET MAXIMUM BENEFIT FROM YOUR PERSONAL RECORDS

Each record you keep should be tested against these three criteria:

1. Will it serve an important purpose?
2. Will it help you achieve top-level selling?
3. It is simple and easy to keep?

To get maximum value from your records, you must look upon them as an integral part of your earnings objective, not as "paperwork to get done." Only by keeping and using records *with your earnings goal in mind* can you get the maximum profit from them.

This chapter provides forms to help you

- Keep records of personal information on prospects
- Keep records of prospect calls and callbacks
- Record when you've called on prospects and when they might be ready to reorder
- Use your records to plan your calls
- Use your records to plan your route
- Analyze your activities, so that you can improve your productivity and increase your earnings

WHAT TO DO

1. From the sample forms in this chapter, select those that suit your needs. If your company supplies a particular form that serves the same purpose as one of the forms printed here, use the company form instead.

2. Make whatever changes are necessary in the form to suit your needs. Remember, each suggested form is merely a guide. Some of them may suit your needs perfectly just as they are; others might need slight changes.

3. Once you have tailored the forms to your specific needs, have a supply of them run off on a duplicating machine.

4. Record the information accurately and regularly.

5. Use the information you compile; think about it; *take action* to improve your selling record.

RECORDING PERSONAL INFORMATION ON YOUR PROSPECTS

If your selling requires you to gather personal information about your prospects, you should keep some type of card or sheet on each of them that classifies the information and records the calls you've made. Exhibits 10.1 and 10.2 are adaptable for this purpose. The survey information, of course, is determined by what you sell. This form contains sufficient detail to enable you to design a similar card to meet your needs.

EXHIBIT 10.1

Prospect Personal Information Card (front)

1 2 3 4 5 6 7 8 9 10 11 12 13 14 15 16 17 18 19 20 21 22 23 24 25 26 27 28 29 30 31
(MR. MRS. MISS)

| STREET | APARTMENT |

| CITY | ☐ MARRIED ☐ WIDOW—ER |
| | ☐ SINGLE ☐ DIVORCED |

| BUS. CONNECTION | OCCUPATION | MO. EARNINGS $ |
| | | ACTUAL EST. |

HOME ☐ OWN ☐ RENT	OTHER INVESTMENTS	BOY	GIRL	CHILDREN'S NAMES	AGE	AGE
☐ SINGLE	SB $					DATE	AP. AGE
☐ DUPLEX	BL $					
☐ FLAT	GB $					DATE OF BIRTH
☐ APARTMENT	ST $					DAY	MONTH	YEAR
MORTGAGE $	RE $					
	TOTAL $	WIFE'S NAME			
INTEREST RATE %			
SOURCE	☐A ☐C ☐B ☐V ☐R—FROM

EXHIBIT 10.2

Prospect Personal Information Card (back)

	ADDITIONAL PERSONAL INFORMATION	NOTES:
	OTHER DEPENDENTS:	
	FRIEND OF:	
	LODGE CHURCH	
	HOBBIES, RECREATIONS, ETC.	

DATE	INTERVIEW RESULT			FURTHER ACTION			REMARKS	TIME WITH PROSPECT	RADIA-TION NAMES
	OUT		SOLD	KILL	C.B. DATE	LIT.			

Numbers 1 to 31 at the top identify the days of the month, to be flagged for follow-up purposes.

SB: savings banks

SL: savings and loan accounts

GB: government bonds

ST: securities

RE: real estate

NOTE In the blank boxes opposite "Source" use your own code letters to identify the source of your prospect.

Exhibit 10.2 is the reverse side of Exhibit 10.1. There is room at the top to insert additional personal information that you may want to include. In the "Interview Result" column, insert in the blank columns remarks similar to "out" and "sold" that tell you what happened. In the "Further Action" column, if you need something more than "Callback (C.B.) Date," and "Literature (Lit.)," you can add other columns. The column "Radiation Names" is a reminder to you to get the names of possible prospects from your contact.

KEEPING RECORDS OF PROSPECT CALLS AND CALLBACKS

Recording Ideas Discussed

If you make callbacks on the same prospect, it's important to know which product or product benefits you have already elaborated on. Your prospects will be much more impressed, and more eager to listen to your proposition, if you always come up with new features that benefit them.

Exhibit 10.3 provides a sample form for recording this information. At the top of the chart, insert the items to be discussed with your prospect. The ideas are numbered. As each idea is discussed, insert the date in the proper block under the appropriate number. Under "Name," list the name of the company and the individual that you called on. Then on each call, this chart will tell you what you have already discussed and what ideas you have left to discuss.

EXHIBIT 10.3

Sample Record of Ideas Discussed with Prospects

PROSPECT CONTROL RECORD
(Note: Insert opposite the numbers below the items to be talked about.)

1.	6.	11.	16.	21.
2.	7.	12.	17.	22.
3.	8.	13.	18.	23.
4.	9.	14.	19.	24.
5.	10.	15.	20.	25.

NAME	1	2	3	4	5	6	7	8	9	10	11	12	13	14	15	16	17	18	19	20	21	22	23	24	25	REMARKS

This chart is also a tickler follow-up on your calls. On one chart, for instance, you can list all customers that should be called on twice a month. On another chart, you can list those that should be called on monthly. You can have another chart for those to be called on every six weeks and still another for those to be called on every two months. File these charts in a tickler file according to the next date they are to be called on, by week. Then, when any given week comes up, pull out the charts for that week, and you'll find that much of your week's work has been preplanned.

RECORDING DATES OF CALLS AND POSSIBLE REORDERS

A record like that shown in Exhibits 10.4 and 10.5 enables you to determine when to call back on a customer and what items the customer will be interested in reordering *at the specified time.* For example, before calling on a prospect, fill out the card in Exhibit 10.4 with the name of the organization, zone, type of business, and rating. When you call on the prospect, get the name of the buyer as well as the names and titles of other executives whom it might be advisable to see. Enter this information on the card in the space under "Memoranda and Remarks," with the date of the call. In the "Follow-up" column, insert the date when you should follow up.

EXHIBIT 10.4

Record of Calls (front)

JAN.	FEB.	MAR.	APR.	MAY	JUNE	JULY	AUG.	SEP.	OCT.	NOV.	DEC.	
FIRM NAME						SALESMAN					Zone	
STREET ADDRESS						BUYER(S)					Rating	
CITY				P.O. Zone	State						Bus. No.	
TYPE OF BUSINESS				Telephone No.		RECORD OF SPECIAL MAILINGS						
						Dept. Store Forum	Ind. Forum	Dist. Forum	Ret. Forum			

RECORD OF CALLS

Date of Call			MEMORANDA AND REMARKS	Follow-Up	
Mon.	Day	Yr.		Mon.	Yr.

SALES CONTROL PLAN   SALESMAN'S WORK CARD   FORM No. 378

Exhibit 10.5 is the reverse of Exhibit 10.4. Use it as a customer sale and inventory record. Enter the items that the customer has bought, under "Record of Sales." Enter the customer's inventory of the various items in the upper half of the card.

> **NOTE** Salespeople must, if possible, ascertain and note the quantity on hand of each different product used that their company can supply. If the prospect will not permit an actual count of the stock, the salesperson explains that by looking over the inventory he or she can offer suggestions on forms that might not have been thought of previously. If this fails, the

salesperson notes on the card the prospect's or customer's estimate of how long the present stock will last. In any case, the salesperson marks on the card the month and year in which he or she wants to follow up the account.

EXHIBIT 10.5

Record of Inventory—Record of Sales
(Reverse side of Exhibit 10.4)

					RECORD OF INVENTORY						
Item No.	Form No. or Name	Type or Style of Stationery	Mfg. By	Average Monthly Usage	DATE AND QUANTITY ON HAND						
1											
2											
3											
4											
5											
6											
7											
8											
9											
10											

					RECORD OF SALES						
Item No.	Date	Quan.	Price	Item No.	Date	Quan.	Price	Item No.	Date	Quan.	Price

PROPERTY OF THE SHELBY SALESBOOK COMPANY, SHELBY, OHIO

USE YOUR RECORDS TO PLAN YOUR CALLS

Exhibit 10.6 also helps you plan your daily calls, the objectives of each call, and the means to achieve them. The information you record after completing your calls becomes part of your permanent files. It gives you a capsule history of what you have accomplished and what remains to be done to make the sale.

EXHIBIT 10.6

Today's Plan and Call Record

TODAY'S PLAN and CALL RECORD

DATE . . . .

TODAY'S PLAN
This is my plan for the day, to be made out in advance of calls.
List calls in the order I plan to make them, including more than I expect to make.

CALL RECORD
At the end of the day, record the results of my call. Cross off calls not made; add those made but not previously entered.
List classifications (N-R-U). Transfer pertinent data on each call to my permanent prospect and customer records.

CALLS		NO.	SUMMARY	NO.	ORDERS TAKEN					
					PRODUCT		PRODUCT		PRODUCT	
						NO.		NO.		NO.
New	(N)		Demonstration							
Repeat	(R)		Proposal							
Users	(U)		Close							
TOTAL										

LOCATION	COMPANY	INDIVIDUAL	OBJECT-IVE	SALES TOOL	CLASS N. R. U.
RESULTS					
RESULTS					
RESULTS					
RESULTS					
RESULTS					
RESULTS					
RESULTS					
RESULTS					
RESULTS					

OBJECTIVES						SALES TOOLS	
Inquiry	(INQ)	Survey	(SURV)	Complaint	(CPLT)	Order Form	(O. F.)
Referral	(REF)	Proposal	(PROP)	Others--		Sales Manual	(S. M.)
Canvass	(CANV)	Close	(Cl)	(Specify)		Literature	(LIT)
Demo	(D)	Maintenance	(MAINT)			User List	(U. L.)
Competition	(COMP)	Instruct	(INST)			Movies	(M)
		Price Change	(P. C.)			Testimonials	(T)

How to use Exhibit 10.6 as a plan for daily calls

List in the appropriate columns the names of the companies, locations, and individuals you want to call on the following day. Beside each name, in the "Objective" column, add the specific objective of that particular call from the list of "Objectives" at the bottom of the form. Under the "Sales Tool" heading, list the selling aid you plan to use to achieve your objective. (Notice that the "Objectives" and "Sales Tools" are codified. If you add other objectives or sales tools, make an appropriate abbreviation. Entries on the record are by code letters.)

How to use Exhibit 10.6 as a record of your calls

After each interview, indicate in the "Class" column whether the individual you called on was a new prospect, a callback, or a user of your product. Also note the results of each call. Delete names of persons you were unable to see; add nonplanned calls.

How to use Exhibit 10.6 as a selling aid

At the end of each day,

- Transfer the total of each class of calls to the "Calls" section at the top of the form. This section tells you whether you have made a sufficient number of calls on new prospects to assure a continued supply of fresh business. A large number of callbacks without closing might indicate a need for more careful consideration before a callback is made.

- Use the summary of objectives, next to the "Calls" column, to record the number and kind of different objectives you actually reached. These figures tell you whether you are achieving your goals; whether your interviews are aimed at closes, demonstrations, and so on, and not at less profitable objectives.

- If you are a multiproduct salesperson, refer to the "Orders Taken" section to see just which products you're selling and whether you're neglecting any items in your line.

- Note the objective and result of each call to help you plan a new objective for your next call.

- Save your daily plan and call reports for a week or a month. Analyze the figures to see just how you spend your interview time, the percentage of goals you achieve, where your planning is falling short, the products you need to sell harder, and so on.

- Transfer important information from your daily record of calls to your permanent prospect and customer records (this is important).

USE RECORDS TO PLAN YOUR ROUTE

If you work your territory by zones, arrange your cards in each zone so that you can work up one side of the street and down the other. For follow-up purposes, tab the cards at the months indicated at the top. On the first of each month, go through the tabs, which are already arranged by zone, and pull those that are to be followed up.

Exhibit 10.7 can help you plan your itinerary for the coming week if you spend most of your time "on the road:"

- Enter the names of the towns you plan to stop at during your coming week's itinerary.

- Record the date you plan to arrive and when you will leave.

- If you drive, add a "Mileage" column (filled in beforehand by referring to a map) to tell you just how far you have to go to get to your next destination.

- List the hotels where you plan to stay. (Leave a copy with someone who can get in touch with you if necessary.) If you go into a new territory, list and rate your hotels as you go along. The next time you go that way, a glance at your previous route schedule will tell you whether to stay there again or try somewhere else. Knowing where you have stayed is also useful if you leave something behind during your trip or if you must send for a forwarded item that you missed.

EXHIBIT 10.7

Sample Route Schedule Form

ROUTE SCHEDULE
Week Beginning_____, 19___

DATE	ARR.	TOWN (S)	STATE	HOTELS	LEAVE	WORK PLAN

ADVANCE SCHEDULE FOLLOWING WEEK

NOTES:

- Under the "Work Plan" heading, list the names of the people you plan to call on during your stay in town.

- Use the bottom half of the form to prepare an advance schedule for the following week. After changes, this becomes your new week's schedule.

- Use the "Notes" section at the bottom of the form to record any unusual road conditions or information you will want to remember for your next trip.

ANALYZE YOUR WEEK'S ACTIVITIES TO ASSESS YOUR PRODUCTIVITY

Analyze yourself by filling out Exhibit 10.8. Your record of the week's accomplishments will show you how good you really are. The result, good as you may be, may open avenues of effort and new possibilities for increasing sales. The self-questioning at the bottom of the form is designed to make you find the new possibilities.

> **NOTE** This form does not have to be filled in every week. Use it at regular intervals to assure a complete checkup on performance. Save your record and compare it with the preceding one, as well as with those you filled out several months or a year back to see what kind of progress you're making.

A periodic checkup, say, the first of every month, using a form that lets you rate yourself on various personal questions should be part of every salesperson's self-improvement program.

Exhibits 10.9, 10.10, and 10.11 provide three questionnaires to help you assess the overall impression you make on sales prospects.

EXHIBIT 10.8

Weekly Work Analysis Sheet

THINGS I ACCOMPLISHED DURING THE WEEK ENDING ....

	Monday	Tuesday	Wednesday	Thursday	Friday	Saturday
No. of accounts called on						
On how many of the above calls did I get to the man or woman I wanted?						
No. of future appointments made						
No. of presentations made to NEW accounts						
No. of presentations made to REGULAR accounts						
No. of orders taken						
$ value of orders taken						
No. of contacts made in connection with merchandising activities						
No. of times sales portfolio was used						
During the past week have I worked out any new, unusual sales presentations which helped my business or created new INTEREST or ENTHUSIASM on the part of the buyer?						

As soon as you have recorded the week's activities, look this over and ask yourself these questions:

1. Am I planning my time AHEAD so that I can contact as many Buyers, Merchandise and Advertising men as possible EVERY DAY?

2. At the rate I am going, will I accomplish all I am CAPABLE of doing this year?

3. Am I applying TOO LITTLE effort to one or more important phases of my work?

4. Am I applying TOO MUCH effort on some relatively unimportant phase of my work, so that more important matters suffer as a result?

5. Does the above week's record show that I am USING MY TIME to the best possible advantage?

EXHIBIT 10.9

Personal Assessment Questionnaire 1

Give yourself a 4 on any question where you sincerely believe you are above average, 3 for good or average, 2 for fair or mediocre, and 1 for poor or weak. Rate yourself honestly, it will seriously impair your chances for self-improvement if you do not respond to the following questions as objectively as possible.

Goals

☐ Do I really want to be successful?

☐ Do I have determination and the will to win?

☐ Am I willing to put forth concentrated effort and work hard?

☐ Am I willing to sacrifice some pleasures and comforts if need be?

☐ When adverse conditions arise, do I steadfastly continue my efforts?

☐ Do I have a clear picture of my ultimate major objective?

☐ Am I setting small personal objectives as stepping-stones to more easily and surely attain my goal?

☐ Am I constantly adding knowledge to make my efforts more effective?

Attitude

☐ Do I have a positive attitude?

☐ Do I enjoy my work?

☐ Do I feel loyalty toward the company for which I work?

☐ Am I completely "sold" on the products I sell?

☐ Do I have faith in and teamplay with my management?

☐ Am I considerate?

☐ Do I cooperate with my coworkers?

☐ Am I aware of all the motives that should impel me toward success?

☐ Do I have properly balanced motivation?

Customer Relationships

☐ Do I really understand my customers, associates, and friends?

☐ Do I consistently try to promote the customer's feelings of adequacy and gain his or her goodwill?

☐ Do I command the confidence and respect of my customers?

❑ Do I see the customer's point of view and settle any differences of opinion by reasoning and diplomacy?

❑ Do I bend over backwards to give my customers service?

Total Score: A total score of 70–88 means that you are above par and this is undoubtedly reflected in your present performance. If your score is 55–70, it shows that you are an average individual, and can easily and readily improve yourself by conscientiously trying. A score of 40–55 indicates that self-improvement should be started at once and diligently continued. And a score below 40 signifies that you are in real danger of failure and should adopt drastic, concentrated action to improve.

EXHIBIT 10.10

Personal Assessment Questionnaire 2

Again check yourself conscientiously and rate yourself honestly. Award 4 for excellent, 3 for good, 2 for fair, and 1 for poor.

Personal Appearance and Personality

❑ Am I neat and clean, pleasant and friendly, smiling and cheerful?

❑ Am I sociable and generally well liked?

❑ Do I create a pleasant first impression?

❑ Do my speech, mood, and actions enhance this first impression?

❑ Is my telephone personality outstanding?

❑ Do I avoid such bad habits as poor personal taste and improper speech and actions?

❑ Am I conscious of, and do I control, annoying nervous habits?

❑ Have I eliminated all speech hesitancy, and do I avoid interrupting the customer's conversation?

❑ Do I check myself periodically to determine if I have erased any old bad habits or have acquired any new ones?

Sales Techniques

❑ Do I use my company's advertising and promotion to promote more sales?

❑ Do I, where possible, use "suggestion selling" and tie in wanted or needed related merchandise?

❑ Do I, when advisable, "trade up" or "trade-down" a sale—whichever will give the buyer the most satisfaction?

Prospect/Customer Approach

❑ Are my initial greetings cordial and friendly?

❑ Do my approaches get attention and arouse interest?

❑ Do I occasionally ask "self-answering" questions to qualify my sales talk and check the customer's interest level?

❑ Do I ask questions to find out my customer's wants and needs?

❑ Do I understand and use the basic motives that create desire?

❑ Is my explanation concise, clear, accurate, and informative?

❑ Do I prevent many complaints by explaining clearly and completely?

❑ If complaints arise, do I always handle them cheerfully, quickly, and properly?

Total Score: A total score of 70–80 means that you are in the top 10% bracket, 55–70 is good, 40–55 means that you're on the borderline and need extensive improvement, and under 40 means "act now" before it's too late.

EXHIBIT 10.11

Personal Assessment Questionnaire 3

Rate yourself 4 on each question in which you are outstanding, 3 for good, 2 for fair, and 1 for poor.

Presentation Skills

❑ Do I increase the value of my explanation with demonstration and visuals, where possible?

❑ Do I have a complete knowledge of my products?

❑ Can I intelligently answer any and all questions about my product to the customer's satisfaction?

❑ Do I state the benefits and features (in that sequence) of each product as I sell it?

❑ Do I know my stock, where it is, and what I actually have on hand?

❑ Do I have ample confirmation available and use it frequently to substantiate my sales talk?

☐ Can I overcome sincere objections effectively without arguing or causing customer displeasure?

☐ Can I eliminate sales resistance and unearth the real "nonbuying" reason?

☐ When in doubt, do I "test" before trying to close?

☐ Do I use two or three different closes on each sale before giving up?

☐ Do I express and show real appreciation to every customer?

☐ Do I have genuine self-confidence, because I have a thorough knowledge of myself, my selling skills, and my company's products?

Continual Improvement Efforts

☐ Have I eliminated indecision, discouragement, and anxiety?

☐ Am I aware of my limitations as well as my capacities?

☐ Am I doing anything constructive to eliminate my shortcomings?

☐ Am I consistently trying to enlarge my capacity to "think creatively"?

☐ Am I honest, sincere, and dependable?

☐ Do I work with a minimum of supervision and follow instructions cheerfully and implicitly?

☐ Do I always plan my work and work my plan?

☐ Is my plan always worked out in an organized, systematic fashion?

Total Score: Again, 70–80 is tops, 55–70 is average, 40–55 is weak, and below 40 shows urgent need for self-improvement. Anyone who cannot rate a total of at least 55 definitely lacks initiative and may be either too lazy to acquire sufficient knowledge or too self-satisfied to realize his or her own shortcomings.

HOW TO FIND INFORMATION ABOUT PEOPLE AND COMPANIES

This Appendix provides you with the key reference sources other top salespeople use to find helpful information about prospects and customers. As every top salesperson can testify, the more you know about your prospect before you approach him or her, the easier it is to make the sale.

The reference sources explained in this Appendix are published regularly by organizations whose business it is to gather and prepare important information about people, companies, and the products they make—information you can put to work in your day-to-day selling. You can find most of these works in public and college libraries.

"FINDER" FOR ESSENTIAL INFORMATION

In the publications discussed in this section, you can find the following information about people, companies, and their products:

547

- Addresses (company)
- Addresses (residence)
- Affiliated companies
- Biographies
- Branches
- Chamber of Commerce members
- Credit ratings (company)
- Directors of a company
- Executives of a company
- Financial strength (company)
- History (company)
- Industry data, trends, and the like
- Key personnel (company)
- Manufacturers of a product
- Maps (local)
- Number of employees
- Officers of a company
- Parent companies
- Plant locations of a company
- Products of a company
- Purchasing agents
- Subsidiaries

STANDARD & POOR'S REGISTER OF CORPORATIONS, DIRECTORS AND EXECUTIVES

Standard & Poor's Register is designed to provide easy access for whatever reference is being made. It is arranged in three volumes and also includes cumulative supplements:

Volume 1—*Corporate Listings*

This is an alphabetical sequence by business name of over 55,000 corporations including the following:

- Address
- Telephone numbers
- Names, titles, and functions of approximately 500,000 officers, directors, and other principals
- Names of company's accounting firm, primary bank, and primary law firm
- Stock exchange(s) on which company's stock is traded
- Description of company's products/services
- Standard Industrial Classification (SIC) codes
- Annual sales and number of employees where available
- Division names and functions
- Subsidiary listings separate, with reference to parent companies
- Principal business affiliation and address of executives, if other than the subject company.

Volume 2—*Individual Listings, Directors and Executives*

This is an alphabetical list of over 70,000 individuals serving as officers, directors, trustees, partners, and so on. Provides principal business affiliations with

- Official titles
- Business addresses
- Residence addresses
- Year and place of birth (where obtainable)
- College and year of graduation (where obtainable)
- Fraternal memberships (where obtainable)

Volume 3—Indexes

This volume is divided into seven color-coded sections:

Section 1—Standard Industrial Classification Index (Green Pages) explains the organization and use of the SIC code numbers and lists these numbers by major groups and by alphabetical and numerical division of major groups.

Section 2—Standard Industrial Classification Codes (Pink Pages)—lists corporations under the four-digit SIC codes, which are arranged in numerical order. Approximately 900 different SIC codes provide a defined breakdown by a company's line of business.

Section 3—Geographic Index (Yellow Pages)—lists companies appearing in the Register geographically by states and by major cities.

Section 4—Corporate Family Indexes (Blue Pages)—consists of

- A *Cross-reference Index*, which lists subsidiaries, divisions, and affiliates and links them to their ultimate parent company in Volume I.

- The *Ultimate Parent Index*, which lists ultimate parent companies with their subsidiaries, divisions, and affiliates and indicates each unit's relationship to their parent.

Section 5—Obituaries (Green Pages)—records the deaths of which the publishers have been notified in the past year.

Section 6—New Individual Additions (Buff Pages)—contains a complete alphabetical list of individuals whose biographies appear in the *Register* for the first time.

Section 7—New Company Additions (Buff Pages)—contains a complete alphabetical list of companies appearing in the *Register* for the first time.

WHO'S WHO IN FINANCE AND INDUSTRY

Who's Who in Finance and Industry provides you with information on top-ranking executives throughout the country.

The **"Who's Who"** section—gives career sketches of leading businesspeople and other noteworthy individuals in the field of commerce and industry. The type of information varies slightly. A typical sketch might give you these data:

- Name
- Address
- Position (such as "utility official")
- College and degree
- Companies associated with
- Dates of association
- Positions held in various companies
- Memberships in organizations
- Memberships in clubs

The Roster of Ranking Executives—provides an alphabetical listing of individuals.

The Indexed Catalog of Selected Principal Businesses is located near the end of the reference and lists names of selected companies in alphabetical order. You can find the names of the company's key executives, then refer to their biographical listings in the *Roster of Ranking Executives*.

Dun & Bradstreet's Million Dollar Directory® Series

The *Dun & Bradstreet's Million Dollar Directory*® Series provides information on the headquarters and single locations of 160,000 companies. Every company included meets at least one of these criteria:

- A sales volume of over $25 million
- 250 or more employees
- A net worth of at least $500,000

The listings include the following:

- Company name
- Subsidiaries
- Address
- Phone number

- Names and titles of principal officers
- Number of employees
- Sales volume
- Primary and secondary SIC codes (up to six levels)
- Line of business
- Primary bank

Top 50,000 Companies—is an abridged version of the entire series. As the title indicates, it provides information on the top 50,000 companies in the United States. All entries are fully cross-referenced geographically and by industry classification.

Reference Book of Corporate Managements™—profiles officers within 12,000 top U.S. companies and contains biographical information and work histories.

America's Corporate Families® and *America's Corporate Families*® and *International Affiliates*—is a two-volume set that traces corporate linkage and ownership throughout the world.

Dun's Industrial Guide® and *The Metalworking Directory*™—is a three-volume directory that profiles manufacturers and serves as a nationwide industrial directory of 71,000 manufacturing plants and distributors whose business involves metals in any way.

Dun's Directory of Service Companies—provides details on 50,000 of the largest service enterprises with 50 or more employees in the following lines of business:

- Accounting, auditing, and bookkeeping
- Advertising and public relations
- Amusement and recreation
- Architecture and engineering
- Consumer services
- Executive search
- Health
- Hospitality
- Management consulting
- Motion pictures
- Repair

- Research
- Social services
- Law firms

MOODY'S INDUSTRIAL MANUAL

Moody's Industrial Manual contains two volumes (A–I, J–Z) and provides the following information about listed companies:

- Name
- Address
- History of the company
- Primary holdings
- Officers' names and title of office held (chairperson, president, vice president, treasurer, secretary, etc.)
- Directors' names and city
- Number of employees
- Number of stockholders
- Business and products
- Principal plants and properties: location by city, type of operation
- Subsidiary's name, city, and business
- Financial statement (income account, sales and earnings, balance sheet, and capital stock)

THOMSON BANK DIRECTORY

The *Thomson Bank Directory* (formerly called the *Rand McNally Bankers Directory)* describes nearly 15,000 U.S. banks and their 45,000 branches and 60,000 foreign banks around the world. Entries are arranged geographically by state and city. (There is also an alphabetical index in Volume 1.)

For every headquarters location there is an extensive array of data provided in addition to name, parent company, address, phone, and names of key executives that includes the type of bank and form of charter, founding date, summary financial information, and more.

MOODY'S BANK AND FINANCE MANUAL

Volume 1 of the *Moody's Bank and Finance Manual* covers banks and trust companies, savings and loan associations, and federal credit agencies. Volume 2 covers insurance, investment and finance companies, real estate companies, and real estate investment trusts. Information for each company that has standard coverage usually includes

- Brief financial history
- Officers and directors
- Comparative income statements
- Balance sheets
- Information on capital stock
- Record of dividend payments
- Recent stock price range

POLK'S WORLD BANK DIRECTORY

Polk's World Bank Directory contains a geographic list of world banks, giving officers and directors, correspondents, out-of-town branches, assets, and liabilities. Supplementary information includes

- NameMaps for each state
- State banking officials
- Legal holidays
- List of bank holding companies
- Transit numbers

- List of bank-related associations
- Ranked list of largest banks

THOMAS' REGISTER OF AMERICAN MANUFACTURERS

Thomas' Register of American Manufacturers is a 23-volume reference that is set up into a three-part system.

Products & Services, Volumes 1–14, contain detailed sourcing information under each of more than 50,000 separate product and service headings. Volume 14 also includes a product index.

Company Profiles, Volumes 15 and 16, includes capabilities and contact information on more than 145,000 U.S. companies. Volume 16 also includes a brand-names index that can be used to find the owner company when you only know a brand name. Companies are listed alphabetically and information includes

- Addresses
- Phone numbers
- Asset ratings
- Company executives
- Locations of sales offices, distributors, plants, and service/engineering offices

The catalog file, Volumes 17–23 contains nearly 10,000 pages of catalog data from more than 1,400 companies. The catalogs are arranged alphabetically by company name and are fully cross-referenced within both the Product & Services section and the Company Profiles section.

STATE AND REGIONAL INDUSTRIAL DIRECTORIES

Many states and regions of the country (for example, *Directory of New England Manufacturers*) have industrial directories that are usually listed by city or town or by industry (SIC code). Some directories have more than one volume and contain both types of listings. In state and regional directories, you'll find the following types of information about companies in a particular area:

- Name
- Address
- Phone number
- Number of employees
- Principals
- Products
- Gross sales

TRADE DIRECTORIES

Trade directories are published by professional and industry associations, trade journals, or other commercial publishers and focus on a specific type of industry. They usually contain the following information:

- Name
- Address
- Kind of business
- Telephone number
- Officers
- Directors
- Key personnel
- Affiliations

WORLD CHAMBER OF COMMERCE DIRECTORY

Chambers of Commerce are good sources of information. You can find the addresses and phone numbers of chamber offices across the country through this directory.

The information you'll receive from a chamber will vary, but they can usually provide information on some or all of the following for the area they serve:

- Company names
- Company addresses
- Name of the head of the company
- Names of chief management personnel
- Name of the purchasing agent
- Number of employees, usually within categories such as 25 to 100, 100 to 500, more than 500
- Products and services available from members
- History of the company
- Individuals to see in particular departments
- Local maps

INDEX

Q

R